UNDERDAWGS

HOW BRAD STEVENS AND
BUTLER UNIVERSITY BUILT THE
BULLDOGS FOR MARCH MADNESS

DAVID WOODS

Originally published as *Underdawgs: How Brad Stevens
and the Butler Bulldogs Marched Their Way to the Brink
of College Basketball's National Championship*

SCRIBNER
New York   London   Toronto   Sydney   New Delhi

SCRIBNER
A Division of Simon & Schuster, Inc.
1230 Avenue of the Americas
New York, NY 10020

First Scribner trade paperback edition February 2012

SCRIBNER and design are registered trademarks of The Gale Group, Inc., used under license by Simon & Schuster, Inc., the publisher of this work.

For information about special discounts for bulk purchases, please contact Simon & Schuster Special Sales at 1-866-506-1949 or business@simonandschuster.com.

The Simon & Schuster Speakers Bureau can bring authors to your live event. For more information or to book an event contact the Simon & Schuster Speakers Bureau at 1-866-248-3049 or visit our website at www.simonspeakers.com.

Manufactured in the United States of America

1   3   5   7   9   10   8   6   4   2

Library of Congress Control Number: 2010036176

ISBN 978-1-4516-1057-4
ISBN 978-1-4516-1058-1 (pbk)
ISBN 978-1-4516-1059-8 (ebook)

See page 303 for insert photograph credits.

ALSO BY DAVID WOODS

The Butler Way:
The Best of Butler Basketball

Dedicated to the Woods,
Rettberg, and Jordan families.
Even those who aren't basketball fans
love a good story.

CONTENTS

FOREWORD
BY LUKE WINN

There are upsets that happen by chance, underdogs who enter the national consciousness due to some rare cosmic event, but the story of Butler's back-to-back trips to the national title game—the greatest story of college basketball's modern age, never mind that it didn't include an actual championship—is one with a deep foundation. Spending time around the program is less likely to make you feel part of a fairy tale than it is to make you appreciate just how thoroughly Brad Stevens's Bulldogs have their act together, and how exceptional achievements can result from prolonged adherence to a certain set of values. One such value was preparation: When I passed through Butler's locker room last October, before the start of the 2010–11 season, I saw a sign in each player's locker with the heading "How We Prepare." It challenged them on points of precision, instructing them to "engage yourself in deep practice," and on points of character, asking, "If you couldn't play at all, would you be a valuable teammate every day?" It challenged them to be the best preparation team in the country.

Most of us were unprepared for what Butler accomplished over the past two seasons. Being assigned to cover their last four games of each NCAA Tournament run for SI.com was a privilege, because all a writer roots for is an inspiring story, yet I was ashamed for not picking the Bulldogs to survive past the first weekend on any of my 2010 or '11 pool sheets. Even those closest to the team were amazed: I remember seeing the *Indianapolis Star*'s David Woods, this book's author and the team's lone beat writer, outside the media hotel in Houston on the night he arrived for Butler's Final Four encore. He'd just emerged from travel hell (he hadn't planned in advance to be in Houston, and his flight reservation home from the New Orleans Regional had somehow been botched, so he'd improvised a route to Reliant Stadium using Amtrak and taxis), but still had a sense of wonder about him. "Can you believe that we're doing this all over again?" he asked me.

Butler's run to the 2010 Final Four in its hometown of Indianapolis made them America's Team; few fans could resist the appeal of a real-life version of *Hoosiers* emerging from Hinkle Fieldhouse to take on the Goliaths at Lucas Oil Stadium. Beneath that story line, though, was the fact that each of Butler's upsets was not a miracle but the culmination of the kind of "deep engagement" that Stevens preached. Their man-to-man defense had become so stout—the result of rotations honed and honed to perfection in early-morning practices at Hinkle, starting before light broke through the fieldhouse's upper windows—that it held every NCAA Tournament opponent but Duke to less than one point per possession. Mistakes that led to unchallenged shots were few and far between, creating immense frustration for higher-seeded foes Syracuse, Kansas State, and Michigan State.

The Bulldogs' coaches took it upon themselves to match the level of preparedness they demanded from their players, combining data analysis—Stevens talked about using kenpom.com statistics to help figure out the "puzzle" of an opponent—with old-school scouting to create comprehensive game plans. When Butler beat K-State in the 2010 NCAAs and Pitt in 2011—two teams that were among the country's best in offensive rebounding percentage, a metric viewed as a high success indicator among the advanced-stats crowd—it wasn't a coincidence that the Bulldogs held them to their worst percentages of the season. It was a concerted effort to diminish an advantage. Likewise, when Butler met Wisconsin in the 2011 Sweet Sixteen, Stevens and his assistants knew how efficiently point guard Jordan Taylor and the Badgers' sweet-shooting big men functioned in pick-and-roll situations, so the Bulldogs devised a plan to corral Taylor with a double team off the screen, with help defenders rotating over to cover shooters. It was not a fluke that the Badgers had their worst offensive outing of the year, and it was reasonable to believe, after seeing that game, that Butler *was* the best preparation team in the country.

There were also less measurable elements of the Butler formula, one of them being the energy that its key players brought to every game, regardless of the stakes. At the Horizon League Championship in 2010, I saw then-junior Matt Howard dive into the stands for a loose ball, knocking over chairs and risking injury—when the Bulldogs *were up by 24 points on Wright State in the second half.* Stevens praised Howard that night, saying that the play "speaks to who [Howard] is, but it also speaks to who we all want to be every day." The next year in the NCAA Tournament, when I saw Howard, hustling for an offensive rebound and buzzer-beating putback to beat Old Dominion in the first round, then hustling to draw a game-winning foul (and free throws) against Pitt, I couldn't help but remember what he did against Wright State. That play, in the scope of that game, was meaningless; but that mentality, maintained over time, would eventually keep a season alive.

Howard was the consummate teammate, with his unrelenting hustle and his willingness, during his junior year, to cede the spotlight to sophomores Gordon Hayward and Shelvin Mack, who were emerging as the team's new stars. There was a kind of special chemistry on that first Butler club that I rarely encountered while covering teams all over the country. The Bulldogs had a mutual respect for one another and allowed each player to fill his best possible role—such as Ronald Nored, a defensive stopper who, despite being just a sophomore, functioned as a sort of spiritual leader, delivering inspirational messages in pregame huddles. His late father had been a preacher, and Stevens predicted that Nored would someday run for president. The staff's commitment to recruiting high-character players made the team more likely to lift itself up in crucial moments than fracture from within.

The coaches—and those who preceded them, namely Barry Collier, Thad Matta, and Todd Lickliter—prepared the foundation from which the Bulldogs could make history, but above all, it required players who genuinely bought in to the Butler Way. And it's difficult to grasp, as a journalist, how much time goes in to creating those sorts of bonds, although occasionally you do get hints. Such as this past summer, when I was in Riga, Latvia, covering the FIBA under-19 World Championships, and Butler sophomore-to-be Khyle Marshall was there as part of the U.S. team, which finished fifth. He'd just appeared in the national title game a few months earlier and was a bit frustrated by the un-Butler-like way the Americans were playing in the tournament—neither locking down on defense nor sharing the ball effectively on offense. But each day, he would either come to the arena early or stay late, to sit with parents he'd just met and cheer on their son, who was the point guard for the Australian national team. Their son was Jackson Aldridge, who'd signed a letter of intent to play for the Bulldogs and would be arriving on campus later in the summer. I asked Marshall why it was so vital to see those games, and his expression suggested that he hadn't even considered the alternative. "I'm here," Marshall said, "because he's going to be my teammate."

UNDERDAWGS

TWO MINUTES FROM GLORY

The sun set in the west, spring showers were falling, and the Duke Blue Devils were on the verge of a national championship. It was April 5, 2010, and normalcy had returned to college basketball.

Duke was overriding a fictional tale with the facts. The Blue Devils were too big, too talented, too tough, and too well coached to lose to a small-college team that began the NCAA Tournament as a 200-to-1 shot.

It did not matter that most of the 70,930 in attendance on a Monday night at Lucas Oil Stadium—a $720 million palace built for the National Football League's Indianapolis Colts—were cheering for Butler. Or that most wanted to witness American sports history. Indiana's governor, Mitch Daniels, said he was anticipating the greatest upset "since Lake Placid," where an underdog USA hockey team beat the Soviet Union at the 1980 Winter Olympics.

Downtown was bustling all weekend with fans wearing Butler gear and shouting, "Go Dawgs!" That contrasted to the previously tepid fan support for the Bulldogs in their home city. In college sports, this was as close to rags to riches as it gets. Butler once considered abandoning major college basketball, sent teams traveling in an old limousine called the "Blue Goose," played before crowds of fewer than 1,000, and didn't cover the full cost of players' scholarships.

Among college basketball Goliaths, Butler was a David, except without the stone.

Butler had the smallest school (enrollment: 4,200) in the NCAA championship game in 40 years. This was a real-life version of Hickory, the fictional team in the movie *Hoosiers*, based on the true story of Milan

1

High School, which beat an opponent with an enrollment 10 times larger to win Indiana's state tournament in 1954. Movie scenes were filmed in Hinkle Fieldhouse, the 82-year-old arena where the Bulldogs played.

Hollywood wasn't in control, though. Duke was.

The Blue Devils were ahead, 60–55, and fewer than two minutes remained. It had been tense, taut, tenacious labor. The teams were never separated by more than six points.

Butler had trailed in the second half of all five of its 2010 NCAA Tournament victories, but not by this many points this late in the game. In the tournament, Duke had become the first to score as many as 60 points against the Bulldogs. Since this tournament expanded to 64 teams in 1985, no other team had held five successive opponents under 60. You couldn't solve the Dawgs' defense. You tried to survive it.

Duke's defense proved to be similarly impenetrable. This was old-school, possession-by-possession, hard-nosed basketball. And Duke could play that way better than anyone. Coach Mike Krzyzewski hadn't come this far to be denied a fourth national championship, second only to the 10 by UCLA coach John Wooden.

Duke forward Kyle Singler, toward the end of a 19-point night, uncharacteristically was called for traveling with about two minutes left. Butler point guard Ronald Nored dribbled around the half-court, nearing the basket, but was swarmed. He passed the ball out to Gordon Hayward, the Bulldogs' marvelously versatile 6-foot-9 sophomore. Hayward dribbled toward the basket before looping a pass over his head to Matt Howard underneath. Howard's layup bounced off the rim and through with 1:44 on the clock.

Duke 60, Butler 57.

Duke ran 25 seconds off the shot clock before Nolan Smith's left-handed attempt rolled off the rim. Nored cleared the rebound for Butler, pushed the ball upcourt, and passed to Shelvin Mack, who was alone near the 3-point line. Such 3-pointers in transition were Mack's specialty. This one missed.

The 6-foot-8 Howard, whose participation had been in doubt because of a mild concussion, was hustling as always. He outfought everyone else to rebound the ball. Howard passed out to Hayward, who passed to Nored, who sent it over to Mack. This time Mack bounced the ball for a while, then located Howard on a pick-and-roll play. Again, Howard laid it in. Fifty-five seconds remained.

Duke 60, Butler 59.

If the pro-Butler crowd had despaired moments before, the momentum had reversed. Seventy thousand voices reverberated under a stadium roof that was retractable, and perhaps that top did move a centimeter or so.

Time-out, Duke.

That allowed 33-year-old coach Brad Stevens to gather his Bulldogs on the sideline and say what he always did in such moments: "Stay poised. We're going to win this game."

After the time-out, Duke worked the ball to Singler, who was unguarded at the right of the foul line. His jump shot was short, grazing the rim. There was a scramble underneath as Duke's 7-foot-1 center, Brian Zoubek, attempted to shove Howard away. Official Ted Valentine signaled Butler possession, pointing that the ball went off Zoubek's foot. Thirty-four seconds remained.

Duke 60, Butler 59. The scoreboard had not changed.

History beckoned. Butler had the ball, and the chance to win a national championship. Destiny, not Duke, was the opponent.

Hayward passed inbounds to Nored, who dribbled right to left after crossing midcourt. Nored passed to Willie Veasley, then received a return pass and drove into the foul lane. Cut off by Duke's Jon Scheyer, Nored passed back to Veasley, who in turn passed to Mack. Mack dribbled backward, then saw an opening and headed for the free throw line. He stopped. Veasley was open in the left corner, but Mack's pass was deflected out of bounds by Zoubek.

Time-out, Butler. Thirteen and six-tenths of a second remained.

Hayward tried to pass the ball inbounds from the left corner, but with Zoubek in front of him, found no one available. Hayward placed his hands in the shape of a T.

Time-out, Butler. As before, 13.6 seconds remained.

Stevens wanted the ball in Hayward's hands. Twice during the season—against UCLA and Detroit—Hayward had been fouled at the finish and saved games by making free throws. Not that Butler's coach expected a reprise of those scenarios.

"I didn't think they'd call a foul," Stevens said. "My thought was, 'Shoot a pull-up if you have it.' You would just have to get creamed in the national championship game to get a foul call."

On a second out-of-bounds play, Howard began with the ball. Mack would have been an option, but he was stationed in the right corner and not in position to catch an inbounds pass. Howard passed high to Hayward, who leaped to catch the ball about 30 feet from the basket.

Hayward, guarded by Singler, started left, dribbled behind his back, and veered right. There was not a clear path to the goal. Singler stayed with his man, directing Hayward toward the baseline and Zoubek. Hayward stopped, leaned back, and arched a shot over Zoubek's outstretched left arm.

Hayward had made only two of nine attempts until then, but as he shot the ball with seven seconds left, this one looked true . . . but was not. The ball struck the back rim and bounced directly to Zoubek. Mack fouled him.

Duke 60, Butler 59. The scoreboard had not changed.

Players walked to the other end and took their places along the foul lane, waiting for Zoubek to shoot. From the sideline, Krzyzewski motioned where he wanted the Blue Devils positioned along the foul lane. He and Duke players stood, seconds away from what they hoped would be a national championship. Butler forward Avery Jukes, whose 10 first-half points had kept the Bulldogs in the game, was a picture of concentration as he kneeled in front of his bench. CBS cameras panned to worried looks of Butler cheerleaders, all of them adorned with a Bulldog painted on their faces.

Zoubek dribbled three times, squared his shoulders, and released. Swish.

Duke 61, Butler 59, with 3.6 left on the clock.

Then Zoubek executed a calculated risk by Krzyzewski. The Duke shooter intentionally missed the second free throw.

The Duke coach did not want to go into overtime, figuring the hometown Bulldogs would have an edge in an extra five minutes, especially with Duke in foul trouble. Krzyzewski reasoned that a missed free throw would make it difficult for Butler to retrieve the ball, advance it, and attempt a shot—more difficult, in fact, than scoring on an inbounds play. The strategy was defensible, with one caveat: a 3-pointer, maybe from half-court, would beat Duke. But what where the chances of that happening?

Hayward, with no Duke player between himself and Howard on the inside position of the foul lane, leaped and easily collected Zoubek's miss off the back rim. Hayward took two short dribbles and two long ones as he advanced the ball. Howard stopped to set a screen before the mid-court line, and Singler crashed into him so hard that he fell backward. Hayward took another long step and a half, and he aimed from half-court, about 45 feet away.

The 70,930 onlookers inside the stadium, 48 million TV viewers, and more millions online in 178 countries, watched expectantly. The ball they were watching was not thrown wildly. Hayward released with a running start, and the basketball had the proper trajectory.

"Hey," was the simultaneous thought, "that looks good."

CHAPTER 1

RISE, FALL, AND REBIRTH

Tradition is difficult to revive when it's been gone so long. Late in the 20th century, Butler University leaders reasoned that its basketball program could be restored and perhaps have a positive influence on the entire campus. But some suspected Butler was deluded.

Basketball at Butler was in a sorry state by the late 1980s. It was in as much disrepair as its old arena, Hinkle Fieldhouse. Crowds rarely exceeded 2,500. During the mid-1970s, there was discussion of reassigning all Butler teams to the NCAA's Division III, joining schools that don't offer athletic scholarships, and thus participating at the lowest level of college sports. Butler instead forged ahead, trying to compete in Division I—the highest level—with a Division III budget.

Past glories were distant memories.

Butler is an Indianapolis university that opened with high ideals and low funding, a condition that persists to this day. Although Butler is no longer a church-affiliated university, biblical principles are woven into its fabric, and especially into the 21st-century basketball program.

The pre–Civil War force behind the university was Ovid Butler, an abolitionist and attorney. He was the son of Chauncey Butler, a preacher for the Disciples of Christ. Because of poor health, Ovid Butler gave up his law practice, but not his crusading nature. Members of his denomination wanted to build a university, which was approved on January 15, 1850, by the Indiana General Assembly.

Doors opened at what was then North Western Christian University on November 1, 1855, at a site at 13th Street and College Avenue on the near-north side of Indiana's capital city. It was a modest start. There was a janitor, two professors, and no president. There was a mortgage, too. Money would forever be an issue. In 1875, the university moved to a 25-acre location in the Irvington area of Indianapolis and was renamed in honor of its founder.

As George "Mac" Waller wrote in his book *Butler University: A Sesquicentennial History,* "From its earlier days, Butler harbored the dream of becoming something more."

Butler University's first season of basketball can be traced to 1892–93, although no results are available. By the 1920s, the school was becoming more serious about athletics, and especially basketball. Although the sport was invented in 1891 by James Naismith at a YMCA in Springfield, Massachusetts, nowhere did it become more popular than in Indiana. The first statewide high school tournament was held in 1911, and basketball became a rallying point for communities from South Bend to Evansville, Richmond to Terre Haute, and all stops in between.

Harlan "Pat" Page became Butler's basketball coach in 1920. He was a three-sport star at the University of Chicago and once averaged 10.3 points a game, then an amazing figure.

In 1924, Page coached an upstart Butler team that presaged the national tournament run 86 years later. In the final game of the regular season, on February 28, the Bulldogs had a 6-7 record when they traveled 20 miles south to face Franklin College, then a national power. Franklin High School's "Wonder Five" is a storied team in Indiana, having won state championships in 1920, 1921, and 1922. The players stayed in town and enrolled at the local college to follow their coach, Griz Wagner. Franklin's Fighting Baptists won 36 consecutive games over two seasons.

Unexpectedly, Butler won 36-22. Franklin star Robert "Fuzzy" Vandivier was held to eight points on a single field goal and six free throws.

"My boys were 'off' tonight, and Butler was definitely on," Wagner said. "It's bound to happen."

Despite a 7-7 record, Butler earned an invitation to the Amateur Athletic Union Tournament in Kansas City, Missouri. There, the Bulldogs defeated Schooley-Woodstock 34-29, Hillyards 35-29, and Kansas State Teachers 40-21 to reach the championship game. In the climactic game before a crowd of 10,000, Haldane Griggs scored 12 points to lead Butler over the Kansas City Athletic Club 30-26, resulting in a national title.

The Bulldogs went 20-4 in 1925, setting a school record for wins that lasted 37 years. Success was accompanied by tensions, however. Page resigned abruptly in 1926. He had significantly increased the athletic budget, and there was speculation he quit because he would have to relinquish control of the fund.

Page's greatest contribution to Butler athletics was to bring in Paul "Tony" Hinkle as an assistant coach in 1921. Hinkle was to remain at the university for 71 years.

UCLA's John Wooden has been called the greatest coach of all time, any sport, though he disagrees with this popular wisdom. Wooden once suggested that Hinkle was the greatest because Hinkle coached more than one sport. Indeed, the fact that Hinkle could coach football, basketball, and baseball is probably what kept him at Butler so long.

"He loved to coach all three sports," said Hoosier historian Herb Schwomeyer, who served at Butler in various capacities for 38 years.

Hinkle was born near Logansport, Indiana, on a farm owned by his mother's parents. His family moved around before settling in Chicago. In high school, Hinkle played basketball, baseball, soccer, and golf. (His school had dropped football.)

Hinkle's father, Edgar, directed him toward the University of Chicago, whose campus was four miles from his home. Page, Hinkle, and Fritz Crisler, who became the University of Michigan's football coach, were the only University of Chicago athletes to win three letters each in football, basketball, and baseball. Hinkle was an all-conference guard in 1919, and the next season he helped Chicago win the Big Ten basketball championship.

In his sophomore year, Hinkle acquired his nickname. On a road trip, he came out of a restaurant carrying an extra serving of spaghetti and meatballs. Page called him "Tony," as if he were Italian.

After Page left Chicago for Butler, Amos Alonzo Stagg appointed himself acting basketball coach. Hinkle assisted him as he finished courses for a degree in oil geology. Page asked Hinkle to join him at Butler in February 1921, and to Stagg's surprise, Hinkle left for Indianapolis.

In 1926, Hinkle took over as Butler's acting head coach in football and basketball and served as athletic director. Butler soon hired George "Potsy" Clark as football coach and athletic director, so Hinkle was removed from those two posts. He stayed as basketball coach, however, for 41 seasons, interrupted only by World War II. After retiring in 1970, he continued serving Butler as a special assistant to the president. He was 93 when he died. If the university had allowed it, he might have coached until then.

Hinkle won games—even a national championship—but was more influential outside of his coaching duties. He was enshrined in the Naismith Basketball Hall of Fame in 1965 not as a coach, but as a contributor. He was on the national rules committee in the mid-1930s, when the center jump after each basket was rescinded. He originated the orange-colored basketball, replacing dark brown. Hinkle worked with the Spalding Company to introduce the new ball, which was tested at the 1958 Final Four in Louisville, Kentucky, and approved by the NCAA.

When built in 1928, the fieldhouse that bears Hinkle's name was the largest in the country and remains a memorial to its namesake. What was known as Butler Fieldhouse—the name was changed in 1966—is a hangar-shaped edifice made of red brick built for $800,000, or the equivalent of $10.2 million in 2010 dollars. The big barn on West 49th Street was the first building finished at the university's new location. It is a National Historic Landmark, and has been called the basketball equivalent to baseball's Fenway Park or Wrigley Field.

The Bulldogs, coached by a 30-year-old Hinkle, made their first full season in the fieldhouse memorable. They opened against Pittsburgh, which was coming off a national championship, on December 13, 1928. Future major-league pitcher Oral Hildebrand scored 18 points, and Butler erased a late 6-point deficit to end Pittsburgh's 27-game winning streak, 35–33.

Butler edged Purdue, 28-27, in the game in which the fieldhouse was dedicated, then climbed to 14-1 before losing to Notre Dame, 24-21. In the rematch, at Notre Dame, the Bulldogs crushed the Fighting Irish, 35–16, to finish a 17-2 season. Months later, the Veterans Athletic Association of Philadelphia declared Butler the 1929 national champion.

Yet Hinkle wasn't sure that was his best team. Two years later, in the 1930–31 season, Butler was again 17-2. In 1948–49, Butler was led by the backcourt combo of Ralph "Buckshot" O'Brien and Jimmy Doyle. The Bulldogs went 18-5 and made it into the inaugural Associated Press rankings—something that wouldn't happen again for 53 seasons.

Butler made its first appearance in the NCAA Tournament in 1962, winning 13 straight in a 20-5 season. The Bulldogs' starters were all from small to midsized Indiana towns, except for 5-foot-8 guard Gerry Williams, of Indianapolis. They averaged 6-foot-1. Even half a century ago, that was small.

"We're easy to underrate," Hinkle said.

Butler was led by 18-point-scorer Tom Bowman, rugged rebounder Jeff Blue, and Williams. In the 25-team NCAA field, the Bulldogs were assigned to play No. 8-ranked Bowling Green at Lexington, Kentucky. Butler's campus—then with 1,900 students—held rallies for the team. Bowling Green featured two future NBA stars, Howard Komives and 6-foot-10 Nate Thurmond. But Butler took a 56–53 lead on Williams's two free throws with 33 seconds left, then held on to win 56–55. Thurmond had the numbers—21 points, 14 rebounds—but Butler had the Sweet Sixteen berth.

In the Midwest Regional at Iowa City, Iowa, the Bulldogs trailed No. 3 Kentucky, 37–36, at halftime. Kentucky pulled away in the second half and beat Butler 81–60. There was a third-place game in regionals then, and Williams's late layup gave Butler an 87–86 victory over Western Kentucky.

The Bulldogs wouldn't play in the NCAA Tournament again for 35 years. They wouldn't win in the tournament for 39 years.

Buckshot O'Brien was among Hinkle's notable protégés. The 5-foot-9 O'Brien was a college All-American and played two seasons in the NBA with the Indianapolis Olympians and Baltimore Bullets from 1951 to 1953.

But the Butler player with the most enduring legacy is Bobby Plump. The real-life Jimmy Chitwood of *Hoosiers,* his basket sent tiny Milan High School over Muncie Central 32–30 in Indiana's 1954 state championship game, and he has been interviewed about that moment ever since. Plump was a good college player, too, setting a school record of 41 points in a 1958 game and ending his career with what was then a school-record 1,439 points.

The only other Butler player to reach a U.S. pro-basketball league in the 20th century was Billy Shepherd, whose career scoring average of 24.1 remains the Butler record. He played three seasons in the ABA, from 1972 to 1975. Shepherd played for Hinkle's last team. Before the coach's final game, on February 23, 1970, a ceremony honoring him included an ovation lasting two and a half minutes. Notre Dame and Butler played what was then the highest-scoring game in fieldhouse history before an estimated 17,000, exceeding capacity. Austin Carr scored 50 points and Collis Jones 40 to lead the Irish to a 121–114 victory. Shepherd scored 38.

Hinkle would soon turn 71, but he wasn't ready to go. Hoosier historian Schwomeyer said the university president, Alexander E. Jones, pushed for the change because "he was totally jealous of Hinkle." Others have corroborated that version of events. Prominent alumni circulated a petition asking that Hinkle be retained as coach, but he resigned himself to the fact that the university wanted him out.

Hinkle finished with a record of 560-392, a .588 winning percentage, and was the seventh-winningest coach in college basketball history when he retired. Toward the end of his life, he was asked to identify the best players he ever coached.

"We never had any great players, only great teams," he replied. "The kids did what I told them, and we played as a team. That is why we could win so often."

Following Tony Hinkle's retirement, Butler went into a two-decade decline. The university was ill prepared for the transition, even though President Jones hastened it.

George Theofanis, who played for Hinkle and had been a successful coach at Shortridge High School in Indianapolis, succeeded his mentor in 1970. Theofanis's contribution was bringing in more black players, notably all-time Butler rebounding leader Daryl Mason, at a time when there were few black students on campus. However, the coach's efforts didn't produce many victories. In seven seasons under Theofanis, the Bulldogs were 79-105, a percentage of .429.

The university's leadership was always conservative, according to former football coach and athletic director Bill Sylvester. And there was never much money.

"But it wasn't just in athletics," Sylvester said. "Other things hurt during that time, too."

In an era in which the Baby Boomers were reaching college age, student enrollment should have climbed. Butler's fell. The figure in 1972 was 1,731 when the university could have accommodated 1,000 more. In 1973 and 1974, the university ran a budget deficit, and the endowment shrank to $8 million.

The NCAA separated into divisions in 1973, with Division I featuring the biggest universities and highest level of competition. Division II granted athletic scholarships, but fewer of them. Division III offered none.

At a meeting of the Indiana Collegiate Conference, other university leaders asked Jones to bring Butler into a lesser division. He considered it, according to Sylvester. Such a move would have represented a seismic change in athletics and had a ripple effect upon the university for decades.

"What he was thinking about was the money," Sylvester said. "He didn't have the vision to know what athletics would really do for Butler."

Simply put, it was not a good time to be a Bulldog. However, this period produced a figure who helped pull the Bulldogs from quicksand: Barry Collier. The junior college transfer from Miami played just two years at Butler but later devoted himself to elevating the basketball team, athletic program, and entire university.

Collier's coach was Theofanis. Eventually Theofanis despaired of what he confronted. He had no recruiting budget. He recruited Collier sight unseen, relying on the recommendation of another coach. The team traveled not on a conventional bus but on a past-its-prime black limousine painted blue, the Blue Goose. Collier was a passenger in the Goose, a hand-me-down from Purdue.

Finally, Theofanis told athletic director Bill Sylvester that he would resign.

"I can't win without players," Theofanis said. "And I can't recruit without money."

That was 1977, the same year President Jones resigned. Butler brought in a new president, John G. Johnson, and a new basketball coach, Joe Sexson. Sexson was a Purdue assistant coach who had been a star player there.

Old problems festered. Athletics operated at a continuous deficit. Butler didn't have a secretary for the athletic department until 1970, a sports information director until 1981, or a marketing director until 1989. And it was never just about athletics. A 1984 report pointed out that Butler lagged behind other universities in fund-raising and recommended a campaign to raise $75 million. Tuition had been underpriced for years, compared to similar institutions.

"For the '70s and '80s, it was a Division I school in name only," said Chris Denari, the first sports marketing director and former radio voice of the Bulldogs.

A positive development was inclusion in a new conference of private schools, the Midwestern City Conference, beginning with the 1979–80 season. Of the six original members—Butler, Loyola, Oral Roberts, Oklahoma City, Evansville, and Xavier—only Butler and Loyola remain. Nonetheless, the MCC cemented Butler's status as a Division I program.

It would be hard to identify a Division I school with a more pitiable introduction to its conference. From 1980 to 1991, Butler lost in the first round of the MCC tournament every year: a 0-12 record. The sports information director, Jim McGrath, became so accustomed to losing that he didn't pack a change of clothes for the tournament because the Bulldogs always headed home soon after they arrived.

Sexson was 143-188 in 12 years, a percentage of .432, about the same as Theofanis. Sexson declined to speak about his Butler tenure, perhaps not wanting to criticize anyone at the university. His recruiting budget was $3,000, or a tenth that of the second-lowest figure in the Midwestern Collegiate Conference. Butler basketball was such an anachronism that so-called full scholarships excluded cost of books and other fees. Knowledgeable insiders never blamed Theofanis or Sexson for Butler's decline.

"They were trying to eat dinner on a dime," Collier said. "It wasn't a fair fight."

John G. Johnson improved Butler's stature during his 10 years as president. His administration reversed Butler's drift, setting up successor Geoffrey Bannister in 1989.

Bannister was not a sophisticate of basketball, an American invention. He was born in England and raised in New Zealand, where he was a champion cyclist. But Bannister's vision for Butler basketball in the 1990s resembled that of Notre Dame football in the 1920s—a marketing tool that could remake the university. The vapid nature of the campus extended even to Butler's stationery. Instead of blue, the school color, it was beige.

"We were dying slowly," said Bruce Arick, who has been at the university since 1990 and later became vice president.

If Butler was going down, Bannister said, it would go down fighting. The most visible changes were capital improvements and campus landscaping. Bannister hired 34-year-old Barry Collier as coach, and the president was the force behind a $1.5 million renovation of Hinkle Fieldhouse. Collier said the "same peeling paint" that was on the walls when he first arrived on campus in the 1970s was still visible in 1989.

The fieldhouse's decrepit basement locker room was upgraded, windows replaced, seatbacks added, offices installed, and the parking lot repaved. Seating capacity was reduced to 11,043, and later to 10,000.

"The university had gone into a quiet, retiring phase where people had forgotten its name," Bannister said in a 1991 interview. "Basketball is such a big part of our history, and it was a way to remind people we were back at work."

Bulldog basketball was not exactly a sports entertainment priority in Indianapolis. In Sexson's final season, 1988–89, eight of the Bulldogs' home games had attendance under 2,500. There were only 15 paid season tickets the next year, according to Denari. The 597 other season tickets were giveaways. Media coverage reflected the apathy. The only radio coverage was from the student station, and the *Indianapolis Star* had no beat reporter assigned to the Bulldogs.

Collier accepted the challenges. He was prepared for his job interview, and his 45-page proposal was persuasive. Coincidentally, both Collier and Bannister were born in England. What might not have been as evident in the process was this: Collier loved Butler.

It was a love that stemmed from his earliest days on campus. Collier, a transfer student, was fewer than three weeks into his first semester as a business major in 1974. He asked whether it was too late to transfer into education and was surprisingly ushered in to see the dean of education, Joseph Nygaard. It was near the end of the school day, so the dean told him to see him the next morning.

When Collier reported back, Nygaard handed him a revamped schedule and told him his next class was in half an hour. Any problems, the dean said, check back with him. The incident changed Collier's life.

"I'm sure that has a lot to do with why I think so much of Butler," Collier said.

As a player, he averaged 15.2 points and 7.5 rebounds in his senior season, 1975–76, for a 12-15 team. He and Bill Lynch were cocaptains and Lambda Chi fraternity brothers. Lynch remembered Collier as smart, tough, and physical. Lynch returned to Butler in 2011 as an associate athletic director.

"From the day he walked on campus, you could tell he [Collier] was a special guy," said Lynch, who has been head football coach at Butler, Ball State, and Indiana. "You could tell he knew what he wanted to do, and he set out to do it."

UNDERDAWGS 15

Collier started the requisite apprenticeship for coaches, serving as an assistant at Rose-Hulman, Seattle Central Community College, Idaho, Oregon, and Stanford. He sought head coaching jobs at Idaho (twice) and the University of the Pacific but was rebuffed. He was with Stanford at the Pac-10 Tournament when he heard Butler was seeking a new coach, and he immediately applied. During the 1989 Final Four, Collier met with Denari, who was about to take Butler's new sports marketing job, in a Seattle hotel room.

"I was really captivated," Denari said.

The best thing that ever happened, Collier said, was not getting one of those other coaching jobs. Yet he did not begin auspiciously.

The Bulldogs were 6-22 in his first season, 1989–90, and set a school record for losses. The next season, led by MCC player of the year Darin Archbold, the Bulldogs were 18-11 and made the NIT. Collier earned the first of four awards as conference coach of the year. There were other great moments—notably a 75–71 upset of coach Bob Knight's 10th-ranked Indiana Hoosiers on November 27, 1993—but the seasons were ultimately unsatisfying. To Collier they were, anyway. He yearned for the Bulldogs to play in the NCAA Tournament and became convinced his up-tempo style would not get them there.

At a 1995 summer retreat, Collier and Bowling Green coach Jim Larranaga spent two days with newly named Wisconsin coach Dick Bennett. Collier admired the way Bennett's Wisconsin–Green Bay teams played but didn't believe he should ask for trade secrets in the same league. Bennett was no longer in the conference, and Collier no longer wanted business as usual. The coaches met in an attempt to refine their philosophies.

"Not that you coach by," Larranaga said, "but that you live by."

Larranaga brought 107 pages of notes, and Bennett told him everything important could be reduced to one page. Collier adopted five principles—humility, passion, unity, servanthood, and thankfulness—that came to be known as the Butler Way. That was a foundation for everything that followed, even when Collier was no longer Butler's coach.

Larranaga took what he learned to George Mason University. He led George Mason to the Final Four in 2006, featuring upsets of Michigan State, North Carolina, and Connecticut along the way. George Mason was the first true mid-major to make the Final Four since 1979, but the Patriots lost to eventual champion Florida in a national semifinal at Indianapolis.

To Collier, the 1995 retreat represented an epiphany. He had "pieces of the puzzle," he said, but had not put them together. In basketball terms, the Bulldogs became better defensively and recruited more efficiently. More personally, Collier found that his Christian principles coincided with winning basketball.

"I wasn't perfect. Far from it," he said. "But that helped."

Butler won what was then the Midwestern Collegiate Conference Tournament in 1997 and 1998, earning spots in the NCAA Tournament. Collier recalled that after the first championship, his immediate thought was, "Is that it? I don't know what it was I had been expecting."

More important than winning, he said, was playing in such a way as to win. The path walked is more important than the destination. That's right out of 1 Corinthians 9:24: *You know that in a race all the runners run, but only one wins the prize, don't you? You must run in such a way that you may be victorious.*

At the end of the 1999–2000 season, Butler was victorious, game after game. The Bulldogs' winning streak reached a school-record 15 as they headed into the NCAA Tournament. Their 23-7 record earned them a No. 12 seed—each of four regions has 16 teams ranked from 1 to 16—and a game against No. 5 seed Florida at Winston-Salem, North Carolina.

The Bulldogs surprisingly led by seven points with four minutes to play in what was shaping up as a 12-over-5 upset, which had become a near-annual occurrence in the tournament. The Gators rallied, sending the game into overtime tied at 60. Butler twice led by three points thereafter, and was ahead 68-67 when Bulldog forward LaVall Jordan was fouled with eight seconds left. Jordan was an 83 percent foul shooter, nearly automatic. He missed twice.

Florida's Mike Miller took a pass on the left wing and headed toward the hoop. He avoided a collision with Butler's 6-foot-11 Scott Robisch and shot from five feet. The ball climbed over the rim as time expired. Butler lost 69-68. Florida advanced as far as the championship game—held in Indianapolis—but none of that mattered in the moment.

Jordan dropped to the floor, disappointment piled on top of grief. On the day NCAA pairings were announced, his great-aunt Jetha Jeffers had died.

The loss gnawed at the Bulldogs. It always will. Collier said watching a retelecast makes him sick, and he doesn't like to relive the game or talk about it. The game is hard to escape, though. It is often retelecast on

ESPN Classic. Collier has conceded that "our team played the way you want Butler teams to play."

As devastating as the defeat was, the outcome galvanized the Bulldogs in a way victory could not have. Adversity challenges, molds, and humbles. Prosperity rarely does any of that. The Florida game was perhaps the most important played by Butler in the 2000s because the ripple effect was felt in every subsequent season by every player and every coach.

Florida turned out to be Collier's last game as Butler's coach. He was soon hired by Nebraska, where he was 89-91 in six seasons before returning to Butler in 2006 as athletic director. As good as Butler's leadership has been in the 2000s, however, the program evolved from coach-centered to player-centered.

In the summer of 2000, players stayed on campus and practiced together without coaches' supervision, something that had not been routine. Henceforth, returning players instructed newcomers in the Butler Way. Open gym did not come with a license to launch 3-pointers or practice dunks. Inside Hinkle Fieldhouse, summer school was in session.

"They're playing for all the guys whose shoulders they're standing on before them," former cocaptain Mike Marshall said of Butler players over the past decade.

Bannister ended his presidency on May 31, 2000, so he wasn't around to see his vision become reality. His assessment was that the university had "every capacity but one for greatness—great financial strength."

After Collier left, athletic director John Parry didn't prolong the search for a new coach. Collier wanted Butler to promote 33-year-old Thad Matta, an assistant coach. So did the Bulldogs' players, many of them recruited by Matta. Ultimately, Parry sided with the players.

"Okay," Parry told them. "Show that I made the right decision."

Matta played for the first Butler team coached by Collier. Matta called that forgettable 6-22 season the worst year of their lives.

Matta was not going to deviate from the Butler Way. Collier introduced the five principles, but it was Matta who actually coined the phrase the "Butler Way." Matta's coaching debut wasn't as dreadful as Collier's, but there were bumpy patches.

When the Bulldogs began 11-6—and 2-3 in the conference—there seemed little chance of winning another title. But Butler showed what it was capable of by going on the road January 30 at 10th-ranked Wisconsin and shocking the Badgers 58–44. Wisconsin became the highest-ranked team beaten by Butler since a 79–64 upset of No. 3 Michigan on December 22, 1965.

The Bulldogs won their final five conference games to claim the regular-season title, then won the MCC Tournament by beating Detroit 53–38. The tourney MVP? Jordan, who was so despondent the year before.

The Bulldogs were seeded 10th in the NCAA Tournament and assigned to play No. 7-seeded Wake Forest in the Midwest Regional at Kansas City, Missouri. Butler players repeatedly said returning to the national tournament was not enough. They were there to win. They showed how emphatic they were.

Early on, Butler spurted ahead of Wake Forest 17–2, building the margin on four consecutive 3-pointers. Matta turned to his coaches, including administrative assistant Brad Stevens, and asked, "Are we really ahead 17–2?"

Matta asked for confirmation of the score four times in that half.

Soon it was 25–3. Midway through the first half, 30–5. By halftime, 43–10. It was an unimaginable deficit for a Wake Forest team once ranked No. 4 in the nation. The 10 points were the fewest in one half of an NCAA Tournament game since 1941.

"I think we played a little bit scared with that big lead," Matta said. "I knew I was scared. I didn't know what to tell the team."

Wake Forest never crept closer than 16 points in the second half, and the Bulldogs won 79–63. It was their first NCAA victory since the two in 1962. Coincidentally, the victory came in Kansas City, where Butler won the national AAU tournament in 1924. On hand for Butler history was Collier, who sat among a cheering section of about 400 Bulldog fans.

The second round pitted Butler against Arizona in a pairing that, by tournament guidelines, should not have occurred. The bracket was supposed to prevent rematches until the Sweet Sixteen, so the Bulldogs were no surprise to Arizona. Butler led 22–15 in the first half, but even its system could not overcome the Wildcats' talent. Arizona won 73–52 and ultimately reached the championship game (losing to Duke 82–72).

The Bulldogs' nine-game winning streak, and 24-8 season, were over. So was Matta's one-year tenure. He left in May to coach at Xavier, and later moved on to Ohio State.

Besides the two losses to Arizona, the Bulldogs' six other losses were by a cumulative 15 points. Jordan didn't complain about the draw.

"If we played again tomorrow, we'd have a chance to win, no matter who we played against," Jordan said. "We're confident in our system and our program, and that's just the way we are at Butler. We always think we have a chance."

The Bulldogs again wanted one of their own. That's what players told John Parry when Collier left, and the same message followed Matta's departure. The athletic director made the same decision he had made the year before: Promote an assistant coach.

On May 4, 2001, Todd Lickliter, at 46, became the Bulldogs' head coach. He and Matta were sons of coaches, graduates of Butler, and Collier assistants. At a news conference, Lickliter's voice broke several times as he expressed gratitude to the players. Everyone called it his dream job.

"He's really the brains of the operation," declared sophomore center Joel Cornette.

Lickliter was in his third stint on Butler's staff. He was an Indianapolis native whose father, Arlan Lickliter, was a longtime coach at North Central High School. Todd had played for Butler in the 1978 upset of Ohio State commemorating the fieldhouse's 50th anniversary.

His humility was revealed in self-deprecating humor. He liked telling the story about scoring poorly on a fitness test while at Butler. An assistant coach told him he was "the worst athlete ever to play Division I basketball."

Lickliter's score as a first-time head coach was much higher. The Bulldogs won the Top of the World Classic at Fairbanks, Alaska, overcoming an 18-point deficit to beat Washington 67–64 in the championship game. Nine days later, Rylan Hainje, who was born in Lafayette, Indiana, and grew up as a Purdue fan, carried the Bulldogs from 14 points behind to beat the Boilermakers 74–68. Hainje scored 25 points. Butler hadn't beaten Purdue since 1967, hadn't won *at* Purdue since 1953, and hadn't been 5-0 since 1930.

After reaching 11-0, the Bulldogs' early Christmas present was their first national ranking in 53 seasons. Their status intensified the buildup for the Hoosier Classic at Conseco Fieldhouse, home of the Pacers and a $183 million building that architects modeled after Hinkle Fieldhouse.

Host Indiana was 38-0 in its own tournament, winning those games by an average of 25 points.

Hainje didn't score in the closing 30 minutes—he went out early in the second half with an injured ankle—and Indiana pulled ahead of Butler 51-42. The Bulldogs came back, as they did against Washington and Purdue. With the score tied at 64 and time expiring, Butler's 5-foot-9 Thomas Jackson dribbled close enough to attempt a five-footer. The ball hit the glass, then the front rim, then bounced high. Cornette was there to slam the ball through the hoop with 3.4 seconds left.

Final score: Butler 66, Indiana 64.

Butler completed its nonconference schedule with a 13-0 record but fostered skepticism after losing three of its first six conference games. The Bulldogs won the next eight, finished 12-4 in the MCC, and won a third straight regular-season title.

Now all that was left was to win another league tournament. Not that it should have been needed for invitation to the 65-team NCAA Tournament. Butler, at 25-4, was first in the nation in wins away from home (15), fourth in wins (25), and seventh in winning percentage (.862). The problem was Butler's No. 66 ranking in a computer formula—Ratings Percentage Index (RPI)—that the NCAA committee used to help select and seed the tournament field.

The Bulldogs traveled to Cleveland for the league tournament. Fewer than 12 hours before tip-off, there was tragedy on a team that was as close as family. At about 3:30 A.M., a phone call brought news that the mother of junior forward Rob Walls had died. Walls's mother, Maxine, was 50. His roommate was Hainje. All the players were grief-stricken when they gathered for breakfast at 7:45.

Those who watched Butler meet eighth-seeded Green Bay in a noon quarterfinal saw a team that was barely recognizable. The Bulldogs trailed 23-10 late in the first half. They pulled themselves together and went ahead 48-40 with two minutes remaining. But in the final 64 seconds, Butler missed the front end of three one-and-one chances—six potential points resulting in zero—and were overtaken by Green Bay's closing 9-0 spurt.

The 49-48 defeat eliminated the Bulldogs and prompted a nationwide debate on whether they belonged in the NCAA Tournament. The committee delivered a verdict eight days later: no.

Lickliter was numb and the players devastated. Butler was accepted into the NIT, beating Bowling Green 81-69 before losing at Syracuse

66–65 in overtime. A season that started with promise in Alaska ended in anguish in upstate New York.

These Bulldogs were forever known as the Snub Team. They almost certainly changed college basketball more than if they had actually made the NCAA Tournament. Did they belong? Well, they defeated Indiana, which reached the national championship game.

NCAA insiders acknowledged to Parry that Butler's omission was a mistake. The RPI formula was amended to give greater weight to road wins. The MCC, soon renamed the Horizon League, changed its tournament format to reward the regular-season champion with home-court advantage. None of Butler's biggest wins—Washington, Purdue, Ball State, Indiana—was televised. The Snub Team predated ESPN's *Bracket-Buster* series, which featured TV games pairing mid-major teams. The Snub Team left a legacy exceeding that of championship teams.

"I think that team did something for college basketball," Lickliter said.

Butler began the 2002–03 season without the gifted duo of Rylan Hainje and Thomas Jackson. What the Bulldogs lacked in talent they compensated for in experience—and agitation. The snub stung. It always would. All the Bulldogs could do was make sure it didn't happen again.

For the second year in a row, Butler started 10-0. That streak ended in Hawaii, which turned out to be no paradise. In the championship game of the Rainbow Classic, Butler led by 21 points in the first half and by 15 with four minutes left. The host Rainbow Warriors forced enough turnovers to create a 66–66 tie at the end of regulation, although witnesses said the officiating was an embarrassment. Hawaii won 81–78 in overtime.

"It was the worst 'homer' job I have ever seen," said longtime broadcaster Chris Denari. "They were making stuff up."

Upon returning to the mainland, the Bulldogs picked up where they left off. They ran their record to 15-1 before losing 69–65 at nemesis Milwaukee. They bounced back with a 68–53 victory at Green Bay, then headed to Durham, North Carolina, for a nonconference game at fifth-ranked Duke.

The Blue Devils had won 22 in a row at home. Since 1986, under coach Mike Krzyzewski, they had been to the Final Four nine times and won three national championships. The Bulldogs were within six, 26–20, before halftime. Yet after Duke scored the last six points of the first half and the first six of the second, it was 38–20 and effectively over. Duke won easily, 80–60. The game had an NCAA Tournament atmosphere, Krzyzewski said.

"Butler is a tremendous school . . . beautiful kids, well coached," he said. "It was an honor for us to play them."

The Bulldogs stumbled once more in the league, losing at Loyola 73–63, but kept pace with Milwaukee in a two-team race to the finish. Heading into a finale at Hinkle Fieldhouse on March 1, 2003, both teams were 13-2. Only the winner, and champion of the regular season, would be in position for an at-large berth in the NCAA Tournament.

A sellout of 11,043 packed the arena. The Bulldogs led by 15 points in the first half and 16 in the second, but there was never security against a team coached by Bruce Pearl. The Bulldogs' lead gradually eroded, and they fell behind 74–73 with 4.2 seconds left. Butler called time-out.

On the Milwaukee bench, Pearl reminded the Panthers about the shooting range of Butler guards Brandon Miller and Darnell Archey. Mike Monserez had the ball to throw inbounds. He ran along the baseline, searching for an open teammate. With little choice, he passed to a freshman, Avery Sheets, on Butler's side of half-court.

There was no defender to impede Sheets as seconds ticked away. He kept dribbling until he was outside the 3-point arc, to the left of the key. His shot rippled the nets.

Final score: Butler 76, Milwaukee 74.

Fans swarmed onto the court, jostling some Milwaukee players. The Bulldogs had won a fourth consecutive league title, an uphill climb requiring five victories in 10 days. The old barn throbbed as it had in so many moments past. Sheets walked among the fans for nearly two hours. He was still wearing his uniform, as if taking it off would make the magic disappear. Cornette choked back tears.

"You can't tell me this was just a game," he said. "It's so much more."

The rematch came 10 days later. The league hadn't yet switched to its new tournament format and, coincidentally, it was Milwaukee's turn to be host school. So it was the Panthers versus the Bulldogs in the championship game to determine an automatic berth in the NCAA Tournament.

The five previous Butler–Milwaukee games had been decided by a total of 13 points, four times on the final shot. The sequel wasn't as compelling. Milwaukee led 14-0, 21-4, and 38-16. The Panthers' 69–52 victory sent the Bulldogs to another agonizing wait on Selection Sunday. Miller, so sick he had lost 14 pounds, was off form. Cornette was tearful and alluded to the snub.

"I really hope this isn't it," he said. "I hope people really take a look at what we've done and put us in the dance. Because we deserve it."

Butler was 25-5 in 2002–03, the same as in 2001–02. The difference? Its RPI was 37th, or 40 places higher. Butler's five losses—to Duke, Hawaii, Milwaukee (twice), and Loyola—were to teams with a cumulative home record of 50-3. Was Butler really better than the year before? It all seemed so capricious. Archey kept telling himself Butler was in, just so he could sleep.

Butler *was* in. Barely. Butler and Brigham Young, both No. 12 seeds, were the two lowest at-large teams. Butler was possibly the last team admitted to the tournament. The Bulldogs were dispatched to an East Regional game against No. 5 seed Mississippi State at Birmingham, Alabama. Mississippi State was a trendy pick to reach the Final Four, having come off a 64–57 loss to No. 2 Kentucky in the Southeastern Conference Tournament.

Cornette had grown out his hair for 15 months, but he agreed to shave it off in a display of solidarity with teammates. Otherwise, the national stage featured the same old Dawgs: rigid on defense, deliberate on offense. With Butler trailing 46–45 and the shot clock expiring, Miller threw the ball out of bounds with 1:04 on the clock. But after a Mississippi State miss, Miller grabbed the ball and kept it. Lickliter paced the sideline in his first NCAA Tournament game as a head coach but did not call time-out.

Miller found an opening in the lane and arched in a running one-hander, a shot he had often practiced in the off-season. The ball went through with 6.2 seconds left and sent Butler ahead 47–46. A 3-pointer by Mississippi State missed at the buzzer, and Butler won. Miller ran around pumping his fist in the air, and Monserez jumped onto a press table in jubilation.

It was the most notable upset of the first round and paired the Bulldogs against No. 4 seed Louisville. Louisville's Rick Pitino had coached in four Final Fours—with Providence in 1987 and with Kentucky in 1993, 1996, and 1997—and had a team good enough to go that far again. As for the Bulldogs, they were playing not only for themselves but for the 2001–02 seniors.

"We feel like we were owed one from last year anyway, getting snubbed," Cornette said.

The Louisville game supplied two enduring images in Butler basketball lore:

- One was of Archey alone in the left corner, sinking another 3-pointer. He was 8 of 9 from the arc, including 6 of 6 in the second half, and scored 26 points.
- The other was of Rob Walls's shoes. Late in the game, Cornette dove into his bench trying to retrieve a loose ball. He knocked over two water coolers, one with a sports drink that left his shoes oozing blue liquid. Walls, without hesitation, pulled off his size 15s and passed them to Cornette. Butler called a 20-second time-out so Cornette could change. He called them Cinderella's slippers.

"That's just a small example of what the Butler Way is," Walls said.

Butler, after trailing by 15 in the first half, came back to beat Louisville 79–71. The Bulldogs had returned to the Sweet Sixteen, 41 years after Tony Hinkle took them there. Cornette reiterated the defiance that had been fueling the Bulldogs, chiding the media for not giving them a shot.

"And we're still playing for a national championship," he said. "And we are still *here*."

Butler fans celebrated as if they were national champions. The smallest school and lowest seed in the Sweet Sixteen endured a media blitz that was perhaps more stressful than the games. The folksy elements of the program were underscored when Cornette and Archey, both business interns, were on the phones selling tickets to fans traveling to Albany, New York, for the East Regional. Cornette conducted informal tours of the historic fieldhouse.

Next up was top-seeded Oklahoma, which was more prepared than the previous two opponents. Sooners coach Kelvin Sampson discarded film of the Mississippi State and Louisville games, saying those teams didn't know how to play Butler. Instead, Oklahoma's coaches studied league games against Milwaukee. The strategy was obvious: Don't let Butler's 3-point shooters shoot.

Ebi Ere scored 25 points, and the Sooners' defense limited Butler to 4-of-13 shooting from the arc. The Bulldogs were within 5 points until late, finally losing 65–54. They were deflated afterward, and not only because they lost. They finished 27-6—a school record for victories—but weren't satisfied with what others considered a tremendous achievement.

"Not just to get to the Final Four, but to win the whole stinking thing," Monserez said. "Why would you set your goal to lose?"

A small college in a small conference with a small budget can't win big all the time. Certainly, Butler could not.

Out of 13 scholarship players on the 2002–03 roster, 6 were seniors. The Bulldogs couldn't reload fast enough. Through 13 games in 2003–04, they were 4-9, or as many losses as they had in the previous two regular seasons combined. Lickliter didn't get the accolades he received the previous year, but he was no less of a coach. Butler went 12-5 thereafter to finish at 16-14, extending its streak to 11 consecutive winning seasons—the Bulldogs' longest run since the 1920s and '30s.

That ended with a 13-15 record in 2004–05. After the season, four players left the program. The start of 2005–06 was little better: Butler was 9-8. Brandon Polk, the league player of the year, and junior forward Brandon Crone would not allow a slide to become a free fall.

"We just had a lot of guys who didn't have a winning mind-set," Crone said. "At the end of the '05–06 season, we really started establishing ourselves."

Butler could have earned a league cotitle and brought the Horizon Tournament to Hinkle Fieldhouse by winning the finale at Detroit. The Bulldogs sank 18 3-pointers, a school record, in a 73–71 defeat. Their bid to return to the NCAA Tournament was foiled by an 87–71 loss at Milwaukee in the league championship game. But at the end of a 20-13 season, a winning attitude had been restored.

Still, after losing three 1,000-point scorers, the forecast for Butler in 2006–07 was unfavorable. A preseason poll picked the Bulldogs for sixth in the Horizon League. Paradoxically, the last time they lost three senior starters, after 2002, they reached the Sweet Sixteen the next year.

What no one could have foreseen is what a difference two transfers, point guard Mike Green and 3-point specialist Pete Campbell, would make. They complemented returning Dawgs: junior guard A. J. Graves, forwards Crone and Brian Ligon, and sophomore wing Julian Betko.

After an opening 77–37 victory at Tulane, the Bulldogs played in the 2006 NIT Season Tip-Off. The former preseason NIT was divided into four regionals that sent survivors to New York City for a final four. Butler, Notre Dame, Indiana, and Lafayette were assigned to the Midwest Regional at Conseco Fieldhouse.

Notre Dame had discontinued the Butler series after 1995, largely owing to a streak of five straight losses. In this renewal, Notre Dame held a 69–68 lead with 90 seconds left. What happened then set in motion the greatest prolonged run of success in Butler history. On the fateful play, Green passed the ball into the right corner. Graves caught it, behind the arc, and arched in his eighth 3-pointer.

Neither side scored thereafter, and Butler emerged with a 71–69 victory. Graves scored 28 points, and Green had 19 points with a career-high 12 assists. This was "big-time," Green said in a postgame news conference. He had spent his first two seasons at Towson University, playing on losing teams before small crowds.

That set up a meeting with Indiana, now under Coach Sampson. The Hoosiers built a 47–35 lead in the second half. But Butler overtook them, and Graves banked in a late 3-pointer as the shot clock expired. With a 60–55 victory, the Bulldogs were bound for Broadway.

In a Madison Square Garden semifinal against Tennessee, the Bulldogs fell behind by 13 against a team coached by nemesis Bruce Pearl. As they did against Indiana, the Bulldogs surged from behind. They limited Tennessee to 3-of-29 shooting in the second half and won 56–44. Gonzaga upset No. 2-ranked North Carolina 82–74 in the other semifinal, setting up a championship between two teams from outside the major conferences: Butler and Gonzaga.

"I have no problem with that," North Carolina coach Roy Williams said. "I think it's what makes our game the best game there is."

Butler had been winning with defense, but the script changed against Gonzaga. Butler sank 8 of 12 3-pointers in one stretch, extended its lead to 17 points, and won 79–71. Graves scored 26 points and was voted the NIT's most outstanding player.

"They outplayed us in any facet and every facet that I can possibly think of in basketball," Gonzaga coach Mark Few said.

The Bulldogs had prevailed in the tournament by winning four games against opponents favored to beat them. Their New York celebration was muted because they had another game in a few hours. The NIT finals were so unexpected that a game had been scheduled the next night against Kent State in Indianapolis.

The team's charter flight was delayed, and the Bulldogs didn't arrive home until about 3:00 A.M. Lickliter slept for a few hours on his office couch, never going home. The weary Bulldogs again fell behind, this time by 8 points, and were fortunate to send the game into overtime tied at 57. Graves's 3-pointer tied the score at 67 with five seconds left in the first overtime, and his free throws in a second overtime secured an 83–80 victory. Graves, who scored 22 of his 26 points after halftime, said playing in this game was the toughest thing he had ever done. Butler had won three games in 75 hours, with a flight in between.

"I'm about half amazed that these guys could do what they've done," Lickliter said.

In the next Associated Press poll Butler climbed to 19th, or its highest national ranking since 1949. Skeptics waited for the Bulldogs to flounder, but they won 23 of their first 25 games. Graves scored 25 in a 68–65 victory over Purdue at Conseco Fieldhouse, 29 of his 31 after halftime in a 73–67 overtime loss at Illinois–Chicago, and 26 in a 70–66 overtime win at Loyola. Campbell shot 58 percent from the arc in league games, making 8 of 11 3-pointers in a 92–50 victory at Cleveland State. As a team, the Bulldogs set a school record for 3s, making 20 of 33.

But after Cleveland State, the Bulldogs lost four of eight heading into the NCAA Tournament. They twice lost at home—to 16th-ranked Southern Illinois and to Loyola—and twice at Wright State, including the Horizon League Tournament championship game. However, the Bulldogs' November excellence was rewarded in March, and their 27-6 record merited a No. 5 seed in a Midwest Regional game at Buffalo, New York. The committee that snubbed the Bulldogs in 2002 was disparaged for awarding them such a high seed in 2007.

Butler made the committee look prescient. The Bulldogs beat Old Dominion 57–46, pulling away when Campbell came off the bench to sink three 3s in 92 seconds. Then Graves scored 19 points, including a late 3-pointer that padded Butler's lead to 5 points, in a 62–59 win over No. 4-seeded Maryland. In New York State, the Bulldogs validated their triumph in New York City. For the second time in five years, Butler was in the Sweet Sixteen.

"We've shown all year that when 12 players play together, anything can be done," Brandon Crone said.

Anything?

That would be put to a test in St. Louis. Awaiting Butler was Florida, the defending national champion, No. 1 seed, and featuring a roster of six future NBA players. It was Florida that spoiled the Bulldogs' upset bid in the 2000 NCAA first round.

"It still hurts," said LaVall Jordan, who became an assistant coach at Butler.

The Bulldogs led by as many as nine points in the first half, but Florida reclaimed the lead at halftime 35–29. Yet after Drew Streicher converted both ends of a one-and-one with 3:33 on the clock, Butler led 54–53. Impossible was plausible.

At the end, the Gators reasserted their superiority. They went on a 10–1 spree, scoring their final six points on free throws, and survived, 65–57. Coming so close to the eventual national champion—Florida would not be as challenged in any other tournament game—was of no solace to the deflated Dawgs.

"We didn't come here to give them a scare, man," Green said. "We came here to win."

Florida was the last game Lickliter coached at Butler, just as Florida was Collier's last game. Lickliter soon left for Iowa, accepting a contract for $8.4 million over seven years—and lasted three years.

Beginning with Collier and continuing through Matta and Lickliter, there had always been a coach ready to take over at Butler. Now it was Brad Stevens's turn.

CHAPTER 2

THE MAKING OF A COACH

After eight months on the job as Butler's athletic director, Barry Collier faced a momentous decision: Who to hire as basketball coach? Butler has football, too, but doesn't award scholarships in that sport and doesn't play major college football. Butler is a basketball school. Basketball is not only the flagship of athletics, but for many students, alumni, and Indianapolis residents, the front porch of the university.

Todd Lickliter's departure for Iowa was announced on a Monday in which, coincidentally, a former Butler coach was trying for a national championship. Thad Matta's Ohio State Buckeyes lost 84–75 to Florida, the team that rallied late to beat Butler. That night, Butler assistant Brad Stevens called Collier to voice interest in the head coaching job.

There was an expectation that the next head coach would be one of the assistant coaches. That's what players said they wanted. The position was as precious as an heirloom, and could be passed down only to family.

The three assistants were young: Stevens was 30, Matthew Graves 32, and LaVall Jordan 26. By the next night, Collier had interviewed all of them. After a campus rally the next day, Collier and the coaches gathered at the home of university president Bobby Fong for a luncheon. Also invited was Mitch Daniels, the Indiana governor. Daniels spoke to the assistants and surmised that one would be the next coach. The governor was formerly an executive at the Indianapolis pharmaceutical giant Eli Lilly, so he had something in common with Stevens, a former Lilly marketing associate.

"If you stood them up in a lineup, he's not who I'd have picked," Daniels said of Stevens. "Not because he wasn't very impressive, just 'cause he looked like the waterboy."

By that night—April 4, 2007—Stevens had become the second-youngest head coach out of more than 300 in major college basketball. Most of Butler's best head coaches had been young when hired: Pat Page was 33, Tony Hinkle 27, Collier 34, Matta 32. The Bulldogs' formula for success had been to hire one of their own, and they didn't deviate from that.

"It was a whirlwind before, it was a whirlwind those two days, it's been a whirlwind ever since," Stevens said.

The hiring process took less than 48 hours. Yet as far as Collier was concerned, Stevens's audition lasted much longer.

"I was at practices. I was at games," Collier said. "I was watching them interact and communicate with the team. It was because we just knew he was the right guy."

Chris Koumpouras thought so, too. Koumpouras, a pharmacist, was once Stevens's manager at Lilly. Coaching was not Stevens's original career path. Upon graduation from DePauw University with an economics degree, he was employed by Lilly.

It wasn't until after a year at Lilly that Stevens pursued his ambition to coach. After Lickliter resigned, Koumpouras turned to his wife and correctly predicted that Stevens would be Butler's next coach.

"I knew that no matter what he threw himself at, he'd excel," Koumpouras said.

As a youth, Stevens threw himself into sports. He was born October 22, 1976, in Greenville, South Carolina. Three years later his family moved to Zionsville, Indiana, a bedroom community northwest of Indianapolis. Serendipitously, the Stevenses moved into a subdivision populated with potential playmates. On Brad's first day of school, several first-grade boys showed up at the same bus stop. Some remain among his best friends.

"It was a lot of fun to grow up there, and I wouldn't trade it for anything," Stevens said.

He was an only child but never lacked for companionship. He was the kid who brought everyone together, whether it was touch football, pickup basketball, or home run derby. He was a people person, and nearly everything he did involved others.

An exception was the solitude of reading. Some summer hours were devoted to Chip Hilton books written for adolescent boys by basketball coach Clair Bee. The books were published in the 1950s and '60s, so family and friends purchased them for Brad at stores stocking used books. The series hero is not only a three-sport star but also tries to persuade teammates to share his virtues. Stevens carried a love of reading into adulthood, devouring volumes about leadership and recommending books to his players.

Football was the sport of choice in Zionsville, which won state championships in its high school classification in 1987 and 1996. It was not the sport for Stevens, even though his father, Mark, played football for Indiana University. Brad was into soccer, baseball, and golf, and he ran the 400 meters in track. But that was all secondary to basketball.

When he was five, he spent mornings watching videotapes of basketball games before attending afternoon kindergarten. On his eighth birthday, his mother bought him a hoop and came home from work early to see the expression on her son's face. The first game he can remember watching is the 1985 NCAA championship game, in which Villanova upset Georgetown 66–64. He accompanied his father on drives to Bloomington, where he watched coach Bob Knight's Indiana Hoosiers. Stevens spent winter days in the basement, playing with a minibasketball goal. He pretended to coach the Hoosiers, using a chalkboard on the wall.

One of Stevens's treasured memories is of visiting the home of Jim Rosenstihl, who coached Rick Mount in Lebanon, Indiana. Mount was such a phenom that in 1966 he was the first high school athlete ever to appear on a *Sports Illustrated* cover. Rosenstihl narrated film of Mount's games.

"Basketball was always my first love," Stevens said. "It's hard not to be when you're a kid growing up in Indiana in the '80s and '90s, because basketball in this state was pretty darn good at that time."

A favorite hangout was the home of Brandon Monk, who moved to the neighborhood from Terre Haute, Indiana. The backyard had a 40-foot-by-40-foot concrete court with glass backboards on each end, and free throw and 3-point lines painted on it. Stevens frequently rode his bike there, and the friends shot for hours, using an automatic rebounding device. Boys, even from rival schools, brought their own provisions, and Monk's mother supplemented with grilled cheese sandwiches.

After games of one-on-one or H-O-R-S-E, the neighborhood boys rode bikes to Dairy Queen. The loser had to treat the winner to a Mr. Misty slush, and Brad rarely, if ever, had to buy. One friend, Brian Flickinger, developed a virtual sibling rivalry with Stevens. They competed in everything, from sports to board games.

Although summer basketball has developed an unwholesome reputation for exploitation of players and recruiting abuses, Stevens's memories of those days are all good. He was on teams chosen from all over central Indiana and practiced at Rhodius Park in Indianapolis. Even at a young age, he traveled in basketball circles and could always find a pickup game. Anywhere he played, Stevens knew someone, or knew someone who knew someone.

Because he was around adults so much, he was always mature for his age. When he was 12, he played in a national tournament in Salt Lake City. With as many as 2,000 watching from the stands, he exuded confidence.

"I don't see many kids who have that," recalled his mother, Jan Stevens. "That's when it struck me. 'My gosh, what an incredible gift for him.'"

Stevens has often said his most valued possession is a key to Hinkle Fieldhouse. His affinity for old gyms didn't begin when he arrived at Butler, either. As an eighth-grader, he asked if a junior high tournament could be moved to Zionsville's Varsity Gym, a vintage Indiana bandbox that Stevens called a "mini-Hinkle." The gym eventually was torn down to make way for a library addition, but at the time it was where the high school Eagles played. The 14-year-old Stevens lived his dream of playing there, too.

"I used to say I love the way his mind worked," his mother said. "It was a lot of fun to grow up with him."

Even when he was playing the game, he was thinking the game. In the state championship game of a summer tournament, Stevens's Municipal Gardens team was down to four players in the second half. Injuries, foul-outs, and absences left the team shorthanded.

Municipal Gardens employed a triangle-and-one defense in which Stevens chased the opponent's top guard. Teammate Damon Frierson, later an Indiana Mr. Basketball, went on a shooting spree that propelled Municipal Gardens to victory.

"Brad's smarts really came through, and his basketball IQ," coach Red Taylor said. "He was a coach on the floor at that particular point."

Stevens was a star player in high school. His Zionsville pal, Brandon Monk, was the point guard. Monk said it was his job to pass the ball to Stevens. If there was ever any confusion about that, Stevens would declare, "Just give me the ball."

Stevens was not a selfish player and had the respect of his teammates even as a freshman, according to then coach Dave Sollman. The coach said Stevens was an exceptional shooter but that sometimes he had to nag him to shoot more.

"If he was inside the doors of the gym, he was in range," Sollman said.

The road to Indiana's state finals starts with sectionals, and Zionsville was ready to end a drought of sectional titles in 1994, when Stevens was a junior. The Eagles lost, and they were devastated. Monk hadn't been home five minutes when he heard a knock on his door, and Stevens was there. They retreated to the backyard court, where they had spent so many hours, talking and shooting hoops late into the night.

"At that point, Brad had forgotten the loss," Monk said. "He was already focused on next year."

The next year represented a Zionsville breakthrough. Stevens scored 97 points in three games, leading the Eagles to their first sectional championship since 1986. It remains their *only* sectional championship since 1986.

The 6-foot-1 Stevens set several Zionsville records, including season scoring average (26.8) and career points (1,508), assists (491), and 3-pointers (138). At a senior class dinner, Stevens awarded Sollman with a special gift: underwear with the rear end missing.

"That was for the four years of chewing his hind end off when he played basketball for me," Sollman said. "It was one of the funniest things any of my players has ever done."

Stevens's mother was more gratified by her son's off-court growth than his basketball achievements. He graduated No. 7 in a class of 165. Twice he went on mission trips, to Texas and Louisiana, with youths from Zionsville United Methodist Church.

Once while driving on a stormy night, the teenager slid into a car in his subdivision. Many cars were parked along the street because of a bridge game going on in one of the homes. Rather than ignore the incident and drive away, Stevens went to the door of the host and explained what happened.

"That made me feel good as a mom, that he did that," Jan Stevens said.

Stevens was neither quick enough nor athletic enough to play big-time college basketball. He was not recruited by Butler. But he wanted to continue playing. He had family ties to DePauw, where his grandfather graduated, and connections through Zionsville, which sent many students to the small liberal arts college in Greencastle, Indiana.

DePauw has high academic rankings and a prominent faculty. Alumni include actors, authors, musicians, journalists, governors, congressmen, and Fortune 500 CEOs. Notable graduates include baseball commissioner Ford Frick, Urban League president Vernon Jordan Jr., Vice President Dan Quayle, statesman Lee Hamilton, Angie's List founder Angie Hicks, ESPN founder Bill Rasmussen, and authors Barbara Kingsolver and James B. Stewart.

DePauw didn't offer athletic scholarships and played in Division III, the lowest rung of NCAA basketball. But the total package was attractive to Stevens. At DePauw he was a management fellow, in an honors economics program whose graduates often go on to study business at Stanford or law at Harvard. He was a member of the Alpha Tau Omega fraternity.

"One of the things that happens is, you get in a situation like this where you're around a lot of high-achieving guys," DePauw coach Bill Fenlon said. "There's this kind of expectation that you're going to be master of the universe in some way. That's probably the reason that Brad wasn't immediately drawn to the coaching thing. 'How am I going to go out and make a lot of money and have a great life?' "

Stevens made the dean's list but described himself as a stubborn student. Economics professor Mary Dixon remembered him as being confident but not cocky. He credited her for setting him straight.

"Brad, if you want to do anything, you'd better start doing things you don't like," Dixon told him.

There was not a lot to like about the DePauw Tigers during Stevens's four years there. They were a cumulative 56-45. Twice they had losing seasons, and only one other time has that happened under Fenlon, who has been DePauw's coach since 1992. Because the Tigers' talent declined, Fenlon asked more of Stevens than he ordinarily would have during his sophomore and junior seasons.

Then, as a senior, Stevens's playing time and scoring average (5.4) diminished. He became a mentor for freshmen Mike Howland and Joe Nixon. Stevens won the Coaches' Award, the only award that DePauw has in basketball, as the player who cared most about the team.

"That's what you're looking for all the time," Fenlon said. "It's easy to start and play 35 minutes a game. Being the other guys is tough. Those guys find out what they're made of."

Three years later, Howland and Nixon led DePauw to a 24-4 record, No. 4 national ranking, and a place in the Elite Eight. A couple of different bounces, Fenlon said, and the Tigers could have been national champions. The coach credited Stevens for helping reverse the program's downturn. The experience influenced Stevens's interest in coaching. He said his years at DePauw taught him how to play a role.

"You're working with guys who are 18 to 22 years old. They're as crazy as bedbugs half the time," Fenlon said. "Even the good ones are crazy. They're not fully formed people, even though they think they are. That's what I like most about what we do. We help guys grow up a little bit.

"We can get guys to embrace selflessness. If you can get them to do that, they have a jump start to the rest of their life."

The rest of Stevens's life started at Lilly, where he first won a prestigious internship. Corporate America was a natural progression. His job description was metrics and incentives for a sales group. He said the months at Lilly were exciting and rewarding, although he conceded he was "itching" to be part of basketball.

A Lilly director gave him what he considers the best advice he ever received: Do your best on the job you have, and good things will happen.

Stevens stayed connected to basketball as a volunteer assistant at Carmel High School, an assistant coach for Municipal Gardens, and as a coach at Butler's summer camp. He might have become a high school coach but did not have a teacher's certificate, so that wasn't a viable option. Eventually he reached a crossroads. He could maintain a comfortable lifestyle where he was, or quit and accept an offer from Thad Matta to become an unpaid volunteer in the Butler basketball office.

Stevens discussed a coaching career with girlfriend Tracy Wilhelmy, a DePauw soccer player he had dated since they were sophomores. Perhaps she should have seen it coming. On their third date, Stevens took Tracy to a high school basketball game in Anderson, Indiana, which was 92 miles from campus. She was certainly acquainted with Stevens's competitive nature. On one vacation trip with his parents, everything was a contest—laps in the pool, shuffleboard, tennis, miniature golf. One of his favorites is Scrabble. Finally, Tracy beat Brad. She calculates that he leads the series 500–2.

This basketball bug was not going to disappear. At a dinner with Tracy and Stevens's parents, he said he had made up his mind. He was taking the unpaid basketball position.

"It was so obvious that's what he should be doing," Tracy said.

Stevens's parents were not as enthusiastic. His father, an orthopedic surgeon, said he "about flipped out." His mother reasoned lost income could be recouped over time.

Fenlon encouraged his former player to go for it. The coach didn't think it was crazy or risky, and told Stevens's father that. With no wife, no children, no mortgage, and no car payments, the 23-year-old was in a position that he would not be in 10 years later.

"It's not like if it didn't work out you'll be sleeping under a bridge somewhere," the coach told Stevens.

Stevens accepted a job at Applebee's and planned to live in a friend's basement. Then, just before he was to start waiting tables, Matta promoted him to director of basketball operations in 2000. The job opened after an assistant coach, Jamal Meeks, was arrested for soliciting a prostitute and drug possession. Meeks resigned, although two charges were dropped and he was acquitted of a third.

It was an odd way to enter college coaching.

Stevens joined the staff in time for Butler's team trip to Finland. He told Tracy he should go, but that he would thus miss the wedding of Tracy's brother, Albert. This reinforced the fact that a coach's life was bumpy and unpredictable. For two hours the couple was no longer a couple.

"I was furious," Tracy recalled. "That was actually the only time Brad and I ever broke up, for those two hours."

He returned to her Indianapolis residence. She had thought about things, about what he had in front of him, about what they might have in front of them.

"I thought, 'Okay, I love him,'" she said.

She was independent before they met. She could do things, go places, by herself. She was "all in," as she put it.

Tracy continued working at a nonprofit housing development agency while studying for law school admission. She returned to her native Cleveland area in 2001 so she could be with her mother, Mary Kay, who had been diagnosed with cervical cancer. Tracy attended law school at Case Western Reserve University. For two years, Tracy made five-hour weekend trips to Indianapolis in her Jeep Cherokee to see Brad. While driving, she listened to law books on tape. Time away pulled them closer together.

In October 2002, Stevens proposed marriage on the lakefront a few blocks from Tracy's home in Rocky River, Ohio. He said he was "shaking in my boots," conceding he was eager to rid himself of the ring he had purchased. He got down on his knees, and she said yes.

She and Brad wed on August 8, 2003. Ten months later, and fewer than three months after Tracy graduated from law school, her mother died. The decision the couple had made in 2000 allowed Brad time to adjust to coaching and Tracy to enjoy precious time with her mother.

"I had two years with her, and we had this fantastic relationship," Tracy said. "It was an absolute gift."

The couple are parents of two children, a son, Brady, born in 2005, and a daughter, Kinsley, born in 2009. For five years, Tracy was employed by the Bingham McHale law firm and specialized in labor and employment. She examined each of Stevens's contracts before he signed them. There are advantages for a coach to be married to a lawyer, who he says is his agent.

"Which means I'm the only coach in the country paying 100 percent to his agent," he joked.

DOBOs can grow up to be head coaches. DOBO is the acronym for director of basketball operations, a long title with a long list of responsibilities that do not include coaching. The primary job is to arrange team travel and lodging, but it also includes monitoring players' academics, planning community service, organizing summer youth camps, and fund-raising.

Stevens was a DOBO, as were Thad Matta and Todd Lickliter. In his year in that position, Stevens lived in a house in the Broad Ripple area with friends who allowed him discounted rent. Matta remembers Stevens being mostly quiet but absorbing everything. The new guy on staff was "a basketball sponge," as Brandon Monk characterized his former high school teammate. Stevens was with the Bulldogs when they beat Wake Forest in 2001 for their first NCAA Tournament victory since 1962.

"It may have been as enjoyable a year as I ever had," Stevens said. "I didn't know what was going on. I was just so happy to be here."

He was no pushover, though; he was too competitive for that. Former Bulldogs center Joel Cornette remembers that they "would get into it constantly," playing cards or arguing over hoops minutiae.

Stevens thought he knew basketball until he became a full-time coach. So much more went into it than he realized, and there was always something to learn. Matta encouraged him to "think like a head coach" every day. It made him understand how small tasks fit into a bigger picture.

"That's something I really, really ran with," he said.

He could always run numbers through his mind. No one taught him that. Tracy said her "math geek" recalls phone numbers and addresses without looking them up. Brandon Miller, a former Butler player and assistant coach, said Stevens remembered numbers like the savant from the movie *Rain Man*.

Stevens studies game films as other coaches do, but also relies on analysis from sources such as kenpom.com, a college basketball website that uses statistics to evaluate teams' offensive and defensive tendencies and efficiencies.

He regards numbers as powerful, but he also understands the importance of words. His Hinkle Fieldhouse office has a library of books about coaching and leadership. He quotes from Bill Bradley's book *Values of the Game*—champions have a bond "that selflessness forges," Bradley wrote—and has been influenced by *As a Man Thinketh*, the classic by James Allen published in 1902.

Matta and Lickliter left templates to follow—so much so that players referred to Stevens as "Little T," or Little Todd. The coach asked incoming players to read *QBQ! The Question Behind the Question*, a book by John G. Miller about personal accountability, because that's what Lickliter did. Stevens cultivated a relationship with then Indianapolis Colts coach Tony Dungy.

"I hang on every word he says or texts me," the Butler coach said.

Stevens developed a preternaturally calm sideline demeanor, standing and watching with arms folded. However, fire burns within. Officials feel his wrath, and sometimes players. He doesn't resist being hard on them, but said he doesn't do so "unless they deserve it."

He was once so angry at the players that he broke a clipboard in a huddle. What made the incident memorable, though, was that he immediately apologized. Nick Rodgers, a nonscholarship player, said Stevens uses a velvet glove to discipline.

"He doesn't yell a lot," Rodgers said. "When he does, he means business."

Bobby Plump, the all-time Butler great whose shot lifted tiny Milan to Indiana's high school state championship and inspired the movie *Hoosiers*, said Stevens reminded him of his high school coach, Marvin Wood. Plump said Stevens was as good as anyone he had seen in years.

"He proves you don't have to shout and stomp your feet," Plump said. "To me, he's in the mold of three of the greatest college coaches ever— Mr. Hinkle, John Wooden, and Dean Smith."

Stevens's tenor of control and confidence transmitted to players, who believed they would win because they were so well prepared for each opponent.

By the time Stevens became head coach, he had been on the Butler bench for eight NCAA Tournament games and two Sweet Sixteen teams. There were distinguished head coaches at larger programs who had never lived through so much success.

In the days after the announcement, Stevens stayed awake until 4:00 A.M. answering e-mails from home. He slept a couple of hours and returned to his office. He could be so absorbed in summer recruiting that he would have breakfast at 7:00 A.M. and forget about eating the rest of the day. He loved mornings because the Bulldogs usually practiced at 6:30, avoiding possible conflicts with classroom schedules.

"It's certainly not my team," he said as the Bulldogs opened practice in October 2007. "I'm just blessed to be a part of it."

The Bulldogs were expected to win, and win big. The veteran team was coming off a 29-7 season. There were inevitable wisecracks about the players looking older than the coach, but the truth was that few college teams were as experienced.

Butler began with five senior starters: Julian Betko, 24; Pete Campbell, 23; and Drew Streicher, A. J. Graves, and Mike Green, all 22. Their average, 22.6 years, made them nearly as old as the NBA's youngest lineup, the Atlanta Hawks, whose average was 23.6.

Stevens said his sole responsibility was to coach basketball. The Bulldogs weren't newbies in need of nurturing. They were mature, nearing the end of college and preparing for careers. Graves's older brother, Matthew, was one of the assistant coaches. Players and coaches both knew the system. Seniors called the coach "Brad." It would have been illogical to be overbearing with such a group.

"I will be thankful to them for a long time," Stevens said. "Not for how good a basketball team they are or all their accomplishments. But how easy they were to coach. That showed itself to the younger players. They could have easily not been that way. 'Hey, this is something we all believe in, and we're all on the same page.' It probably gave us credibility."

The Bulldogs took a 3-0 record to the Great Alaska Shootout, a tournament introduced in 1978 in Anchorage and televised live back to the Lower 48 on ESPN networks. The Dawgs didn't wow anyone upon arrival from a 3,000-mile flight. All the players walked toward baggage claim. Stevens was last in line. He was asked if he was with Butler.

"Where's your team?" someone asked.

"That gives you an idea of what we look like," Stevens quipped.

At a pretournament gathering the next day, Stevens and his boyhood idol, Bob Knight, sat at adjacent tables. The 67-year-old Knight had more wins than any coach in college basketball history, leading Stevens in that category 892-3. Knight, then coaching at Texas Tech, had twice brought the Hoosiers to Alaska; they finished 1-2 in both 1978 and 1995. He enjoyed those trips, he said, adding, "The disappointing part of that is, my fishing over the years has been a hell of a lot better than my coaching."

Unexpectedly, the championship game matched Knight and the kid who used to cheer Knight's Hoosiers. Stevens was born about seven months after Knight won his first NCAA championship with Indiana's 32-0 team in 1976. The Bulldogs reached the Alaska championship game by beating Michigan 79-65 and Virginia Tech 84-78 in an overtime semifinal. In the other semifinal, Texas Tech upset No. 14 Gonzaga 83-73.

As a nine-year-old, Stevens was in Indiana's Assembly Hall when Knight famously threw a chair to protest a referee's call. In Alaska, Knight took time before tip-off to speak to the five coaches on the Butler staff, all of them former high school players in Indiana.

"Coach Knight recognized that he probably had a huge influence on all these guys," Stevens said.

Texas Tech might have had an edge in years coaching, but Butler had the edge in years playing. The Bulldogs had been burying opponents under a barrage of 3-pointers, and they continued doing so against the Red Raiders. Butler was 16 of 24 from the arc, setting championship game records for 3s made and percentage (.667), and rolled to an 81-71 victory. Green, with 60 points and 20 assists in three games, was voted most outstanding player. Among those awarding the Bulldogs the trophy was Alaska's governor, Sarah Palin, some nine months before she was chosen to be the running mate for Republican candidate John McCain in the 2008 presidential race.

Butler's total of 47 3-pointers was a tournament record, making the Shootout a shootout. Knight was never a proponent of the 3-pointer but said if he were a fan, he would love watching the Bulldogs play. He devoted almost all of his postgame news conference to Butler rather than Texas Tech.

"That Butler team really deserves to be complimented, and the best compliment I could give them is I wish that we played as smart as they do," Knight said.

Coming from Knight, Stevens said, those words meant something. Before the game, Stevens told Knight that he set a standard for team play.

"And for doing things right and for doing tough things. And never accepting anything less than the best," Stevens said. "He helped set that standard for this business."

Not that anyone would mistake Stevens for a Knight acolyte. For instance, as ingenious as Knight could be, he wasn't exactly known for his sense of humor when his team fell behind. But that was a ploy Stevens used in the Bulldogs' very next game.

In a rare visit by a Big Ten opponent to Hinkle Fieldhouse, Matta brought Ohio State to face Butler before a sellout of 10,000. In a reversal of Anchorage accuracy, the Bulldogs began 0 of 15 from the 3-point line and fell behind by 14 points in the first half.

At halftime, Stevens crumpled up some paper, gave each Butler player a wad, and asked him to toss it in a trash can. Shooting can be that easy, the coach said.

"Everybody laughed, and it was a good thing because we were down at the time," Green said.

Butler outscored Ohio State by 29 points in the second half and won 65–46. The downside was a knee injury to Campbell, whose 3-point shooting was a weapon and spread the floor for Butler teammates. That cost the Bulldogs in a 43–42 loss at Wright State. More costly than Campbell's absence was the coach's anxiety. Stevens said he felt he was "on edge" in that game.

"I felt like our team played on edge," he said. " 'From that point on,' I said, 'I don't want to lose a game because of my approach.' "

Another eight-game winning streak lifted the Bulldogs to 16-1. The streak ended at Cleveland State, 56–52, and the aftermath illustrated why this Butler team didn't need a butt-chewing coach. Players said things about one another that Stevens would never say publicly.

"You just have to go out there and be man enough to play," A. J. Graves said. "And half of our team wasn't man enough to play, and we got beat."

Green concurred.

"Everybody is not doing their jobs," he said.

After climbing to 25-2 and a No. 8 ranking, the highest in school history, Butler lost at home to No. 16 Drake 71–64. That would prove to influence NCAA seeding but not anything else. Two home victories netted the Horizon League regular-season championship, and two more the postseason title.

In the regular-season home finale, fans stayed for a short ceremony honoring the seniors. Characteristically, Stevens said the kind of people they are exceeds any playing achievements.

"Be proud that they are Butler," he said.

Stevens was ever mindful of Butler tradition. Before the league tournament's title game, won 70–55 over Cleveland State, he kept in his pocket a piece of net cut down when Butler won what was then the Midwestern Collegiate Conference Tournament in 2001. Players did cartwheels at midcourt, an old Butler custom for huge victories.

The transition from Lickliter to Stevens had been so seamless that news outlets still called Butler to ask for Lickliter. They had to be reminded that Lickliter left for Iowa.

Even though Stevens was more big brother than father figure—indeed, Streicher's older brother once played against Stevens in high school—the young coach had made the proper decisions and pushed the appropriate buttons.

"We've meshed together better than what you would have thought with a new leader, new coach, new team, five seniors trying to bring sophomores and freshmen together," A. J. Graves said.

Perhaps the season's greatest disappointment was something over which Stevens's Bulldogs had zero control. Despite a 29-3 record, No. 11 national ranking, and No. 16 RPI, they were a No. 7 seed in the NCAA Tournament. That meant the selection committee placed them between 25th and 28th. The loss to Drake was so damaging that nothing could compensate for it.

Butler was paired against 10th-seeded South Alabama in an East Regional opener at Birmingham, Alabama. The teams played evenly for 14 minutes; then the Bulldogs began sinking 3s as they did in Alaska. Butler sank 15 3-pointers and led by as many as 27 points in an 81–61 blowout.

Campbell scored a career high of 26 points in 20 minutes played, shooting 8 of 10 from the arc. Stevens became the youngest coach in 57 years to win 30 games in major college basketball.

"It's been fun to be a part of," he said, "but it's more fun because of the people you're doing it with."

It would not be fun for Butler (30-3) to meet No. 2 seed Tennessee (30-4). It was the first time in tournament history that two 30-game winners were matched as early as the second round. Butler players didn't say so at the time but acknowledged that they felt slighted, and Julian Betko later said Tennessee was the worst possible matchup. Four weeks before, Tennessee was the nation's No. 1 team.

But even after the Vols surged ahead 13-2, they could not distance themselves from the Bulldogs. Willie Veasley's tip-in with 37 seconds left pulled Butler into a tie at 63, and the game went into overtime. Graves's driving layup sent Butler ahead 68-66 with less than two minutes left, but Tennessee reasserted control and won 76-71. Green had the kind of totals that made him the league's player of the year—15 points, 7 rebounds, 5 assists—but shot 4 of 17 and committed 6 turnovers.

Butler's historic season, and Stevens's first season, was over. It was painful to accept, yet there were no complaints.

"You know what, last week we just decided this is what's been given to us, and we've got to go out and play," Stevens said.

Vols coach Bruce Pearl called it the best Butler team he had seen, and he coached against Butler's best while at Wisconsin–Milwaukee and Tennessee in 2002, 2003, 2007, 2008. Stevens would not be lured into those comparisons, only allowing that Butler "can play with anybody."

Although the Bulldogs won two national titles in the 1920s, and had twice advanced to the Sweet Sixteen in the 2000s, this was arguably the best team they ever assembled. They aimed at a Final Four and a national championship, even if they didn't announce it. No other mid-major since Indiana State in 1979 had won 30 games and finished the regular season in the Top 10 (coaches' poll).

For schools such as North Carolina, Duke, Kentucky, Kansas, and UCLA, there would be frequent seasons in which a Final Four was reachable. Not so at Butler. Maybe in the 2100s. A once-in-a-century opportunity seemingly was lost.

CHAPTER 3

FINDING PLAYERS WHO FIT

Butler does not have a glitzy new $20 million basketball practice facility, as Indiana University does. It does not have a $575,000 recruiting budget, as Kentucky does. Moreover, Butler's $59,644 recruiting budget for 2008–09 was merely third in the Horizon League.

Yet it would be a mischaracterization to claim that the Bulldogs managed to win without good players. No successful coach is so delusional that he believes he can win without talent, and no Butler coaches purported to do so. From 2002 through 2010, Butler had five postseason league players of the year, and two others who were preseason players of the year. Butler coaches didn't recruit as if they were handicapped in any way.

"Resources are not dollars," Brad Stevens said. "Resources are people. And we have great resources here."

What Butler coaches managed to do is locate players, perhaps overlooked by others, who they believed would prosper in college. Butler was not swayed by where high school prospects were ranked. Nor should it be, according to recruiting analyst Dave Telep.

"They are at the top of the food chain in terms of how they project guys into their system," Telep said. "If everyone was as good as they are at that, higher-level basketball teams would have a better success rate than they do. They never sacrifice character for talent."

In a *New York Times* study commissioned by Telep, 32 all-league players from mid-major conferences were evaluated. Those analyzed were admired at their high schools and had high basketball IQs. In other words, they fit the Butler prototype.

Telep's summation: Butler recruits with a rifle, not a shotgun. That is, Butler identifies a small number of players to recruit and pursues the ones it can sign. To devote time and money in a spirited recruiting battle, only to finish second to another school, "doesn't do you any good," Stevens said. A small private school with an 11-to-1 student-to-faculty ratio appealed to some players, he said.

"Couple that with the fact you're in a town and in a state that is mad about basketball," he said. "Add on top of that, that you play in a building that every basketball purist in the world wants to go through at one time or another.

"Does that work for every kid? No, it doesn't work for a lot of 'em. You bring a kid in that loves Hinkle Fieldhouse, that means he appreciates tradition, he appreciates history, and is likely a good teammate because he appreciates what's gone on in the past. I think those are things that have added up. All that put together creates a niche that we have to continue to try our best to recruit to."

When Stevens was promoted to head coach in April 2007, one of the first things he did was to meet with incoming freshmen Matt Howard and Zach Hahn, who affirmed their commitment to Butler. By phone, Shawn Vanzant told the coach the same thing.

Next, Stevens had to assemble a group of new players who would arrive on campus in 2008. Recruiting never stops in college basketball, but this would be a particularly important class. The Bulldogs were losing five seniors at the end of Stevens's first season, and would be virtually starting over.

Stevens targeted a spindly 6-foot-8 forward from nearby Brownsburg, Indiana, an all-state tennis player named Gordon Hayward. Assistant coach Brandon Miller was keeping watch on a 6-foot-3 guard, Shelvin Mack of Lexington, Kentucky, who was ignored by his hometown Kentucky Wildcats.

Butler's staff had once been interested in Ronald Nored, a 6-foot guard from the Birmingham suburb of Homewood, Alabama. That was essentially a lost cause. Nored was headed to Western Kentucky University.

No big-time schools were recruiting Gordon Hayward. No small-time schools, for that matter. Why would they?

He was a skinny white teenager from Brownsburg, a Hendricks County town of 19,000 off Interstate 74. Its residents were 97 percent white and its culture quite distinct from that of neighboring Indianapolis. An example of how distant Indy seemed: Hayward used to think Butler was a Division II or III school, not one of college basketball's rising Division I powers.

People didn't look at Gordon Hayward and think Larry Bird. They thought Opie Taylor. The kid himself aspired to be Steve Nash. He thought he was a point guard.

When Hayward was a 5-foot-11, 125-pound freshman, he would stand in front of a mirror, rehearsing what he would tell his basketball coach: I quit. He was thinking of dropping the sport altogether and concentrating on tennis.

"I was just thinking ahead, and thinking realistically, 'I probably don't have a good chance to play college basketball right now, and maybe I should concentrate on tennis,'" Hayward said. "But I stuck with it."

His mother encouraged him to give it another year. Results were not initially spectacular. A growth spurt was. Hayward's parents, Gordon Sr. and Jody, were both 5-foot-10, but a doctor speculated Gordon Jr. might reach 6-foot-3. Hayward was 5-foot-9 at the end of eighth grade, making him as tall as twin sister Heather. Two years later, he was 6-foot-4. By the time Butler began recruiting him, he was 6-foot-6, and he had two more inches to grow.

"You look at pictures of me when I was in eighth grade, and I look completely different," Hayward said. "You just have to thank God for what He's given me."

As a sophomore in high school, he averaged 5.9 points a game. The summer after that, he broke his wrist, missed most of the AAU circuit, and thus was out of sight of college coaches. As a junior, he averaged 13.6 points for a 14-9 team that didn't get out of its sectional. Butler assistant coach Matthew Graves was watching, though, when Hayward performed well in a high school tournament. Hayward could create shots for himself and for teammates. Virtually no other college had him on its radar.

The month after the high school season ended, Hayward participated in an Indianapolis workout for juniors across the state and attended by college recruiters. Toward the event's completion, he was playing on the end of a Ben Davis High School court by an exit. As coaches were leaving, they couldn't help but notice what was happening.

"He was making shots. He made a nice dunk on one play," Butler assistant coach Micah Shrewsberry recalled. "He kind of piqued everyone's interest. 'Who is this guy?'"

Soon thereafter, Stevens attended a workout at Brownsburg. Other witnesses included coaches Matt Painter of Purdue and Jim Beilein of Michigan. Hayward could shoot, dribble, pass, and rebound. And he was 6-foot-6 and growing.

"I was blown away with him," Stevens said.

His prospects evolved so quickly that Hayward said it was almost as if he were never recruited at all. He was invited to visit Purdue, alma mater of both parents, where he attended summer camps. Although there was no scholarship available, Painter encouraged him to come up anyway.

Toward the end of the family's visit, the Purdue coach surprised them by offering a scholarship after all. A Boilermaker player had become academically ineligible, leaving the opening. Academics became a pivotal issue because Painter did not encourage an engineering curriculum for the alums' son. Too many conflicts with basketball.

Hayward kept thinking about Purdue's offer on the drive south on I-65. There was no enthusiasm. He was analytical by nature, and the feelings were hard to process.

"Because it was always my dream," he said. "But it just wasn't the right place for me."

Maybe Michigan would be. He would fit neatly into Beilein's perimeter-oriented system. Hayward's mother made him drive the 295 miles home so he could "see how far it's going to be." Halfway to Brownsburg, he decided it was already too far.

Meanwhile, Stevens was making Hayward a priority. The coach was winning over the parents with regular handwritten letters. Stevens told Gordon Sr. that he thought his son could someday play in the NBA. Later, in a meeting with Hayward, Stevens told the player that. Besides his obvious gifts, Hayward could make the right play at the right time, even if that wasn't evident on a stat sheet. Everything Hayward could do would translate into college basketball. Eventually, maybe, the NBA.

"Going into that meeting, playing in the NBA was just a dream," Hayward said. "It was kind of eye-opening, though, to have someone say you could accomplish that dream."

Stevens called the Municipal Gardens coach, Tony Safford, and pleaded not to showcase Hayward on the summer circuit. Do that, Stevens said, and every coach in the country will want him. Hayward had planned to concentrate on tennis that summer anyway, aiming at a state singles championship in the fall season. He accompanied Municipal Gardens to a spring tournament, the Kingswood Classic in Houston.

Hayward had "a monster tournament," Safford recalled. Recruiters wondered who Hayward was, where he'd been, when he joined the team. He had been on the roster since fourth grade and played on four national championship teams. Never as the star, though.

"If he had grown sooner," Safford said, "he probably would have been top 10 in the country."

Hayward's father had seen enough. AAU basketball can be physical and loosely officiated, and he didn't want his son injured in that environment and ruin all chance at a scholarship. He encouraged his son to select a school—Butler, Purdue, Michigan, and IUPUI (also in Indianapolis) were all options—and end the recruiting process.

On June 1, 2007, while on a Florida vacation to Disney World, Hayward called Stevens and committed to Butler. Butler felt like family. Hayward came from a close-knit family, could study engineering, and could perhaps play right away. It all made sense.

"I've said many times that's one of my best days of the first three months," Stevens said.

Gordon Daniel Hayward can simultaneously be called an early prodigy and a late bloomer. Although the growth came late, the aptitude came early. How else to explain a four-year-old disrupting a youth league?

Hayward's father started him with a foam ball and a tiny hoop, then signed him up for an Indianapolis league at age four because Brownsburg didn't start organized basketball that early. Although Gordon Sr. subsequently helped coach his son's teams, he was a spectator in the Garfield Park league, which used small basketballs and six-foot goals. Late in the first game Gordon Jr. ever played, the score was close as time was expiring.

"Get Gordon the ball, get Gordon the ball," his coach pleaded to the peewee players. "Get Gordon the ball."

No one remembers the final score. But after that, no scores were kept in any of the games. Garfield Park leaders decreed a scoreboard made the games too competitive for four-year-olds.

Competitiveness came naturally to Hayward, a quiet child who was more comfortable in action than conversation. His parents remember announcing when their twins were three-year-olds that sports would not rule the family's lives, but soon they were shuttling them from one game to another. Hayward was always burning calories, so there was little wonder that he craved his mother's macaroni and cheese or Oreo milkshakes.

His parents, both from Brownsburg, also were athletes. Gordon Sr. was cut from the high school basketball team but participated in tennis, swimming, and baseball. He grew to love basketball in rec leagues, and has continued playing into his 40s in Sunday-morning games against other weekend warriors.

Jody Hayward was into tennis, volleyball, basketball, track, and softball. She was a center in basketball and led the team in assists. Sometimes she passed off too often. In a regional game, a teammate passed the ball inbounds to her. Jody immediately passed it back to her teammate—who was standing out of bounds.

The nurturing of kids in sports was a way of life in Brownsburg, where purple street signs were adorned with the high school's Bulldog mascot. The town won two state titles in football in the 1980s, had a 35-0 baseball state champion in 2005, and sent teams to the Little League World Series in 1999 and 2001. Hayward's cousin, Zach Koontz, played on the 1999 Little League team.

Hayward played everything: basketball, baseball, football, soccer, tennis. Or, if there was no formal game, it was video games, capture the flag, street hockey, Foosball, cards.

"Everything he picks up, he will beat you," said childhood pal Blake Hall.

An example of that came when Hayward attended a cookout at the home of an assistant high school basketball coach. The teenagers, several of whom went on to play college football, were wrestling in the backyard swimming pool and holding each other underwater. Naturally, it became a contest, and the skinny sophomore who was outsized ended up winning. Hayward hated to lose, no matter what the game was.

"He's always had this moxie about him," said high school basketball coach Joshua Kendrick.

The one sport Hayward abandoned after a few months was football. As a fifth-grader, he was an option quarterback going up against sixth-graders. He was hit "every single play," he recalled. His mother covered her eyes so she wouldn't see the collisions. He told his father that football was a lot more fun on TV.

Hayward's intensity rarely boiled over, so it was memorable when it did. Another longtime friend, Mark Conover Jr., said he and a buddy once heard Hayward spout a cussword while playing a video game.

"We looked at each other and said, 'Did that just happen?'" Conover said.

On another occasion, Hayward was disgusted during a tennis match and threw down his hat. It was so innocuous that it could have gone unnoticed. Unnoticed, that is, by anyone other than his mother. She angrily left the courts and walked away rather than continue watching her son.

"I was so mad," she said. "In my mind, when you walk on the court, you're a role model. Behavior and attitude, to me, are important."

There was little for the parents to worry about. The twins were acolytes at Messiah Lutheran Church, where their maternal grandmother was a charter member. At dinnertime there was a jar in the middle of the table where they deposited coins if there was a violation of good manners. Homework had to be completed, and on time. When they graduated from high school, Heather ranked 8th in the class and Gordon 11th.

"They push him hard and have high expectations for him, and Gordon always lives up to them," Hall said.

Hayward had his own high expectations. As a five-year-old, he compiled what came to be known as The List. He was so young that his father had to write it for him. Hayward kept it posted, and checked off goals completed. Years later, The List had a corner missing, the ink was fading, and the paper was crinkled. On it were Hayward's eight hoop dreams:

1. Play in NBA.
2. Major contributor on D-1 college team.
3. Make Indiana All-Stars.
4. Start at Brownsburg High School (20–30 ppg as senior).
5. Start as junior and sophomore.
6. Varsity as freshman.
7. Start on seventh/eighth-grade teams.
8. Start on sixth-grade team.

Hayward was so scrawny as a kid that he said he looked like a "white Kenyan." One of his travel team coaches, Brett Comer, called him "Stickboy." Hayward was never without kneepads. Comer, the high school football coach, told him, "There are two words in your future, son: 'weight room.'"

Coaches saw more than that in Hayward's future, although they complained he didn't shoot enough. Another travel team coach, Mike Dove, said the boy's basketball knowledge and ballhandling skills were phenomenal for one so young. Hayward was mindful of what was going on, where teammates were, what the defense was, how a play should be run. Conover said it was like his boyhood pal had a sixth sense.

"I told somebody in fifth grade, 'That's a Division I ballplayer right there,'" said Dove, the Brownsburg police chief.

Red Taylor, founder of the Municipal Gardens teams, coached both Hayward and Stevens in summers. Taylor counted 8 Mr. Basketballs and 71 Indiana All-Stars among those passing through the program. He placed Hayward on his all-time starting five as a point guard. The four others all became NBA players: power forward Shawn Kemp, small forward Alan Henderson, center Eric Montross, and shooting guard Eric Gordon.

Taylor said Hayward's strengths were a calm demeanor and mental quickness.

"You don't have to be the 100-yard-dash track star if you have mental quickness," Taylor said. "How fast can his mind put his body in motion?"

Still, Hayward had limitations. He was small, and Municipal Gardens assembled some of the top players in the Indianapolis area. There were summer tournaments in which he sat on the bench and watched his peers play. That was a hard adjustment. He was "a boy among men," his father said.

The growth spurt changed everything. In one summer game after Hayward's sophomore year, he was running on a fast break, caught the ball, and dunked left-handed. No one had ever seen him dunk, not even in warm-ups or practice.

Teammates sitting on the bench "went crazy, they went crazy," said Safford, the coach.

Hayward can remember the incident as if it were a video posted to his brain. The game was at Warren Central High School in Indianapolis, and he said, "I could tell you which court it was on."

Later that summer, a broken left wrist sidelined Hayward. That caused Karen Starkey, one of his tennis coaches, to despair about the upcoming fall season. But the injury forced Hayward to work on a backhand slice, a maneuver he had never used, and made him a more complete player.

Hayward finished with a 22-2 singles record. The season made him wonder if, with more concentration on tennis, he could win a state championship.

"It really showed he could adapt to adversity," Starkey said. "He was a quick learner. It actually helped him rise to another level in the game."

The next summer, after committing to Butler and playing in the Houston basketball tournament, Hayward devoted an off-season to tennis. In style of play, he resembled 6-foot-9 American star John Isner. Watching Isner "is kind of like me out there," Hayward said. Stevens attended one of Hayward's high school matches and, uncharacteristically, Hayward lost.

By that senior tennis season, Hayward was becoming more difficult for those on the other side of the net. He was quick for his height and his serve was powerful.

"It was tough when the ball would bounce up so high because he was serving from such a high contact point," said Dalton Albertin, an opponent from Lawrence Central. "When he came to the net, it was pretty hard to get the ball by him."

Albertin ended Hayward's state championship quest, winning 3–6, 6–2, 6–1 in a regional. The basketball player ended with a 23-3 record. Albertin went on to finish second in the state tournament.

The only state title Hayward could win now was in basketball.

Joshua Kendrick became Brownsburg's basketball coach when Hayward was a freshman, and the coach noticed Stickboy the first time he saw him in the gym. The young guard had skills and poise. More memorable, though, was an e-mail the coach received later that night.

The coach asked the players to do all they could to win a sectional. Hayward e-mailed that the Bulldogs could win the state. That's bold for a freshman, Kendrick thought.

Kendrick challenged the boys and was intolerant of nonsense. He asked them to write down goals, instructing them not to include playing in the NBA, "because none of you guys is going to play in the NBA."

As a freshman, Hayward played on the varsity. As a sophomore, he was backup to shooting guard Seth Fair, who went on to be a standout golfer at the University of Indianapolis. In a sectional game, Brownsburg's backup point guard was out with an illness, and the starting point guard immediately picked up two fouls. The coach trusted Hayward to run the point and the team.

Brownsburg was building toward its 2007–08 team, which featured six seniors. Besides Hayward, the Bulldogs had another major college recruit in 6-foot-8 Julian Mavunga, who was headed to Miami of Ohio. Mavunga, a native Zimbabwean, didn't start playing basketball until moving to Brownsburg before his freshman year of high school. The two were friends and complements. Hayward call Mavunga "a monster" and Mavunga called Hayward "an athletic freak."

As Hayward's size and skills grew, so did the demands placed on him. In practice, the coach vexed Hayward by asking teammates on the other side to foul him. Every play, bump him, thump him.

"I hated it," Hayward said. "I just hated it at the time and almost got in fights in practice because they'd just be fouling on purpose. I think it helps in the long run. You can't be frustrated by it or flustered."

Other Bulldogs willingly became role players. Hall's job was to set screens for Hayward. Everyone filled in around Hayward and Mavunga. The teens were all friends, so it wasn't a hard sell. The coach's toughest task was getting Hayward and Mavunga to dominate.

"I've never been around a group that spent so much time together off the court," Kendrick said. "They liked being around each other."

Brownsburg unexpectedly began 0-2, then won 15 of 16. However, in losing their last two regular-season games by three points each, the Bulldogs weren't even in the Class 4A Top 10 when the postseason began. Forget it, the Brownsburg players told one another. It's a new season.

After opening the Brownsburg Sectional with a 59–54 victory over Ben Davis, Brownsburg squandered a lead against Pike, which closed within 36–35. However, Hayward scored on three successive possessions then passed to a teammate for a 3-pointer just before the third-quarter buzzer. Brownsburg's 10-point lead turned into a 65–48 victory.

In the championship game, seeking its first sectional title since 1997, the Bulldogs were favored against a Decatur Central team that was 11-10. Brownsburg trailed 35–34, and Hayward was surrounded by defenders as time was expiring. Rather than shoot, he passed to open teammate Austin Fish, whose 3-pointer with six seconds left supplied a 37–35 victory.

"I see him do it every day," Hayward said afterward. "Fish and I shoot 100 3-pointers every day after practice."

Regionals in Indiana bring together four teams to decide the survivor in one day. In the first semifinal, at Southport High School in Indianapolis, Hayward nearly had a triple-double—14 points, 19 rebounds, 9 assists—as Brownsburg won, 62–58, over a North Central team that had beaten the Bulldogs 12 days before. Mavunga added 26 points and 19 rebounds. In the championship game, Hayward had 21 points and 11 rebounds in Brownsburg's 63–59 victory over No. 5-ranked Carmel. Brownsburg claimed its first regional title since 1995, and was two wins from a state championship.

"Gordon took it upon himself to be assertive, and he was just fantastic at that," Kendrick said.

In the semistate, played at Southport before a capacity crowd of 7,200, Brownsburg faced No. 1 New Albany, which was 27-0. The Bulldogs trailed 18–13 at halftime, and were deflated when Mavunga went to the bench with three fouls early in the third quarter. Hayward nearly single-handedly reversed the momentum.

The Bulldogs played confidently when the ball was in Hayward's hands, and he delivered. He scored 13 of his 24 points in the fourth quarter, grabbed 16 rebounds, and led Brownsburg to a 51–41 upset victory.

"I'm so proud of him for stepping up," Kendrick said. "He's really improved his game in just this postseason."

Brownsburg had been meeting, and defeating, some of Indiana's most storied programs on the way to the state championship game. Ben Davis, Pike, North Central, Carmel, and New Albany had won a cumulative eight state championships, and next up was Marion. The Giants, with seven state titles, were trying to tie the record eight won by Muncie Central.

In the climactic game, at Conseco Fieldhouse, Brownsburg was ahead 35–29 midway through the fourth quarter, but the lead quickly shrank. J. D. Cosby's free throw gave the Bulldogs a precarious 38–36 edge with 24 seconds left. Then Marion guard Julius Mays dribbled against Hayward near midcourt before driving toward the basket. Mays passed out to Scott Wood, whose 3-pointer put Marion ahead 39–38 with 2.1 seconds left.

After the teams combined for four time-outs, Fish threw a one-handed inbounds pass three-fourths of the length of the floor. Mavunga jarred the ball loose from a Marion player, redirecting it to Hayward. He put the ball on the rim, and the shot rolled in as the clock ran out, resulting in a 40–39 victory and sparking a wild celebration. It had not been one of Hayward's greatest games—10 points and 5 rebounds—but represented his greatest moment.

"I don't know how I was open or how I caught it," Hayward said. "But, I mean, it went in."

For an exclamation point, he won the Mental Attitude Award from the Indiana High School Athletic Association. When the Bulldogs arrived in their home gym for a postgame celebration, Hayward was serenaded with "Happy Birthday." It was past midnight, officially March 23. He was 18.

Hayward and his mother refer to incidents such as the state championship game as "can you believe it?" moments. They record such thoughts in a book of handwritten letters that the twins started as 10-year-olds on Mother's Day. Jody, in turn, writes letters to the twins.

The letters were bound and saved as family treasures. The twins didn't write as often upon becoming teenagers, but they submitted as many as four a year.

"If something ever happens to me, they would always have letters from me showing how much I loved them, and the things we did," Jody said.

Hayward was close to his family, and especially to Heather. When he was a fifth-grader, he was assigned to write a paper about someone showing good character. Gordon wrote about Heather. It was their mother's proudest moment.

"The moms all went, 'Aw-w-w,'" Jody recalled.

The twins were kept in different classrooms in grade school because the district wanted to foster individuality. Jody, also a twin, asked the policy to be revisited. The twins reunited, to the benefit of both.

Gordon pushed his sister in sports, and Heather pushed her brother in academics and spiritual growth. They were practice partners in more than tennis, according to Starkey, who coached both. They were Brownsburg's 2008 male and female athletes of the year.

"They were always together," Starkey said.

Gordon was so protective that intimidated boys were leery of asking Heather on dates. Their father acknowledged that Gordon didn't want her to date at all. Knowing that, some tennis players provoked Gordon at a fall dance when they *all* decided to dance with his sister. Later, at a season-ending banquet, the boys wore T-shirts with I DANCED WITH HEATHER imprinted on the back. A photograph shows the shirts' lettering and Heather with palms raised in a "what can I do?" pose. Gordon's arms are folded, and he has a disapproving look.

"He did not find humor in it," the twins' mother said.

The years did not diminish the twins' relationship. Heather, who has an artistic side, assembled a montage of the twins' photos, affixed them to block letters spelling out N-B-A—Never Believe Alone—and gave them to Gordon on his 20th birthday. At Butler, Heather joined the women's tennis team. The twins would not be separated.

"Sometimes I forget how good he is," she said, "and I think, 'That's my brother.'"

Although Shelvin Mack played in Lexington, Kentucky, for his high school, Bryan Station, as early as eighth grade, he was not considered an elite prospect. Mack told Butler in January 2008 that he would enroll there, even though he couldn't sign a letter of intent until April. His high school coach, Champ Ligon, said Mack was a man of his word and that Butler had recruited him the hardest.

"I think Butler is getting a steal. I think people have overlooked this guy," Ligon said.

Ligon spoke as much about nonbasketball traits as about Mack's hoop achievements. The coach cited work ethic, intangibles, and B-plus grades. Mack's chief physical characteristic wasn't strength or quickness, but a wide smile illuminating everything around him.

"He's a perfect kid," Ligon said.

Mack was a gym rat. But a more accurate testament to his devotion to basketball was conveyed when he mimicked a disoriented gym bat.

As a five-year-old, little Shelvin wanted to dunk. He leaped from a chair toward a seven-foot goal mounted on the side of a deck. The attempt resulted in him stuck, hanging in the net—by his teeth. He was rushed to a Lexington hospital for a root canal.

"I thought he would be done with basketball," said his mother, Victoria Guy. "It did not stop him at all."

As a youth, Mack was rarely without a basketball. In a modern culture of dunks, behind-the-back passes, tattoos, and trash talk, Mack somehow developed fundamental skills: dribbling, passing, midrange shooting. He was so old-school that in face and frame he resembled a smaller version of a 1960s college basketball star, Cazzie Russell of Michigan.

Mack's mother credited her grandmother—his great-grandmother—for her son's humility. He addressed adults as "sir." He has always been that way, his mother said.

Mack's mother emphasized schoolwork so much that when he once received a C on a midterm, she benched him for the next game. He cried, and the coach pleaded to let him play. Mom stood firm. Grades came first.

"He's better than that," she told the coach.

Turns out he was a better ballplayer than many thought, too. Two recruiters once visited an open gym and left disappointed because Mack did not dominate play. Ligon said Mack didn't do so because he was trying to make teammates better.

Mack represented Cincinnati's D-I Greyhounds in summer ball. That AAU club featured future NBA players O. J. Mayo and Bill Walker, along with high school All-Americans William Buford and Darius Miller.

"You have to go out there and work hard every day and prove people wrong," Mack said.

He could be so self-critical that he once wrote the initials "F.I." and taped them to his sneakers. The letters stood for "Forget It," so he wouldn't dwell on a missed shot or poor play.

He visited Butler and liked the coaches, small campus, proximity to home, and opportunity to play. He asked his mother to pick a school because he couldn't make up his mind. His mother's reply? It's your life, your decision.

Mack kept his commitment to Butler after Kentucky showed interest. As a senior, he began challenging good friend Darius Miller for the state's Mr. Basketball honor. Mack averaged 23.7 points, 7.7 rebounds, and 7.5 assists in leading Bryan Station to a 30-3 record and No. 1 state ranking.

Not that there was ever any chance of Mack growing an outsized ego.

"He needs to remain humble and remember the struggles he's gone through," his mother said.

Ronald Nored was born in Indianapolis. His grandparents lived on 40th Street, less than a mile from Hinkle Fieldhouse. Yet he had no intention of enrolling at Butler, even though his grandmother prayed that he would.

Delores Kennedy-Williams was told by her daughter, Linda Nored, that Ronald was going to Western Kentucky. The Noreds lived in Homewood, Alabama, a suburb of Birmingham, and Western Kentucky would be closer to home. Stubbornly, the grandmother continued to pray that her grandson would go to Butler.

"You can pray all you want," Linda said. "He's going to Western Kentucky."

Harvard had actively pursued Nored, too. That was flattering. It was hard to determine what would be best. After a stressful recruiting process, Nored signed with Western Kentucky in November 2007. The decision was a relief to the family.

That all changed when Darrin Horn left Western Kentucky to become coach at South Carolina. Nored's grandmother said he felt betrayed, and Western Kentucky released Nored from the commitment. The recruiting process was to start all over again.

Stevens was familiar with Nored, although their first meeting wasn't propitious. Nored, visiting his grandparents during a spring break, was shooting baskets at Hinkle Fieldhouse. It was a so-called noncontact period, and not wanting an NCAA rules violation, then assistant coach Stevens told Nored he had to leave.

Stevens was eager to have Nored around this time. The point guard had an all-state season—averaging 15.3 points, 6.9 rebounds, and 5.2 assists—and led Homewood High School to the Class 6A state championship game. He also was a graduate of Point Guard College, which enrolls aspiring high school and college point guards at locations across the United States and Canada. Five-day sessions included classroom training, video study, and on-court instruction. Coincidentally, Kendrick, the Brownsburg coach, saw Nored at one such session in Anderson, Indiana.

"He owned the gym," Kendrick recalled.

Stevens couldn't book a flight on short notice, so he drove 490 miles to Birmingham, where his Bulldogs lost to Tennessee weeks before in the NCAA Tournament. Everything the Butler coach knew about Nored was reinforced on the recruiting visit. Nored promptly committed to Butler.

"I just knew anyone would follow him," Stevens said.

Grandmother knew Who was responsible.

"I think it's just God's hand," Kennedy-Williams said.

One of the Butler Way's principles, servanthood, wasn't introduced to Nored at Butler. That virtue was taught by his father, the late Ronald Nored Sr., an African Methodist Episcopal pastor. Nored's father led a church and community that transformed a Birmingham neighborhood.

Nored's father, a former pitcher for the Lane College (Tennessee) baseball team, was a TV news anchor before becoming a pastor. In 1987 he went to Bethel AME Church in the Ensley area of Birmingham. The church was in Sandy Bottom, named in the 1950s for the ash that fell on the area from steel mills. When the mills closed in the 1970s, thousands became unemployed and the shotgun houses in which the workers lived began crumbling. Lots were weed-infested and filled with trash. Sewer and drainage systems were poor, and utility lines hung at eye level. Sandy Bottom was populated by transients, drug dealers, and bootleggers.

Ronald Nored Sr. described the neighborhood in his 1999 book *Reweaving the Fabric.* The book featured a photograph of seven-year-old Ronald Jr. on the cover and was dedicated to the pastor's sons. The pastor wrote:

"Sandy Bottom faced nearly all the problems that a neighborhood can face—from drugs to economic decline, from poverty to youth in trouble, from unemployment to absentee landlords. The community fabric was in shreds, torn by landowners' neglect, lack of adequate social and public services, and the indifference of people who passed through the neighborhood. Years of abandonment, betrayal, and broken promises had made residents very suspicious of outsiders, and unfortunately, that included church folk!"

The pastor wrote that he felt God calling his church to rebuild a six-block area surrounding it. He and Clarence L. Brown cofounded Bethel-Ensley Action Task, Inc., which raised millions to do just that. Forty new homes were built. More important, lives were rebuilt.

"It was a complete 360," Ronald Jr. said.

The son accompanied his father when he went into the area to work on housing. Every Christmas morning, Ronald and brother Randall didn't awaken and begin opening presents under the tree. First, they went with their father to distribute gifts to needy children. If people needed a meal, they could eat at the Noreds' home. If someone needed money, Ronald Sr. would reach into his own pocket and hand over as much as $200.

"He was an awesome person to be around," Ronald Jr. said. "If you really, really got to know him and listen to him and hear him talk and hear what he was about, it was a wonder."

The pastor was honored as Birmingham Citizen of the Year and posthumously given the Martin Luther King Jr. American Dream Award.

Ronald Nored Sr. was diagnosed with pancreatic cancer in July 2002, soon after returning from a trip to South Africa. He was told he had six months to live. As ill as he was, he watched from a wheelchair when his sons played in basketball and football games. The pastor told his wife he wasn't afraid to die but would miss seeing his sons grow up.

Ronald Nored Sr. died October 11, 2003. He was 43.

That was a painful period for the sons, who were especially close to their father, according to mother Linda. While she attended law school, her husband was the primary caregiver. When his father died, Ronald Jr. was in eighth grade and a star running back. He created an uproar when he quit football, which is king in Alabama, to concentrate on basketball.

Later, Dad wasn't around to help with the recruiting process. But he was always in his sons' souls.

"The real gift that both of them got is they have such fond memories of their dad," the mother said. "Not everyone has that."

Ronald Jr. says that he if can accomplish in his lifetime half of what his father did in 43 years, he will have accomplished a lot. The son could speak about his father without sadness, saying his father's life was something to celebrate, learn from, and live by.

"I can only be proud to say that I'm his son," Ronald Jr. said.

Enrolling at Butler brought him full circle to the Circle City. He was born in Indianapolis because his mother once worked at Methodist Hospital there. She traveled from Alabama so she could deliver her first child at that hospital. Nored's aunt, Lenore Williams, was the pastor at St. John African Methodist Episcopal Church, at the corner of 17th Street and Columbia Avenue in Indy.

Nored never expected to be attending classes on a campus where he spent summers riding bikes past Holcomb Gardens and Atherton Union. Upon arriving for his first semester at Butler, he walked past all those familiar places and relived those days.

Then he went to live out new memories.

There was a characteristic common to those in Butler's 2008 recruiting class. All five players had been to a state championship game in high school or played for a No. 1-ranked team. Hayward's shot won a state title, Mack's 30-3 team reached No. 1, and Nored's team made it to the championship game.

"We wanted to get a class that could come in and be as competitive as possible without forfeiting the team-first, improve-today mentality," Stevens said.

Another recruit, Garrett Butcher, led Edgewood High School of Ellettsville, Indiana, to a Class 3A No. 1 ranking when he was a junior. Edgewood was 45-4 in his final two seasons. Butcher became Monroe County's all-time leading scorer, surpassing NBA player Sean May.

Chase Stigall became the fifth guard in the 2000s from New Castle, Indiana, to choose Butler. He and the Bulldogs' Zach Hahn helped New Castle win a 3A state championship in 2007.

Four of Butler's incoming freshmen were chosen for the prestigious Indiana–Kentucky All-Star games—Hayward, Butcher, and Stigall for Indiana, and Mack for Kentucky. In the first game of the all-star double-header, played in Indianapolis, Indiana overcame an 11-point deficit to beat Kentucky 83–82 despite Mack's 24 points. Hayward had 11 points and 8 rebounds for Indiana. Two days later, in Louisville, Mack scored 16 points as Kentucky ended a streak of eight straight losses in the series 95–78.

The record showed the Indiana–Kentucky series even: 1-1. But there was one winner: Butler.

CHAPTER 4

BUILDING FOR ETERNITY

Coach Brad Stevens's second Butler team was nothing like his first. The teams could not have contrasted more.

Stevens's 2007–08 Bulldogs were so old that the players weren't much younger than their 30-year-old coach. In a public event before Halloween, Stevens joked about the youth of the '08–09 team. He said the Bulldogs were so young that:

- "I don't get asked how old I am anymore,"
- "Every practice we have nap time *and* recess," and
- "On Friday we have to cut practice short to end at five because trick-or-treating starts at six."

Butler was the fourth youngest of 344 college basketball teams. There was not a senior on the roster. Two juniors, Willie Veasley and Avery Jukes, were on scholarship. There were five freshmen and four sophomores. The team leader was a sophomore, 6-foot-8 Matt Howard. So it was justifiable for a preseason poll to pick Butler fifth in the Horizon League.

To surpass such low expectations, some of the five freshmen—Gordon Hayward, Shelvin Mack, Ronald Nored, Garrett Butcher, and Chase Stigall—would have to come through. All summer, returnees and newcomers played informal games. Former Butler forward Mike Marshall was so impressed with the recruits that he told Stevens, "You're going to start three freshmen." The coach was skeptical. That wasn't the way it was done at Butler.

• • •

The young Bulldogs contradicted forecasts about the program's demise, winning their first eight games. Their streak ended in a December 13 loss at 21st-ranked Ohio State, 54–51. The Bulldogs trailed by 13 before Hayward's seventh 3-pointer of the game tied the score at 51. He was nudged by Ohio State's David Lighty on a 3-point attempt as time expired. It wasn't a flagrant collision, and no foul was called. Hayward scored 25 points but would have gone to the free throw line with a chance to shoot three and send the game into overtime.

"It could have been a foul," Ohio State's Evan Turner conceded afterward. "We'll take it."

The Bulldogs returned to Ohio 10 days later for a momentous date at No. 14 Xavier. The Bulldogs had lost four straight against Top 25 opponents, and this would be their last chance against a ranked team in the regular season. The Musketeers had become such a power that they advanced to the Elite Eight in 2004 and 2008, and once dominated Butler's conference so much that they left for the Atlantic 10. The Bulldogs made the two-hour bus trip east before freezing rain around Cincinnati made travel hazardous and shut down highways. Then, the Bulldogs shut down Xavier.

After going ahead 29–26 at halftime, Butler never relinquished the lead. The Bulldogs were 26 of 30 on free throws in the second half and ended Xavier's 15-game home winning streak, 74–65. Howard (19 points, 14 rebounds) and Hayward (19 points, 10 rebounds) both had double-doubles.

"The fact their freshmen and sophomores executed the way they did in our arena is really phenomenal," Xavier coach Sean Miller said.

The freshmen were adjusting not only to college basketball but to college life. They took the classroom seriously. So seriously, in fact, that Hayward and Jukes engaged in a heated squabble inside the locker room.

About a physics problem.

"It was pretty animated," Jukes recalled. "We're both opinionated."

The two engineering students were debating how to solve a problem from a physics test. They wrote it out on a board and left their calculations there, leaving Stevens to wonder what it was all about.

"Physics is a hard class. If I remember right, we were both wrong," Hayward said. "But parts of each of us was right. Neither of us got the whole answer."

Bobby Fong, the university president, and many professors supported the basketball team unreservedly because some players were genuine scholars. Hayward once took a graph theory class from longtime mathematics professor Prem Sharma.

Hayward is "a brilliant student who can flawlessly sketch in his mind a meandering path through a complex grid of almost 17 million nodes spread in 24-dimensional space," Sharma once wrote in an e-mail. "Most people see in Gordon glimpses of a greatness in basketball; they know not abstract universes reside in his brain."

The New Year did not interrupt the run by the Bulldogs, who climbed the national rankings and extended a new winning streak to 11. Heading into February, Butler's 19-1 record was the school's best ever through 20 games. Its 21-game league winning streak tied a record held by Wisconsin–Green Bay.

"That was almost ridiculous that we were 19-1," Stevens said later. "Obviously, we shouldn't have been."

The Bulldogs weren't good enough nor seasoned enough to win indefinitely. The streak ended on a Monday night at Green Bay, 75–66. The 11th-ranked Bulldogs became the highest-ranked team ever beaten by Green Bay, and jubilant students in the crowd of 6,978 poured onto the Resch Center floor.

Yet the Bulldogs showed the resilience of youth, regrouping in road wins at Detroit, 66–61, and Wright State, 69–51. A 2-1 week in which the Dawgs traveled nearly 1,500 miles was more than satisfactory.

"That's as tough as any stretch that I've heard of in league play anywhere," Stevens said.

In their first game after returning to Indianapolis, the Bulldogs wore black patches on their uniforms in memory of Lorin Maurer. She was the girlfriend of Kevin Kuwik, the Butler coordinator of basketball operations, an administrative post Stevens first held. Maurer was among those who died in a jetliner crash near suburban Clarence, New York. Kuwik spent much of that long night calling friends and sending texts. Butler players gathered in the morning to hear the news from Stevens. By the time Kuwik awoke from a nap, he had received texts from about half the team, including some "really deep, meaningful" messages he did not expect.

Kuwik asked one thing of the Bulldogs: play with passion. They did that and more, leading by 19 points in the first half of an 80–61 victory over Illinois–Chicago.

It is not possible to quantify how grief influences sports events, which are not life-and-death issues. So there was no way to determine what effect, if any, the tragedy had on Butler players in a Sunday game against Loyola two days later. But the Bulldogs were inexplicably lethargic. Loyola, which had lost to Butler by 23 points earlier and was a 19-point underdog, led by as many as 18. Despite Howard's career-high 30 points, the Ramblers ended Butler's 16-game home winning streak, 71–67.

"Everything I love about basketball happened tonight," Stevens said. "It just didn't happen on our side."

The upset was the Horizon's biggest since No. 1-seeded Butler lost to No. 8 seed Green Bay, 49–48, in the 2001 league tournament. Coincidentally, that loss followed the death of the mother of Butler player Rob Walls, who learned the news in the middle of the night. Another dispiriting loss—to Florida, 69–68, in overtime in the 2000 NCAA Tournament—came days after the death of the grandmother of another Butler player, LaVall Jordan.

Butler had gone 111 games without back-to-back losses. But the Bulldogs' downturn extended to Milwaukee, where they fell behind by 13 and lost for the third time in six games, 63–60. Stevens rejected a suggestion that his star freshmen, Hayward and Mack, were tiring. Instead, the coach saw a team that, for the first time, demonstrated anxiety. Butler, at 22–4, had declined enough that an at-large bid to the NCAA Tournament was no longer a certainty.

Thus Butler versus Davidson in a *BracketBuster* game—one of the televised mid-major pairings arranged for ESPN—became something of a bust. Both teams were coming off losses, and Davidson junior Stephen Curry was coming off an ankle sprain. Curry, after leading Davidson to the 2008 Elite Eight, was one of the sport's biggest stars.

Curry wore an ankle brace but decided to play. The 5,223-seat Belk Arena in Davidson, North Carolina, was sold out but didn't witness a Curry breakout. Instead, Hayward took center stage, scoring a career-high 27 points in Butler's 75–63 victory. In one 10-minute stretch—including 3 minutes spent on the bench—Hayward scored 20 of the Bulldogs' 30 points.

Curry was obviously impaired. He missed his first eight shots, finished 6 of 23, and scored 20 points, or 9 below his nation-leading average. Nored ran himself dizzy, chasing Curry everywhere.

"Ron could hardly walk on his way in here," Stevens said in the interview room.

The Bulldogs secured No. 1 seed for the Horizon tournament by closing the regular season with home wins over Youngstown State, 78–57, and Cleveland State, 58–56. The outcome gave the Bulldogs a third straight Horizon regular-season title and seventh in 10 years. They had not followed the program's template: winning with upperclassmen assimilated into the Butler Way. They won with practically a new team.

Afterward, Cleveland State coach Gary Waters was already looking ahead to a third meeting in the league tournament. He prophesized: "Fate's coming, and it may happen in the tournament. Fate comes. Just remember that."

As No. 1 seed, Butler was host for the tournament and advanced directly to a semifinal. In a third meeting with Wright State, the Bulldogs built an 11-point lead in the second half before winning 62–57. In the other semifinal, Cleveland State erased a 12-point deficit and defeated Green Bay 73–67. Butler was assured of going to the NCAA Tournament, as an at-large entry if not the league's automatic representative. Cleveland State, at 24-10, had no such assurance. The Vikings had to win. And they hadn't been in the NCAA Tournament since 1986.

The lack of urgency, nine o'clock tip-off, and absence of students (away on spring break) contributed to a small crowd of 5,107 for what should have been Butler's game of the year. For once, the Bulldogs could not rise to the occasion. Cedric Jackson sank a 3-pointer to put the Vikings ahead for good, 50–48, in a game they eventually won 57–54. Jackson, who made it to the NBA a year later, shot 7 of 12 from the field and earned tourney MVP honors with 19 points and 8 assists.

The math was simple. On 3-pointers, Cleveland State was 10 of 19 and Butler 4 of 19. That's a 30-12 variance.

"Sometimes I think we overanalyze these things," Stevens said. "Cleveland State is a terrific team."

Fate came.

For the NCAA Tournament, Butler (26-5) was a No. 9 seed and assigned to play No. 8 seed Louisiana State (26-7) in the South Regional at Greensboro, North Carolina. Besides Butler, the only teams outside the six major conferences to earn at-large spots were Xavier, Dayton, and Brigham Young.

In the final Associated Press poll, LSU (26-7) was 21st and Butler 22nd. The Bulldogs lost home games to Loyola and Cleveland State, so they had little rationale to complain about the seeding. But LSU coach Trent Johnson conceded the Tigers felt spurned after winning the regular-season title of the Southeastern Conference.

LSU exploited the Bulldogs' inexperience. Before the game was two minutes old, Butler committed three turnovers and trailed 9–0. Marcus Thornton, the SEC player of the year, scored all nine points in another 9–0 run as LSU extended the lead to 31–18. Butler was fortunate to be within 35–29 at the half.

The Bulldogs had overcome deficits of 12 or more to beat Northwestern, UAB, and UIC, and they ultimately overtook LSU. Butler led by one point on three separate occasions. Howard had to leave the game with five minutes left because he was bleeding, so Zach Hahn came in to shoot his free throws. Hahn sank both ends of a one-and-one to tie the score at 58. However, LSU reasserted dominance, making seven straight free throws in the final 47 seconds of a 75–71 victory.

Howard, in 25 minutes, finished with 22 points. Thornton, another player who was in the NBA a year later, was the difference. He scored 30.

"They had the best player on the court. Clearly. Not even close," Stevens said. "Marcus Thornton was a hard guy for us to stop."

An SEC team eliminated the Bulldogs for the fourth time in a decade, following losses to Florida (2000 and 2007) and Tennessee (2008). Butler had been 4-0 in first-round games since 2001, so the defeat was humbling.

"We probably weren't quite as good as everyone thought we were," Stevens said. "But we were a good basketball team that had its moments."

The Bulldogs resolved to get better. It was their way.

Over the summer, Hayward and Mack were selected by USA Basketball to try out for a national team to play in July's under-19 World Championship in Auckland, New Zealand. Almost immediately, Hayward created a buzz at the trials. Someone that size who could shoot, rebound, handle the ball . . . selectors and NBA scouts all saw what Brad Stevens saw two summers before. Hayward had grown quickly, and his confidence was catching up to his height.

"Sometimes I feel I'm still little, underneath with all the big guys," Hayward said. "But I'm not little. Especially on offense, it's a weird feeling."

Mack didn't make as much of an impression in scrimmages as he did at all other hours. He endeared himself to the coaches by arriving early to shoot, then staying late. He wasn't posturing. He always did that. He wasn't quite the point guard Team USA wanted, but selectors decided they needed his attitude as well as his skills. Mack, a leader by example, became team captain.

"Shelvin Mack has got substance," said Purdue coach Matt Painter, an assistant on Team USA.

At Auckland's 4,200-seat North Shore Events Centre, Hayward acquired a small number of New Zealand "groupies," young girls who baked cakes for him. They held signs with his name, sticking out their tongues like Maori warriors. Hayward consented to a few autographs, and teammates teased him unmercifully.

Hayward scored 20 points in a 93–73 quarterfinal victory over Canada and 15 in an 81–77 semifinal victory over Croatia. Auckland has a contingent of Croatian immigrants, some of whom fled conflict in the former Yugoslovia, and they cheered lustily for their homeland team. Hayward's 3-pointer sent the Americans ahead 70–66, and then he drove the baseline for a dunk that gave them the lead for good, 72–70. Both plays were featured in a 63-second Hayward highlight video posted by FIBA, the world governing body for basketball.

In the gold-medal game, Greece's strategy was apparently to restrain Hayward. That plan succeeded. Content to let teammates shoot, he missed the only two shots he attempted and did not score in 25 minutes. But the Americans built a 16-point halftime lead and easily won the gold, 88–80. They completed a 9-0 run through the tournament, winning by an average of 22 points. Hayward was a stat-stuffer. In 22 minutes a game, he was third on the team in scoring average (10), second in rebounds (5.7), third in total 3-pointers (12), and fifth in assists (16). That earned him a place on the All-Star Five selected by a media panel.

"You see the USA flag is rising over everyone else's when they play the anthem," Hayward said. "It was the trip of a lifetime and a great experience."

In a photograph of celebrating Americans, Mack was easiest to identify because of his gleaming smile. For someone who wasn't supposed to be on the team at all, he made himself indispensable.

After New Zealand, the Bulldogs' summer itinerary didn't end. The team embarked on an August trip to Italy. Although it would help any team to have extra practices and exhibition games, Stevens viewed the tour as a chance to enhance the players' education and compatibility. The biggest off-season concern was the condition of point guard Ronald Nored. His left leg had been sore for much of two years, dating to his senior season of high school. He kept thinking it was shin splints, but X-rays on his tibia revealed it was more than that.

"It looked like someone cut out a piece of his tibia," Butler trainer Ryan Galloy said. "It was the worst stress fracture I've ever seen. He's one of the toughest athletes I've been around. We almost had to put a rod in his leg."

Nored did not play in Italy. His duties were confined to cheering, holding a clipboard, carrying his teammates' cameras, and taking pictures.

The team arrived at its hotel in late afternoon and went on a 45-minute walking tour of Como, located by Lake Como and near the Alps. The Bulldogs rode a mountainside cable car to the small village of Brunate and were treated to a breathtaking view of the city. They had their passports stamped and bus inspected when crossing over the Swiss border into Chiasso, where they played Switzerland's national team less than 30 hours after arrival. Butler lost to the Swiss 76–72, and again the next day, 100–90.

After the second game, the team traveled south about five hours to Venice, stopping for dinner in Verona. The bus rides and shared experiences brought a close-knit team even closer. In a foreign country, and without cell phones, players interacted. They spent hours with "Catch Phrase," a game in which players used words and gestures to get a teammate to guess a word or phrase. The players hooted and hollered from the back of the bus.

In Rome, players toured two 2,000-year-old structures, the Colosseum and Pantheon temple, plus St. Peter's Square and the Sistine Chapel. The architecture and workmanship caused Stevens to reflect on Roman construction, basketball, and his own team. He told the players that ancient engineers and artists intended for their work to last. Last for eternity. Stevens said Butler's program was built that way, too.

So the coach introduced a slogan: "Build for Eternity." Those words were imprinted on gray T-shirts as reminders of what the Bulldogs were trying to do.

CHAPTER 5

UNDERDOGS OR UNDERACHIEVERS?

Soon after the start of classes, in August 2009, Brad Stevens called a meeting with Butler players. All coaches at all colleges in all sports do likewise. Stevens didn't want this to be routine, however. He wanted the Bulldogs to be especially attentive. What he told them was this:

I sold you short last year. I'm not doing that again. If you do everything right, if you go to class, if you are a good teammate, if you pay attention to every detail, you can be playing for the national championship on April 5.

"I don't know if I believed it," Stevens acknowledged months later. "I don't know if *they* believed it."

They did. A national championship "was literally the thinking from day one," Ronald Nored said. The coach had been correct so often, and had shown so much faith in them, that the Bulldogs internalized Stevens's goal.

"Him saying that made us even more motivated and made us feel we had a chance to do something special," said Willie Veasley, who was about to begin his senior season.

Butler mounted an aggressive season ticket campaign, too, using players to deliver the message in a televised commercial.

Gordon Hayward: "We're at Butler . . ."

Shelvin Mack: "To compete for championships . . ."

Veasley: "To play against the best in the nation . . ."

Matt Howard: "To build on the tradition."

Stevens wasn't alone in his belief in the Bulldogs, although he suspected that preseason accolades might simply be trendy. College basketball websites needed content over the summer, and with Hayward and Mack performing so well for the under-19 gold medalists, Butler supplied reporters with something to report. On October 29, the major preseason polls were released, and Butler was ranked 11th by the Associated Press and 10th in the ESPN/*USA Today* coaches' rankings.

Never in their history had the Bulldogs been ranked in the preseason, and here they were in the Top 10. ESPN.com reporter Pat Forde picked Butler to go to the Final Four, as did ESPN analyst Mark Adams. In a July 2 blog, Adams wrote: "I can't explain it, but THE BUTLER WAY is a lifestyle, a commitment, a brotherhood like no other in college basketball, and trust me, THE BUTLER WAY works!!! This season it just might work all the way to the Final 4. Yes, I am dead serious!"

For what was believed to be the first time, a Butler player was featured in a preseason magazine. Howard appeared in a regional edition of *Athlon Sports,* sharing the cover with Indiana and Purdue players. Butler's customarily restrained athletic director, Barry Collier, said Butler could have its best team ever. Pete Campbell, who played for the 30-4 team in 2007-08, said he had never seen so much talent at Butler.

"Flattery is like perfume," Stevens told fans after one intrasquad scrimmage. "It's okay to smell. Just don't drink it."

In public, Butler players said the right things. That is, the rankings and expectations didn't mean anything. They hadn't played a game. They hadn't done anything yet. Et cetera, et cetera, et cetera. They didn't back away from forecasts, either. Hayward said in July that Butler's goal was to win a national championship.

Yet even Hayward recognized restraint should be exercised. During one lunch hour before the season, he told some friends, "Fox Sports has me going 10th in the [NBA] draft. But that's not happening."

Someone at the table said, "They're on crack."

There was reason to wonder: Could Butler handle the hype? The Bulldogs had never had to do so. Even those heaping praise upon them asked if the Bulldogs could prosper under pressure.

One of Butler's student managers, Ryan McLaughlin, was called "McLovin," named for a character in the teen comedy film *Superbad.* McLovin filmed practices. During one such session, he questioned how anyone could pick Butler to make the Final Four. Those words ended up making the audio track of the videotape.

"We're good," McLovin said. "But we're not that good."

In a couple of preseason games, they weren't. They beat DePauw 77–45 and Taylor 75–44, laboring against overmatched small-college opponents. Stevens scheduled the teams out of respect for the coaches, Bill Fenlon at DePauw and Paul Patterson at Taylor. Fenlon was Stevens's college mentor. Stevens often called Patterson "to pick his brain" about people issues, practice drills, and teaching methods.

"I don't know anything about what a Top 10 team is supposed to look like," Patterson said. "But that's one, if I'm voting."

The good news for Butler was that Nored was cleared to resume playing in mid-October after five months of no weight-bearing on his left leg. His exercise had been limited to swimming and riding a stationary bike, plus putting up a few shots in the gym. He was so impatient that one day he lied to teammates, said he had a doctor's okay, and played in open gym. Stevens and trainer Ryan Galloy scolded him for that.

Nored's tibia took so long to mend that Butler concealed the possibility that he might miss the entire season to injury. Galloy speculated that all the walking Nored did on his protective boot in Italy accelerated the healing process.

"I think he dodged a surgery bullet," Galloy said.

Nored remained a team leader. However, the Bulldogs started the season with a different starting point guard: Shawn Vanzant.

Some news articles compared Shawn Vanzant's life to that of Michael Oher, the football player whose life was dramatized in the movie *The Blind Side*. Both were teenaged black athletes who came to live with a white family. But Vanzant resented any comparison between his life and Oher's. In fact, Vanzant said he would personally apologize to Oher if they met.

"I feel my situation was nowhere close to how his story was," Vanzant said. "I had clothes on my back. I had money in my pocket."

More than that, Vanzant had love all around. His tale is one of triumph over tragedy.

Vanzant ended up at Butler in a roundabout way that can occur in college basketball recruiting. From age 12 he was coached by David Bastian on a summer team in Tampa, Florida. Bastian, an accountant, played at North Central High School in Indianapolis under Arlan Lickliter, father of former Butler coach Todd Lickliter. That connection led to the Bulldogs' pursuit of Vanzant, whose Wharton High School team was 29-2 when he was a senior. Lickliter left Butler after that 2007 season, but Vanzant honored his commitment to the school.

"I can adjust to anything," Vanzant said.

He did so many times.

His mother, Effie, died on October 9, 1990—10 days before his second birthday. He carried a photo of her in his gym bag. His father, James, moved his two sons, Wesley and Shawn, from Cleveland to Omaha, Nebraska, in 1992 because he didn't want to live in that house anymore.

In Omaha, James moved in with a girlfriend, Marie Ward, and her two children. Ward's daughter, Stacia, was a basketball star and the one who first piqued Shawn's interest in the sport. On the night of Stacia's birthday in her junior year of high school, a drunk driver rear-ended the car she was driving. She missed her senior season. Colleges that had been recruiting her stopped doing so. Life can be fragile, as young Shawn was learning. Somehow he was also learning to steer clear of trouble.

"I never had to worry about Shawn," his father said. "When I put that basketball in his hands, that was it."

Wesley nurtured his younger brother's ability, once buying him a new basketball and playing one-on-one. Shawn's competitive streak was obvious. After losing to his brother, he punted the new ball into a pond.

James Vanzant separated from his girlfriend and moved his sons again, this time to Tampa, in 1997. When the father was diagnosed with diabetes and encountered financial problems, Shawn moved in with Wesley, who is seven years older but looks like a twin. Wesley ran into trouble with the law but made sure his younger brother did not. Shawn called his brother his other half. "Wes" was tattooed on Shawn's right arm.

"Basically a parent and a brother and a friend all at once," Shawn said. "I'd do anything for him."

On February 1, 2006, Wesley was arrested on seven charges, six of them felonies and one for selling cocaine. He eventually headed to jail. Shawn feared heading to his brother's apartment because his brother's drug-dealing buddies would inevitably come looking for money. It would be safer to sleep in his car. So Shawn did.

Vanzant told his Wharton coach, Tommy Tonelli, that he would have to move to Cleveland and live with his grandmother. The coach tried to reassure Vanzant that a solution could be found, although he had no idea what it might be. That day, the solution pulled up to the school in a black Cadillac Escalade. Lisa Litton arrived to pick up her son, Zach, from junior varsity practice.

"It was like God sent a guardian angel," Tonelli said.

The coach explained Vanzant's predicament to Litton. The mother absorbed it all and invited Vanzant to stay with their family of five. It was supposed to be temporary, but it soon became evident the arrangement would be more. If his father approved, Shawn could move in.

"I took a deep breath, closed my eyes, and said, 'Okay,' " said James Vanzant, who also had a four-year-old son to support.

Shawn might not be a Michael Oher, but Lisa Litton resembled the take-charge southern woman portrayed by Academy Award winner Sandra Bullock in *The Blind Side*. Leigh Anne Tuohy welcomed a black teenager into her white family, as Lisa Litton did with Shawn. When Lisa saw the movie, she "cried like a blubbering idiot," she said.

Lisa had a tough side and a tender side. Tough, as someone simultaneously fighting lupus, an incurable disease that attacks the immune system, and breast cancer. Tender, as the team mom, cooking pregame meals and transporting boys to games.

Mothering was her mission. When she was eight, she and her six-year-old sister were left by their mother at the Miami airport. The girls never saw her again. That experience inspired her to take in Shawn.

"I didn't want him to feel like he had no place to go," she said, "because I've been there."

Her husband, Jeff Litton, reflected on what Lisa told her when they were engaged. They would raise four boys, she announced. She gave birth to Josh and Zach and Chase. Then a doctor told Lisa she wouldn't be able to have more children.

Then along came Shawnie, as she called him.

"She understood where I came from," he said. "I understood where she came from."

Jeff, an assistant general manager of a Cadillac dealership, lost a parent, too. When he was 18, his alcoholic father committed suicide. That was tough. Welcoming a fourth boy into the house was not. Shawn called him "Pops" and Lisa "Moms."

"I guess to some people, it's different," Jeff Litton said. "For us, it has become natural."

The culture clash wasn't black versus white. It was total freedom versus house rules. Soon after Shawn moved in, he went out with friends and stayed out late. Very late. Way too late for the family's 1:00 A.M. curfew. When he arrived home at about 5:30 A.M., there was Lisa, waiting on the stairs.

Shawn looked down and knew he was in trouble. He said his cell phone died. Did everyone's cell phone die? she asked. There were rules in this house, she said.

"I told him that's the right way for a mother to raise her son," she said. " 'We love you. But you play by our rules.' "

Vanzant's brother agreed with the discipline. Jeff Litton once suspected Shawn of drinking alcohol at a party. Wesley Vanzant, then living in his Tampa apartment, came to the house for a meeting. Jeff dreaded a confrontation.

"I'm looking out for you. This has got to stop," the father told the fourth son. "There are too many people out there who are waiting to see you fail."

He didn't need to say more. Wesley piled on Shawn. Listen to Mr. Litton, the brother said. Do what he says.

"It was almost like we were ganging up on Shawn," Litton said. "That really impressed me."

Relationships aren't formed instantly. It takes time. Before Vanzant's first Christmas with the family, he was asked to list what gifts he wanted. He returned a blank paper. He revealed to Lisa that he hadn't received Christmas gifts since seventh grade.

On Christmas morning, Jeff, Lisa, and the four boys took turns opening packages. Saved for last, for Shawn, was a box containing a watch. To him, it was as exciting as a buzzer-beating basket.

"It was the very first time that Shawn and I exchanged an emotional connection," Lisa said. "Because he was so overwhelmed, he didn't look at me. He got up and hugged me and would not let go."

They remained as tight as that embrace. After he went off to college, Lisa texted him constantly. Even with her medical condition, Shawn said, she was always there for him. One morning, when home from Butler, Vanzant sat quietly at the breakfast table. Lisa knew he wanted to say something, and he hesitated.

"He finally said he understood why I was so hard on him when he came to live with us," Lisa said. "And he appreciated it so much. Then he said, 'I now know what it means to miss someone who loves and cares for me so much.' I'll remember that always."

Just as distance did not disconnect Shawn from Lisa, prison walls did not separate him from Wesley. Shawn regularly spoke by phone to his brother, an inmate at the Marion Work Camp in Lowell, Florida. Shawn visited him there, too. Wesley was scheduled to be released August 3, 2011.

Over the years, Shawn grew close to Chase, the youngest Litton brother, who was just 10 when Shawn arrived. Their personalities were similar, and both were fiercely protective of their family. And both happen to be basketball talents. As a 6-foot-5 eighth-grader, Chase was already attracting attention on the 2010 hoops circuit. For an important tournament, Shawn took a flight to Tampa so he could support him. Chase wore the same No. 2 jersey that Shawn did.

"He's going to be a lot better than I ever will be," Shawn said.

As a ballplayer, maybe. But Shawn was more than a ballplayer, more than a brother, to his adoptive family. He was their inspiration.

"He's our guiding light," said Josh, the oldest son. "Obstacles don't matter, not if you want something badly enough. He taught us all that."

Butler opened the season at home against Davidson, which didn't have Stephen Curry anymore but had the same coach, Bob McKillop, and the same system. Brad Stevens said he dreaded the game for six months, and it wasn't coachspeak. He meant it. Davidson reminded Stevens of Butler's senior-led teams from 2003 and 2007. Those teams were projected to go nowhere and ended up in the Sweet Sixteen of the NCAA Tournament.

"They had a chip on their shoulders, they were chock-full of winners, and they played with great, great purpose," Stevens said. "You replace guys in a program, and those guys have a program."

Still, there was no replacing Curry, who left college a year early for the NBA. In leading Davidson to the 2008 Elite Eight, he energized the campus in a way "that probably won't happen again in my lifetime," the 59-year-old McKillop said. Some were calling for that kind of run by the Bulldogs, but all Stevens would address was Davidson.

Hinkle Fieldhouse had changed little since construction in 1928, but Butler added one new element for the season: a scorer's table featuring a video board that showed photos, graphics, statistics, and sponsor ads. Attendance for Davidson was 6,713, the most for a home opener since 1998.

The scoreboard showed something Butler fans rarely saw: the Bulldogs behind by 10 points. Through 12 minutes, the nation's 11th-ranked team trailed 20–10. With two and a half minutes left in the first half, Butler still trailed by 10 points, 33–23.

The Bulldogs reclaimed the lead at halftime, 37–35, and went on a 17–2 run late in the second half. They held Davidson scoreless for more than seven minutes and persevered to win 73–62.

"Now that it's over, it's probably a good thing for us," Stevens said.

Hayward scored 17 points, although he didn't attempt a 3-pointer for the first time in 33 college games. Mack was limited to 5 second-half minutes because of leg cramps, something that would become a recurring issue. He sat on the bench ingesting fluids. Nored played 28 minutes off the bench and contributed 8 points and 5 assists. He was back.

In 30 minutes, Vanzant scored 10 points, reaching double figures for the second time in college. In a game in which the Bulldogs had trouble starting, he charged their batteries.

"It doesn't matter if I play 20 minutes, 5 minutes, whatever," Vanzant said. "I'm going to do what Coach needs me to do."

The Bulldogs enjoyed the afternoon because their next six games were on the road. Many national powers rarely travel in November or December, and some never play on an opponent's court until January. Large programs can pad their records and revenues by remaining home, offering guarantees as large as $100,000 to visiting teams they expect to beat.

Beyond that, Butler must play a demanding nonleague schedule to prove it is worthy of an at-large berth in the NCAA Tournament. The automatic berth, through victory in the league tourney, is never a certainty. So the Bulldogs kept their bags packed before New Year's.

"There's not a coach in the country who would prefer to play six games away from home in a row in the preseason," Stevens said. "But that's the schedule we have."

Butler's second game, at Northwestern, produced an oddity before tip-off. Never before had Butler been nationally ranked and favored while visiting a Big Ten arena. Yet the trip to Evanston, Illinois, loomed as one of Butler's toughest pre-Christmas tests.

In Indianapolis the year before, the Bulldogs overcame a 12-point deficit to beat Northwestern, whose Princeton-style offense creates backdoor cuts for layups. Northwestern went on to beat three nationally ranked opponents, tying a school record, but failed to secure what would have been their first NCAA Tournament appearance ever. That left them more angry than discouraged, according to coach Bill Carmody.

"We know we can hang. Let's see if we can do more than hang in there," Carmody said.

The Wildcats were dealt a setback when 6-foot-8 Kevin Coble, a star forward, injured his foot and was declared out for the season before their first game. Stepping into his role was John Shurna, who was Hayward's Team USA roommate in New Zealand during the under-19 World Championship. The two exchanged a few trash-talking texts before the game.

Stevens changed tactics from the previous year, keeping Butler defenders farther away from Northwestern players. That prevented those back-door plays the Wildcats exploit. Michael Thompson foiled Butler's strategy, sinking three 3-pointers in the opening nine minutes. But after that he didn't score for 28 minutes.

Early in the second half, Vanzant was poked in the eye and had to leave the game. Predictably, text-happy Lisa Litton immediately sent Vanzant the following:

Shawnie, Do you want me to come to Butler and kick that guy's ass?

Minutes later, Vanzant called to say he was on his way to the hospital to have his eye examined. But there was no impairment in the eyes of his teammates. The Bulldogs sank four 3-pointers in less than four minutes, including two by Avery Jukes. It was 50–30. Hayward's dunk on a fast break expanded that to 57–36.

"Butler did a good job of moving the ball," Thompson said. "They had us running all over the place."

Mack scored 15 points and delivered 8 assists in Butler's 67–54 victory. Hayward scored 14, the same as Shurna. The Bulldogs had been 0-12 at Northwestern in an intermittent series that began in 1934, so the outcome ended a 75-year drought. It also raised Butler's record to 6-1 in the past seven games against the Big Ten.

Hayward said the Bulldogs didn't heed conference affiliation and "just play Butler basketball." They shot 47 percent, committed 10 turnovers, and smothered a Northwestern team that won its next nine games and climbed into the Top 25. The Bulldogs' season lasted many more games, but this one stood out as one of their most complete performances.

"For 40 minutes, everybody who checked into the game played hard," Veasley said. "They went out and held themselves accountable."

Vanzant didn't accompany the team down I-65 to Indianapolis, staying in a Chicago-area motel overnight with trainer Ryan Galloy. Vanzant made it to practice late the next afternoon with goggles to protect a scratched cornea. Teammates called him "Amar'e Stoudemire," after the Phoenix Suns star (now with the New York Knicks) who dons such eyewear.

Everyone on Butler's team was susceptible to ridicule, and nothing was off-limits: girlfriends, school, gaffes, appearance, apparel, hometown. Roommates Hayward and Garrett Butcher had a running gag about whether Butcher was raised on a farm. He's from Ellettsville, Indiana (population 6,000), but was not a farmboy.

"It's that brotherly love," Vanzant said. "We all care about each other."

Two days after the trip home from Evanston, Butler players were on a bus again for a Saturday date at Evansville. The game was the first of 13 televised on Channel 23 in the Indianapolis area by WNDY. With an abundance of cable outlets, it was rare to have a local station anywhere produce games. WNDY sent a crew of 14 to Evansville, including play-by-play announcer Anthony Calhoun, the sports anchor of WISH/Channel 8 (a CBS affiliate), and Ralph Reiff, a former Butler trainer and longtime radio analyst.

Butler received exposure but no rights fee. Still, the agreement was a landmark for Butler, which would have all but four games televised. For several years, partly due to a Horizon League agreement, ESPN had televised Butler games on one of its networks: ESPN, ESPN2, or ESPNU. In the Indianapolis TV market, Butler nearly pulled even with Big Ten giants Purdue and Indiana.

"The economic times right now make everything more difficult than normal," said Jeff White, president and general manager of WNDY and sister station WISH. "Historically, you could probably sell something on the emotion and getting someone on board with Butler. Now, you have to deliver the audience."

Against Evansville, the Bulldogs didn't deliver as advertised. Travel might have been a factor. They bused nearly 200 miles to Evanston on a Tuesday, played Wednesday and arrived late in Indianapolis, arose early for classes Thursday, bused 185 miles to Evansville on Friday, and played Saturday night. The Bulldogs looked lively and sharp in the morning shootaround at Roberts Stadium, then couldn't locate the basket.

The Bulldogs missed 14 shots in a row and finished at 28 percent (14 of 50). Howard's shots kept rolling off the rim, and he was 1 of 9. Butler led 55–42 with less than two and a half minutes left and 56–46 with a minute left. Not a problem? Not exactly.

Freshman guard Colt Ryan sank a 3-pointer—Evansville's first of the game—and then completed a conventional three-point play on which Howard fouled out. That trimmed the margin to 58–52 with 48 seconds on the clock. Hayward's two free throws made it 60–52, and then action became exasperating for Butler fans watching on TV. Ryan hit another 3-pointer, then stole the ball and hit another. In less than four seconds, Butler's lead had been pruned from 62–54 to 62–60. Seventeen seconds remained.

Mack made one of two free throws, but with a three-point lead, Butler wasn't secure. Ryan missed a potential tying 3-pointer, and Hayward was fouled with 3.6 seconds on the clock. He missed the first free throw. Still not secure. He made the second.

The Bulldogs escaped what would have been an ignominious defeat 64–60. It was their 23rd consecutive November victory, dating to 2005. Ryan scored 12 of his 17 points in the final 60 seconds.

"At the end of the game, we got too lax," Veasley said.

Stevens maintained the Bulldogs did "a lot of good things" or they could not have won. They were 31 of 44 on free throws but missed six in the closing four minutes. The 28 percent shooting was their worst in 414 games—since December 1996. Hayward said the Bulldogs wouldn't fret about shooting.

"Law of averages," he said, repeating a Stevens maxim.

College basketball often prevents college players from being home with family on holidays, but it wasn't a terrible hardship for Butler players. Their team was like family. Before traveling to Anaheim, California, for the 76 Classic—where the Bulldogs would appear on national TV on Thanksgiving night—players gathered at the home of Brad and Tracy Stevens for a holiday meal. NCAA rules allow for occasional visits.

The coach's wife hadn't traveled to Italy, so she hadn't seen the interaction there. But now she sensed the camaraderie she had witnessed on previous championship teams at Butler.

"You could see the team as early as Thanksgiving starting to come together," Tracy said. "The thing that I love the most is seeing these guys off the court and getting to see them grow up, essentially.

"They come in as 18-year-olds. They're shy, they're timid. By the time they're seniors, they're in the kitchen, talking to us. They're talking as adults. How lucky are we that our kids get to grow up around these fantastic young men."

The made-for-TV event at the Anaheim Convention Center, less than a mile from Disneyland, assembled the strongest field of any in-season tournament that year: No. 8 West Virginia, No. 12 Butler, No. 19 Clemson, No. 22 Minnesota, plus Texas A&M, UCLA, Portland, and Long Beach State. The collective record was 23-2, and five of the teams would go on to the NCAA Tournament.

It was a high-risk/high-reward venture for the Bulldogs, who would be judged more on how they played in this 3-game tourney than in 18 Horizon League games. Veasley said he could understand the scrutiny, although it was not the kind of thing the Bulldogs dwelled on.

The Minnesota Gophers supplied enough to worry about. They won their first three games by an average margin of 34 points, despite the absence of three suspended players, and were coached by veteran Tubby Smith.

Butler players and coaches attended a Wednesday welcome dinner at Disney's California Adventure theme park. On Thanksgiving, the morning shootaround was not at the arena, but at Orange Lutheran High School in Orange, California. Butler was the only non-California entry to bring cheerleaders. The Bulldogs were supported by a large fan contingent, made conspicuous by the light attendance of 2,697—and that amounted to a 76 Classic record in the 7,500-seat arena. There were too many holiday distractions in Southern California to squeeze in college basketball.

The Bulldogs started auspiciously against Minnesota, using Hayward's 8 points to build a 13-7 lead through 6 minutes. He virtually vanished thereafter, going scoreless for the next 32 minutes. The Gophers, with a deep team that came at opponents in waves, had one player Butler could not contain: 6-foot-10 Colt Iverson, who had 11 points and 10 rebounds off the bench in leading Minnesota to a 32-28 halftime lead.

The Bulldogs' errant shooting—they were 6 of 20—persisted, and they had an uncharacteristic nine turnovers. In the locker room, Butler's coaches reminded the Bulldogs they hadn't played well and yet still had a chance. Howard scored Butler's first 10 points of the second half, tying the score at 38. But he picked up his fourth foul seconds later, sending him to the bench. With him went that chance.

Minnesota expanded the margin to 10 points. Although Butler twice closed within 4 in the final two minutes, Minnesota closed out an 82–73 victory that gave credence to Butler skeptics. It was Butler's sixth loss in seven games against Top 25 opponents, dating back to the 2007 NCAA Tournament.

Butler's 21 turnovers—including 7 by Mack and 6 by Hayward—were the most in seven years. The 82 points were the most scored against Butler in Stevens's 70 games. The coach wasn't worried about others' expectations.

"Our goal is to be team first. Those are our expectations," Stevens said. "That's the only way you can maintain any form of a program over the course of a long season, in my opinion. What people outside of our program say, we can't control."

On the plus side was the Bulldogs' ability to induce fouls, resulting in a tournament record of 36 free throws (in 45 attempts). Howard set a tournament record for free throws made (15) and attempted (18), and he finished with 23 points in only 22 minutes played. On the minus side was Butler's shooting through four games: 37.7 percent, or 316th out of 347 teams in NCAA Division I.

Butler was not only dispatched to the losers' bracket the next day, but also, in a worst-case scenario, was paired against UCLA in UCLA's backyard. If the Bulldogs were deflated, the Bruins were embarrassed. UCLA lost to Portland 74–47 in the most lopsided defeat in coach Ben Howland's seven-year tenure. Howland took the Bruins to three Final Fours, but after losing five underclassmen to the pros in three years, he could not reload fast enough. The fact that UCLA retained three Top 50 recruits coming out of high school underscored the folly of recruiting ratings. Senior forward James Keefe called Butler a "must win" for UCLA.

Butler coaches reviewed film of UCLA, as they did of every opponent, but Stevens deviated from custom before a tip-off that started close to midnight in Indianapolis. Rather than write keys to the game on the locker-room board, he reiterated Butler's core values. Then he printed two words: BE BULLDOGS. It was a succinct message.

The crowd of 3,027, again a tournament record, didn't see the bumbling of the night before. Butler's offense clicked, with Nored returning to a starting role at point guard.

Mack made his only two 3-pointers consecutively, stretching Butler's lead to 30–16 in the first half. Howard sat out the final 15 minutes of the half after picking up his second foul, but Mack's 14 first-half points staked the Bulldogs to a 42–35 halftime lead. There was no letdown. These weren't John Wooden's Bruins, or even the Bruins of recent vintage. But as Mack put it, "It's UCLA. Who can't get up for UCLA?"

Butler carried an eight-point lead into the closing five minutes but couldn't close it out. With 1:40 left, UCLA's Nikola Dragovic banged into Mack, who fell and was called for blocking. That provoked an animated response by Stevens, who stomped down the sideline. Dragovic's two free throws trimmed Butler's lead to 62–60. Butler led 64–60 when Nored drove for a layup . . . but he missed. The Bruins sandwiched two baskets around Zach Hahn's two free throws, pulling them within 66–64 with 14 seconds left. The Bruins weren't crumbling.

With 12.4 seconds left, Mack was fouled. He missed his first attempt, and the second teetered on the rim before dropping.

Butler 67, UCLA 64.

UCLA could tie the score on a 3-pointer. Stevens chose not to foul because too many seconds remained. Then Jerime Anderson's 3-pointer did tie it with 8.6 seconds left.

Time-out, Butler.

Stevens wanted the ball in the hands of Hayward so he could make something happen. Hayward dribbled upcourt and went all the way to the rim, drawing a foul with six-tenths of a second on the clock. He made the first throw. He tried to miss the second to allow time to run out . . . but the ball went in anyway. He had failed to score or draw a foul on previous forays to the goal, but he didn't hesitate to drive again at the finish of Butler's 69–67 victory.

"When I looked up and had the ball, I didn't realize we didn't have that much time left," Hayward said. "I saw there were seven seconds left, so I just tried to take it down the floor and to get to the basket."

Hayward had an inelegant 11-point night, shooting 3 of 14. The Bulldogs' errant shooting continued (39.6 percent). But they were 24 of 33 on free throws, played the first 11 minutes of the second half without a turnover, and received 21 points from Mack. Butler survived with Howard limited to 16 minutes and fouling out for the fourth straight game. It had been 50 years since Butler beat UCLA.

"I thought UCLA was a huge, huge step for us," Nored said. "We did embrace those values."

After victory, the next stop was Disneyland—for some players, anyway.

They toured the park on a day off after practicing at another area high school. Other players went on a drive down the Pacific coast, and another group headed for the beach. As if the weekend weren't stressful enough for Stevens, infant daughter Kinsley was admitted to a hospital after she developed an allergic reaction to medication for a head-to-toe rash. The coach's wife and mother kept him posted on his daughter's condition.

There were no easy opponents in Anaheim. Butler tried to stay in the Top 25 by beating Clemson. For most of the consolation game, the Bulldogs maintained control. They led by 12 late in the first half and early in the second.

However, Butler lost the ball on three successive possessions, allowing the Tigers to pull within 44–43. Later, Demontez Stitt's 3-pointer put Clemson ahead 55–53. Hayward's emphatic dunk sent the Bulldogs into a 60–57 lead, and that gap grew to five points inside the three-minute mark.

Hayward could have put Butler ahead by four by converting both ends of a one-and-one, but he missed the first attempt. Everything was unraveling. Andre Young's 3-pointer returned the lead to Clemson 68–67 with 1:32 left. A tip-in briefly gave the lead to Butler, 69–68, but Mack missed a chance to expand that when he missed with 14 seconds left. Clemson had the ball, down by one.

Stitt was Clemson's go-to player, but he was 20 feet from the basket and fumbling the ball when Veasley fouled him with 3.3 seconds on the clock. Veasley said he "felt like it was a clean strip." Stitt made both free throws for his 18th and 19th points, sending Clemson to a 70–69 victory.

With the college basketball media focused on them, the Bulldogs lost two of three. The calendar hadn't reached December, but for the doubters, the verdict was in on Butler. The Bulldogs just weren't that good. They were not a Top 25 team.

Stevens tried to prevent an overreaction, explaining that if the Bulldogs had managed one last stop, "it's all jubilee and everything's perfect and everything's gravy." One possession, he reiterated.

"That's why your margin for error in a season, between great seasons and championship seasons, is very slim," Stevens said.

Hayward made the all-tournament team after a 20-point, 12-rebound night, but he shared in the Bulldogs' frustration. Oddly, Butler shot 54 percent in defeat after shooting 28 percent in victory (over Evansville). Clemson shot 58 percent in the second half, an unacceptable figure for Butler, a team built on defense.

The facts were these: Butler lost twice in six games, after not losing for a second time until the 21st game the season before.

"It showed we weren't as prepared as we thought we were," Veasley said. "We weren't even as good as everyone thought we were at the time."

West Virginia routed Portland 84–66 to win the 76 Classic championship. The Bulldogs weren't in the Mountaineers' class.

Whether pollsters showed grudging respect or unwillingness to concede they were wrong, they kept Butler in the Top 25 (23rd by the AP, 20th by coaches) when new rankings were released. No other ranked team had as many as two losses. On the other hand, no other ranked team had played just one home game.

The Bulldogs were determined not to make it three losses. Their week included games against Ball State and Valparaiso, two in-state rivals that Butler was expected to beat. Indeed, Butler had won 13 in a row over Indiana opponents. But Stevens and the Bulldogs took nothing as given, preparing for the next game as if it were the season's most important— which is what they always did anyway.

After Monday's daylong travel, the Bulldogs held an unusual Tuesday-night practice. They usually arrived early at a road arena, but they didn't leave for their Wednesday-night game until late afternoon. They stopped for a walk-through at Pendleton Heights High School, off Interstate 69 on the way to Muncie, Indiana.

"We wanted to prove to ourselves we were a good team," Veasley said. "That week of practice might have been the hardest week we practiced all year."

At Ball State, the Bulldogs atoned for Anaheim's sins. Before six minutes had elapsed, the outcome was effectively decided. By then, Mack had four 3-pointers and Butler had a 13–4 lead. The crowd of 6,996, including a large Ball State student turnout, was mostly silent after that. Butler was ahead 29–11 at halftime, holding Ball State to 19 percent shooting.

"Butler came out and hit us hard early," Ball State coach Billy Taylor said. "I think our team got down and got deflated, and didn't do a good job of rebounding from that run."

Butler won 59–38. Not since 1952 had Ball State scored so few points in one game. Mack conceded that Anaheim "woke us up."

The Bulldogs returned to a campus on which, oddly, they shared attention with the football team. The afternoon basketball game against Valparaiso was rescheduled for Saturday night because Butler was playing Central Connecticut State in the Gridiron Classic at the Butler Bowl. The football Dawgs, playing in the postseason for the first time since 1991, scored their first postseason victory ever 28–23.

The Pioneer Football League champions finished 11-1, winning seven games by a touchdown or less. It was a stunning reversal from an 0-11 record just four years before. Basketball wasn't the only sport on campus enjoying a renaissance.

The hoop Dawgs, meanwhile, began defense of their league championship in their first home game in three weeks. Hinkle Fieldhouse rims were more friendly than those on the road, and Butler's accuracy markedly improved. The Bulldogs shot 57 percent—and 69 percent in the second half—in an 84–67 victory over Valparaiso.

Although the Bulldogs allowed 53 percent shooting, they negated Horizon League scoring leader Brandon Wood, whose 7 points were 16 under his average. Valparaiso had previously played national powers North Carolina and Michigan State, and veteran coach Homer Drew said Butler belonged on that level. Indeed, Drew seemed eager for Hayward to move to the next level.

"I can just give you three letters for this guy. He's an NBA player," said Drew, whose son Bryce played six NBA seasons.

Of course, no matter what Butler did inside the league, it was graded by what it did outside. It would be so again in the week ahead, against 15th-ranked Georgetown and 13th-ranked Ohio State. The Bulldogs traveled to New York City to face Georgetown in the Jimmy V Classic at Madison Square Garden. The doubleheader—Indiana versus Pittsburgh was the other game—was held annually in memory of North Carolina State coach Jim Valvano and raises funds for cancer research.

If the Bulldogs were under scrutiny in Anaheim, that was accentuated in New York, the nation's media capital. The *Washington Post* devoted a lengthy story to the Butler Way. An informal panel of national media didn't call it a make-or-break week but acknowledged the importance.

Joe Lunardi, an ESPN.com analyst who carved a niche with predictions of what the NCAA Tournament bracket will be, wrote it was premature to "seal the fate" of Butler or any other team. Clark Kellogg, the lead analyst for CBS television, contended that the committee would pay attention to what happened in the Horizon League and in other leagues.

He said Butler was going through a learning curve, living as the hunted instead of the hunter.

"We're in such an age where we evaluate everything game by game, minute by minute," Kellogg said. "I know what age we're in, but it's not really fair. There's a lot of work to do and a lot of changes are going to happen between now and Selection Sunday."

The Bulldogs practiced at Hinkle Fieldhouse on a Monday and had no delay on their charter flight despite a rush-hour snowstorm in Indianapolis. The team checked into a Times Square motel, a few blocks from ESPN Zone, where large screens in the restaurant showed images of Stevens being interviewed. Before tip-off, about 200 Butler fans, many of them East Coast alumni, gathered at Stout NYC, a pub near the Garden. For 1980s grads it was an opportunity to cheer a winning team, something that didn't often happen when they were in school.

Georgetown's coach, John Thompson III, was the son of the coach whose Hoyas were famously upset by Villanova in the 1985 NCAA championship game—the first game that Stevens could recall watching. Butler–Georgetown wouldn't have that TV audience, but the ESPN telecast did expose the Bulldogs to the nation. Georgetown exposed them, too.

Butler couldn't guard Greg Monroe, a 6-foot-11 sophomore center. His basket started the Hoyas on a 10–0 surge that built their lead to 20–11. The Bulldogs trimmed the margin to 31–27, only to see all their work negated by Monroe. He scored eight points over the closing 85 seconds of the half, including a basket off a lob that made Georgetown's halftime advantage 39–31.

Stevens was revolted by what he was seeing. The customarily calm coach was out of character, yelling at players. There was little the Bulldogs were doing well, especially on defense. They were getting out-toughed, an intolerable shortcoming. The Hoyas flung Butler players aside to grab rebounds without fouls being called.

Early in the second half, Stevens walked to the end of the bench and signaled to Nick Rodgers, a nonscholarship senior who almost never played.

"If this doesn't change in a few minutes," Stevens said, "get ready to go!"

Rodgers was startled. He didn't know what he would do if he went in. But Rodgers knew Butler's system better than anyone and was respected by everyone. If that was what the team needed, well, he would try to supply a spark. Stevens sent him in, replacing Veasley.

"If nothing comes of it, I'm going to make sure they see that I worked hard," Rodgers thought.

Soon after Rodgers checked in, Georgetown's 6-foot-9 Julian Vaughn rebounded a miss, then plowed into the 6-foot-2 walk-on. It was an offensive foul. The little Dawg had done his job.

"I don't think he saw how small I was," Rodgers said.

His 45 seconds completed, he returned to the bench and was replaced by Zach Hahn. Later, Stevens wished he had left Rodgers in longer. At least Rodgers knew what he was doing. That wasn't true of everyone.

Soon thereafter, the Hoyas expanded their lead to 52–35. What was supposed to be the Bulldogs' time to shine was becoming a dark night. Hayward attempted to prevent a debacle, scoring 18 of his 24 points in the second half. Injury was piled on top of insult. Mack hurt his right shoulder on a drive to the basket, and he grimaced afterward. No foul.

Mack had to have the shoulder taped for weeks, but he reentered the game and soldiered on. The Bulldogs never gave up the chase, futile though it was. Hahn's 3-pointer pulled them within 67–62 with 41 seconds left. Ultimately, Monroe's 25 points and 14 rebounds overpowered Butler 72–65. His center counterpart, Howard, was bothered by the long-armed Hoyas and shot 1 of 9. Again, Howard fouled out.

"It's just a frustrating night. Him, and our entire team, I thought," Stevens said.

This was a Top 25 test, and the Bulldogs flunked. Again. They were 0-3 against the Top 25, and 1-8 since 2007. After a formal news conference, Stevens patiently answered more questions from the media throng outside the locker room. He reasoned that even though the Bulldogs played poorly, they had a chance to win.

"So what I felt when we left that gym was, 'We've got a chance to be pretty good,'" Stevens said months later. "Meanwhile, everybody else was taking the expectations off."

Inside the locker room, the scene was not so serene.

Ronald Nored wasn't one of Butler's formal captains, but he was someone the Bulldogs followed. And they had never seen him so agitated. The point guard spoke so loudly that in the adjacent locker room, through the wall, Indiana coach Tom Crean heard Nored's voice. At first Crean thought it must be a Butler coach.

"We are not playing Butler basketball!" Nored shouted. Referring to Rodgers, he continued, "He did his job. Everyone needs to do your job!"

Nored's tirade lasted several minutes, surprising himself with his own ferocity. He rebuked everyone. Keep this up, he said, and the Horizon League will kill us.

"I've never been more fired up in my life," Nored said months later. "The more I yelled, the more fired up I got."

Initially, the players were shocked. No one reacted for a moment. Then, one by one, teammates had their say in what became a players-only meeting. Conversation continued to be heated. Stevens could hear their voices, so he let them alone. There is a time to "let go of the reins," he said.

As impassioned as the discussion was, Rodgers said, it did not degenerate into personal attacks or accusations. That was not the Butler Way. The Bulldogs would succeed, or fail, collectively. Rodgers spoke up, as did another walk-on, Alex Anglin. Hahn and Mack and Jukes took turns. No one was excluded.

"I'm not going to go against Coach," Jukes said. "I think we are playing hard. We're not playing smart, especially on defense. It doesn't matter if you're playing 100 percent if you're not playing smart."

Jukes and Nored identified a key issue: defense. In such a symbiotic system, everyone relying on everyone else, the Bulldogs would pull together or come apart. Nored theorized that there were personal agendas on defense. That could not happen. The players' consensus was that they had worked too long and hard through the summer and fall to allow the season to deteriorate. When they emerged from the locker room, they didn't reveal what happened inside. Hayward hinted at it, saying the Bulldogs needed to change "everything we're doing" in comments to reporters who waited for them.

The Georgetown game did change everything. For Butler. For its season.

"It was our 'coming to Jesus' moment," Nored said.

Coming home did not offer the Bulldogs any relief. No. 13 Ohio State was the highest-ranked visitor to Hinkle Fieldhouse since No. 11 Indiana in 1993. It was the Buckeyes' first game without 6-foot-7 Evan Turner, the national player of the year. He fell and injured his spine in their previous game, and his absence detracted from the pairing. Yet Ohio State's roster remained loaded with high school or junior college All-Americans, a testament to the recruiting of Thad Matta, the former Butler coach.

The Bulldogs were being battered on the court, on the message boards, and in media accounts. The hype that was once intoxicating turned noxious. Veasley said they were aware of the critics.

"We're all at fault here," ESPN's Andy Katz said in a telecast, asserting that the media overrated Butler on the basis of a small résumé.

Stevens carried a countenance of calm in the storm. With justification, he could attribute the 6-3 record to multiple factors: seven of nine games away from home, three ranked opponents on neutral floors, five games against teams from power conferences. Nonetheless, the schedule was what the Bulldogs needed. It was honest.

"We don't have time to sulk. We don't have time to worry," Stevens said. "We only have time to prepare for the next game."

The athletic department prepared by announcing a free shuttle for the expected large crowd. For those who couldn't find parking in Butler lots or neighborhood streets, there was space at the varsity athletic fields, across the waterway canal in Rocky Ripple. Students lined up outside the fieldhouse by 8:00 P.M. Friday for Saturday's noon game. And fans weren't the only ones descending on campus. Even with Turner sidelined, credentials were issued to 18 NBA scouts.

Stevens never told the Bulldogs that this was a must-win game. He merely asked them to abide by the standards set in the program. Then he attempted to lighten the mood before tip-off.

"Who in sports has a better opportunity than Butler?" he asked his players. "With the way it's going to be with the sun shining through those windows? It's just special."

All Butler needed was a special performance. So did Ohio State, for that matter. Matta told his Buckeyes that any time you're on the road, you need to be 6 points better than the opponent—except this time, you need to be 12 better.

The Bulldogs kindled excitement in the near sellout of 9,338, bolting ahead 21–10. That energy dissipated, and Howard went to the bench with two fouls. Ohio State outscored them 16–0 late in the half to go ahead 34–28. Butler pulled within 36–34 when Hayward scored on a lob from Mack before halftime.

After midway through what had been an even second half, it was Butler's turn to burn. Five different Bulldogs scored in a 15–0 run, creating a 67–50 margin with less than five minutes left. Ohio State forced a series of turnovers and caused a scare by cutting that to 69–66 in the final minute. Then Veasley sank four straight free throws to conclude a 74–66 victory.

Hayward scored 24 points and Veasley 15. Howard endured 3-of-12 shooting but drew enough fouls to finish with 13 points. Howard's presence inside freed teammates for open shots, and the Bulldogs kept feeding him the ball.

"They stuck with the horse," Matta said.

Howard fouled out for the sixth time in nine games, but nothing could spoil his afternoon. Not after the Bulldogs ruled the rebounds 40–27. Not after ending the Top 25 drought. Howard told himself to have fun, as he did in grade school.

"And I tell you what, I was a fouling machine back then, too," he joked.

Nored neutralized Ohio State's 6-foot-6 guard Jon Diebler, who was averaging four 3-pointers a game. Diebler went 38 minutes without a basket and scored 7 points, 10 under his average.

Not since a 2001 victory over No. 10 Wisconsin, when Matta was coach, had the Bulldogs beaten a team ranked so high. Matta called Butler's schedule "ridiculous" and reminded listeners that the season was long. Jay Bilas, a TV analyst who was at courtside for ESPN, claimed Butler had not been a disappointment. Furthermore, Bilas said fans and media should not clamor for teams to assemble tough nonleague schedules, then pillory them if they lose a few games.

Hayward said games such as Ohio State "don't mean anything," contradicting his coach, who often stated it was *not* all about March. The sophomore was realistic, though, given a culture that weighed success or failure by NCAA Tournament results.

"We're just worried about March," Hayward said.

March could wait. Butler's unrelenting schedule featured two more December tests, Xavier and Alabama–Birmingham. Not to mention classroom tests. Howard, a finance major, had final exams in database design, operations management, and marketing before a Thursday-night practice. Finals week was awkward for Butler, which frequently was flat or out of sync in games played following exams.

With Bob Knight returning to Hinkle Fieldhouse, there were more media requests for the Xavier game than for Ohio State. Knight, the former Indiana coach, was teaming with Brent Musburger on the ESPN2 telecast. Knight's 11th-ranked Hoosiers lost to Butler 75–71 on November 27, 1993.

Knight is a celebrity in the state, and though security officers kept fans away from him, a Butler cheerleader managed to secure his autograph. During the game, Lambda Chi Alpha fraternity brothers chanted, "Bob-by, Bob-by, Bob-by," from the north balcony, and Knight waved to acknowledge them.

Xavier was making its first visit to Butler since 1998, and had won seven in a row there. The Musketeers were capable of extending that to eight, even after Butler went ahead by 15 points. Xavier scored the last 4 points of the first half and the first 11 of the second to seize a 43–39 lead. Musketeers guard Jordan Crawford, who transferred to Xavier from Indiana, ignored fans taunting, "IU dropout!"

The Bulldogs fell behind by six before finally reclaiming the lead 65–64 when Mack made the second of two free throws with 1:51 left. Crawford scored the last 2 of his 20 points on a jump shot with 48 seconds remaining, restoring the Musketeers' lead to 68–65. Mack made two more free throws to bring Butler within 68–67, setting up one of the most chaotic finishes imaginable.

Hayward tied up Xavier guard Mark Lyons with 37 seconds on the clock, perhaps fouling him. Instead, the possession arrow returned the ball to Butler. Mack missed a 3-point attempt, but Butler cleared the rebound. The ball was knocked out of Mack's hands and bounded past midcourt. Nored and Xavier's Dante Jackson went sprawling into the backcourt, and an official signaled the ball was tipped so that there was no violation. Mack ran to retrieve the ball.

Mack dribbled back into the frontcourt, drove into the lane, and passed out to Veasley, who missed a 3-point attempt from the left wing. Veasley, on his knees, grabbed the loose ball and shoveled it to Hayward, who also had been on the floor. Hayward dribbled once and scored on a layup, sending Butler ahead 69–68.

The clock showed 1.2 seconds remained. Not so.

With 14.7 seconds on the clock—when the ball was deflected past midcourt—timekeeper Gary Nash mistakenly stopped the clock. He immediately realized his error, restarting it.

"I could swear I heard a whistle. I'll go to my grave claiming that," said Nash, a 63-year-old teacher who had served at Butler in various capacities since 1964.

Before he could bring the stoppage to the attention of officials, they were asked by Xavier to look at the TV replay. Officials wanted to determine how long the clock was off. Nash offered to let officials use the stopwatch mode on his wristwatch, but they wanted a conventional stopwatch, as required by rule. The timekeeper felt bad because officials had commented before the game that there was no need to worry about Butler's scoring table because there were never any problems.

Mike Freeman, one of Butler's assistant athletic directors, was dispatched to find a stopwatch in the basement office of the weight training room. He was startled when he arrived because he awakened Ethan, the strength coach's Rottweiler, who slept there. A bulldog was one thing. But a Rottweiler . . .

"I didn't really know where the stopwatch was," Freeman said. "I don't know how I grabbed it."

By now, the delay had lasted nearly 15 minutes, with fans unsure of what was happening. Freeman hurriedly took the stopwatch upstairs to the officials, who timed the replay and determined that the clock was off for 1.3 seconds. Hayward released the ball with 1.8 seconds left—in time—and the ball went through the net with 1.2 left. Deducting the 1.3 from 1.2 meant: game over.

Knight and Musburger contended that since the home timekeeper made the error, Xavier should have been allowed to play the 1.2 seconds. It was a coincidence that John Adams, the NCAA supervisor of officials, was in the building. Though he did not intervene, Adams said the officials got it right. During the long wait, Stevens realized Hayward's basket might be disallowed. He told Butler players to "go out there with class" and shake hands with Xavier players, win or lose.

Xavier players were understandably outraged by the abrupt ending. Xavier coach Chris Mack railed at the refs, and at least one Xavier player had to be restrained from going after a heckling fan. Witnesses said small fights broke out in the stands, but no arrests were reported. Security personnel escorted the Musketeers off the floor. The timekeeper heard the angry words, but there was no one "in his face," he said.

"There was a lot of commotion going on and yelling, but none of it directed toward me, specifically, that I heard," Nash said.

A Xavier player tore a drinking fountain off the wall outside the visitors' locker room. Xavier's administration apologized for the incident and offered to pay for damages. No Xavier players joined Coach Mack at the postgame news conference. The coach calmed considerably by the time he addressed reporters, and he said failure to put the game away was more disappointing than the bizarre finish.

It was a familiar finish for Hayward, who was in the right place at the right time. He won the 2008 state championship for Brownsburg High School with a last-second shot out of a scrum.

"It was kind of a scramble at the end," he said. "I feel like I've said this before: Just take the ball up and try to score as fast as I could."

Hayward finished with 22 points and 14 rebounds. The timing error was a blip, but a home loss to Xavier would have been much bigger than a blip. After being thoroughly dominated in the second half, "it's kind of a wonder that we won that game," Veasley said. Stevens was asked how stressful the afternoon was.

"Ah, shoot. This is fun," he replied. "Our guys enjoy it."

Butler's last pre-Christmas game, and last before resumption of Horizon League play, was a homecoming for Ronald Nored. The Bulldogs were playing the Alabama–Birmingham Blazers, near his hometown of Homewood. The Dawgs practiced Monday at Hinkle Fieldhouse, bused to Louisville, Kentucky, and took a flight to Birmingham for the Tuesday-night game.

Despite losing three players to European pro teams, the Blazers were 10-1 under coach Mike Davis, their best start in 16 seasons. They had 30 consecutive nonleague victories at home. Not that everyone inside Bartow Arena was for UAB. Nored had a cheering section of 155 fans from Section 226 in the arena's upper level, all from the youth group of Trinity United Methodist Church.

"I could have brought 170. I just didn't have the tickets in hand," said David Thompson, pastor of student ministry at the church. "We wanted to come and support him and show how much we loved him."

Nored was a leader in the church's student ministry. He never met a stranger, according to close friend David Hayes, a high school classmate.

"Everyone he talks to is automatically friends with him," Hayes said. "He can make a connection with anybody."

Although UAB began slowly and fell behind 21-15, a 9-0 spurt changed that quickly, igniting the near-sellout crowd of 8,367. The Blazers expanded a six-point lead to 32-22 by halftime, and they didn't relent in the second half. The margin widened to 51-35. This was becoming a repeat of the Georgetown game. Veasley later conceded that Butler underestimated UAB.

"We didn't guard them very well," Nored said. "They got comfortable. After that, there was nothing we could do about it, no matter what we did to try to change it."

The Bulldogs charged back, cutting UAB's lead all the way to 57–55. But they missed their final seven shots, including a layup by Howard that would have tied the score with two minutes left.

"They turned it up a notch in those last two minutes, and boy, I tell you what, it felt like they were all over the floor," Stevens said. "It felt like there were more than five guys out there."

UAB won 67–57, handing the Bulldogs their largest margin of defeat in 87 games. Dating to February 2, Butler was 15-9 over 24 games, not the ledger of an elite program. ANOTHER BLEMISH was the headline published in the next day's *Indianapolis Star*.

The Bulldogs' dreary shooting continued, and they finished at 34 percent. Epitomizing their plight was a dunk by Hayward that went through the rim and popped out. The basket was disallowed for offensive goaltending. Howard fouled out again, and for the first time in 48 games, he did not attempt a free throw. He was frustrated with himself but said the Bulldogs hadn't lost confidence. Still, they kept losing games.

"We don't have time to sulk," Stevens said. "We're not bad. No way. If we are, then we've got our priorities and our focus in the wrong place. We've played 12 games and a lot of really good teams in a lot of great venues."

Butler's nonleague schedule was rated No. 4 in difficulty, with the four losses coming to teams that had a collective record of 40-7. That was its only favorable rating. After 19 rating periods and 364 days, Butler fell out of the AP Top 25 when rankings were released on Monday, December 28. Two Butler opponents, No. 24 UAB and No. 25 Northwestern, pushed Butler out.

The Bulldogs' pre-2010 schedule had been neither total success nor utter failure. At 10–2 or 6–6, it would have been easier to define them. Their evolution was incomplete.

CHAPTER 6

UNDEFEATED

The Butler locker room was stripped bare. Chairs were gone. Trophies were gone. Slogans were gone. Quotes were gone.

Brad Stevens's tolerance was gone.

There was one symbol left in the middle of the room: the second-place trophy from the previous year's Horizon League Tournament. The players, seated on the floor, listened intently to Stevens's message: Keep this up, and this is what we'll be. Runners-up.

It was as angry as Stevens had been in three seasons as a head coach, although he spoke in a normal tone. He asked players to point to different spots and recite what slogan, or inspirational saying, had hung there. Slogans such as "Great teams have great teammates." Many remembered the spots. All hangings were placed with purpose. They were daily reminders of the cost of success.

"This stuff is not on the wall just to be on the wall," Stevens said. "And they knew it."

If they forgot, small individual second-place trophies were placed in each locker stall.

The Bulldogs reconvened after Christmas break, and they were coming off a loss. There had long been an expectation at Butler: No bad practices after a loss. And what the coach had seen was bad. The focus wasn't there, replaced by sloppiness.

Stevens's response wasn't impulsive. Assistant coach Micah Shrewsberry texted Nick Rodgers, the senior walk-on, to ask what he thought of Stevens's plan. Let me think about it, Rodgers texted back. He was torn. Ultimately, he approved.

"In the end, I think it was good," Rodgers said.

Practices became good. Better than good. Wall adornments were restored.

"Our practices, when we came back from Christmas, were unbelievable. Every practice," Nored said. "We got *so* much better."

Especially on defense. It was the foundation of the Butler program, and it would be the foundation of this Butler team. It needed to be. The most glaring decline from the previous season was in field-goal percentage defense. Butler was seventh in the NCAA at .385 the year before, and now it wasn't in the top 250 at .458. Stevens, a numbers analyst, reasoned that with three more stops a game, Butler would be at .398, "and nobody's talking about it."

Nobody in the national media talked about the Bulldogs when they resumed Horizon League play. One characteristic the best Butler teams shared, though, was application to the task at hand. They prepared as diligently for Youngstown State as for Ohio State, as steadfastly for Loyola as for Georgetown. Stevens was on staffs of teams reaching the Sweet Sixteen in 2003 and 2007, and collectively those Bulldogs lost more games inside the league than outside. The Horizon was not a major conference, but its members created major obstacles.

"Those people know you," Stevens said. "They *really* want to beat you. When you go in their arena, it's their biggest game of the year."

The coach reminded the Dawgs of that heading into a New Year's Eve date with Wisconsin–Green Bay. Stevens showed film of the ending of the previous season's game at Green Bay, where students stormed the court in celebration of a 75–66 upset of the 11th-ranked Bulldogs. Renewal of this rivalry came at Hinkle Fieldhouse, and Green Bay was missing injured point guard Rahmon Fletcher.

The Bulldogs took out the frustration of the UAB loss, and the 8-4 start, on the unfortunate Phoenix. Butler led by 11 points in the first half, 18 early in the second, and 25 before it was over. The Bulldogs held Green Bay to its lowest output in 96 games and rolled to a 72–49 victory.

"We really stressed playing as five people, as a team, and not playing as five individuals," Veasley said.

Green Bay's Tod Kowalczyk, a candid and outspoken coach, singled out one individual: Gordon Hayward. Although the Butler sophomore had modest numbers on this night—13 points, 6 rebounds—Kowalczyk called him one of the best players in college basketball.

"He's complete. He's as good a player as this league has ever seen, or ever will see," Kowalczyk said.

Matt Howard scored seven points in 16 foul-plagued minutes, but strong play off the bench by 6-foot-11 freshman Andrew Smith compensated. Smith said he and Howard "definitely don't go easy on each other" in practices.

The Bulldogs had it easy two days later, using Shelvin Mack's career-high 25 points to beat Wisconsin–Milwaukee 80–67. The two teams had won or shared the previous 10 regular-season league titles, although Milwaukee wasn't the power it was under former coach Bruce Pearl. Butler was, well, what Butler is. Milwaukee coach Rob Jeter alluded to the dialogue of a popular beer commercial:

"I almost said, 'They are who we thought they were,'" Jeter said.

Howard was not putting up numbers for Butler like he did the year before—he had eight points and five rebounds—but would not complain about aches and pains he endured all season. He took solace in victory, never mind the stats.

"Really, I feel like in other areas, I'm doing my job—boxing out, sealing for guys to get layups, and doing little things like that," Howard said. "I don't mind if I'm the one scoring or other guys are scoring, as long as we're putting up points and winning."

Winning is what Butler was about. That was the only agenda of a demanding January sequence: six of eight games on the road, four of them in succession. Indeed, the next trip—to Wright State and Detroit—represented the two most difficult Horizon road games of the season.

Wright State was picked to finish second behind Butler. Until the previous season, Butler had lost seven straight to the Raiders at Dayton, Ohio. Wright State was on an 11-game home winning streak, including the last 6 by an average of 23.5 points. Raiders coach Brad Brownell—a DePauw University graduate, as Stevens was—knew Butler's system as well as Butler's players did. The Detroit Titans were on the rise under second-year coach Ray McCallum, and they lost to Butler by 4 and 5 points the year before.

Predictably, Brownell said nothing to rile the Bulldogs, but he correctly observed that with the schedule they played, they never had a chance to "pad" stats. He saw little difference from previous Butler teams.

"They're still doing all the same things that Butler teams do that win,"

Brownell said. "They get to the free throw line. They don't turn the ball over that much. Their rebounding is as good or better."

Unfortunately for Brownell, his assessment was prescient. Playing in front of a near-sellout crowd of 9,674, Butler seized a 14-point lead in the first half, made 23 of 24 free throws, and defeated Wright State 77–65. Brownell was so aggravated that he shed his coat after the Raiders fell behind 37–26 at halftime.

"Our guys knew this was really important," he said, "and our guys wanted to win badly."

Strain was evident on both sides. On one second-half possession, officials stopped the clock when Wright State guard Vaughn Duggins went down, nullifying a Butler basket. Thirty rows up, Tom Crowley, a Butler assistant athletic director, shouted, "He's hurt! He's not dead!" Momentarily mortified, Crowley sat and vowed not to allow runaway emotions to get the best of him again.

Mack scored 21 points, including 10 in a two-and-a-half-minute span of the first half. Hayward scored 20, ignoring the taunts of "Towel Boy" from Wright State fans, who had a reputation for being caustic. He set career highs for free throws made (13) and attempted (14), scoring 10 of Butler's final 19 points. It was as if Hayward were the anchorman in a relay race, carrying the Bulldogs to the finish line first.

Wright State crept within five points with fewer than five minutes left, but all that did was alert Zach Hahn, the Raider-killer. Hahn, who sank five 3-pointers at Wright State the year before, shot one in over a zone defense to restore Butler's lead to 65–57.

"That was a big-time shot," Hayward said. "Crowd was really into it, and we were kind of struggling a little bit."

Struggles were infrequent. Butler's four league wins were by 17, 23, 13, and 12 points. Stevens didn't need to remind the Bulldogs that Detroit would be different. Not after the year before, and not after so many previous epics at 58-year-old Calihan Hall, the league's only other vintage gym besides Hinkle Fieldhouse.

McCallum, formerly head coach at Ball State and Houston, landed at Detroit after leaving the Indiana staff in the wake of a rules violation scandal involving Hoosiers coach Kelvin Sampson. Following McCallum to Detroit were two transfers from Indiana, Xavier Keeling and 6-foot-10 Eli Holman. Stevens said guarding Holman, one of the nation's leaders in field goal percentage and blocked shots, "takes an entire team's focus."

Holman wasn't the Bulldogs' problem; fouls limited his productivity. But Detroit, like Butler, was a team with multiple weapons. The Bulldogs led by seven points early in the second half but never could pull away, especially with Titans guard Chase Simon on his way to a career-high 23 points. Butler led by five with less than three minutes left but couldn't build a comfortable lead.

Simon's jumper tied the score at 53. Veasley was fouled with 20 seconds left and made the second of two free throws, pushing Butler in front 54–53. Then Detroit guard Woody Payne made a nifty left-handed layup, supplying the Titans with their first lead since the first half, 55–54. Only five seconds remained.

Time-out, Butler.

Stevens wanted the ball in Hayward's hands again, similar to the UCLA scenario, hoping for a similar outcome. Hayward caught the inbounds pass in the backcourt, and as he neared midcourt, Howard set a screen that knocked a Detroit player off his feet. Hayward dribbled nearly to the rim and, as he stretched to release the ball, an official emphatically called a foul against Keeling. There were four-tenths of a second on the clock. Hayward gathered himself at the foul line and swished the first free throw.

Butler 55, Detroit 55.

On the second free throw, Hayward rimmed it. The Bulldogs headed into their only overtime game of the season. With about three and a half minutes left and Butler trailing 60–57, Veasley was struck in the face and went to the bench so the bleeding could be stopped. Briefly, his vision was so blurred that he was blinded. Garrett Butcher came in to replace him, and stayed in. With three minutes left, Hayward sank a 3-pointer from the left wing to tie the score at 60.

"How about the mental toughness to miss that free throw and then hit that 3 when we were down three? Big-time play," Stevens said afterward.

There were more big plays to come. Another jumper by Simon returned the lead to Detroit before Nored's two free throws tied it again. Mack's pull-up jump shot with 59 seconds left pushed the Bulldogs in front 64–62.

In a scrum with eight seconds left, an official appeared ready to whistle the ball dead. Instead, play continued, and Keeling had an uncontested 3-point attempt to win for Detroit. His shot clanged off the rim. Butler won, and was 5-0 in a league in which all others had two or more losses. It wasn't pretty, which suited Howard. Don't want pretty, he said.

"This league is tough, and is really tough on the road," he said. "We're going to have to grind out a lot of them if we're going to get wins."

McCallum spoke on the same theme. Butler is skilled, he said, but wins by being so competitive.

"You aren't always going to bring your 'A' game," Mack said, "but you can always bring your heart when it comes to games like this."

No team in the country was creating as much divergence of opinion as Butler. That Butler could win twice on the road and receive so little support showed that Horizon results were largely ignored. Butler climbed two places in the coaches' poll, to 22nd, but was 39th in the AP writers' voting. No other team was separated as widely as 17 spots. Part of the difference could be explained by the fact that 25 of the 31 coaches voting belonged to mid-major conferences and might have been predisposed to vote for one of their own.

"Our league was all about business," Ronald Nored said. "At that point, people had completely discounted us. We just stayed focused on what we had to do."

The Bulldogs' string of road games was interrupted by a home pair against Cleveland State and Youngstown State. Cleveland State was the only team to have beaten Butler in each of the past two seasons, so the matchup qualified as a budding rivalry. Cleveland State coach Gary Waters didn't necessarily emulate Butler but studied its program closely. For example, he employed four guards around one post player, resembling what the Bulldogs did around Howard.

There was anxiety at Butler because Hayward developed an upper respiratory infection and was treated with intravenous fluids at St. Vincent Hospital. He was not approved to play until several hours before tip-off. Hayward was sluggish, and for most of the first half, so were the Bulldogs. So, too, were the 5,383 fans, a season low. Indianapolis attention was on a televised Indiana basketball game and the Colts' impending game against the Baltimore Ravens in the NFL playoffs.

Cleveland State, a 15-point underdog, beat only a Division III opponent in a 10-game span earlier in the season. The Vikings lost to the likes of Kentucky, Virginia, West Virginia, Ohio State, and Kansas State, so they were as battled-tested as Butler. Cleveland State led 31–22 before Butler scored the final eight points of the first half.

Stevens "got into us" at halftime, Veasley said. "When we were down, we just realized we weren't defending and weren't playing our style of basketball."

The Bulldogs made 10 of their first 13 shots to start the second half, finally taking control in a 64–55 victory. Veasley scored 16 points and Mack 15. Hayward scored 8, the first time all season he had been out of double figures. Waters was dismissive of Hayward's contributions, calling Mack the Bulldogs' best player.

"I mean, they'll go to someone else. A person like Mack is just a player," Waters said. "He finds ways to get the job done. And then you've got to deal with Howard."

Two days later, Youngstown State was unable to deal with Mack or Howard. The Penguins were 0-9 at Butler since joining the league, and their 10th visit quickly became lopsided. Mack scored 22 points in the first half to nearly equal Youngstown State, which fell behind 49–26.

Butler shot 57 percent, made a season-high 12 3-pointers, and reached its highest point total in 95 games by winning 91–61. Mack settled for 24 points. Asked how the Bulldogs compared to previous Butler editions, Youngstown coach Jerry Slocum said they had the potential to be better. Howard was certainly better—his 22 points featured a career-high four dunks—but said it had nothing to do with shedding the T-shirt he usually wore under his jersey.

"I've done it on the road, and I like the way it feels," Howard said. "So I might keep doing it."

During the game, Stevens and other Butler coaches went barefoot to help raise awareness for Samaritan's Feet, a charity that distributes shoes to needy children worldwide. College basketball coaches around the country became involved through the efforts of another Indianapolis coach, Ron Hunter of IUPUI.

At 7-0 in the league, and with six successive victories, Butler was so overwhelmingly dominant that it ranked first or second in the Horizon in 14 of 17 meaningful team statistics. As impressive as that was, Butler had played only two league opponents on the road, albeit those two were Wright State and Detroit. Butler hit the midpoint of the league season in a weekend trip to Chicago. More important, it was an opportunity for seniors Willie Veasley and Nick Rodgers to achieve a Butler milestone.

• • •

Butler's program celebrates teams over individuals. But inside the locker room is a wall of honor. Photos are prominently displayed in a gallery. To qualify, four-year players must be on teams winning 80 or more games. Two-year players must have won at a rate of 70 percent.

With more than 80 victories each, Willie Veasley and Nick Rodgers were already on the wall. The school record was 100, by four 2003 seniors: Joel Cornette, Darnell Archey, Lewis Curry, and Mike Moore. They were 100-28. The 2010 seniors were 99–21.

Veasley's contributions were such that Brad Stevens compared the 6-foot-3 forward to Shane Battier of the Houston Rockets. Battier's influence could not be measured in conventional ways, but he helped his team win. The dynamic was so applicable to any organization that Butler's College of Business was studying the "Battier Effect," based on a *New York Times* analysis of the NBA player. Rockets general manager Daryl Morey called Battier "Lego" because all the pieces fit together when he was on the court. That was Veasley, too.

"I would tell you that every other team in this league would love to have him," Loyola coach Jim Whitesell said. "I think he would be an impact guy. He's just a marvelous player, and really a guy who's evolved in their system."

Coaches in the league marveled at Veasley's emergence as a scorer. When he was a sophomore, he shot 42 percent on free throws. Now he was shooting close to that on 3-pointers.

Veasley's commitment to winning was evidenced the season before. Upon Gordon Hayward's arrival, Stevens told Veasley that he and Hayward would be interchangeable. So in every practice, Veasley deferred to Hayward.

"That's a junior for a freshman. That doesn't happen," Stevens said.

On another occasion, a video clip at a practice showed Veasley helping every teammate on defense while never leaving his own man unguarded. Except for those knowing the intricacies of Butler's defense, it would have been impossible to detect.

"The No. 1 quality of a leader, in my opinion, is somebody's willingness to serve others," Stevens said. "And he is clearly one of the best servant leaders we've had here."

Veasley was raised in Freeport, Illinois, a town of about 25,000 located 20 miles south of the Wisconsin border. Adolph Rupp coached at Freeport High School before leaving to become a legendary figure at the University of Kentucky. The town commemorates an 1858 Lincoln-Douglas debate, but Veasley was no speaker. He kept most of his thoughts to himself. The only boy in a family of seven siblings, his father was his best friend until junior high school.

Veasley's talent was obvious to all. The wife of his high school coach, Jeff Lawfer, once told her husband that she had Freeport's next great player in her classroom. Willie was in second grade. His mother, Rose, remembered her son sitting on the front steps with a basketball under his arm, waiting for Dad. After returning from his job as an ironworker in Rockford, Willie Sr. would play against his son until both were too weary to continue.

One day, a car in the driveway blocked the path to the hoop. The car had a standard transmission. When Rose arrived home, the car was in the street and Willie was playing ball.

"It was kind of scary for the mother of an eight-year-old," Rose said. "That was probably the worst thing he's ever done."

Willie made trouble mostly for opponents. By seventh grade, he could dunk. In eighth grade, his summer team went 44-0. As a freshman, he was called up to the varsity of the Freeport Pretzels, so named for the snacks introduced by German immigrants settling in the area. Veasley broke the school's all-time scoring record and averaged 25 points for a 24-5 team. Letters from colleges recruiting him filled three bins.

Veasley wanted to go to Marquette, about 130 miles away in Milwaukee. Marquette instead offered a scholarship to a taller player.

"I knew he was hurt," his father said, "but he went on."

When Veasley visited Butler, his future teammates took him bowling and made him feel comfortable on a small campus that reminded him of his hometown. Later, when the other prospect rejected Marquette, the offer to Veasley was renewed. He declined. He had committed to Butler.

"I gave my word," he told his father.

As a freshman, Veasley was attentive to what upperclassmen told him. In his third game, he guarded Indiana's 6-foot-9 D. J. White, a future NBA player. Her son could handle that, Rose Veasley said, "because he guarded someone who weighed 100 pounds more than him for most of his life."

Veasley's stone-faced expression on the court rarely changed, irrespective of circumstance. He had been through it all, and he had a calming effect on those around him. Teammates listened when he did speak. So did his six sisters, even though all but one is older.

"The girls all look up to him," their mother said.

Yet Veasley had a sentimental side. Before every game, he phoned his mother for a kiss. Over the line, she sent him one.

Freeport teachers remembered their former student so fondly that many attended Butler games, including a busload that once made the trip to Milwaukee. When Veasley was an athletic director's aide, he sorted mail, changed file boards, and filled water jugs. And he was the star of the school.

"Willie has made some lasting impressions on people," his mother said.

At Butler, it was the Veasley Effect.

Before the Bulldogs took the floor at Loyola's Gentile Center, there was an upset. Their locker room was next to that of the Loyola women's team, and they heard the Ramblers whooping and hollering after their first victory ever over a Top 25 opponent. Before the men's game, Loyola's women beat 17th-ranked Green Bay 65–63, ending a 35-game league winning streak.

Loyola's men, on the other hand, hadn't beaten a ranked opponent at the Gentile Center since 1986. Against Butler, 20th in the coaches' poll, there was little chance of that changing.

Yet this was one of those nights on which the Bulldogs couldn't assert any dominance. The crowd of 4,372 was nearly double the total for the next most attended Loyola home game, and Veasley said it was the loudest gym in which Butler had played.

Butler took the lead midway through the first half and held it, but the halftime margin was just 30–26. With less than seven minutes left, Hayward's 3-pointer sent the Bulldogs ahead 46–43. It was their last field goal. It was not their last stand.

The more shots they missed, the more their resolve increased.

"Hey, just keep guarding," Stevens told them in a sideline huddle. "Keep doing what we do. Guys, this is one of those games that we're supposed to lose. Why not win?"

Loyola's only field goal of the final seven minutes was a 3-pointer by Terrance Hill, tying the score at 47 with 47 seconds left. Veasley was fouled with 34 seconds left, and he made the second of two free throws to push Butler ahead 48–47. A Loyola turnover returned the ball to Butler, but Mack dribbled out of bounds, which gave it back. With time expiring, Hill rimmed a 3-pointer, and a tip-in rolled off. Just as they had survived a last-second shot at Detroit, the Bulldogs survived at Loyola.

The 48–47 victory was a milestone 100th for Veasley and Rodgers. It was clunky, but it was a victory.

"The free throw, I guess, makes it that much more special," Veasley said.

Butler scored a season low in points, shot a season-worst 15 percent (3 of 20) on 3-pointers, and was outrebounded by 13. Howard did not attempt one free throw. To Butler fans, that was as distressing as fingernails across a chalkboard.

"To win games like this is how you move forward," Stevens said. "Every championship team, or every team that competes for a championship, has to win games like this."

Rather than question the Bulldogs' capabilities, ESPN analyst LaPhonso Ellis said, "What you saw tonight was an ability to grind out games."

What TV viewers saw, too, was Butler's defense in lockdown mode. For that reason, the 1-point win over Loyola was more meaningful than the 30-point win over Youngstown. The latter was easy. What happens when it is hard? For two months, that was the Butler question.

Excluding Butler, visitors in the league were 7-9. Butler was 3-0 in league road games. It *was* hard.

Usually hard, anyway. Butler made it look easy two days later in an 84–55 romp at Illinois–Chicago. The Bulldogs shot 56 percent and did not commit a second-half turnover. Butler had a strong contingent of Chicago alumni, and Dawg fans filled most of three sections in the lower level of UIC Pavilion. The Flames were so badly overmatched that their scoring leader, Robo Kreps, was held to 4 points—11 under his average.

Hayward was dazzling. He scored inside and outside, right- and left-handed, dunked, rebounded, passed, and blocked shots. He scored 25 points in 27 minutes. In keeping with the Butler Way, the only applause from teammates came when he went to the floor, digging out a ball like a back-row volleyball player.

"This shouldn't be the case, but I probably need to get on the floor more often," Hayward said, smiling. "So they all kind of gave me some jokes about that."

The victory gave Veasley and Rodgers No. 101, breaking the Butler career record. It brought the Bulldogs to 9-0 halfway through the league season, renewing speculation that they might reach a perfect 18-0. After the Wright State–Detroit road sweep, kenpom.com gave Butler a 22 percent chance of going unbeaten in the league. Kenpom, a college basketball website dedicated to statistical analysis, raised that figure to 30 percent at the schedule's midpoint.

UIC coach Jimmy Collins said the Bulldogs would need some luck, but yes, they could do it. ESPN.com's Andy Katz wrote that Butler "is looking like it won't lose in the league." ESPN's Joe Lunardai estimated the chance at 67 percent, and CBS analyst Clark Kellogg at 40 percent.

It was not the kind of discourse Stevens wanted to hear. Going unbeaten had "never been a reasonable thought," he said. There had been enough burden on this team already, and he didn't want to load on more cargo.

"Any talk of going undefeated is not only premature, but uninformed, in my opinion," Stevens said.

He realized how thin the margin of error was. For instance, in going 14-2 in 2003, Butler won six league games by four or fewer points or in overtime. In the league's 31-year history, three teams had gone unbeaten. One, Loyola, played just five games in the inaugural 1979–80 season. None of the three won the league tournament, either.

As the winning streak lengthened, nonplayers made superstitious contributions. Radio announcer Joe Gentry always wore a gray suit, and analyst Nick Gardner the same white Bulldog polo. Stats-keeper Chris McGrath wore the same Moxsters canvas shoes. Stevens's four-year-old son, Brady, kept wearing a No. 21 jersey—Veasley's number. Butler's male cheerleaders wore the same armbands and socks, and they maintained a morning routine on game day. While waiting for breakfast, they went around the tables chanting the "Butler War Song," line by line.

A Chicago attorney who was an alum realized he had been watching all the wins seated on a stool bearing a Butler logo and proclaimed, "It's the stool." Gotta be the stool.

One Butler fan, 54-year-old Pat Gallagher, wasn't superstitious at all. By late January he was already counting down how many victories it would take for the Bulldogs to remain unbeaten and win the national championship.

"If you're going to dream," Gallagher said, "you might as well dream big."

Butler coaches continued to prod the Bulldogs.

"We have goals to win a championship, but why lose?" assistant coach Micah Shrewsberry asked them. "Why let up and lose a game? Why not go undefeated?"

Why not? Green Bay and Milwaukee, for two reasons. The Bulldogs lost at both Wisconsin sites the year before, and both opponents were competent, irrespective of earlier losses at Hinkle Fieldhouse. The Bulldogs scheduled an early Thursday practice before a charter flight to Green Bay, but the practice went poorly. When it didn't get any better, Stevens called it off.

The Bulldogs reconvened upon arrival in Green Bay and went to the Kress Events Center for a second practice next to the campus arena where the Butler and Green Bay women's teams were playing. The Bulldogs weren't going to the game. They were going back to the gym.

"If we have more work to do," Stevens said later, "we've got to do it."

The Phoenix had won 16 straight league games at home—their last loss was to Butler—and had already beaten 20th-ranked Wisconsin there. They were hyped. Point guard Rahmon Fletcher was back, and he was ready. The Bulldogs . . . were not.

Stevens began the game standing, and continued standing. An official warned him not to leave the coach's box. Green Bay took the lead, and Stevens took Hayward out.

"You're in la-la land!" the coach shouted at his sophomore star.

Hayward picked up two fouls within the opening three minutes and sat down, soon to be followed by Howard, also with two fouls. The suddenly outsized Bulldogs, now used to being less reliant on the 3-pointer, needed field goals from the arc to stay close. They made them. They scored the final six points of the half, including Zach Hahn's third 3-pointer, to forge a 33–29 halftime lead.

Butler went on a 13-3 spurt to open the second half, and Green Bay crumbled. The lead grew to 14 points, then 18, then 21. The crowd of 6,237, anticipating an upset like the year before, quieted. Howard scored 14 of his 18 points in the second half of what became a 75–57 demolition. His emphatic one-handed slam was chosen as one of ESPN's top 10 plays of the day. Veasley supplied 13 points, 8 rebounds, and his usual immeasurables.

"When we're on the court, it's the five guys there," Veasley said. "We need to help each other, talk to each other, hold each other accountable."

If NCAA rules allowed it, the Bulldogs could have been cast in TV commercials for tires or trucks. They were road-tough. Their 8-1 record on opponents' courts was bettered by just two other teams in all of major college basketball: St. Mary's (8-0) and Syracuse (5-0). In preparing the Bulldogs for each game, Stevens never addressed location, only opponent. It's not like one game is worth more than another, he said.

Milwaukee's U.S. Cellular Arena had been a punishing venue for the Bulldogs, who were 2-7 in the last nine visits. Even mediocre Panther teams were fierce there. Compounding the challenge this time was foul trouble ensnaring Butler's front line.

Some of the season-high 5,012 fans in Milwaukee taunted Howard, who was accused of flopping to induce fouls. The detractors needn't have bothered. Butler teammates said it was impossible to embarrass or unsettle Howard. They knew because they had tried. When you grow up in a family of 10, as Howard did, you don't sweat the small stuff.

With the Bulldogs ahead 40–39, Howard picked up his third foul three minutes into the second half. Avery Jukes and Garrett Butcher already had three fouls each, and eventually fouled out. Hayward was assigned to defend 6-foot-7, 230-pound Anthony Hill, who had 19 points by early in the second half. Hayward, though slender, was long-armed and nimble, and he virtually removed Hill from Milwaukee's offense.

"It's tough to get by him," Hill conceded.

Hayward, who had been so ineffective at Green Bay, turned assertive on offense, too. After Butler fell behind 49–42, he scored 15 of his team's last 31 points over the closing 14 minutes. His 10-foot shot expanded the Bulldogs' lead to 69–64 with 1:35 left, and they finished off a 73–66 victory.

Nored, rarely a scorer, contributed 11 of his career-high 13 points in the second half. Hayward was 13 of 16 on free throws, scoring 23 of his 25 points in the final 25 minutes. A fourth road win in 11 days completed a 9-0 January.

"They have a pro," Milwaukee coach Rob Jeter said. "A lot of times, that's the difference. With Gordon Hayward on the court, they're able to make some plays that you just don't coach."

A swelling undercurrent to the Butler season was speculation over whether Hayward would leave school after two years and submit his name for the NBA draft. A few months before, that would have been a preposterous notion. He wasn't one of those prospects who since age 14 had been told how great he is. But NBA scouts were appearing at every game, and Hayward's future was on the minds of the youngest Butler fans.

"Is Gordon going?" a small child asked Hayward's father, Gordon Hayward Sr.

Hayward Jr. gave obligatory responses to such questions, saying he was concentrating on his studies and Butler basketball. By all indications, he was. He was leaving the research to his father and Stevens. Hayward's father was taking calls from agents leaving messages. When his mother, Jody, heard the same messages, she cried.

Yet it was prudent to explore the process, so the father began educating himself about projected draft range. Only those taken in the first round had guaranteed contracts, and then only for two years. Stevens spoke to general managers and scouts who were fascinated by the skills in someone as tall as the 6-foot-9 Hayward. The kid was 19 and still adjusting to his height, after all.

"The one thing with Gordon that may not be the case with some of those other guys who are in the discussion is he wasn't in this position three years ago," Stevens said. "He wasn't even fathoming that it's a possibility. I know this. Butler is very important to Gordon. I know that high-level education, and his engineering degree, are very important to Gordon and very important to his family."

Hayward's father acknowledged he couldn't shield his son from the NBA talk and wondered aloud if it was all premature. How could any atmosphere in the NBA, for instance, equal that inside Hinkle Fieldhouse for Ohio State and Xavier? Hayward's mother worried about the temptations of an NBA lifestyle. The family resolved to put the situation in the Lord's hands, praying about the outcome.

"If Butler does really well and he blows up," Hayward's father said, "then we'll have to sit down and talk about it."

It took a 10-game winning streak, but the Bulldogs began February by returning to the AP Top 25 at No. 23. To stay there, they had to sweep 3 home games within five days. Detroit traveled to Indianapolis as a 15-point underdog, which was absurd by any calculation. Detroit, at 14-8, had lost 6 games by an aggregate 13 points. If the 2-point outcomes were reversed, the Titans would be 10-1 in the league and Butler 9-2.

"Without question, they're one of the most talented teams we've played," Stevens said.

Playing Detroit at Hinkle Fieldhouse was no easier than it had been at Calihan Hall. The Titans hadn't beaten a ranked opponent on the road in 31 years, and Butler represented a chance to do so. Although the Bulldogs bolted ahead 10–0, Detroit overtook them midway through the first half 16–15.

After Detroit closed within 45–44 in the second half, Hayward converted 3-point plays on successive possessions. Nored, although vexed by a career-worst 6 turnovers, scored 6 of Butler's final 10 points and tormented Chase Simon. After averaging 24.2 points in Detroit's previous six games, Simon scored 15 on 5-of-16 shooting. The Bulldogs won 63–58, and never mind the point spread. Butler would assuredly remember the Titans.

"They're a really good basketball team who could beat a lot of teams on a given day," Stevens said.

Just not Butler. Not on this day. No one was beating Butler on any day. In the 118-year history of the basketball program, Butler had never been 12-0 in any conference—Missouri Valley, Mid-American, Indiana Collegiate, or Horizon.

That this was a different kind of Butler team was underscored by the fact that it went two games with two 3-pointers each. In a program known for 3-point barrages, these Bulldogs were sometimes difficult to embrace by longtime fans. Their offense was more conventional and more efficient: points inside, off the dribble, and on free throws. Those components were there more often on a nightly basis than the 3-pointer.

With six games to play, the Bulldogs were on the verge of securing a share of a fourth-straight regular-season title, an active streak exceeded only by Gonzaga (nine in the West Coast Conference) and Kansas (five in the Big 12). They were "the gold standard of the league," Loyola coach Whitesell said.

They had a golden touch in an ESPN2 game against Wright State. The Bulldogs shot 67.5 percent in a 74–62 victory, and a staggering 79.3 percent on 2-pointers. They made 27 of 40 shots from the field, and one more field goal would have broken a 16-year-old school record for shooting percentage.

Brownell, the Wright State coach, said Butler was stronger than the Raiders and overpowered them on drives to the hoop. He twice called time-outs early in the second half as Butler expanded its lead to 14.

"I didn't come up with any brilliant ideas in those 20 seconds over there," Brownell said. "I just stopped the crowd from clapping for a few minutes."

Five Bulldogs scored 10 or more, led by Veasley's career-high 19 points on 9-of-9 shooting. Nored had 7 more turnovers, but also a career-high 8 assists. Stevens could feel the pulse of his team, so he didn't belabor the Bulldogs' 17 turnovers.

"I want them to play with free minds," he said, "and play with an attacking mind-set."

Such thinking was not original, and actually was consistent with the philosophy of Hoosier legend John Wooden at UCLA. It is what Wooden had been taught by coach Piggy Lambert at Purdue.

"I believed if you were not making mistakes, you were not doing anything," Wooden wrote in his book *My Personal Best*. "You need to *do* something to make things happen."

Howard was always trying to make things happen but wasn't as productive as in the previous season, when he was the league's player of the year. In Butler's first 10 games he shot 42 percent, resembling a golfer who inexplicably developed yips on the putting green. However, it was no coincidence that as his fouling decreased and shooting percentage increased, Butler's winning streak lengthened.

As self-critical as Howard was, the coaches' regular response was to express confidence in their big man. The trust was warranted, as Howard showed in delivering 20 points in a 62–47 victory over Loyola.

"To me, he looks back to being the MVP of our league like he has been," Loyola coach Whitesell said. "I always think Butler starts with Matt Howard."

In clinching a championship share, the Bulldogs finished the three-wins-in-five-days sweep and extended their winning streak to 13. They missed as many shots (13) in the opening 10 minutes as they did in the entire game against Wright State.

The Hayward-Mack duo was uncharacteristically ineffective. Neither scored for 27 minutes, and they totaled 13 points. The two sophomores had played almost nonstop for 16 months, including the USA Basketball experience and Italy tour. After scoring in double figures for 21 straight games, Mack averaged 7.7 in the three-game home stand. Hayward shot 0 of 13 from the 3-point line over four games. Stevens bristled at a suggestion that the two were tiring. Hayward said the solution was to keep shooting.

"I think I'm just thinking about it too much and not going out and shooting it," Hayward said.

He appeared anything but weary three days later at Youngstown State, although the same wasn't true of all the Bulldogs. After leading early, they allowed Youngstown to outscore them 23–4 and go ahead 28–20. Butler never trailed over the closing 19 minutes, pulling away after Hayward drove in for a dunk midway through the second half. Butler sank eight straight shots down the stretch, and the margin reached 17 points in a 68–57 victory.

Hayward scored 22 points, and his 17 rebounds were the most by a Butler player in 20 years. He made two second-half 3s to end a streak of 16 successive misses from the arc. Hayward was "phenomenal," Stevens said. "Phenomenal."

With a 15-0 league record and outright title, No. 1 seed for the tournament, and 14-game winning streak, the Bulldogs turned their attention to Cleveland State. Hayward said they would look at the Vikings' 2009 championship banner for motivation.

Indeed, the banner supplied more stimulus than the Vikings intended. Stevens and some of his players noticed a banner hanging in Cleveland's Wolstein Center that proclaimed HORIZON LEAGUE CHAMPIONS, rather than tournament champions. That was a technicality, but to the Bulldogs, it was a provocation. Furthermore, the Vikings carried a 14-game home winning streak in Horizon play, and TV and magazine journalist Seth Davis picked Cleveland State to win.

Although the Vikings led by six in the first half and trailed 29–27 at halftime, the outcome was inevitable. In the first half, Butler had 17 defensive rebounds and Cleveland State no offensive rebounds. The Bulldogs secured every missed shot under their own basket, a statistic almost never seen in the sport. Cleveland State, despite a reputation for being tough and physical, was simply overpowered 70–59.

Howard (21 points, 13 rebounds) and Hayward (19 points, 11 rebounds) each had a double-double. Butler outrebounded Cleveland State 46–20. When the Bulldogs were troubled by the press, they let Hayward bring the ball upcourt. He dribbled more than half the length of the floor to score as the first-half clock expired. He hadn't scored more than 9 points in four previous games against Cleveland State, but ace defender D'Aundray Brown said he couldn't restrain Hayward "no matter what we did."

The 15th consecutive victory tied a school record, set in 2000, and matched Murray State for the nation's longest active streak. At 16-0, the Bulldogs were 2 away from an unprecedented 18-0 league season. Coach Waters promised the Vikings again would meet Butler in the league tournament at Hinkle Fieldhouse. Stevens indicated the Bulldogs were promised nothing, even though a 23-4 record made an NCAA Tournament berth probable.

"As long as you have season left, then the best moments should not be behind you," Stevens said. "You need to keep getting better and striving for better."

With three games left in the regular season, the most consequential was not in the league, but rather a *BracketBusters* pairing against Siena of the Metro Atlantic Athletic Conference. Before the Siena matchup, Butler muddled through a 73–55 victory over a UIC team that was winless on the road. Although the Bulldogs were anything but crisp, they committed a season-low six turnovers, limited UIC to 31 percent shooting, and broke the school record with a 16th-straight victory.

"Hopefully, it's just one of those games you have to get through," Howard said.

It wasn't one Butler got through without calamity. Veasley sprained his left knee late in the game. The injury came at an inopportune time because Siena (22-5) loomed as the most formidable foe for Butler (24-4) since UAB. Coincidentally, 13 days after New Orleans beat the Colts in the Super Bowl, it was Saints versus Indianapolis again.

Siena had virtually the same group that won NCAA Tournament games over Vanderbilt in 2008 and Ohio State in 2009. So most of the Saints had played in 4 NCAA games, and most of the Bulldogs had played in only 1. The Saints recently had a 15-game winning streak stopped at Niagara 87–74, and Stevens said "it really bothers me" that they would be downgraded for that. There were no reprieves for mid-major programs, and Siena was more in need of a victory than Butler. Stevens, as usual, avoided debate over March ramifications.

"If you focus on anything but Siena," he said, "you're in trouble."

Veasley warmed up in hopes of playing, and though his condition improved, he was not ready. Trainer Ryan Galloy said the last thing he wanted to do was to have Veasley, with his parents in attendance, watch the Senior Day game in street clothes. Yet that was most judicious. Because Veasley was going to be sidelined, he surprised some Butler fans by mingling with them in the fieldhouse's Wildman Room before the game.

He was replaced in the lineup by another senior, 6-foot-8 Avery Jukes, who never thought he would wait until the end of his college career to be a starter. Jukes transferred from Alabama, where he stayed a semester. Someone coming from the Southeastern Conference was expected to become a key figure at Butler. He did, but off the bench. Jukes sometimes met with Stevens privately to discuss his role. Jukes invariably toiled out of his natural position, forward, because Butler needed him to reinforce Howard at center. And Jukes wasn't going to displace Veasley or Hayward at forward.

"Sometimes I felt like, 'Oh, I can't really control it,'" Jukes said. "Other times, I thought I should get more playing time. That was kind of the most frustrating part. When I did get the time in a game, I would play well. And in the next game, I would play five or six minutes."

Butler needed him to play well against Siena, and he did. Jukes sank two 3-pointers in the opening four minutes, helping Butler surge ahead 16–7. That incited the crowd of 9,111, most wearing white in compliance with a whiteout request to fans. The hysteria didn't last long. Siena featured four candidates for MAAC player of the year, and the one with the hot hand was junior guard Clarence Jackson. He scored 14 of the Saints' first 16 points, and they overtook Butler by halftime 31–28.

Howard was assessed his third and fourth fouls a minute apart early in the second half. That sent him to the bench, leaving Butler without two starters and facing a 34–32 deficit. Butler had lost home *BracketBusters* games to Southern Illinois in 2007 and Drake in 2008, and was in jeopardy of another such deflating defeat.

Yet when forced to employ a smaller lineup, the Bulldogs came up big. Hahn's consecutive 3-pointers climaxed a 15–4 run to create a 9-point lead. That was all the separation required. The Bulldogs expanded the lead to 20 in a 70–53 victory that conveyed what they were capable of against a national-caliber opponent.

"If you're going to beat them, you almost have to play a perfect game," Siena coach Fran McCaffery said.

Mack scored 12 of his 23 points in the closing seven minutes. Hayward had a fourth-straight double-double (15 points, 12 rebounds). It wasn't difficult to discern why the Bulldogs built a 42–22 bulge in the second half: They shot 61 percent to Siena's 23 percent. Stevens credited the Bulldogs' resilience for coping with the absence of Veasley and How-ard, and their experience for thriving in an "amped-up" arena.

"Even though they're sophomores and juniors, for the most part, they've played a lot of minutes," Stevens said. "They know what to expect. They know how to handle it and all that goes with it."

The Bulldogs played so impressively that Westwood One radio ana-lyst Bill Frieder, a former Michigan coach, suggested to Stevens that they might receive a No. 4 seed in the NCAA Tournament. Selection Sunday was three weeks away. Hayward said the Bulldogs would let others worry about the consequences of the victory. Besides, there was business to fin-ish in the Horizon League: perfection.

For much of February, Hayward endured soreness in his back. After heat was applied before games, he was able to play unaffected. However, two days before Butler's regular-season finale, at Valparaiso, he developed debilitating back spasms. It was impossible to determine whether the Siena load was responsible, but he had carried the Bulldogs on that vul-nerable back: rebounding, ballhandling, defending every position.

Galloy, the trainer, worked on him for four hours. The trainer called in team physician Joel Kary for additional treatment. They decided to trans-port him to chiropractor Sheila Wilson, who had treated track and field athletes for many years. Hayward was so locked up that the chiropractor generated some audible "pops" in his back. The player was startled.

"It was loud," Galloy recalled.

Hayward felt better the next day, riding a stationary bicycle and jog-ging a little. He traveled with the team north to Valparaiso, but the trainer told Stevens not to count on Hayward. If that weren't worrisome enough, Howard showed up at the afternoon shootaround pale and bil-ious. He was diagnosed with dehydration, a result of food poisoning or intestinal illness. He was sent back to the hotel and given antinausea medication.

Student manager Scott Schmelzer never left Howard's side, deliver-ing a favorable report to the trainer: Matt is okay. He's farting now. Gal-loy could testify to that after returning to a malodorous room. At Butler, even the managers stood their ground.

"Wow, that's toughness," Galloy thought.

It also demonstrated the all-in-it-together approach of everyone, including the managers. Players treated them like teammates, especially senior manager Erick Brown, nicknamed "E. Weezy." Former Butler guard Mike Green came up with that sobriquet, and it stuck. When Stevens occasionally polled players about which of them epitomized various Butler Way values, E. Weezy received votes.

But there wasn't much even the most dedicated managers could do when it came to taking the floor against Valparaiso without Veasley or Hayward or Howard. Valpo coach Homer Drew had said this was the best Butler team he had seen, but that was with an intact lineup.

Veasley's knee had improved enough to allow him to play, and Stevens decided to start Howard, too. Hayward sat on the bench in street clothes, leaving a 17-game winning streak and a 17-0 league record at risk.

"Nobody wanted to lose that game, especially trying to go undefeated," Veasley said. "Everybody knew that we had to play that much better because Gordon wasn't going to be there."

Valpo packed a sellout of 5,266 into its arena, and the Crusaders gave them reason to cheer. The league's highest-scoring team led Butler by eight points midway through the first half and 31–30 at halftime. The Bulldogs led by seven early in the second half but couldn't keep control. Valparaiso restored its edge to 49–46 in the second half.

That's when Veasley, the onetime scattershot who couldn't make a free throw, shot down the Crusaders. He sank three 3-pointers during a 16-3 run to push the Bulldogs ahead 65–52. On the second of Veasley's successive 3s, his coach broke into a smile as wide as the foul lane. Veasley scored a career-high 20 points, and the Bulldogs repulsed the Valpo challenge 74–69. Howard revived enough to add 17 points and 10 rebounds.

It was a perfect ending.

The Bulldogs won their 18th straight. They were 18-0 in the league. They were unbeaten in February, as they were in January. They were six games ahead of second-place Wright State in a league that had never been won by more than four. With No. 1 Kansas losing at Oklahoma State the next day, Butler became the only team in the nation with an unbeaten league record.

"It's a tough task, but it's a real testament to how this team has played and fought through some tough situations," Howard said. "We've been through a lot of different things this year and found ways to win."

As the players boarded the bus for the return to Indianapolis, driver Charles Jones gave them all fist bumps and yelled, "We're undefeated!"

So was the Miller Trailways driver. In 11 games in which he transported the team, Butler was 11-0.

Butler had eight days before a semifinal in the Horizon League Tournament. It allowed more time for treatment on Hayward's back and reflection on what Butler achieved. At 82-14, Stevens had set a record for wins by someone coaching his first three seasons of major college basketball.

When league honors were announced, Hayward, Nored, and Stevens were, respectively, the player, codefensive player, and coach of the year. Hayward, Howard, and Mack made the all-league first team. Joining Nored, who shared his honor with Detroit's Woody Payne, on the all-defensive team was Veasley. There were years in which voting displayed anti-Butler sentiment, but not in 2010. Three first-team selections and recognition of all five starters were unprecedented. Of course, so was 18-0.

None of it made the Dawgs behave imperiously. They practiced early the next morning, as usual, and did so in the West Gym. They relocated because the women's team was scheduled to use the main Hinkle Fieldhouse floor. Hayward didn't scrimmage with the men but busied himself stretching and running under the trainer's supervision. They took a day off Wednesday before resuming preparation Thursday. Butler was well rested heading into the postseason.

Under the league tournament format—introduced after Butler's 2002 snub season—the Nos. 1 and 2 seeds received byes into the Saturday semifinals at Hinkle Fieldhouse. No. 4 seed Milwaukee earned the right to meet Butler by eliminating Cleveland State 82-75. No. 7 seed Detroit beat No. 3 seed Green Bay 62-53, and the Titans advanced to meet Wright State.

As much as they were up against Milwaukee, the Bulldogs were confronting complacency. None of the three previous teams to go unbeaten through this league won the postseason tournament. As if on cue, Milwaukee forged a 10-point lead and was ahead 29-28 at halftime.

At least Hayward was playing again, although he had been rehabbing all week and this was his first game in 14 days. Stevens once looked to the bench to insert him into the game, and he wasn't there. Hayward was riding a stationary bike to keep his back from stiffening. Other than being out of breath, he said he "felt fine."

The Bulldogs couldn't breathe easily until late, grinding out a 68–59 victory behind Howard's 18 points. Hayward (10 points, 13 rebounds) had a fifth-straight double-double, becoming the first Butler player to achieve that since 1974. The game was interrupted by 49 fouls, 28 by Milwaukee, and never had any rhythm.

The 10-point deficit was the largest that Butler overcame since the opener against Davidson. The Bulldogs had waited a year to play in the championship game, and would finally do so Tuesday against Wright State. The Raiders won the other semifinal over Detroit 69–50. Howard called it unfinished business. It was as if life outside the Butler bubble did not exist. Stevens deflected questions about the NCAA Tournament, saying players had not spoken about it.

"And their locker room is right next to my office, and I have not once heard any bracketology or any of that stuff from them," the coach said.

The day before the climactic game, Nored and five teammates—Veasley, Mack, Shawn Vanzant, Alex Anglin, and Grant Leiendecker—joined him for breakfast at the West 40th Street home of Nored's grandparents. Delores Kennedy-Williams's homemade cooking was better than anything on a Le Peep or Bob Evans menu. Eggs, bacon, sausage, French toast, pancakes, biscuits, orange juice, milk.

"We love it," Grandma said. "His teammates will tell him, 'Tell your grandmother to fix me this.' He always says, 'You tell her. She'll do it.'"

The Bulldogs were hungry for more than breakfast. Leading up to the March 9 championship, Stevens had never seen them more wired for a single game. Of course, they all knew they were in the NCAA Tournament, irrespective of the outcome. That was not the issue. The image of that second-place trophy inside a barren locker room was implanted in the Bulldogs' psyche, and it was not something they wanted to revisit.

There were many stopovers on their seasonlong journey, and there would be more later. But nothing else on the itinerary was quite like this. The Bulldogs were edgy, like thoroughbreds in a starting gate.

"We wanted to make a statement," Rodgers recalled.

Hinkle Fieldhouse wasn't filled, but with four busloads of Wright State fans traveling from Dayton, the crowd of 6,065 created a championship environment for an ESPN audience and 100-station Westwood One radio network. Stevens kept pieces of net from Butler's 2001 and 2008 tournament championships in his pocket, something he did not do the year before. Maybe it wouldn't help, but it sure wouldn't hurt.

Brownell, mindful that Butler didn't shoot 3-pointers as accurately as it once did, started Wright State in a zone defense. It would have been shrewd strategy, except Butler made 8 of 13 from the arc in the first half in running out to a 42–28 lead. This looked more like old Butler than new Butler. Not that it mattered. Winning is all that did.

More important than winning was to do everything possible to win on every possession. With the Bulldogs securely ahead by 25 points in the second half, the usually quiet Howard exhorted his teammates: "This is not over! Don't stop playing!"

Howard never stopped. Soon thereafter, he dove into the courtside seats, knocking down a chain barrier and breaking a chair. In doing so, he batted a loose ball back into the hands of Shawn Vanzant. The extraordinary hustle resulted in a Veasley layup and a 27-point lead. Stevens said he would show the play for the next 20 years, that it was the signature moment of the season.

"For him to do that said, 'I care so much about doing the right thing on this possession, the score is inconsequential in my approach,' " the coach said.

Butler concluded a 70–45 victory, one point short of a record margin for the league's championship game. The streak became 20 and their Horizon record 20-0. The Bulldogs' nine 3-pointers gave them 22 straight wins in games making nine or more 3s.

Howard, with 14 points and 9 rebounds, was voted the tournament's MVP. He was disappointed only in that Veasley wasn't voted onto the all-tourney team. That could not spoil the night for Veasley, who said it was "an amazing feeling." All Veasley did was limit Wright State forward Todd Brown, the leading active scorer in the league, to no points.

By earning the league's automatic spot, Butler left no doubt about inclusion in the NCAA Tournament. The Bulldogs could be snubbed in seeding. But this 28-4 team was going to be in the bracket somewhere.

"You don't want to have the same taste in your mouth as last year," Howard said. "You want to make sure you're in."

Wright State made 2 of 20 3-point attempts, and for the 12th time in 14 games, the Butler opponent shot less than 40 percent. The Bulldogs' viselike grip on the defensive end pulled ever tighter.

CHAPTER 7

MARCHING THROUGH THE MADNESS

The week leading up to Selection Sunday coincided with spring break. With no classes, and only so many hours devoted to practice, what's a college basketball player to do with idle time?

Make a hip-hop track, of course. At least that's what Gordon Hayward did. He and Boris Golubov and Gino Calderon, two buddies from Brownsburg, Indiana, wrote and recorded "Too Big, Yo" and released the rap on Facebook and YouTube.

Word of the rap was spread over the Internet by two college basketball reporters, Luke Winn of *Sports Illustrated* and Kyle Whelliston of mid-majority.com. The national attention surprised Hayward, who did not consider himself a celebrity.

"It really was not supposed to be this big of a deal," he said. "It kind of got blown out of proportion."

Nonetheless, the rap became wildly popular on Butler's campus. Hayward was so taken aback that the rap was removed from YouTube, but it was preserved elsewhere on the Internet and remained accessible. Hayward went by "G-Time" in the rap, "'Burg" was Brownsburg, dubs were "Ws" (wins), and " 'Ship" was championship. His lyrics:

> Yo, yo, the name's G-Time
> Big frame, big game, call me big time
> Ball hard every night and day
> From the 'Burg, I rep it in a big way

Come too close, I'll hit you with the blow-by
Straight to the rim, I'm just too high
Stay back and I'll hit the J
Try to stop me, there's just no waaaay

But it's not about me, it's about the team
Going to the tourney with a full head of steam
'Ship's real close, it's at our back door
Get a few dubs, we'll be in the Final Four
Not stopping there, that's not in store
Push it to the limit, we want more

Coach Brad Stevens asked only if the rap was clean and if it was good. The answer to the first question: yes. The second: matter of opinion. The coach himself had not heard it.

Shelvin Mack said he "didn't expect it from Gordon," but liked the rap. Matt Howard's reaction?

"Just as long as he doesn't go Ron Artest on us," Howard said, referring to the NBA player who was a self-styled rap artist.

Howard made his own statement by growing out his wispy blond mustache, a Trash 'Stache. Several players agreed to grow mustaches during the NCAA Tournament as a show of solidarity, but the others abandoned the idea. Not Howard, though. The Trash 'Stache inspired its own Facebook page and a whimsical online diary.

"Once Matt sets his mind on something," Ronald Nored said, "he's not going to change it."

The pretournament blathering about Butler focused not on hip-hop or facial hair, but on seeding. Seeding was an influential factor on how far teams advanced, and Butler received both favorable and unfavorable seeds in previous years. A consensus of mock brackets put Butler in the Nos. 5–6 range. Part of the reason was Butler's No. 12 standing in the computer rankings used by the NCAA selection committee.

Fans were hoping the Bulldogs wouldn't be seeded as low as No. 7, as in 2008, because that pitted them against No. 2 seed Tennessee in the second round. Butler had Final Four ambitions that year but lost to Tennessee in overtime. Stevens expressed indifference to seeding, maintaining that matchups were more important than "the number next to your name."

There was so much parity in college basketball that some wondered whether a mid-major could make a run to the Final Four. For one thing, even though Kansas and Kentucky were regarded as the best teams, there was an absence of superpowers. Teams were "charmingly flawed," as *Washington Post* columnist Michael Wilbon put it. And there was a large pool of threats outside the major conferences.

In 2006, George Mason became the first authentic mid-major in the Final Four since Indiana State and Penn in 1979. One component needed to make a Final Four is callusing so a mid-major "is not in awe of any top-rated teams," George Mason coach Jim Larranaga said. "Because you're going to play some high-powered BCS teams for sure, in the Round of 16 and Elite Eight."

Butler did that in November and December, winning 8 of 12 games. The story line of Butler returning to Indianapolis for a Final Four in Lucas Oil Stadium was irresistible. However, Butler wasn't necessarily the best of the mid-majors.

CBS analyst Clark Kellogg gave New Mexico, Xavier, and Gonzaga better chances. Mike DeCourcy of the *Sporting News* said Butler had the best chance, as long as it didn't have to face teams featuring significant size. DeCourcy said the Bulldogs would not match up well against No. 1 seeds, "so I'd imagine they'd probably need some help to reach the Final Four." To make it that far, according to Gary Parrish of the CBS website, the Bulldogs would have to beat at least three teams better than any team they had beaten all season.

Dan Dakich, a former Indiana University player and assistant coach, was formerly head coach at Bowling Green University, another mid-major. Dakich, a sports radio talk-show host in Indianapolis, said Butler reminded him of Hoosier teams he had been around.

"We knew we were tougher than you, and we were going to beat you in the end because of toughness, culture," Dakich said. "Truthfully, it's the best thing that Butler has had in this entire reign of this whole thing, in my opinion. It's a great sign of growth in the program."

The impact of the NCAA Tournament on American culture can't be overstated. It captures the nation's attention like nothing else. Not even the Super Bowl or the Olympics involves so many fans over so many days. Games might be coming to a city near you. It is not only for New York, Chicago, or Los Angeles. Your team could be playing in Albany or Albuquerque, Boise or Birmingham, Sacramento or Spokane.

The tournament envelops those who aren't sports fans, especially with brackets filled out in office pools across the land. The brackets are plain, neat, and tidy.

Nearly everyone has some connection to at least one of the participating teams. That became possible after the field expanded to 64 teams in 1985. As recently as 1974, there were only 25. In the first round especially, the big-versus-small pairings and inevitable upsets create energy that lasts three weekends and builds to a climax.

CBS had televised the tournament since 1982, and the precious sports property continued to grow in value. Soon after the 2010 tournament, the NCAA announced a 14-year, $10.8 billion agreement with CBS and Turner Sports for the television rights.

Although it initially seemed odd that CBS would air a show simply announcing who is playing whom and where, Selection Sunday has become a fixture on the sports calendar. There is no similar program to announce entries in the Kentucky Derby, for instance. However, everyone has a horse running in the NCAA race.

On the afternoon of the March 14 selection show, Butler players and coaches gathered at Stevens's north-side home on Meadowbrook Drive. Indianapolis media crowded into the house carrying notebooks and cameras. The team's youth theme extended to the coaches, all in their 30s, and their eight children, all age 5 or under. The kids scurried around, squealing and playing, making the occasion like a Christmas morning.

The players had little reaction to seeing "Butler" appear on the TV screen. There were a few fist pumps, a few claps. That was all. As young as the Bulldogs were, they were businesslike, modeling their behavior after that of their corporate-looking coach. Butler was awarded a No. 5 seed, equaling its best ever, and assigned to the West Regional in San Jose, California.

The downside? The opponent was Texas–El Paso, whose 26-6 résumé resembled Butler's. Given that, it was surprising for UTEP to be a No. 12 seed. Another surprise was that the Bulldogs were dispatched to California, where a 1-2 record in the 76 Classic created such skepticism about them.

"I think we've obviously gotten a lot better since California, which is huge," Nored said. "We just have to go out there and prove that we have gotten better and show that we can actually play basketball."

It didn't take long for Hayward and Shelvin Mack to begin exchanging trash texts with UTEP's Arnett Moultrie, a 6-foot-11 forward. All three played on Team USA's under-19 gold medalists.

The four No. 1 seeds were Kansas (32-2) in the Midwest, Syracuse (28-4) in the West, Kentucky (32-2) in the East, and Duke (29-5) in the South. Although RPI aided Butler, it could empathize with teams that were snubbed. Of the six highest RPI teams omitted from the tournament, all were mid-majors. The six all had computer rankings ahead of Florida and Minnesota, which made the NCAA field.

The Bulldogs were eager to play anyone. Through Wednesday, the day before their first-round game, they would go 25 days with three games. In Anaheim, they played that many in four days. Veasley said all that time off allowed the Bulldogs to rest, treat "little nicks," and improve weaknesses. The UTEP game would be his sixth in the NCAA Tournament, tying a Butler record.

"I'm not ready for my career to end, and I'm not ready for this season to be over with this group of guys," Veasley said.

Hinkle Fieldhouse served many purposes besides basketball during its history: World War II barracks, indoor track, Pan American Games, rodeo, graduation ceremonies, presidential addresses. To that, another could be added: coaches' dormitory.

After NCAA pairings were announced, Stevens and Butler's assistant coaches stayed up all night watching film of UTEP and other potential opponents. They slept on couches in their offices, or in the locker room, to prepare for Monday morning's 6:30 practice.

Butler's administration scrambled all day Monday, even past midnight, to assemble band members and cheerleaders to accompany the team on Tuesday's charter flight to San Jose. That fulfilled an NCAA requirement for the tournament, but it also meant that all those students would miss four days of classes. There was no send-off for the two buses carrying the travel party of about 100 to Indianapolis International Airport. While waiting to go through security, Howard carried his size-18 basketball shoes because he couldn't find room in his bag.

Hip-hop wasn't limited to Hayward among Butler students. Two male cheerleaders, Chris Polhamus and Steve Pelych, were bored during the team's flight and recorded a rap video to pass the time and entertain the rest of the cheer squad. Some players saw it and began forwarding it.

Before long, the video was on YouTube, receiving 4,000 hits and supplying background sound and morale-boosting at campus parties.

Upon arrival at the San Jose airport, the Bulldogs bused to Stanford University for practice. The other students, plus alumni and fans, checked into the downtown Fairmont. San Jose was once without what would be recognized as a center. But the city of 1 million revitalized the downtown in the 1980s and '90s, developing hotels, theaters, museums, restaurants, shopping malls, and Guadalupe River Park.

There was light rail service downtown, too, as Ronald Nored discovered nearly too late. He was "running my mouth like usual," he said, as he walked toward a trash can to discard something. He wasn't heeding the horn from a train bearing down on him. In a blog written months after the NCAA Tournament, he said the train was "less than 10 feet away " when Avery Jukes shouted at him to get out of the way.

"Funny story, I almost died in San Jose from public transportation," Nored said.

The tournament site, the HP Pavilion, was a key component of the downtown. Aqua blue was the dominant color inside the lustrous arena, nicknamed the Shark Tank as home of the National Hockey League's San Jose Sharks.

The Fairmont lobby was transformed into an informal Butler headquarters, where everyone gathered to discuss the tournament and Bay Area sightseeing. Other guests repeatedly asked about Butler, what it was, where it was, and why so many people were wearing Butler gear. Butler was as foreign to them as Burundi.

That did not apply to UTEP's coach, Tony Barbee. He was raised in Indianapolis, grew up a Butler fan, played at North Central High School, and was recruited by the Bulldogs. But that was more than 20 years ago, and Barbee headed to the University of Massachusetts to play basketball. Barbee was one of Stevens's friends in coaching.

"For me, it's kind of special, it's neat to be playing against them," Barbee said in a pregame news conference. "But it doesn't affect my guys. They don't get into all that. Maybe I should show them *Hoosiers*. I got to play in Hinkle a few times; it's a great place to play."

Stevens made his customarily impressive presentation. He answered questions about Todd Lickliter's recent ouster at Iowa, perils of leaving for bigger schools, how Butler had sustained success, UTEP's size, the 20-game winning streak . . . and Hinkle Fieldhouse. Stevens was animated in responding to a question by CBS online columnist Dennis Dodd, who asked whether Butler should tear down the fieldhouse and build a new arena.

"I don't know that I would want to still be there," Stevens said. "I think Hinkle Fieldhouse is part of what Butler is all about. It's part of the people, the tradition, it's part of the history, it's part of the 'we' attitude.

"It's bigger than anything new or plush or fancy can do, and Butler is unique, and Hinkle Fieldhouse is a good representative of that."

Few teams in the tournament were mistreated as badly as UTEP, which, as it turned out, barely made the 65-team field. The Miners won 16 in a row before losing to Houston 81–73 in the Conference USA championship game, and they were 25th in the national coaches' poll. Yet as Barbee watched the Southeastern Conference championship game, he heard CBS analyst Seth Davis say a Mississippi State victory would knock UTEP out of the field. Kentucky won 75–74 in overtime, much to the Miners' relief.

Barbee phoned Kentucky coach John Calipari, who coached him at UMass, and told him "that was the first thing he ever did for me in his life." The UTEP coach could laugh about it then, but the Miners were miffed. Barbee had never heard speculation about UTEP being on the bubble, and was expecting a No. 7, 8, or 9 seed. He conceded he was "shocked" by a No. 12.

Butler coaches might have been shocked by such a difficult first-round pairing against the Miners. UTEP featured a 6-foot-9, 275-pound center, Derrick Caracter, and the Conference USA player of the year, 6-foot guard Randy Culpepper. Caracter played in two NCAA Tournaments for Louisville before transferring to UTEP, and it would be almost impossible for the foul-prone Howard to guard him alone. UTEP had more big bodies to bring off the bench.

The Miners were seeking their first NCAA tourney victory since 1992, a prolonged drought for a program with such an illustrious history. UTEP, then known as Texas Western, upset Kentucky to win the NCAA championship in 1966 and inspired the movie *Glory Road*. At least one No. 12 seed had won in the first round in all but three years since 1983, including Butler over Mississippi State in 2003. So even though Butler was listed as a two- to-three-point favorite, UTEP was a popular pick by journalists and analysts.

That viewpoint was probably more a credit to UTEP than an affront to

Butler. Howard said the Bulldogs didn't need to prove anything to other people, and Hayward said they didn't focus on what others said. But some Butler players were annoyed by what they heard and read.

"It was disrespectful, to be honest with you," Nored said. "By that time, we had run up 20 straight, won our league championship by 25. There's a 5-12 upset every year. We were the one they picked."

Butler and UTEP weren't the only teams in town feeling wounded. Murray State was a No. 13 seed despite a 30-4 record. Moreover, the Racers were grieving with reserve guard Picasso Simmons, whose mother was killed in a car crash the day before the team departed for San Jose.

Murray State and fourth-seeded Vanderbilt had the first game of a quadruple-header at the first-round site, and the score was much closer than the seeding. Murray State, trailing 65–64 with 4.2 seconds left, called time-out. Isacc Miles was supposed to shoot off a double screen, but he found himself guarded by two defenders. So he took one quick dribble and passed to Danero Thomas, whose shot from the right wing sent the Racers to a 66–65 upset. Some Murray State coaches rushed to hug Butler band members, who happened to be sitting next to the Murray State bench.

"Things like that happen in this tournament," Miles said. "This time in March, anybody can win."

About half an hour after the first buzzer-beater of the 2010 tournament, the crowd of 12,712 sat back to watch UTEP and Butler. The Bulldogs had started miserably in the first round the year before, falling behind LSU 9–0, but weren't as ineffectual this time. But neither were they clicking as they usually did during the 20-game streak.

After Mack's jump shot tied the score at 10, the Miners ran off the next seven points to go ahead 17–10. Paradoxically, it was the energetic play of Shawn Vanzant that settled down the Bulldogs. Vanzant, who had only 10 3-pointers all season, sank one during a 9–0 spurt. He grabbed two defensive rebounds during the surge and passed to Howard for a fastbreak layup that returned the lead to Butler 19–17.

Then Butler went without a field goal for nearly the final five minutes of the half. Caracter was a behemoth, too wide for Howard to contain. Caracter scored three baskets in the closing five minutes of the half, including a layup before time ran out, and powered UTEP to a 33–27 lead.

"I don't know that I've ever guarded someone quite like him," Howard said.

Not since a 10-point deficit at UAB—the last game they lost—had the Bulldogs trailed by so many points at halftime. Veasley acknowledged that the Bulldogs "might have been just a little nervous." Playing so few games over the last month didn't generate crispness, either. Butler committed 7 turnovers, leading to 9 points by UTEP.

Inside the Butler locker room, Stevens reiterated standard messages: Don't panic. There are a lot of possessions. We don't have to hit home runs. Single, single, single. He also told them a lot can happen in a short time. On that theme, he was prophetic.

On the Miners' first possession, Mack dislodged the ball from Caracter and caused a turnover. Howard later pointed to that seemingly minor incident as a turning point.

"That got into his head a little bit," Howard said of UTEP's center.

A few seconds later, Mack sank his second 3-pointer. About 40 seconds after that, he sank his third. Veasley soon followed with another 3-pointer, and Butler led 36–34.

It's not that they were defying their coach, but the Bulldogs weren't adhering to his baseball analogy. Forget singles. It became home run, home run, home run. Three, three, three.

UTEP briefly reclaimed the lead 37–36, and then the Mack attack resumed. He sank a fourth 3-pointer, then a fifth. Mack, usually undemonstrative during a game, shouted in delight as he ran to the defensive end. Butler led 45–37. After Howard scored on Mack's assist, and Vanzant stole the ball and passed to Veasley for a layup, the margin widened to 49–37.

Butler's 13–0 run lasted less than four minutes, and nearly 12 minutes remained, but there was no light at the end of the Miners' tunnel. Until the midpoint, they had one field goal in the second half. The assuredness they exhibited in the first half, trash-talking to the Bulldogs, turned to quarreling among themselves.

Three more 3-pointers—by Veasley, Mack, and Zach Hahn—grew the gap to 58–41 and culminated a 31–8 run. Fifteen of the 31 points came on five 3s by Mack. Still, the Bulldogs did not relent.

With Butler ahead by 16 and less than two minutes left, Hayward caught up with Culpepper on a breakaway, leaped, and extended his long right arm to block the shot. Culpepper went tumbling out of bounds. UTEP fans booed and cursed Hayward, believing it was a dirty play.

However, a photo by Getty Images was taken at an angle, creating the illusion that Hayward jumped as high as the aqua-draped balcony. The photo showed that: (1) Hayward might not have fouled at all, and (2) he could be spectacularly athletic, refuting critics who asserted that was a weakness.

Over on the bench, Darnell Archey, the Butler coordinator of basketball operations, jokingly told Mack he once made eight 3-pointers against Louisville—a Butler record for an NCAA Tournament game. With 32 seconds left, Mack dropped in his seventh 3-pointer, then looked sheepish afterward.

"I was kind of glad to see he didn't break it," Archey said.

Mack acknowledged he was going for it.

"But it's over with," he said. "Now time to move on to the next game."

Mack's 7 3-pointers and 25 points were career highs in the 77–59 blowout. Butler sank 10 of its season-high 13 3s in a 50-point second half.

"When 3s are falling, we should be a pretty hard team to beat," Hahn understated.

Their defense was hard to beat:

- UTEP's 59 points were 17 under its average.
- Culpepper, dogged by Nored, scored 16 points, and some of those came off turnovers. Culpepper said the Bulldogs did everything possible not to let him touch the ball. "I was trying not to let that get to me," he said.
- Caracter scored 20 points, but his 8 in the second half all came after Butler built the lead. He was visibly frustrated, and sat out for five minutes of the second half. Avery Jukes, outweighed by 60 pounds, effectively backed up Howard in the post.
- Moultrie, astoundingly, was held scoreless by Hayward until 24 seconds were left in the game.

"In the second half, we came out with a little more energy and really executed the game plan," Hayward said. "And then it was just all about guarding."

Barbee said the Miners' communication failed. Their 3-point defense—they had been limiting opponents to 31 percent—was inadequate. Their press was rendered ineffective because they could not score.

Stevens said UTEP was as good as any opponent Butler played early in the season, concluding that "means we got better." For the seventh time in a 21-game streak, Butler trailed at halftime. Every coach's cliché—it's a 40-minute game, not a 20-minute game—was underscored by the Bulldogs.

"It was perfect for us to play such a good team in the first round," Veasley said. "UTEP easily could have beaten us, and they could have beaten anyone else in the tournament.

"A lot of people haven't seen us play. And they pick the team that looks good on paper. Then when they see us play, it's a different story."

One of the most relieved fans in the arena was Dan Wojcik, a Butler graduate who played basketball in the 1960s under coach Tony Hinkle and was a tennis letterman. Wojcik lived in El Paso for 13 years and became a Miners fan while there. A friend bought them tickets for the game, failing to mention that their seats were in the UTEP section. Wearing a long-sleeved Butler T-shirt while surrounded by orange, Wojcik received hateful glares.

The friends made a pact that the fan of the winning team would stay in San Jose, so Wojcik went to the Fairmont the next day in search of a ticket for the Butler–Murray State game. Yes, he revealed, he was the guy cheering in Butler blue in the middle of UTEP orange.

"I instantly became a cross between a rock star and an idiot," he said.

It is why they call it March Madness.

Wojcik survived. So did Butler in one of the most chaotic first rounds in tournament history. All three of Butler's regular-season conquerors—No. 3 seed Georgetown, No. 7 seed Clemson, and No. 11 seed Minnesota—lost. Another mid-major, Ohio University, shockingly upset Georgetown 97–83.

There was one of those compulsory 12-over-5 upsets: Cornell over Temple 78–65. Two No. 6 seeds from the Big East were losers: Washington over Marquette 80–78 and Old Dominion over Notre Dame 51–50. No. 2 seed Villanova, a Final Four team the year before, eked out a 73–70 victory over Robert Morris in overtime.

As Vanderbilt coach Kevin Stallings put it after the loss to Murray State, "This is why this is a great tournament. Because things like this happen."

Neither Stevens nor any Butler player was under the illusion that Murray State would be easier to beat than Vanderbilt. Quite the contrary. Stevens called the Racers "a very, very scary" team to prepare for because of their depth, balance, and guards. Five Murray State players averaged between 9.7 and 10.6 points, a statistical anomaly that would be hard to replicate anywhere in basketball.

The Bulldogs had shown susceptibility to pressure, and few teams in the country could apply it like Murray State. The Racers were 5th in the nation in steals and 11th in defensive field goal percentage.

"They're not on TV as much as some teams, and the irony is they're better than a lot of the teams that are on TV all the time," Stevens said.

Although Butler and Murray State were meeting on the court for the first time since 1976, they had been in competition since February. For most of the month, they shared the nation's longest active winning streak. Murray State's finally ended at 17.

Except for the game between Kansas (33-2) and Northern Iowa (29-4), the Butler (29-4)–Murray State (31-4) pairing had the best cumulative record of the second round. In the 2010 calendar year, Butler and Murray State were a collective 41-1. When one won, so did the other.

"We heard it a lot, and a lot of people would tell me after our game, 'Butler won,' or before the game, 'Butler won,'" Murray State coach Billy Kennedy said. "So I thought, 'We gotta keep winning.'"

One of Murray State's challenges was to regroup from such an emotional victory. Hero Danero Thomas couldn't get to sleep until responding to 70 texts.

The pressure on Butler and Murray State wasn't like that on Kansas and Kentucky—the latter two were absolutely supposed to win—but lingered nevertheless. This Butler team was the most criticized of the 2000s, especially by some of its own fans, who accused the Bulldogs of straying from the Butler Way. The preseason hype morphed into presumptions that had never so burdened another Butler team. Media skepticism persisted.

It wasn't much different at Murray State. To play or coach there was to live with pressure. Basketball in Kentucky was important, and after reaching the NCAA Tournament 12 times since 1988, it was about time the Racers made it to their first Sweet Sixteen.

"When we lose, our guys don't feel real comfortable going out in the community, just being honest with you," Kennedy said. "That's just how it is."

Butler players managed to relax through it all. As others answered questions from reporters on the day between games, Howard was transfixed by *The Price Is Right* on the locker-room TV. As a contestant tried to win a Lexus, he was as fired up as he was in the closing minutes of a tight game. Hayward mentioned the P. F. Chang's in San Jose, not realizing it was a national restaurant chain. Naturally, his teammates mocked him for that. Mack, a native Kentuckian, showed off his "I ♥ KY" T-shirt, a takeoff on the "NY" shirts sold in New York and nearly everywhere else.

Defense would determine if Butler kept its record intact of never losing to a lower-seeded team. Butler and Murray State proved nearly impenetrable to each other.

The Bulldogs didn't score for more than three minutes to open the game but then went on a 12–0 spurt to go ahead 12–3. After Murray State closed that gap, 3-pointers by Hahn and Mack pushed the margin to 18–10.

The teams traded baskets until the final six minutes of the half, when the Bulldogs quit scoring altogether. They held on to a 22–18 lead until Hayward and Mack went to the bench with two fouls each. After a half in which points were so scarce, Murray State scored eight in the final 90 seconds, capped by a 3-pointer that made it 26–22.

Butler trailed at halftime so often, and won, that nothing remarkable needed to be said in the locker room. Stevens saved the oratory for when it was necessary. At least Howard, with one foul, wasn't in trouble.

Howard picked up a second foul early in the second half and, 27 seconds later, a third. Resisting convention, Stevens allowed Howard to stay in the game. Five seconds came off the clock, and Howard had his fourth foul. Finally, he sat.

"I thought I was coming out after the third one," he said. "It was a little bit frustrating at the time."

For the Bulldogs' center to pick up three fouls inside 32 seconds was a fiasco. Howard's absence required Hayward to guard Tony Easley, the Racers' nimble 6-foot-9 center. Murray State soon expanded its lead to 33–26 on B. J. Jenkins's 3-pointer. Irked by what he perceived to be a defensive breakdown, Stevens called time-out.

"Can Ronald Nored guard anybody?" the coach asked in the huddle.

Nored got mad. The Bulldogs got even. There was nothing for them to do except defend their own basket as desperately as a World Cup soccer team does its own goal.

Over the next 10 minutes—equivalent to a quarter—Butler outscored Murray State 20–5. Now it was Butler in front 46–38. Hayward scored seven points in the surge, including his first 3-pointer in a month, and capped it by cradling the ball as he swooped in for a layup. Butler, so adept at closing out games, was 6 minutes away from the Sweet Sixteen.

Suddenly, and shockingly, any comfort the Bulldogs felt was wrenched away.

After going 10 minutes with 5 points, the Racers scored 10 within 60 seconds. Freshman guard Isaiah Canaan sank his fourth 3-pointer—without a miss—to send the Racers in front 48–47. Another field goal completed a 12–1 run, putting Butler behind 50–47 with less than 3 minutes left.

During a TV time-out, Stevens's message was about toughness, not tactics.

"You're soft! You're soft!" he shouted to his Bulldogs, who rarely heard such sideline rebukes. "Where's your guts?!"

When play resumed, Hayward made the first of two free throws. He missed the second. After a Murray State miss, Mack sank a short jumper to tie the score at 50 with 1:22 on the clock. The Racers consumed most of the shot clock but missed again, and Nored rebounded with 51 seconds left.

Nored was never a scorer for Butler, confining his role to defense and playmaking. Yet these were special circumstances, calling for a special play. Nored made a special delivery.

He drove toward the basket, leaned in, and banked the ball in off the glass as he was fouled. His free throw gave Butler a 53–50 lead with 25 seconds left. Miles sank two free throws for Murray State, trimming that to 53–52. On Butler's possession, Mack was trapped, and he called time-out.

When play resumed, Howard was fouled. He made one free throw, and Murray State called time-out. Howard missed the second, leaving Butler ahead 54–52. Seventeen seconds remained.

Miles dribbled swiftly downcourt for Murray State, all the way to the baseline. Hemmed in by Howard and Mack near the basket, he threw the ball out to Canaan. As Canaan looked to pass or shoot, Howard sidled over to guard Miles, who was alone behind the 3-point line in the left corner.

"It was one of the smartest defensive plays I've ever seen," Stevens said. "Matt was basically saying, 'You're not beating us with a 3.'"

Nored picked up Canaan, and Hayward came over to double-team the Murray State guard. Like the tennis player he once was, Hayward extended his left hand like a racket into the doubles alley, deflecting the ball into the backcourt. Hayward and Canaan went sliding after the ball, and the clock ran out. Hayward chest-bumped Mack as the Bulldogs celebrated.

Final score: Butler 54, Murray State 52.

The Bulldogs couldn't keep Howard on the floor nor the Racers off the glass. They couldn't make 3-pointers, and they couldn't stop Murray State from making them. But they made the Sweet Sixteen.

"I'm still trying to figure out how the heck we won," Stevens said.

Butler shot 36 percent, was outrebounded 39–22, and allowed 9-of-14 shooting from the arc. But the Bulldogs committed a season-low 6 turnovers, compared with Murray State's 18. That, plus some clutch baskets and defensive plays, was enough for a 30th victory and 22nd in a row.

"Our little lineup," Stevens said, "boy, were they good."

How tough was it out there? Near the finish, Bulldog mascot "Hink" crumpled to the floor when cheerleaders attempted to lift him. He bounced right back, as did the real Bulldogs.

Nored led Butler with 15 points and 6 assists. How intense was he? The preacher's kid engaged in a little trash talk with the Racers and was told by an official to knock it off.

Afterward, Nored entertained the media with another Hayward story. Stevens once wrote the acronym TGHT on a whiteboard and asked what it meant.

Correct answer: The Game Honors Toughness.

Players' answer: Teach Gordon Hayward Toughness.

"Obviously, he's a tough kid," Nored said. "He made a huge play."

Hayward scored 9 of his 12 points in the second half. The 7-point deficit was the biggest the Bulldogs overcame in a second half all season. They "want to keep playing with each other," Hayward said, and earned the chance to play one more game. That's all they ever contemplated anyway: the next game.

If the Bulldogs were publicly restrained in victory, there were no inhibitions inside the locker room. Stevens walked in and pointed at Emerson Kampen, whose leaping back bumps with Hayward and Mack during lineup introductions came to symbolize the team's unity: a nonscholarship player cavorting with the two sophomore stars. So Stevens jumped and back-bumped with Kampen.

"We let loose in the locker room because we knew we could," said

Nick Rodgers, also a walk-on. "When that door shut, it was all about us. We had fun with that."

While awaiting their plane at the airport, some players, cheerleaders, and band members gathered outside a restaurant to watch the end of the Kansas–Northern Iowa game on TV. Northern Iowa upset the Jayhawks 69–67, dramatizing the unpredictability of the tournament. Kansas, the consensus No. 1 team in the nation, did not get out of the second round. After everyone else was seated on the plane, the coaches powered up laptops to watch film of possible Salt Lake City opponents, Syracuse or Gonzaga, which were playing the next day.

Syracuse was coping with a setback, losing 6-foot-9 center Arinze Onuaku to a knee injury near the end of a loss to Georgetown in the Orange's Big East Tournament opener. Syracuse was 28-2 and ranked No. 1 in the nation until losing at Louisville 78–68 and then to Georgetown 91–84.

Syracuse was good enough to merit the No. 1 seed in the West, however, and validated that in the first two rounds. Playing in Buffalo, New York, about 150 miles from its campus, Syracuse defeated Vermont 79–56 and crushed Gonzaga 87–65. Against Gonzaga, Wesley Johnson had a career-high 31 points and 14 rebounds and Andy Rautins sank 5 3-pointers in a 24-point game.

Naturally, Stevens wasn't going to do anything but compliment the next opponent. But he spoke words that others were thinking in describing Syracuse: "scary" and "as good a team as there is in the country."

Besides, Syracuse was comfortably into the Sweet Sixteen, something other favorites failed to do. Butler was in the Sweet Sixteen for a third time in eight years, and only 12 schools had done so more often over that period.

So far, the tournament was enriched by the close call and the little guy. Thirteen games were decided by three or fewer points, and four in overtime. Cornell was the first Ivy League representative in the Sweet Sixteen since Penn in 1979. For the first time since tournament expansion in 1985, three one-bid leagues—Horizon, Ivy, and Missouri Valley (Northern Iowa)—had teams in the Sweet Sixteen. And for the first time since 1985, four teams seeded ninth or worse survived two rounds.

"Some of those teams that played with the pressure that they needed to win every game just to have a chance to be in the discussion for an at-large bid are now playing great, great basketball," Stevens observed. "Nobody wants to play Northern Iowa. Nobody wants to play Cornell."

Nobody seemed concerned about the travel affecting those playing the games. For the second week in a row, the Bulldogs had to miss four days of classes. It was a source of strife for the cheerleaders and band, particularly, because they weren't as accustomed to interruptions as the players. For a Thursday game, teams traveled Tuesday so they could arrive for Wednesday news conferences. That meant the Bulldogs were on the ground in Indianapolis for all of 60 hours. It was barely long enough to update Butler's postseason media guide before 350 copies were shipped to Salt Lake City.

The players made the most of their available time. Veasley and Mack were at the Fairbanks Center, the technology and communications building, to meet with a professor and attend a class. Howard tried to catch up, opening his laptop at the C-Club food court. He and Hayward, both academic All-Americans, took studies seriously, as did the others.

On Tuesday morning, the day the team was leaving for Salt Lake City, Hayward met his parents and twin sister, Heather, at the campus Starbucks to celebrate his 20th birthday on March 23. His mother had thought carefully about what to give her son, wanting to encourage him spiritually and restore his confidence. So Jody Hayward and Jody's twin sister, Lori, went to a Christian bookstore in search of an item bearing her son's confirmation Bible verse, Philippians 4:13:

I can do all things through Christ who strengthens me.

The women could not locate anything with that verse. So they asked the clerk, who said he would look around. Well, he told them, all he had was a medallion with that verse on one side—and a basketball on the other.

On the morning of his birthday, Hayward opened a greeting card and found the medallion. He kept fingering it and looking at it. He turned it over, back and forth, back and forth.

"Wow. This is so cool," he said.

Later, when asked about the medallion, Hayward said it was a reminder about perspective. That had always been his mother's prayer for him. Before each of his games, she texted him five letters: RWYPF.

Remember Who You Play For. The birthday symbol would help him remember.

"We have a purpose in life," Jody Hayward said. "We really believe God's given him the platform of basketball to be a positive influence."

After a rare night practice, the Bulldogs reconvened Tuesday afternoon at Hinkle Fieldhouse for a return to the airport. The bus passed Lucas Oil Stadium, where the giant banner facing Interstate 70 stated THE ROAD ENDS HERE. By the time the NCAA Tournament bracket narrowed to Indianapolis, 65 teams would be reduced to 4. Stevens turned to his wife, Tracy, in a private moment. How unbelievable would it be, he asked, to return home and play for the national championship: It was a dream too extravagant to contemplate.

Having made a cross-country flight just days before, everyone was used to the routine for the charter to Salt Lake City. The coaches' young children ran up and down the plane's aisles. Four-year-old Abby Graves, daughter of assistant coach Matthew, found a seat with the cheerleaders. Nored sang "Happy Birthday" to Hayward over the sound system.

The West Regional was at a scenic and historic site. Although the games would not be played in the same arena, it was in Salt Lake City where the 1979 NCAA championship game was held, featuring Michigan State and Magic Johnson over Indiana State and Larry Bird 75–64. EnergySolutions Arena was home to the NBA's Utah Jazz and figure skating at the 2002 Olympic Winter Games. A replica torch near the arena's entrance commemorated those Olympics.

The city, at a 4,300-foot altitude and surrounded by the Wasatch and Oquirrh mountain ranges, also was headquarters of the Church of Jesus Christ of Latter-Day Saints. The arena was less than a mile from the manicured grounds of Temple Square. The square, a popular tourist spot of fans following their teams, featured statues of Mormon leaders Joseph Smith and Brigham Young and commemorated Utah's pioneer legacy.

Syracuse versus Butler represented a coaching contrast. Jim Boeheim, 65, became Syracuse's head coach more than six months before the 33-year-old Stevens was born. Boeheim's 829 wins were second only to Duke's Mike Krzyzewski among active coaches, and he was already in the Naismith Basketball Hall of Fame. Boeheim coached the Orange to the NCAA championship game in 1987, 1996, and 2003, winning the national title in '03.

Stevens called Boeheim a leader and role model, especially because the Syracuse coach's involvement extended beyond his own team. Boeheim was active in Coaches vs. Cancer and USA Basketball. He soon would be honored with multiple national coach of the year awards, mostly because the season was so unexpected. Syracuse was picked for sixth in the Big East. At a pregame news conference, Boeheim said Butler's players were probably higher-rated coming out of high school than Syracuse's.

"We've never had a team play any better than this in 34 years in this conference," Boeheim said of his Big East champions. "We've had a few good teams, but this is a special team."

Syracuse was one win away from tying the school record set by the 31-7 team that lost to Indiana in the 1987 championship game.

The trademark of Boeheim's teams was a 2-3 zone defense. It was hard to simulate in practice and harder to solve in games. Boeheim said Syracuse's zone was effective for one simple reason: practice.

"Teams that play man to man don't practice their zone," he said. "They practice it once a week, and they think they can now play zone, and they're surprised when it doesn't work."

Conventional wisdom was that opponents must shoot well against the zone to overcome it. Publicly, Stevens concurred. When his staff and players prepared, though, that was not their plan. The Bulldogs' approach was to stop Syracuse in transition, attack the paint, attack the baseline.

Three-pointers? The Bulldogs did not talk about them. That is, they did not talk about shooting them. They talked about preventing them. As players watched film of Syracuse opponents, they noticed how wide open Andy Rautins was on 3-point attempts.

"They are not going to get those against us," some of the Butler players said to each other at a film session.

Pay attention to every detail, Stevens told them back in the fall. Details matter. It was implanted in them.

Never in hoops history had Butler advanced past the Sweet Sixteen. Throughout the 2000s, the Bulldogs confronted No. 1 or 2 seeds. Each time, they crept closer. They lost to No. 2 Arizona 73–52 in 2001, No. 1 Oklahoma 65–54 in 2003, No. 1 Florida 65–57 in 2007, and No. 2 Tennessee 76–71 (overtime) in 2008.

Jon LeCrone, commissioner of the Horizon League and a former member of the NCAA selection committee, traveled to Salt Lake City and spoke informally to reporters covering the tournament. He had an unusual outlook on the matchup. He said Butler had played a team like Syracuse—that is, Georgetown. Syracuse, he said, had not played a team like Butler. The Bulldogs kept scores low, and Syracuse was 1-2 when scoring fewer than 70 points.

Boeheim said he voted for Butler in his top 10 or 15 teams all season and that league affiliation was irrelevant. And, of course, he was chairman of the committee that selected Hayward and Mack to the under-19 national team. Boeheim said Hayward was as impressive as anyone in national camps during his eight years of USA Basketball involvement.

Veasley said it would be "huge" for Butler's program to beat Syracuse. "People would really start to believe in us instead of always treating us as the underdog," he said.

Stevens denied Butler was at a crossroads, that Syracuse simply represented opportunity. He said he had never once heard the phrase "Final Four" from his players, although back in the fall he asked them to aim for a national championship.

"Certainly, it's a question that we've had to answer," Stevens said. "At least we're up here still with a chance to answer it."

The Bulldogs had long since become accustomed to such skepticism. Some wearied of it.

"What would you say we need to do to become a legit team? Do you have to get to the Elite Eight?" Howard asked. "I guess it's up for debate."

Back on campus, Butler students backed their team against the Orange by boycotting oranges. The fruit was not made available in dining halls. But freshly squeezed Orangemen Juice was served at Atherton Union and the Residential College dorm.

There weren't going to be many Butler fans in the arena, but a very important one was determined to make it: Shelvin Mack's mother. Victoria Guy's Lexington employer paid airfare so she could make the trip—the first flight of her life. She was easy to spot, wearing a replica of Shelvin's No. 1 Butler jersey. It turned out to be the adventure of her life.

The Continental Airlines plane took off Thursday morning from Louisville, Kentucky, but leaked fuel from a wing tank. After a few minutes in the air, the plane returned to the airport. Fire trucks followed the taxiing plane along the ground, past the fire station, and eventually to the terminal. A man wearing a firefighting suit and holding a hose met passengers at the terminal.

After about 20 minutes of checking to confirm there was no fire, Continental announced the flight would continue in a few hours after a part was flown in and the fuel tank repaired. On that timetable, Mack's mother would miss the connecting flight to Salt Lake City and thus the game.

Also booked on the flight was Curt Smith, father of backup center Andrew Smith. Curt Smith and his wife, Debbie, a secretary in Butler's history and anthropology department, were scheduled on different flights leaving Louisville. Debbie was at the terminal, waiting to depart. Mack's mother wasn't sure she wanted to go back up in the air again anyway, but Curt Smith assured her that such a scuttled flight was rare.

After searching for alternatives, the Smiths located one seat—just one—that had a connection allowing for arrival before tip-off. They explained the special circumstance to a Delta Airlines station manager, who agreed to put Mack's mother on the different flight for the same fare. Because Curt Smith wouldn't make the connection in time, he drove home to Zionsville, Indiana, to watch the game on TV. His wife made it to Salt Lake City on a flight through Memphis, Tennessee, and Victoria Guy through Minneapolis. Separately, they sped in cabs from the airport to the arena, leaving luggage behind.

They made it on time.

That was not true of Syracuse. Or at least the Orange didn't rouse themselves on time. Syracuse began sluggardly against Butler, going the first 7 minutes without a field goal. Three-pointers by Mack and Hayward, plus two field goals by Veasley, propelled Butler ahead 12–1. Through 11 minutes, Syracuse had eight turnovers and two baskets. Butler was no fun to play against, *at all.*

"Syracuse likes to play fast, play in transition, so we wanted to make it an ugly game for them," Nored said. "We saw on films, when games were tough and ugly, they weren't as good as when they were out in transition, hitting 3s and getting dunks. And we could see them getting frustrated."

Syracuse climbed within 17–12 after Hayward went to the bench with his second foul. But Mack sank successive jumpers to restore the margin to 21–12. Then he converted a three-point play off a pass from Nored, giving Mack seven points in 67 seconds and Butler a 24–14 lead.

Nored said he ran a marathon in chasing Rautins, and sometimes the defender got too close. Nored fouled the Syracuse sharpshooter behind the 3-point line, and Rautins made all three free throws to bring the score to 24–17. All that did was preface another Butler burst.

Mack also was fouled while shooting beyond the arc, and made two of three free throws. Veasley soon followed with a tip-in. Shawn Vanzant made a 3-pointer from the left corner to extend the score to 31–19, wagging his tongue as he ran back on defense.

Fans in the Butler section erupted. That 12-point lead represented the largest so far. Four minutes remained in the half, and Butler still had no turnovers. By contrast, Syracuse had 10.

It was bewildering to Boeheim. He later said, repeatedly, that there were too many turnovers. Butler outscored Syracuse 14–2 in the first half in points off turnovers.

"Just hasn't been our team. We haven't done that," Boeheim said.

The Orange's 11th turnover came on a steal by Nored, who stripped the ball from Rautins and turned it into a basket. Mack increased his first-half total to 14 points, scoring off an assist by Veasley. Butler increased its lead to 35–23 in the final minute of the half. A rebound dunk just before time expired allowed Syracuse to cut it to 35–25.

Those monitoring scores via television, texts, and tweets were dumbfounded that Butler held a 10-point lead over a No. 1 seed. Butler was "the inferior club, to the naked eye," according to *Syracuse Post-Standard* columnist Bud Poliquin.

Wesley Johnson, a 6-foot-7 All-American—and eventually the No. 4 pick of the NBA draft—was four inches taller than his defender, Veasley. And Johnson managed but three shots and seven points by halftime.

Yet a team as menacing, and as talented, as Syracuse was not going to be easily subdued. The Orange had faced worse, notably an 18-point deficit in a 59–57 victory at DePaul.

Rautins opened the second half with a 3-pointer, then another, in trimming the lead to 39–35. Johnson dunked on a lob from an inbounds pass, and after a Butler turnover, he sank a long 3-pointer from the top of the key. That capped a 17–4 surge that began late in the first half and supplied Syracuse with its first lead, 40–39.

Time-out, Butler. Stevens's steady voice reassured the Bulldogs. Weather the storm, he told them. Syracuse was going to make a big run.

"Now it's time to make our run and get back to how we were playing in the first half," Stevens said.

Hayward, player of the year in the Horizon, countered Johnson, player of the year in the Big East. Hayward was scoreless for 17 minutes, sitting out the closing 9 minutes of the first half. He proceeded to score all of the

Bulldogs' next nine points: a driving one-hander, a dunk off a lob from Mack, two free throws, and his second 3-pointer. Midway through the second half, Butler reclaimed a 48–43 lead.

"The baby-faced assassin is alive and scruffin' in the second half," CBS announcer Gus Johnson said as the Orange called time-out.

Howard soon left for the bench with his fourth foul, and the Bulldogs were left behind. The Bulldogs called another time-out but couldn't blunt a Syracuse surge. Rautins ran to a spot at the top of the key, and Nored trailed too late to prevent a 3-pointer putting the Orange in front 52–50. Kris Joseph's dunk off a fast break capped an 11–2 run. After trailing by 12 in the first half, Syracuse surged ahead 54–50 with five and a half minutes remaining.

Tension was so great that Kristen Johnson, wife of Butler assistant coach Terry Johnson, began hyperventilating and was escorted from her seat. Butler was teetering. However inspiring the Bulldogs were, Syracuse was in control and close to the Elite Eight.

Butler called another time-out, and Stevens reinserted Howard. Syracuse guard Scoop Jardine missed a long 3-pointer that could have been a knockout punch. The Bulldogs wobbled again when Nored threw a pass intended for Howard that was stolen with four minutes left.

Then Veasley retaliated, stealing Rautins's inbounds pass and falling out of bounds as he directed the ball to Nored. The Bulldogs hadn't scored from the field for six minutes, and as the shot clock wound down on their possession, they were in peril of coming up empty again.

Nored caught the ball on the left wing, behind the arc, where he was shooting 17 percent for the season. He might as well have been at half-court. But between San Jose and Salt Lake City, he arrived early at practice to shoot 3-pointers, then stayed late to shoot some more. He spun the ball up there.

"That shot, I knew we needed it," Nored said. "I knew they were going to call the play where I was going to have to catch it. I wasn't going to pass it. I knew I was going to step in and knock it in."

And he did. Instead of falling behind by six or seven, as they nearly did, Nored's 3-pointer pulled the Bulldogs within 54–53. After Howard blocked a Syracuse shot, he caught a pass from Mack on the other end and scored inside.

Butler 55, Syracuse 54.

Nored then stole the ball from Rautins. From the top of the key, Nored spotted Howard with inside position near the end of the shot clock. Howard dribbled once to his left, then located Veasley unguarded in the left corner.

Veasley made the catch behind the arc and shot. Nored, the pastor's son, was praying it would drop. The ball rattled around both sides of the rim, glanced off the glass above the square, and through the net. Veasley could not have duplicated the ball's action if he tried it 100 times. He was backpedaling to play defense because he thought he had missed.

"That's a H-O-R-S-E shot," Veasley said. "I never made anything like that."

Veasley's 3-pointer extended Butler's lead to 58–54 with 1:48 remaining. The game's complexion changed from Orange to Butler blue. After shooting 18 percent from the 3-point line—4 of 22—the Bulldogs had made two straight from there.

Rautins failed on a 3-point attempt for Syracuse. The Bulldogs again used up most of the shot clock before Mack missed. Enter Veasley again. The Veasley Effect was measurable in this instance. He tipped Mack's miss, and the ball bounced on the rim four times before dropping through. Butler's lead grew to 60–54 as the clock dipped under 60 seconds.

With 37 seconds left, Hayward was fouled. He sank the first. The second, he air-balled. No rim. No glass. No net. Nothing. Hayward was an 83 percent free throw shooter, and all Stevens did was laugh and clap his hands. No sweat, kid.

Indeed, Hayward's free throw completed an improbable 11–0 run that built Butler's lead to 61–54. Seconds later, Hayward made two more free throws to restore the seven-point margin, 63–56.

Veasley missed two free throws with 10 seconds left, but that didn't matter. Nored made his fifth steal before the buzzer, and Butler's 63–59 victory was sealed. It was win No. 31, breaking Butler's own Horizon League record.

"And how about this!" Gus Johnson told TV viewers as the clock ran out.

Back at their lockers, Butler players' cell phones began vibrating with text messages. Mack, who had not seen his mother before tip-off, found her afterward. Other players' parents were hugging, or texting friends and family. Stevens and Kampen reprised their locker-room back bump.

In Indianapolis, patrons watching big-screen TVs at Moe & Johnny's, a Butler hangout on North College Avenue, cheered robustly. Sorority sisters who attended Butler in the 1990s gathered at the Buffalo Wild Wings in Broad Ripple, where the atmosphere was electric. At fraternity houses, students jumped on couches and tables. Other students ran into the middle of campus streets, holding one another.

In Lake Placid, New York, a former Butler distance runner, Kim (Kutska) Emigh, was vacationing and watching the game at a bar full of confident Syracuse fans. The bartender chided the solitary alumna, but he relented at the end and treated her to all drinks for the evening. Emigh counted the bartender as a converted Bulldog admirer.

On a business trip to San Francisco, Butler alum Brian Clouse and his wife, Paula, watched on a TV screen from a Jillian's in Union Square, where they, too, were surrounded by Syracuse fans. Afterward, a group of excited men descended on their table, yelling and offering to buy drinks. They had all won cash by betting on Butler in their tournament pools. Walking through downtown San Francisco, with Clouse wearing his GO DAWGS hat and his wife a Butler sweatshirt, cars honked at them. Pedestrians shouted, "Way to go, Butler," and shoppers high-fived. The celebration continued at the Argonaut Hotel, where an enthusiastic young bellman seemed to know everything about the team.

The outcome was hard to accept for Syracuse players, who sobbed in the locker room. Hard for fans in upstate New York. Perhaps hardest for media analysts.

The Orange lost "to the Butler Bulldogs, of all people," Poliquin wrote. ESPN commentators were dismissive of the Bulldogs. Immediately after the game, Butler reserves watched TV in the locker room as CBS analyst Seth Davis explained how much Syracuse missed the injured Arinze Onuaku.

"Man!" they said disgustedly.

Syracuse sorely missed Onuaku. Stevens said as much. So did Boeheim, who lamented Syracuse's 18 turnovers more than the center's absence.

Syracuse outshot the Bulldogs, 44 percent to 40 percent; outrebounded them, 38–28; made more 3-pointers, 7–6; scored more bench points, 14–3, and scored more off fast breaks, 11–4.

The difference? Defense.

Not the 3-pointer. Grit, guile, and grace were the Bulldogs' three points.

Hayward finished with 17 points, including 12 in the second half. Mack scored 14, all in the first half, and Veasley 13. Johnson and Rautins, in their final college game before heading to the NBA, scored 17 and 15, respectively.

"There's talent all over the nation," Hayward said. "If a team comes together and really executes, you can beat a team on any given night."

Butler's 13 steals were a season high and tied its NCAA Tournament record. Syracuse's 59 points were 23 under its average. Syracuse players compared Butler's defense to that of Big East opponents West Virginia or Pittsburgh.

"We've said this word over and over in Indianapolis, and that is 'resolve,'" Stevens said. "These guys have resolve. Hard to measure, but they got it."

Reporters in Salt Lake City, and elsewhere, googled to measure the distance from Hinkle Fieldhouse to Lucas Oil Stadium: six miles. Because the Bulldogs were oh, so close to that far-fetched scenario: to play in a Final Four in Indianapolis.

Now, one victory away, the angle was irresistible. A photograph of a smiling Mack dominated the front page of the next morning's *USA Today*, under the headline BUTLER DID IT. Analogies to Hickory of the *Hoosiers* movie were inescapable.

Predictably, Stevens downplayed that aspect. Long way to go, he said, especially with Kansas State or Xavier coming up next. Butler players acknowledged the obvious.

"Being one game away, that would be great, and I'm sure Indy would love that," Howard said.

As dramatic as Butler–Syracuse was, Xavier–Kansas State exceeded that in the next West Regional semifinal. Either opponent would be challenging, although Xavier would have the motive of reversing the disputed outcome at Hinkle Fieldhouse.

Kansas State and Xavier were tied at 72 after regulation play and 87 after one overtime. After 13 ties and 17 lead changes, Kansas State finally won 101–96 in double overtime.

Kansas State's flamboyant coach, Frank Martin, said afterward that he didn't watch Butler–Syracuse because he never watches another game until his team's own game is over. He left scouting to his assistants, and left to himself whatever inspiration might be required.

"Usually I say, 'How do you get the guys ready to play Saturday?' I say,

▲ Shelvin Mack shoots over a UTEP defender in the first round of the 2010 NCAA Tournament. Mack sank 7 3-pointers and scored 25 points in Butler's 77–59 victory.

▼ Shawn Vanzant's eyes are on–and on top of–the ball against Murray State.

▲ Gordon Hayward stretches to complete a drive to the hoop against Murray State.

▼ Coach Brad Stevens designs a play during a time-out. Willie Veasley towels off, and Nick Rodgers stands with arms folded to Stevens's right. Also standing are trainer Ryan Galloy, directly behind Stevens, and assistant coach Micah Shrewsberry.

▲ Shawn Vanzant received love and support from the Littons, his adoptive family in Tampa, Florida. From left are Zach Litton, Chase Litton, Vanzant, Lisa Litton, Jeff Litton, and Josh Litton.

◄ Bulldog mascot Hink makes sure everyone knows which school he represents.

► Blue II became a popular figure and "America's Dog" during and after Butler's first run to the Final Four.

▼ Students in the Dawg Pound at Hinkle Fieldhouse show support for their Dawgs.

◄ Jake Allen, a freshman from Perrysville, Indiana, brings out a Butler flag during a campus celebration after the Bulldogs reached the 2010 Final Four.

► Butler players, including a leaping Shelvin Mack (1), celebrate after knocking off Kansas State 63–56 to win the 2010 NCAA West Regional at Salt Lake City.

◄ Gordon Hayward, second from right, lowers his head in embarrassment at a news conference during the 2010 NCAA Tournament. Delighting in his discomfort are, from left, Willie Veasley, Ronald Nored, Shelvin Mack, Matt Howard, and, at right, coach Brad Stevens.

► University president Bobby Fong gets a lift from football player Ryan Myers as students on campus revel in the aftermath of the win sending Butler to the 2010 Final Four.

◄ Coach Brad Stevens slaps hands along a line of players after the Bulldogs won the 2010 NCAA West Regional at Salt Lake City.

► Coach Brad Stevens was a calming influence on the Bulldogs throughout the 2010 NCAA Tournament.

◄ Brad Stevens stands near midcourt at Lucas Oil Stadium during the 2010 NCAA championship game. In the background, seated, is Duke coach Mike Krzyzewski.

◄ Ronald Nored dribbles past Duke's Jon Scheyer and heads toward the basket during the 2010 NCAA championship game.

▼ Butler players on the Lucas Oil Stadium sideline lean forward as they watch late moments of the 2010 NCAA championship game. From left are Zach Hahn, Avery Jukes, Shawn Vanzant, Grant Leiendecker, Garrett Butcher, Emerson Kampen, Alex Anglin, and Andrew Smith.

◄ Gordon Hayward follows through on a half-court attempt as time expires in the 2010 NCAA championship game. One calculation was that the potential winning 3-pointer, from about 50 feet, missed going in by 3 inches.

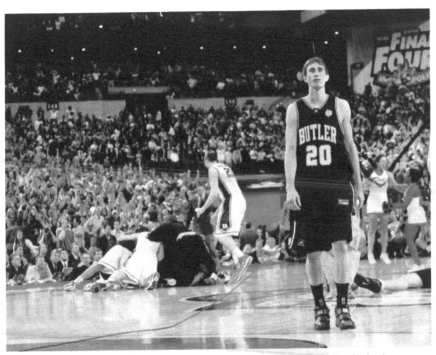

▲ Gordon Hayward walks off a college basketball court for the last time as Duke players pile on one another to celebrate a 61–59 victory that secured the 2010 national championship.

▼ The Bulldogs celebrate after beating Florida 74–71 in overtime, sending them to the 2011 Final Four. No. 1 at right is Shelvin Mack (with bandage), the most outstanding player of the Southeast Regional.

▲ Student fans show what they think of coach Brad Stevens during the 2011 Final Four in Houston.

◄ Matt Howard walks through a Reliant Stadium corridor on the day before the 2011 national championship game.

◄ Shelvin Mack (1) and Ronald Nored (5) exult after Mack's long 3-pointer gave Butler a 22–19 lead over Connecticut before halftime of the 2011 national championship game.

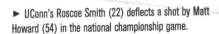

► UConn's Roscoe Smith (22) deflects a shot by Matt Howard (54) in the national championship game.

◄ Matt Howard struggles with his emotions while answering questions after his final college game, a loss to Connecticut in Butler's second consecutive national championship defeat.

'I'll get after them.' I can't get after them tomorrow," Martin said. "We have to coach through their mind, their spirit, enthusiasm, so we can find a way to come out here on Saturday and compete with a big-time Butler team."

Epitomizing the wacky nature of the tournament was the Midwest Regional, in which the Nos. 1, 2, 3, and 4 teams were all ousted before the Elite Eight. But with Xavier, Cornell, St. Mary's, and Northern Iowa eliminated in the Round of 16, Butler was the last of the small-time teams. All the others belonged to major conferences. That included Kansas State, superseding Kansas, the sister school that had so long dominated the state. Kansas State hadn't reached the Final Four since 1964.

One issue for Kansas Sate was how, or if, the players could recover from the Xavier game. In a news conference the next day, they conceded sleep was difficult. The combination of excitement, phone calls, texts, and TV watching prevented most players from going to bed until past 3:00 A.M. Jacob Pullen said he couldn't sleep at all, and that highlights of the game were on virtually every TV channel he selected.

"I laid there staring at the wall," he said.

Pullen was perhaps the outstanding player of the entire tournament, averaging 25.7 points a game. Pullen's patchy whiskers, resembling those of Abe Lincoln, became so popular at Kansas State that fans distributed and wore mock beards in tribute. "Fear the Beard" became the motto of his purple-clad devotees. Denis Clemente, a Puerto Rican, joked that he could communicate with the fiery Martin, who was of Cuban descent, because both spoke Spanish. Pullen and Clemente represented a back-court duo as good as any Butler faced during the 2000s.

Martin and Kansas State players didn't supply Butler any inflammatory quotes to post in the locker room. They said the right things. That is, Butler belongs, Butler is a great team, they play the right way, they're smart, they're tough. Blah, blah, blah. It was impossible to discern whether K State players believed that. Martin seemingly did. Asked whether the Wildcats would look past an opponent that might not look impressive in the layup line, he replied:

"If we make those assumptions, then we deserve to lose. Whether your name is Butler, UCLA, Kentucky, whoever, if you're playing in the Elite Eight game, you're a very good basketball team. You shouldn't be concerned about appearance. You should be concerned about the team."

After going through season after season of moderate attention, even in Indianapolis, the Bulldogs luxuriated in media coverage. Before all Elite

Eight games, the NCAA arranges separate interviews with the coach and all starters from each school so that reporters can gather information for possible Final Four stories. Butler players walked to different areas in corridors of the arena for breakout sessions. Even Howard, once uncomfortable with such scrutiny, was relaxed and candid. Nored called it the greatest experience of his life. Mack recorded a CBS interview with his mother.

Fans back home outfitted themselves in Butler gear. Suddenly that was fashionable. Plans were made for a viewing party inside Jordan Hall, as well as many watering holes around Indianapolis. The student foundation sponsored a birthday bash for Blue II, the bulldog mascot, at the campus Starbucks. Blue II turned six years old on game day, March 27.

"It's fitting that he was born in March," said Michael Kaltenmark, the university's director of development and the dog's adoptive dad.

On game day, the Bulldogs held their customary shootaround before returning to the Sheraton, where they were lodged. There were about 10 people from Butler on an elevator when Avery Jukes boarded. The elevator began to sag, and Jukes jumped off. It was the quickest anyone had ever seen him move. Doors closed, and everyone was stuck there for about 10 minutes. It was nothing new to radio analyst Nick Gardner, who remembered being stuck in an elevator as a player on a trip to Cleveland State. The Bulldogs won that game.

"It was a great omen," Gardner said.

Omens, or inspiration, came in other forms. Athletic director Barry Collier opened a fortune cookie with the following message: "If you stay assertive, you will win the game." Stevens received an e-mail that said, "One more, Ollie." It was dialogue from *Hoosiers,* noting that one more underhand free throw by little Ollie MacFarlane would send Hickory to the state finals.

One more, Dawgs.

Before Butler began the tournament, Nored stopped by Stevens's office for a book to read on the trip to San Jose. The coach handed him *The Last Lecture,* by Randy Pausch, a college professor who in 2008 died of pancreatic cancer, the same disease that took the life of Nored's father. Nored was so affected that he created a Facebook status message based on one of Pausch's passages:

Brick walls are there for a reason. The brick walls are not there to keep us out. The brick walls are there to give us a chance to show how badly we want something. Because the brick walls are there to stop the people who don't want it badly enough.

Nored stored Pausch's quote. He didn't use it before UTEP or Murray State. Or before Syracuse. But for Kansas State, as the Bulldogs waited to take the floor, the moment had come.

How badly do we want this?

Stevens badly did. The calm he emitted to his players, and through the TV screen, contrasted to the roiling inside. Only twice in his young career had he been unable to sleep before a game. The first time was before his head coaching debut, at Ball State, just 28 months before. The second was the night before Kansas State.

The Bulldogs began robustly, as they did against Syracuse. Veasley sank his only field goal, a 3-pointer that banked in, and Vanzant swished a 3-pointer as Butler built a 10–4 lead.

But with less than six minutes elapsed, Howard picked up his second foul, a charging call. Kansas State featured five players 6-foot-7 or taller, so Butler was disadvantaged without its 6-foot-8 center. Howard went to the bench, and as he normally did, Jukes replaced him.

Yet a couple of minutes later, Stevens made a curious substitution. The coach replaced Jukes with Andrew Smith, a 6-foot-11 freshman who hadn't played in any of the three previous NCAA games. Smith's actual minutes played over the past month: three. The Bulldogs borrowed a slogan from their NFL neighbors, the Indianapolis Colts: Next man up. That man was Smith.

"I've felt ready every game, even though I didn't play every game," he said.

Mack grabbed a defensive rebound, dribbled to the top of the key, and sank a 3-pointer. After a Butler miss, Mack regained possession and spotted an open Smith, who caught the pass and laid it in for a 15–8 lead.

Smith was fouled on Butler's next possession and made the first of two free throws. More important, he stayed active, getting his hands on rebounds, staying in front of his man on defense. He batted one rebound to Hayward, who extended his body to score on a layup. When Smith returned to the bench from his five-minute stint, Butler led 18–10.

"The coaches did a great job of telling us exactly what to do, and I just did what I was supposed to do," Smith said. "My teammates helped me out."

After Jukes reentered, he took the ball on the perimeter, drove to the basket, and scored on a layup. If that was a maneuver heretofore unseen, the next was even more so.

Hayward caught the ball on the right wing behind the arc, dribbled once, twice, three times, stepping inside the 3-point line. On the fourth, he bounced the ball between his legs, stepped back from a defender and behind the arc, and swished a 3-pointer. It was an NBA-style play. Internet users used a different description: sick.

The 3-pointer expanded Butler's lead to 23–14. Mack's basket made it 25–14, under the two-minute mark, for the largest margin. The difference was mostly from the 3-point line, where Butler had three baskets to K State's none.

It was an inglorious half for Pullen, defended by Nored, and Clemente, defended by Veasley. Kansas State's guards were scoreless. Curtis Kelly kept the Wildcats close by scoring 12 points. As the half neared the finish, Pullen tipped the ball away from Nored, and Clemente scored off the turnover for the first points by either of the Wildcat guards.

Half: Butler 27, Kansas State 20.

During intermission, CBS's Seth Davis said he didn't realize Butler's half-court defense was so good until he saw it against this level of competition. Every Butler opponent was having the same realization.

Kansas State scored the first six points of the second half, completing a 10–0 run, and pulled within 27–26. Butler responded quickly. To cap a 7–0 spurt, Hayward caught the ball on the right wing in transition and swished a 3-pointer, restoring the Bulldogs' margin to 34–26. Hayward kept his wrist bent in shooting motion, and, in an unusual display of emotion, shouted defiantly as he retreated and chest-bumped Mack.

Pullen stole the ball from Mack and made a layup, but Mack quickly compensated. Off an inbounds play, he nearly duplicated Hayward's step-back 3-pointer, clearing space for himself as he hit from the right corner to send Butler ahead 37–28.

"That's a big-time shot," CBS's Gus Johnson said.

Hayward scored on a pull-up jump shot, and Butler went into the final 10 minutes with a 10-point lead, 42–32. Ten minutes away from a hometown Final Four.

Stevens steadied his Bulldogs throughout the tournament and throughout the season. As suspense grew, he walked to the end of the bench and spoke to players seated there.

"Boy, you guys, this is a lot of fun, isn't it?" the coach asked.

"Yeah, if I don't have a heart attack first," Rodgers answered.

Mack kept the 10-point margin, 49–39, by sinking his third 3-pointer. The Bulldogs stayed in control 51–44 when Hayward hit both ends of a one-and-one with 5:49 on the clock.

But the Wildcats, who were so valiant two nights before in two overtimes, showed no sign of wearing down. Pullen drilled a 3-pointer, then sank both ends of a one-and-one after being fouled by Nored.

Butler 52, Kansas State 49.

The Bulldogs were relying on Hayward to advance the ball, but Clemente poked it away. Not only was Hayward guilty of his fifth turnover, he also fouled Clemente. The Kansas State guard missed his free throw, but the ball was rebounded by teammate Dominique Sutton. Clemente ran around to the right corner, behind the arc, caught Sutton's pass, and unhesitatingly shot.

Clemente's 3-pointer capped an 8-0 surge and supplied Kansas State its first lead 52–51. For the fourth time in as many tournament games, the Bulldogs trailed in the second half.

With 4:14 on the clock, Hayward was fouled after rebounding Mack's 3-point miss. Hey, this is no worse than Auckland, remember? Hayward turned to his Team USA colleague and told him:

"We've got this."

Hayward's first free throw hung on the rim, then dropped. He sank the second. Butler regained the lead 53–52. Howard was fouled while trying to rebound a missed Kansas State shot. With 3:35 left, a TV time-out gave both teams a chance to rest, regroup, and ready any strategy. Stevens spoke with the constancy he had shown throughout the tournament.

"Play your game," he told his players. "Just play your game."

Howard made the first of two free throws, and it was 54–52. But Clemente tied it for Kansas State 54–54 on a drive and an acrobatic teardrop shot over Hayward.

On the Bulldogs' next possession, Hayward slipped behind K State's defense through the back door. He leaped and, though off balance, caught Nored's lob and laid it in before landing on his rump. Butler reclaimed the lead, 56–54.

Kansas State called time-out. But the Wildcats' next shot was an air-balled 3-point attempt by Pullen, returning possession to Butler with less than two and a half minutes left.

Nored took the inbounds pass, moved forward, and kept the ball all around the half-court, never stopping his dribble. Eyeing an open lane, he knifed to the basket and rattled in a left-handed layup as three defenders converged on him. Too late. It was Nored's first basket, extending Butler's lead to 58–54 with barely two minutes left.

The weary Clemente was fouled with 1:33 left, and he missed the first of a one-and-one. Two Butler shots, by Nored and Veasley, were blocked, but Butler retained possession. On the second, Mack saved the ball out of bounds to Howard, who passed it out to Hayward. Hayward took two left-handed dribbles, one long stride, and laid in the ball with his right hand.

Butler 60, Kansas State 54.

With the clock dipping under 60 seconds, time was running out on the Wildcats. Twice the ball was deflected behind midcourt as they struggled for a makeable attempt. On a third loose ball, Nored stripped it from Clemente and passed ahead to Veasley, who in turn sent it to Mack. The Wildcats fouled. They could do nothing else.

"Butler, 18 seconds away from going home! What a team!" Gus Johnson gushed to the CBS audience.

Hayward's mother, Jody, put her head in her hands in virtual disbelief. On the bench, in an atypical outburst, Howard leaped exultantly. He said later that's as high as he could sky. Stevens walked to the end of the bench and signaled to Kampen. Get ready, the coach said. We're doing it. Doing it in front of everyone.

Mack, at the foul line, was shaking. It was a feeling he'd never had before. He'd never been on the verge of something like this before. He missed his first free throw, made the second.

Seconds later, Nored stole the ball again, and though he muffed a layup, a goaltending violation gave him his second basket. That ended a shocking 9–0 run, making Pullen's closing basket inconsequential.

Final score: Butler 63, Kansas State 56.

Forty years after the retirement of Tony Hinkle, who coached the Bulldogs longer than 40 years, they were going to a Final Four. A hometown Final Four.

"Let's go home! Let's go home!" Butler fans chanted, many weeping with joy.

Those included Collier, who two decades ago envisioned what Butler basketball could be, based on what it once was. Butler players dawg-piled into a heap, with a grinning Vanzant on the bottom. Howard jumped into the arms of Smith, representing more than 13 feet and 460 pounds of Hoosier hoop humanity.

The Bulldogs hugged, and screamed, and waved towels. Nored ran to the stands, wrapping his arms around his widowed mother. Later, he performed a move that was something between a front handspring and a cartwheel.

"Thank God," Jody Hayward whispered in the ear of a reporter who waded into the section where parents of Butler players were seated. Victoria Guy, whose harrowing first flight allowed her to share the occasion with son Shelvin Mack, said through tears, "I love him to death."

Curt Smith's flight problems prevented him from attending the Syracuse game, but he had arrived in Salt Lake City to see son Andrew play a career-high 12 minutes and influence a historic victory.

"He wanted to go out and help his team," the father said, his face also damp with tears. "His time came, and he stepped up and did it."

Andrew Smith had his own Jim Valvano moment. Smith said he didn't know what to do, so "I'm just kind of walking around the court." Valvano was the North Carolina State coach who ran around looking for someone to hug after winning the 1983 NCAA championship over Houston.

Ladders were brought out for the ceremonial cutting down of the nets. Players accepted West Regional champion caps and tugged them on their heads. They clapped rhythmically and sang the "Butler War Song." Stevens and Kampen, as they had rehearsed, executed their flying back bump. Kampen teased Hayward that the coach could outjump him.

"Emerson said that? That's what I'm talkin' about," Stevens said, smiling.

Tracy Stevens came out of the stands with the couple's two children, 10-month-old Kinsley and 4-year-old Brady, and kissed her husband. Stevens put Brady, who was virtually a little brother to the Bulldogs, on his shoulders. Kinsley had been her father's film-watching companion, mesmerized by the sights and colors as she sat in Stevens's lap while he analyzed upcoming opponents.

Stevens's own parents, although divorced, were unified in support of their 33-year-old son. Both were in the arena for a moment that Mark Stevens said was every father's dream.

"I'm just stunned. I'm numb," the father said. "I'm so happy for the school. Great group of kids. They deserve it."

Jan Stevens, herself a longtime teacher, said it was her son's ability to teach that made the Bulldogs so prepared for each test.

"He's always been pure joy. Always been pure joy," the mother said.

Hayward scored 15 of his 22 points in the second half, featuring 8 of 11 Butler points in the decisive stretch, and grabbed 9 rebounds. He so often blossomed against the big schools that he was labeled "BCS-killer" by assistant coach Micah Shrewsberry.

Hayward was voted the West Regional's most outstanding player. He said the Bulldogs' dream didn't end at the Final Four.

"We want to win the whole thing," he said.

Mack scored 16 points, giving the two gold medalists 38 of Butler's 63 points. Yet the outcome wasn't decided on the offensive end. Butler beat the Nos. 1 and 2 seeds by holding them to a collective 46 points under their scoring averages. Clemente and Pullen, who totaled 53 points against Xavier, scored 18 and 14, respectively, against Butler. The Bulldogs outrebounded a bigger and supposedly more athletic opponent 41–29.

As usual, Veasley didn't produce numbers, just results. His stifling defense and enduring presence were essential to the immeasurable Veasley Effect.

"I don't know if there's any words to capture how good it felt, how great it felt, that we just proved to the world what everybody but a few thought we couldn't do," the winningest player in Butler history said.

Pullen said the Wildcats were not tired. Tired of playing against the Bulldogs, maybe. Kelly said he felt the Wildcats were in control against Xavier, but never felt that way against Butler. Everywhere Kelly turned, Hayward was there. Martin said the Bulldogs "kicked our tails" and "annihilated us" on the glass.

"It's hard to be happy for someone when you lose," the Kansas State coach said. "But I've got to think it's going to be a great, great week for Butler people and people in the city of Indianapolis to have one of their own in the Final Four."

Indianapolis didn't wait for the team's return to go Dawg wild. On campus, several hundred students watching in Jordan Hall cheered and raised their arms triumphantly. During the game's closing minutes, the noise was so great that students afterward reported that their ears were ringing.

Students spilled into the middle of the campus from every direction, from residence halls and Greek houses. Erik Fromm, an incoming basketball recruit who was a high school senior in Bloomington, Indiana, wanted to be on campus during the game. He watched with a friend from the Delta Tau Delta fraternity, then joined the others who were yelling, running, and hugging people they didn't even know.

"We Are the Champions" boomed from speakers. Outside Atherton Union, students chanted "Final Four, Final Four," and, "Too big, yo." The students deluged Twitter feeds and Facebook pages with "Too big, yo."

Bobby Fong, the university president, appeared outside Atherton Union, prompting chants, of "BoFo, BoFo, BoFo." Matt Werner of the Phil Delta Theta fraternity, across Hampton Drive, carried his iPod into Atherton's Reilly Room, where speakers were set up. He blasted the "Butler War Song" over the sound system.

The crowd closed in around Fong, who was being shielded by football players. Ryan Myers, a 285-pound lineman, asked Fong if he would get on his shoulders amid the uproar. Myers kneeled, and Fong climbed aboard. The Butler president was riding a Butler wave. Fong raised four fingers on each hand to signify Final Four, and cell phones and cameras captured the moment and forwarded photographs around campus.

"It was kind of a thrill-of-the-moment kind of thing," Myers said. "I don't think too many presidents would get up on the shoulders of a rioting crowd."

Fong's mother-in-law, Mary Dunham Nichols, energized her retirement community in Cockeysville, Maryland. Wearing a Bulldogs pin and displaying a B-U-T-L-E-R sign on her sunporch, she turned residents and employees there into fans who cheered, "Go Butler!"

Stevens's father-in-law, Albert Wilhelmy, watched with about 200 other TV viewers at the Harry Buffalo Restaurant in Lakewood, Ohio. The general manager broke out the champagne, Wilhelmy proposed a toast, and the fans sang "Who Let the Dogs Out?"

Viewers at Moe & Johnny's included the Indiana governor, Mitch Daniels. Wearing jeans and a cap, he blended with the crowd. After victory was secured, he exchanged high fives with fans at the bar and grill formerly known as The Bulldog.

"To me, the Butler team personifies the state of Indiana and Indiana basketball," Daniels said. "They have a lot of Hoosier kids, and they play like a team. No one hot dogs, and there's no real ego that you can find. And they're good students. You've got math majors and finance majors on that team, and to see them doing what they're doing—I just think it's a message to every sports fan in America."

In the newsroom of Indy's WTHR, the NBC affiliate on Channel 13, objectivity was momentarily, and justifiably, suspended. Sports anchor Dave Calabro, sports reporter Rich Nye, and newswriter Fred Ramos—all Butler alumni—high-fived and shouted with pride.

Two recent alumni, Adam Hoog and Meg Whelan, had been earnestly following the Bulldogs from Seoul, South Korea. Until they had Internet access, they went to PC rooms for webcasts, cheering quietly while surrounded by computer game sounds and Korean profanity. Or they traveled to foreigner bars near a U.S. military base. When they couldn't access one webcast, they called Hoog's mother and watched via Skype as she directed her laptop toward the Indianapolis telecast. Whelan, and a friend converted into a Butler fan, cried for joy in a Seoul apartment as the seconds ticked away on the Kansas State webcast.

Former Bulldogs playing pro ball overseas watched webcasts, too. Or, in the case of Brandon Polk, on television from Hobart, Australia, where tip-off came Sunday morning. Polk, the Horizon League player of the year in 2006, watched with friends from his living room. He exasperated them by barking like a dog "with nearly each possession," he said. Mike Green, the Horizon's 2008 player of the year, stayed up all night in front of a computer screen at his apartment in Belgium. So did Brandon Crone in Sweden, later booking a flight home for the Final Four.

The outcome was such a big story in Utah that Sunday's edition of the *Salt Lake Tribune* featured Butler across the top of page one, and sports coverage included 8 articles and 16 photographs. The *Deseret News* published similar coverage. *USA Today* featured Butler on page one of its Monday edition.

Back in the locker room, trainer Ryan Galloy took a call from a friend who was so caught up in the euphoria that he said, "This is the greatest day of my life, and I have four kids!"

Stevens gathered the players to talk about the upcoming Final Four week, and they asked what to do about tickets for friends and family. He did not know. He had never been there before, either.

The Bulldogs didn't even know who their next opponent would be. That would be determined in the next day's Midwest Regional final in St. Louis between No. 5 seed Michigan State and No. 6 seed Tennessee. At least Butler would never be playing Kentucky. Later in the day, the No. 1-seeded Wildcats lost to No. 2 seed West Virginia 73–66 in the East final at Syracuse.

Mack, the 19-year-old from Lexington, was in the Final Four. Kentucky, whose five first-round draft picks would go on to set an NBA draft record, was out.

Someone counted the players' text messages and added them up to 458. Nored had more than 120, and Mack nearly that many. The outpouring, in Salt Lake City and around the country, was overwhelming. But the Underdawgs had not seen anything yet.

CHAPTER 8

WELCOME TO INDIANA BASKETBALL

As Butler players walked to the terminal for the flight home late Saturday night, the Kansas State travel party was at the next gate at Salt Lake City International Airport. Butler's charter arrived first. As the airline started boarding calls, one of the Kansas State alumni stood and asked everyone to applaud the Bulldogs. They received an ovation.

If that was the reception they were getting from fans of the team they just defeated, they couldn't imagine what awaited them in Indianapolis. Butler would be the first team to play in a Final Four in its own city since UCLA played in Los Angeles in 1972.

Although the plane was crowded, there was one piece of cargo meriting singular attention. Nick Rodgers carried the West Regional championship trophy, buckling the prize into its own seat between himself and Grant Leiendecker.

The university announced that the team would arrive at Hinkle Fieldhouse sometime after midnight, spreading the word via radio, e-mails, and texts. Students gathered in the parking lot first, soon to be followed by fans of all ages. There were teens and toddlers, grandparents and thirtysomethings, faculty and alumni. Some drove for miles to be there, and others walked over from what was usually a quiet residential neighborhood. Among those waiting were Chrishawn Hopkins, one of the Bulldogs' recruits from Manual High School in Indianapolis, and Gordon Hayward's grandfather, also named Gordon.

The fieldhouse doors were locked, so fans stood outside despite cold temperatures and light showers. Car horns began honking at 12:30 A.M., and a band played in what became an ongoing pep rally. President Bobby

Fong, having survived his spontaneous ride celebrating the Bulldogs' victory, addressed the crowd. Blue II, the bulldog mascot, made the first of what would be 35 public appearances over the next five weeks.

Players received texts reporting what was ahead, but they mostly scoffed. At this hour? Must be an exaggeration.

When the buses rounded the corner shortly before 3:00 A.M., they saw it was not. Reflections of blue and red lights from a police escort signaled that the boys were back in town.

An estimated 3,000 people were there in the mist, cheering as they had eight hours before, when the Bulldogs beat Kansas State. Drummers marched down the parking lot, leading the police car and bus to a stopping place.

"Final Four, Final Four, Final Four," the fans chanted.

Phone cameras flashed, TV video rolled. First to be engulfed by fans was Rodgers, who held the trophy over his head.

"I took that off the bus, and it was one of the coolest things ever," he said. "Plowing my way through, letting them feel that and touch that."

Coach Brad Stevens carried four-year-old son Brady off the bus. He joked that this was Butler's version of midnight madness. For many programs, that's a celebratory occasion marking the first day the NCAA permits practice—hence the enthusiastic midnight start time. But the Bulldogs had never observed midnight madness. This was March Madness, and then some.

"It's sort of nuts," Matt Howard said. "You know, when we came back from the Sweet Sixteen, there were about 20 people here. Look at it now."

Players slowly made their way through the throng, accepting pats on the backs and exchanging high fives. They were genuinely astounded to see such a turnout at such an hour.

"It's like we're rock stars, just wanting to touch us," Gordon Hayward said. "For us, we think we are normal people, so we thought those people were insane."

There was nothing normal about the upcoming week. In a city where the Bulldogs were regularly obscured by other sports news, the daily media message was all Butler, all the time. That wasn't confined to Indianapolis, either.

Panelists on ESPN's *Sports Reporters* were unanimous in respect for Butler. Jim McGrath, the Butler associate athletic director for communication, was deluged by requests for interviews with anyone remotely connected to the team—including two cheerleaders and an assistant strength coach. Play-by-play announcer Joe Gentry was interviewed by 50 radio stations over the next week, from New York to Los Angeles to Hawaii.

The two-person sports information staff, McGrath and Josh Rattray, was augmented by two more. They responded to phone calls and e-mails, but it became obvious that not all media could be accommodated. One minute, the Bulldogs were like a local high school team, covered every now and then. The next, they were Team USA, covered by every outlet in North America.

Butler was again on page one of *USA Today* and was featured prominently on sports websites. The *New York Times* treated the Bulldogs as if they were as important to their readers as the New York Yankees. In "The Couch," a whimsical column by Jason Gay in the *Wall Street Journal*, he essentially ordered all fans to root for Butler:

> Butler doesn't have a single starter taller than 5-foot-2; they travel to away games on mules; and until last year, they played all of their home games by candlelight on a dirt floor. Okay, maybe we're overdoing it on the underdog thing.

Indianapolis media covered the Bulldogs as they did the Colts in the Super Bowl two months before. The *Indianapolis Star* significantly altered pretournament plans for coverage and sales. The newspaper increased the quantity of single copies available downtown and at the airport. Four special sections that were to cover all four teams—for the upcoming Saturday, Sunday, Monday, and Tuesday—instead focused mostly on the hometown Bulldogs. For more than a week, the most-viewed stories on the newspaper's website, IndyStar.com, were about Butler basketball.

Reporters reached out to 81-year-old Buckshot O'Brien, the Bulldogs' last NBA player, who was retired and living in Clearwater Beach, Florida. He granted multiple interview requests, and because he had watched the Bulldogs play several times, he could speak with some authority.

"There were times I've watched them, I thought they'd had it," he said. "But they came back in the final three or four minutes to win."

His former coach, Tony Hinkle, "would love it," O'Brien said.

· · ·

As it turned out, Butler was an appropriate champion of the West Regional. After Sunday's two regional finals, Butler had the westernmost campus of teams in the Final Four. Joining Butler (32-4) and West Virginia (31-6) were Michigan State (28-8) and Duke (33-5). Butler's 24-game winning streak was the longest entering a Final Four since Duke carried a 31-game streak into the 1999 Final Four, in which the Blue Devils defeated Michigan State in the semifinal before being upset by Connecticut in the championship game.

The four finalists were teams without superstars but not without talent. At least that's the way West Virginia coach Bob Huggins saw it.

"Certainly, Duke has pros," Huggins said. "Butler has pros. Michigan State has pros. I think we've got a couple. You know, I think to advance in this tournament, you have to be able to defend. But I think that's all the time."

Michigan State's semifinal opponent was Butler. Neither MSU's Tom Izzo nor Duke's Mike Krzyzewski dismissed the Bulldogs' chances of becoming national champions.

"For one, I think they're very good," Izzo said. "And two, I think the whole tournament is turned upside down. And number three is, they're at home. There's three good reasons."

The Spartans couldn't avoid Butler, as they had earlier in the 2000s. Michigan State was tentatively scheduled to play Butler during coach Todd Lickliter's tenure, but Izzo called to rescind the agreement. The Spartans couldn't afford to lose that home game, and the risk wasn't worth it.

"You're too good," Izzo said at the time.

It was a new era. Different teams had a chance to win, Krzyzewski said.

"It will be like this from now on, which I don't think is bad," he said.

Although fans and students were wildly excited, there were unforeseeable strains on the university. A shipment of 180 T-shirts sold out in an hour at Hinkle Fieldhouse's small Spirit Shop, and 800 preorders were waiting to be filled. At the Follett-owned bookstore, doors opened at 8:30 A.M. Sunday to a crowd of 300 waiting to buy Butler and Final Four merchandise.

Searches for "Butler University basketball" on Yahoo! Sports were up 1,288 percent. On a typical day, the university received 15 inquiries on its admissions website. That Sunday, it received 300. The website later crashed—twice.

"It's been surreal. You cannot be ready for something like this," said Tom Weede, vice president for enrollment.

Ticket sales turned into an unfortunate fiasco. The university notified students via e-mail that $25 tickets would go on sale at 12:30 P.M. Monday. Three hundred were set aside for the team's devoted supporters such as cheerleaders, band members, and those in the Dawg Pound section. At noon, half an hour early, those students were sent a link to online sales. In violation of guidelines, some shared the link with others. By the time other students were supposed to purchase tickets, all were sold.

Snubbed students were outraged. At a time the campus should have been celebrating, all the talk and Facebook postings were about the ticket scandal. The NCAA's decision to process student tickets online proved to be unwise. By Monday night, the university revoked 178 student tickets, allowing others a second chance the next day. The university identified the students who had sent the link and revoked their purchases.

The historic run was bittersweet for students on a semester abroad. Megan Daley, 21, an international studies major from Cincinnati, followed the news from Seville, Spain. She watched the Butler–Syracuse game from a bar where she was mocked by boisterous French rugby fans. After the Bulldogs reached the Final Four, her mother called her at 3:00 A.M. in Italy, where she was on spring break.

"The latter resulted in me possibly being the only person in history to stand on a bridge in Venice at sunset, wishing I was in Indianapolis," she wrote in a poignant e-mail. "The study abroad office made it seem like losing your passport was the worst thing that could happen while studying abroad. But I'm starting to think that watching your school reach the Final Four from 5,000 miles away might be worse."

Ticket buying wasn't as contentious for Butler season ticket holders and Bulldog Club donors, who were allowed two tickets for $280 each. Those at the front of the line arrived at 4:50 A.M., more than seven hours early. About 600 people assembled, some sitting on lawn chairs and others holding leashes of small dogs. The line spilled out of Hinkle Fieldhouse's dimly lit hallway onto the sidewalk.

Matt Howard walked along the queue, delivering high fives to the expectant fans. Among those waiting were composer James Quitman

Mulholland, a professor of music. Mulholland calculated that the Final Four would be worth $100 million of free publicity to the university.

Brad Stevens was attempting to make the week as normal as possible, realizing it would be impossible. He didn't want to detract from the players' experience, either, wanting them to enjoy the Final Four as much as if they were in another city. The city was so transformed, it didn't feel like Indianapolis anyway. Stevens wasn't concerned about the players' being distracted.

"It probably means more to me and the Indiana kids than anybody else because you've lived here your whole life," the coach said. "To watch it being displayed is really unbelievable.

"They're as mature as most seniors I've ever been around. In fact, I'm not so sure they aren't more mature than most 30-year-olds I know. I think they just understand what it's all about. They understand that team is bigger than themselves. I wish I was as mature as some of these guys when I was 20. These guys, they've really bought into each other, most importantly."

Shelvin Mack and Willie Veasley walked around campus with video cameras, recording the buzz. Shawn Vanzant received a standing ovation when he walked into his 9:00 A.M. Spanish class. For a coaching class, the professor asked students to interview Zach Hahn, who spent the entire hour answering questions as prep for the week's media onslaught.

Howard's welcome was more subdued at his 11 o'clock investments class. He was first on the earnings list in a simulated investments game. He gambled on oil, which he said wasn't smart, "but it paid off."

The Bulldogs reported at their customary 6:30 time Tuesday morning at Hinkle Fieldhouse. Although they didn't have a ritzy facility, as more affluent programs did, they almost always practiced on the court where they played home games, which not all college teams did. Among those watching the closed practice were 75-year-old Red Taylor, who coached both Stevens and Hayward in AAU summer ball, and recruit Hopkins.

When the workout ended at 7:45, about 35 media representatives were allowed into the gym for two hours to ask questions and film Stevens and players. The coach had had a busy Monday media schedule, speaking on a teleconference and on four national radio shows. He was busier Tuesday: ESPN's *First Take*, ESPN News, ESPN's *Pardon the Interruption*, a CBS shoot, and another appearance on CBS Radio. He spoke at an additional 4:00 P.M. news conference with Ronald Nored and Shelvin Mack. Stevens said his job was to promote Butler University.

The players showed no sign of stress and were, at times, impish. They reveled in teasing Stevens, who, at 33, was the youngest coach in the Final Four since 32-year-old Bob Knight of Indiana in 1973. The Bulldogs poked fun at their coach's playing credentials and alleged shooting skills.

"He talks like he can play right now, but he never really backs it up," Howard said. "I don't mind if you tell him that, either."

Stevens challenged his players to games of H-O-R-S-E, and sometimes won.

"When he wins," Mack said, "we hear about it. He jaws a lot."

Butler basketball was identified with *Hoosiers* ever since the movie was released in 1986. The native Indiana filmmakers, writer Angelo Pizzo and director David Anspaugh, believed it would have regional appeal.

They wound up making one of the most beloved, and best, sports movies of all time. It was based on the team from Milan High School, with an enrollment of 161, beating Muncie Central to win Indiana's state tournament in 1954. Muncie Central was a four-time state champion with an enrollment more than 10 times that of Milan. Virtually everyone on Butler's team had watched the movie, most of them many times. Mack, a Kentuckian, was a holdout.

"People have been getting on me to watch the movie, but I haven't had time to fit it into my schedule," Mack said at a news conference, prompting a cackle from his coach.

Many players worked at Butler's summer basketball camp, and invariably the youths wanted to watch *Hoosiers* on movie night. *Hoosiers*, week after week, night after night. Nored saw it so often that he could practically recite all the dialogue from memory.

"It's the most annoying thing I've ever experienced in my life," Nored said.

Stevens sometimes embraced the comparison with the fictional Hickory Huskers, especially because they won. Hayward and Howard played along in a 10-question *Hoosiers* quiz posted on an online video. (Hayward won 8–6.) Although Nored had reached the threshold of how many times he could watch the movie, he acknowledged that Hickory's season actually did resemble Butler's.

"They had some tough times at the beginning of the season, and they overcame them," Nored said. "They were tougher because of them. I think we're tougher because of some of the losses we took earlier. We rallied around each other and stuck together, just like you saw in the movie."

The *Hoosiers* script significantly deviated from the actual events it was based upon. Yet at the Final Four, it would have been impossible, even remiss, not to connect the movie to these Bulldogs. The movie was nostalgic, and inspiring, without being syrupy.

It recalled a simpler time when team and town and family and friends were all anyone had in a small community like the one inhabited by the Huskers. Part of the Bulldogs' appeal, besides their obvious underdog status, could be traced to some of the old-fashioned values they lived out on the basketball floor and on TV screens. Perhaps the nation, in an era of economic hardship and political polarization, longed to see a representation of our better selves. In the collective subconscious, the Bulldogs became such symbols.

No matter that all the parallels were inexact. There wasn't a genealogy from Marvin Wood to Norman Dale to Gene Hackman to Brad Stevens. Milan's Wood and Butler's Stevens were young, and Hickory's Dale, portrayed by Hackman, was a middle-aged coach given one last chance long after a scandal had sidetracked his career.

But Butler was a small school from Indiana challenging bigger schools. Butler's gym was Hinkle Fieldhouse, where the climactic scenes from *Hoosiers* were filmed.

Visitors continued to walk into the empty fieldhouse and yell, "Hickory!" anticipating the echo in a reenactment of that movie moment.

The scene in which Hickory player Everett Flatch gets into a fight and is shoved into a glass trophy case was filmed in an old gym in Brownsburg, which was Hayward's hometown. Hickory star Jimmy Chitwood was based on Bobby Plump of Milan. Plump, who went on to play for Butler, owned a restaurant, Plump's Last Shot, in Indianapolis. Maris Valainis, the actor who depicted Chitwood, grew up two blocks from Butler's campus and played pickup ball at Hinkle Fieldhouse.

"We had no idea it would go over as big as it did," Valainis said of the movie. "We thought maybe people in Indiana would embrace it. But the rest of the country recognized what a great story it was."

Milan was Hickory was Butler. Bobby Plump was Jimmy Chitwood was Gordon Hayward. Hollywood blended with Hoosier Hysteria, and the concoction bathed everything with a romantic scent at a Final Four played in Indiana.

As player Merle Webb put it before Hickory took the floor for the championship game, "Let's win this game for all the small schools that never had a chance to get here."

Being thrust into the spotlight wasn't automatically desirable. Light that could reveal crimes, cobwebs, or cockroaches was not the kind of scrutiny anyone would seek.

Yet Butler, a university that from its beginnings sought to be something more, benefited from the exposure. It was cast as a beacon for academicians wondering how to mix the peculiarly American phenomenon of higher education and athletics. Other universities had done so—notably Duke, which also was in the Final Four—but not at such a low cost. Duke's basketball budget for the 2008–09 school year was $13.8 million, compared to Butler's $1.7 million.

In the 2011 rankings by *U.S. News & World Report*, Butler was No. 1 in the Midwest among up-and-coming universities. Butler's ballet and pharmacy programs were rated among the nation's best, and its business school was beginning to receive national recognition.

Of schools that reached the Sweet Sixteen, the highest graduation rates among basketball players were Duke (92 percent) and Butler (90 percent). Five had graduation rates of less than 50 percent: West Virginia (44), Baylor (36), Kentucky (31), Tennessee (30), and Washington (20).

Kadie Otto was head of the Drake Group, an organization for reform of college sports. In examining Butler's team media guide, she was startled to see players in so many different majors: computer engineering, mechanical engineering, economics, accounting, finance, marketing, education. The Drake Group was especially opposed to "clustering," or graduating a high percentage of teammates with the same degree.

Butler players continued to attend classes throughout the week, sometimes shuttling between campus and media obligations downtown. They did not live in special housing or have athletics-appointed tutors.

Howard was honored with a Final Four award, presented to the athlete with the highest grade point average at the finals site of each of the NCAA's 88 annual championships. Howard, a finance major, had a 3.795 average. He and Hayward, a computer engineering major, were academic All-Americans.

"The priority of the kids is such a great example," said Otto, a professor at Western Carolina University. "It's given me a sense of hope."

Butler's president, 60-year-old Bobby Fong, was not some geek or pedant who was antagonistic to sports. Quite the opposite. Fong, the first American-born son of Chinese immigrants, was raised in Oakland, California, and learned about baseball to better understand life in America.

"And I've been overcompensating ever since," he said.

Fong had a collection of 30,000 baseball cards dating to 1951. Although a Bay Area resident as a youth, his favorite player was not the San Francisco Giants' Willie Mays, but New York Yankees slugger Mickey Mantle. Baseball memorabilia filled Fong's Jordan Hall office, including a Norman Rockwell drawing of Brooks Robinson signing an autograph for a child. That seemed fitting, given that Butler's basketball team matched a Rockwellian vision of America.

Fong's undergraduate degree from Harvard and doctorate from UCLA were in English literature, but among his favorite books was *Moneyball*. Author Michael Lewis explained how the low-budget Oakland A's used mathematical analysis and unconventional means to pinpoint overlooked players who could win together. What Butler accomplished in recruiting throughout the 2000s resembled what the A's achieved.

"These are real players. Plus they have the Butler Way," Fong said.

Real students, too.

The hope of becoming something more—nurtured by Butler leaders at various times in the 1800s and 1900s—was coming to fruition in the 2000s. Scholarly pursuits didn't have to be sacrificed to win basketball games.

By the middle of Final Four week, Butler mania had a firm hold on Indianapolis. If anything, it was intensifying.

An estimated 5,000 people, most dressed in Butler blue and some holding signs supporting the Bulldogs, turned out on Monument Circle for a noon rally on an unseasonably warm Wednesday. Temperatures climbed into the upper 70s. Speakers included Mayor Greg Ballard, Fong, athletic director Barry Collier, and Plump. Plump had vitality in his voice, even after conducting phone interviews for seven successive hours the day before.

Butler's pep band, color guard, and cheerleaders performed on the steps of Soldiers and Sailors Monument, in the middle of downtown. Buses transported students from the campus.

With Kansas and Kentucky eliminated, the Final Four was unpredictable. Any of the survivors could become national champion. Even Butler.

"I'm just waiting for the sky to open and the Lord to say, 'This will happen,'" Collier said.

At the end of the rally, Collier and Ballard reprised the Brad Stevens–Emerson Kampen back bump, albeit at lower elevation.

Afterward, Fong and Collier told boosters at the Columbia Club, also on the circle, that the university was in the early planning stages of a $10 million renovation of Hinkle Fieldhouse. Butler intended to move athletic offices so that concourses could be widened and improvements made to restrooms and concession stands.

There were no plans to change what made Hinkle a basketball cathedral, such as the brick facade and raised playing floor. The fieldhouse had "great bones," university vice president Mark Helmus said, but needed modernization.

The fieldhouse was an attraction for visitors, who walked into the building for self-guided tours. Anyone who had seen the movie wanted to see the real fieldhouse. Although athletic department employees tried to be accommodating, it was difficult to work when visitors wandered into their offices to chat or ask questions. It was difficult for professors to maintain decorum in classes elsewhere on campus.

"Nothing got done around here," said Daniel McQuiston, department chair of marketing and management. "We did the bare minimum. We got classes in, and that's about it.

"You could just feel the intensity as it went along. It was palpable around campus. You could just feel it."

Fountains were dyed blue, banners hung from buildings, signs with players' numbers were displayed in yards, blue ribbons wrapped around trees and campus statues, and Clowes Memorial Hall shined at night with a lit bulldog on the wall.

Those in Indianapolis under siege were employees in retail outlets attempting to fulfill the demand for Butler merchandise. It was as if they were digging out of an avalanche with a garden spade.

Retailers weren't totally unprepared—before the season, Butler gear was available for the first time at Dick's Sporting Goods, Finish Line, Kohl's, Wal-Mart, Lids, Kroger, Walgreens, and CVS—but there was no way to anticipate such an outpouring. Strategic Marketing Affiliates, the Butler licensing agency, reported sales of more than $2 million worth of Final Four merchandise in a week.

"In some respects, the sales numbers don't surprise me because of the story behind this school," said John Mybeck, chief operating officer at Strategic Marketing Affiliates. "But a year ago, no one would have ever predicted anything like this."

Revenue from one week at Butler's campus bookstore exceeded that of a normal year. So many customers poured into the store, located in Atherton Union, that students could hardly squeeze through to reach the C-Club food court.

Richard Goodpaster, a Follett regional manager who assisted the bookstore, expanded the workforce from 8 to 50, with reinforcements coming in from Illinois, Ohio, and Kentucky. Employees worked 14 to 19 hours a day to keep up with the demand for T-shirts and hats.

The store welcomed a shipment of 700 Nike hats on Monday, and sold all 700 that day. Online sales were so brisk—including requests from Canada, Europe, and U.S. military bases worldwide—that the bookstore's website temporarily shut down when orders hit 2,000 a day. So many items went online that sellouts occurred before they could be shipped to stores.

T-shirts were wheeled in on utility racks carrying about 400 per rack, still warm off the press. The store went through three to five racks a day. Employees didn't bother placing shirts on shelves, instead asking for sizes and distributing them on the spot. One fan purchased 27 shirts in one order.

Over nine days, the bookstore sold 40,961 more items than in the same time period the year before, representing an astounding increase of 5,364 percent and more than $1 million in sales. In fact, revenue exceeded that of the campus bookstore in Gainesville, Florida, when the Florida Gators won college basketball's national championship in 2006—even though Florida's enrollment (51,000), alumni membership, and fan base far exceeded those of Butler.

"I called it slinging shirts," Goodpaster said. "It's the most phenomenal experience I've ever had in retail."

Employees of the Indianapolis-based NCAA, most of them transplants from other states, caught the fever. During lunch hours, many drove to campus so they could buy Butler gear to wear at the games.

The spending spree wasn't limited to the campus bookstore. Indianapolis-based MainGate printed Russell Athletic orders for Lucas Oil Stadium's Pro Shop and the NCAA Hall of Champions, and sold 120 Butler T-shirts in the first hour Monday morning. The Finish Line, a mall-based chain of 660 stores also in town, sold 2,000 in several styles between Sunday and Wednesday.

Vendors at the stadium ran out of some Butler items, and Butler outsold the three other Final Four schools by a large margin. Butler was going to earn only a fraction of the licensing revenue that major schools reap, but would dramatically exceed the $40,000 from two years before.

Butler mania was so contagious that it spread to two unlikely destinations: Bloomington and Lafayette, where the Bulldogs' Big Ten brethren Indiana and Purdue universities, respectively, ruled. Stores in both college towns scrambled to meet demand for Butler merchandise.

A shipment of shirts to the Finish Line at Bloomington's College Mall sold out three hours after arrival. One Bloomington restaurant, Upland Brewery, had more patrons wearing Butler gear one evening than would typically be seen in Indianapolis.

There was one Final Four figure who forged ahead despite interview requests, TV and radio appearances, game preparation, exercise, and grooming needs: Blue II. For one week, Butler's 63-pound fawn-and-white English bulldog mascot was the most famous dog in America.

The bulldog became useful as a strategic diversion to relieve some of the media load carried by coaches and players. It was stressful because Blue II was accustomed to 8 to 12 hours of sleep a night, plus 3-hour naps morning and afternoon.

Blue II was cared for by Michael Kaltenmark, 30, a Butler graduate and the university's director of development, and his wife, Tiffany. The bulldog was "one big wrinkle" when they adopted him as a seven-week-old from a kennel in Lizton, Indiana, in May 2004. Blue II came to view the university's south mall as his own yard.

Butler players maintained a tradition of petting Blue II during the introduction of lineups at Hinkle Fieldhouse, and the NCAA was allowing that to continue at Lucas Oil Stadium. At home games, Blue II ran across the floor to a bone that awaited him in the Dawg Pound under the north basket, but the NCAA required him to stay on the Butler side of the floor.

"His favorite thing to do on campus is anything sports-related," Kalten-mark said. "If you say, 'Hinkle,' he'll bring his ears back or tip his head. It means he gets to be in the spotlight, and he loves that type of stuff."

With Kaltenmark as spokesman, Blue II was "interviewed" by national media outlets such as Yahoo! Sports, the *Bob and Tom Show,* CBS Sports, the CBS *Early Show, Sports Illustrated's* website, and the Associated Press. The bulldog's photo appeared on the home page of ESPN.com and in *USA Today,* the *New York Times,* and the *Wall Street Journal,* among other newspapers. Later he appeared on the cover of *Indianapolis Monthly* magazine's pet edition.

Blue II enjoyed a bath at a party held for him in the Good Dog Hotel and Spa in the Broad Ripple district. He visited the *Indianapolis Star* to be interviewed for an online video, and was a big hit in the newsroom. He ambled down the same hallway where Hillary Rodham Clinton walked during the 2008 presidential campaign, attracting a much larger audi-ence. The bulldog hid under desks, making sure reporters didn't separate him from his new bone.

The number of his followers on Twitter (twitter.com/butlerblue2) more than doubled, to 1,800. On several days during Final Four week, he received 9,000 photo views a day.

"I tweeted my fingers off just keeping up with Blue," Kaltenmark said.

Blue II eventually acquired his own sponsorships and partnered with a company to make more Butler-licensed dog accessories available for sale. For months, the bulldog made public appearances and was asked for interviews. For Blue II, even the dog days of summer were busy.

"I think we have a new 'normal,' " Kaltenmark said.

The confluence of circumstances—Butler's presence, 70,000-plus seating at Lucas Oil Stadium, new off-court fan events, and summerlike temper-atures—turned the Final Four into a weeklong festival. Local residents poured into downtown, filling restaurants and bars. This was the sixth Final Four to be held in Indianapolis, at a third different venue, but it was like none other.

"This is the next evolution of the Final Four," said former sports col-umnist Bill Benner, director of communications for the Indianapolis Convention & Visitors Association, referring to all the activity connected to the Final Four. He said that before the NCAA Tournament began—before he knew Butler would be there.

Some experts speculated Butler would actually lower the projected $50 million economic impact of the tournament on Indianapolis because of fewer visitors paying for overnight lodging. However, city leaders, NCAA officials, and local hoteliers had no public complaints. The consensus was that Bulldog buzz would compensate for any monetary losses—if, in fact, there were any. The Indianapolis Zoo, located two miles from the stadium, drew nearly 10,000 visitors in a day, or 2,500 more than usual for spring. Shapiro's Delicatessen reported a 30 percent increase over the highest sales for a Colts home game, and its most customers since tourists descended on Indianapolis for the 1987 Pan American Games.

The Crowne Plaza at Historic Union Station, where Butler's team was lodged, and the Omni Severin, where Michigan State was headquartered, were fully booked. So was the Hilton, which was Duke's hotel. Butler fans kept calling hotels, trying to find downtown vacancies so they could be in the middle of the party. Downtown restaurants adopted each of the Final Four teams, including the RAM Restaurant & Brewery for Butler. Hosts taking reservations answered phones by saying, "Go Butler Bulldogs!"

The showcase site was Bracket Town, a 140,000-square-foot amusement area at the Indiana Convention Center. Fans tested their own hoop skills, attended clinics, played interactive games, retrieved autographs, and took photos. Slam-dunk and 3-point shooting contests for college players also were held at Bracket Town.

The Bulldogs entered the downtown maelstrom under police escort Thursday. Fans lined the streets on the bus ride from campus, waving and giving thumbs-up signs. The team rode in a bus driven by their unbeaten driver, Charles Jones. He wore a new Butler hat given to him by the Bulldogs.

"I smell a championship," he said to players and coaches as they boarded the bus.

Lucas Oil Stadium was home to the NFL's Colts, but engineers and architects had basketball in mind when it was built. The Bulldogs went through a closed practice there, plus a formal news conference, and checked into the Crowne Plaza. Players said shooting in the stadium was much like playing outdoors, with nothing but open space beyond the baskets. They conceded it would take time to adjust, but they had another practice scheduled Friday and a shoot-around Saturday morning before the semifinal against Michigan State.

Stevens was stopped by a security guard who mistook him for one of the players. That had happened before to the youngish coach, although not for a couple of years. He said he didn't mind. The guard obviously didn't see him shooting or running, Stevens joked, or he would have asked what he was doing there at all.

Stevens didn't want the Bulldogs to be excluded from the Final Four atmosphere just because they were in their home city.

"I got so many chills in one weekend, it was ridiculous," Nick Rodgers recalled. "I did my best to look around and take it all in and put it in slow motion so I don't forget anything."

Stevens attempted to do the same, although preparation for Michigan State consumed his thoughts. "Stealing moments with Brad" is what Tracy Stevens called time spent with her husband.

"I just would look at him. He was working hard," she said. "There were a few moments here and there, I could see the smile, I could see the joy. He would at least take a few minutes to realize how special this was."

On Thursday night, fans held a Butler-Tarkington neighborhood rally at 56th and Illinois streets. Downtown, the Bulldogs were transported to Weber Grill, where they received a standing ovation from diners. Days before, there might not have been anyone in the restaurant who recognized any of them. Saturation news coverage changed all that.

Mack had been feeling ill but did not divulge his condition. He vomited that night, and trainer Ryan Galloy accompanied him in a taxi from Weber Grill to the Crowne Plaza. Mack lay on the bed, ate some Tums, and took antinausea medication. It was not an ideal scenario for Butler's second-leading scorer to be immobilized less than 48 hours before a national semifinal.

Friday dawned with a controversy involving Mike Krzyzewski and the *Indianapolis Star*. About 30,000 early editions of the newspaper were distributed with graffiti-like marks on a photograph of the Duke coach above a story with the headline DESPISING DUKE. There was an ink-drawn mustache, dark teeth, devil's horns, and a target on Krzyzewski's forehead. Most editions were published with a Krzyzewski portrait minus the artwork. The illustration became a much-discussed national topic because it was featured on various websites.

The story, by Jeff Rabjohns, chronicled how the Blue Devils engender so much hostility among college basketball fans. Duke center Brian Zoubek acknowledged, "We're used to being the hated ones."

But they weren't used to such cartoon treatment. At his news conference that day, Coach K called the illustration "juvenile" and said his seven grandchildren didn't enjoy looking at it.

"We have great kids who go to school, they graduate. If we're going to be despised or hated by anybody because we go to school and we want to win, you know what, that's your problem," Krzyzewski said. "If you don't like it, keep drawing pictures. Try to do them a little bit better than that, though."

Rabjohns, who had nothing to do with the artwork, said he was "horrified that it was above my byline." He first learned about it after receiving e-mails and voice mails early in the morning. Editors from the newspaper met with Krzyzewski, his wife, and Duke officials in the stadium locker room after Friday's practice to apologize. Dennis Ryerson, the *Star*'s editor and vice president, wrote a column of apology in Saturday's editions.

It was oddly coincidental that the April 10 cover of the *Economist* magazine, released at about the same time as the Final Four, featured cartoon treatment—devil's horns, beard, and tail—of the three prime ministerial candidates in Britain's upcoming election. No apology was forthcoming. Coach K was more esteemed than politicians across the Atlantic.

In another coincidence, Butler cheerleaders were featured on the Friday telecast of *The Price Is Right*, a CBS game show that was giving away a trip to the Final Four. Steve Pelych, one of the rappers, and Haley Hileman introduced the prizes. The show was taped February 20, the day the Bulldogs beat Siena and 22 days before Selection Sunday. Cheerleaders from Butler, Michigan State, Duke, and Kansas read the lines, so the show's producers unintentionally had three Final Four schools represented, a higher rate of success than most fans filling out tournament brackets.

In keeping with Stevens's aim to maintain normalcy, five Butler players attended classes Friday morning: Hayward, Shawn Vanzant, Zach Hahn, Andrew Smith, and Chase Stigall. Hayward attended his nine-o'clock math class, spending the final half hour signing autographs and posing for photos. Before that it was "pretty normal," he said.

Little about the week was normal. Hayward's overburdened cell phone filled with voice mails, but one in particular was "really cool," he said. It was from tennis superstar Andy Roddick, who evidently learned that Hayward, a former high school tennis star, was a fan of his.

Butler's noon practice at Lucas Oil Stadium on Friday was open to the public. Free admission was a goodwill gesture by the NCAA, thus allowing those who did not have game tickets to feel a part of the Final Four. Fans walking south on Illinois Street, passing under Union Station on the way to the stadium, could hear the "Butler War Song" blaring on tunnel speakers.

There was gossip that Butler would reenact the movie scene in which a Hickory player stood on a ladder to measure the height of the basket from the floor at Hinkle Fieldhouse. The verdict? Ten feet. Just like the baskets back in Hickory, coach Norman Dale told the Huskers.

"No, we're not doing it," Stevens said with a smile as he walked briskly through a stadium corridor.

Although the 50-minute workouts usually didn't amount to much, the extraordinary turnout for Butler's practice was one of the week's highlights. Doors opened at 11:00 A.M., and seats began filling like a fast-forward version of a time-lapse photo sequence. Stevens conceded that the players—as well as himself and coaching staff—were "wide-eyed" when they walked in.

Two seven-year-old Cub Scouts from Noblesville, Indiana, Sam Van-Meter and Jacob Renner, were told to sit in the front row, near center court. VanMeter's cousin was Nick Rodgers, who heard his name shouted, looked over, and waved to the boys.

By the time the Bulldogs finished practice, the lower bowl that seated 29,000 was nearly full. That represented nearly triple the capacity of Hinkle Fieldhouse, and more than the number of spectators who watched each of the games in San Jose and Salt Lake City. As Stevens told CBS sportscaster Jim Nantz, "But this is Indiana."

Stadium director Mike Fox was genuinely amazed by the scene, calling it "unbelievably memorable." Witnesses said there were more fans in the stadium than attended Michigan State's open practice at Detroit's Ford Field the year before. Avery Jukes said the full lower bowl gave the Bulldogs an idea of what it would be like the next night, against Michigan State.

"You don't get the game feeling in practice," Jukes said. "I think that was an advantage, having all the people there. You knew what it was going to be like the next day, or almost what it was going to be like. When I first walked in, I was like, 'Wow. There's a lot of people.' "

Butler finished more than five minutes early. One by one, players walked around the court and waved to the crowd, which responded with a roar. No one could recall such a sentimental scene during open practice at the Final Four.

Mack stuck to his usual routine. He shot from different spots on the court as assistant coach Terry Johnson rebounded for him. Mack's final shot flipped through the net.

"It was a great feeling that I never thought I would have a chance to experience," Mack said of the setting.

Players' exits were slowed by autograph seekers. Howard signed basketballs, T-shirts, cards, and hats. When he accidentally knocked a pen from a youth's hand, he picked it up and returned it with a smile. The boy smiled back.

Many fans attended from Howard's hometown of Connersville, Indiana. One was his former history teacher Mark Beard, 54, who arranged for 2,500 "Matt Howard/Final Four" pencils to be sold at the high school for 25 cents each. Three of Howard's friends—Tyler Risch and Drew Savoy, both 18, and Brandon Krammes, 23—were in the crowd. Risch arrived an hour early so he could get three seats in the front row.

Krammes was in a life-altering car collision in 2004. He did not need many words to express his excitement.

"I kind of live my life through Matt now," he said.

About an hour after the Bulldogs wrapped up practice and media interviews, they moved six blocks, to Conseco Fieldhouse, to meet perhaps the most devoted supporter of their team. Or of any team, any time.

More miraculous than the Bulldogs' run to the Final Four was that Matt White was alive. More miraculous than that, he was in Indianapolis to witness the games.

White's was the trip of a lifetime, a lifetime he knew would end soon.

He was a high school track star in North Manchester, Indiana, when he was recruited by Butler in 1985. The Bulldogs' upset basketball victory over Notre Dame shortly before his visit to campus influenced his decision to enroll. The former half-miler remembered winning three state college indoor championships and learning that winning was not all about talent.

"The good runners were all talented and worked hard, but the best runners were able to use their talent fearlessly in competition," he said.

He graduated from Butler in 1989 and was employed by Emmis Communications. By age 32 he was general sales manager for a large and profitable Chicago radio station. But in January 2000, days after his 33rd birthday, he was diagnosed with amyotrophic lateral sclerosis, or Lou Gehrig's disease. He was supposed to die within four years.

The degenerative condition had no cause and no cure. White soldiered on despite deteriorating health. An avid golfer, he undertook an odyssey with friends to some of the great courses in Scotland—St. Andrews, Carnoustie, Turnberry—and around the United States. Emmis chairman Jeff Smulyan heard about the golf tour and used his connections to allow White to play Augusta National, home of the Masters.

In 2003, White played his final round at Cypress Point. His friends arranged for him to play one additional hole, the scenic par-3 seventh at Pebble Beach, overlooking Monterey Bay, at twilight. He needed three shots to reach the green, and missed his bogey putt. He rolled in a 15-footer for a glorious double bogey. What followed were cheers and tears, champagne toasts, and the most beautiful sunset anyone there would ever see.

White had to give up golfing. And walking, talking, eating, and all independence. But not thinking. His nimble and contemplative mind was a candle removing any darkness.

White moved to Cape Haze, Florida, to live out his final days near his parents. He was confined to a wheelchair, breathed with a respirator, and took food through a stomach tube. Improbably, he found romance.

When he was in high school, he met a girl named Shartrina on a blind date and dated her for six months. Twenty years later, she gave a presentation in Florida. The same friend who set up the blind date went to visit White and suggested Shartrina tag along. Shartrina did not know what ALS was but, after visiting, began corresponding with White via e-mail. Hundreds of letters ensued. Shartrina, who had two sons from a previous marriage, married White in 2006.

"I have the most treasured gift that I will always have, and that's his letters to me," she said. "They are beautiful. How could I not fall in love with him, and once I had, how could I not marry him?"

White lived to see the Bulldogs play Florida Gulf Coast, in nearby Fort Myers, in December 2007. Through Shartrina, he addressed the team before the game. Afterward, the Bulldogs thanked him and presented him the game ball on his 41st birthday. He told them he wanted a Final Four game ball. What an optimist he was.

White followed Butler's 2010 tournament progress with increasing excitement. If his beloved Bulldogs made it to the Final Four, he announced, he was going. A joke, right? In six years since leaving the hospital, he had been away from home two nights, and never for more than four hours. Joy reigned over the Whites' home when the Bulldogs actually did make it. That sparked the beginning of another odyssey—involving basketball, not golf.

"I thought he was going to jump out of his chair," Shartrina said. "I thought if there is a cure for ALS, it's got to be Butler going to the Final Four."

Arrangements for the trip were made hastily, but carefully. In an e-mail to Stevens, White wrote that it would be "the greatest honor for me" if he could address Butler's team, as he did two seasons before. White's e-mail to Stevens began:

> congratulations on another great win. I don't know bow [how] you stay as cool as a cucumber om thw [on the] sideline. just like larry bird coaching the pacers. that guy was ice.

An anonymous donor allowed use of a private Learjet. White arrived in Indianapolis on Thursday with his wife, an uncle, and a physician. Two Delta Tau Delta fraternity brothers drove White's van, which had liquid food supplies and machines, from Florida to Indiana.

White could communicate with his wife through alphanumeric codes and eye blinks. It took days to write a speech for the Bulldogs that Shartrina delivered and was posted on White's website, cureals.org. Using a special headset, White tapped out each letter on the computer with tiny facial movements. His address began:

> Thank you for letting me be a part of your day. It's nice to see many of you again, and great to meet the rest of you.
>
> One of my favorite characters from history is polar explorer Ernest Shackleton. An amazing man, his selfless acts of courage are better known and marveled at today than when they occurred almost 100 years ago. I like Shackleton because he repeatedly overcame impossible odds in a hopeless situation.
>
> In 1914, two years after losing the race to the South Pole, Ernest Shackleton set out to cross the entire continent of Antarctica, a trip of almost 2,000 miles. He and his crew of 27 men left Buenos Aires, Argentina, in

mid-December, late spring in the Southern Hemisphere. On approaching land, Shackleton and crew encountered much more ice than they thought they would. Soon their ship, the *Endurance,* was hopelessly stuck in the ice pack. The crew spent the rest of that Antarctic summer in a futile attempt to dig themselves free.

Finally, efforts were abandoned and preparations made to winter on the ship. Locked within the ice, the *Endurance* drifted, all the while being crushed by the moving ice. The ship was sinking. As it did, the men left the relative comfort of their ship behind. With three small lifeboats and all the provisions they could carry, the men set off across the ice in search of navigable water or land. With little food and meager shelter, the men faced near-certain death in the hostile environment.

Against all odds and with another winter upon them, they finally made it to the northern edge of the pack. Encountering open water, the men sailed the three small lifeboats to a remote and barren island called Elephant Island. There was no hope for rescue, so Shackleton chose five men to accompany him on a desperate mission. The closest inhabited island was South Georgia Island, 800 miles away. In a 22-foot lifeboat, they accomplished the impossible, surviving a 17-day journey in the dead of winter, through the world's worst seas. Unbelievably, they made it to South Georgia Island. From there, Shackleton commandeered a larger ship to rescue the men he'd left behind.

Throughout the entire two-year ordeal, not one man was lost.

Much has been written and said about Shackleton and his men. How did they do it? Facing certain death time and again, how did they all survive? I think it was their tremendous resolve to survive. To keep moving on, regardless of the obstacles they faced. They also lived in the moment, never looking back or too far forward. They dealt with only what was in front of them and moved on. They never panicked, either. Regardless of the situation, they trusted in Shackleton and in each other completely. They were a tremendously courageous group of men.

So, why am I here, and why did I tell that story? Quite simply, I'm here because you're going to win a national championship, and I want to be here to see it. And the story? The story is all about you, and maybe a little about me.

Speaking through Shartrina, White continued by telling the Bulldogs it was 10 years ago that he was diagnosed with ALS, that he could expect

to live four years. He made it, he told them, by living like Shackleton and
his men. He told the Bulldogs he tried to live like they play, and that they
were his inspiration.

He continued,

> You have tremendous resolve to survive, to keep moving on, regardless of
> the obstacles you face. You also live in the moment. Never looking back or
> too far forward, you deal with only what is in front of you and you move
> on. You never panic, either. Regardless of the situation, you trust in Coach
> and in each other completely. You are a tremendously courageous group
> of men.
>
> Thank you for inviting me to address you today. I count this opportu-
> nity as one of my greatest honors, and I hope you have gotten even a frac-
> tion of the benefit that I have gotten from being here.
>
> Thank you.

The players applauded. They approached the Whites, one coach, one
player, after another. Nored thanked them for inspiring the Bulldogs.

"I'll always remember this," Nored said.

Nored remembered it vividly enough to tell his teammates before tip-
off against Michigan State: Let's give Matt White a reason to know it's
great to live for two more days, at least.

Matt White's journey to reach the Final Four was like none other. So was
Rob Chapman's.

Chapman, a 1987 Butler graduate, taught band students at Concordia International School in Shanghai, China, where he lived with his
wife and four-year-old son. He had been rising in the middle of the
night—there was a 12-hour time difference—to watch Butler's tournament games online.

After the Bulldogs made the Final Four, he asked himself if he could
get there to see it. A four-day weekend was coming up, but it was against
school policy to extend that with personal leave. On Monday morning
he went to ask the school principal anyway. The principal was out for the
day, but before Chapman could explain, the assistant principal asked him:
"What can we do to get you back to the Final Four?"

It was up to the administrative team to decide. Within a day, the head
of the school approved Chapman's trip. Chapman's wife, a former Long

Beach State cheerleader who had been to two women's Final Fours, encouraged him. The *Hoosiers* angle resonated with him because he was an extra in the movie, cast with others in Butler's pep band as the South Bend Central band.

Chapman had his photo taken with Butler attire in front of the Concordia school sign, and later had his photo taken in front of a Butler sign wearing Concordia attire. He found airfare for less than $1,000 for a 7,000-mile flight to Chicago that took 14 hours. In Indianapolis, he slept on the princess-themed bed of a friend's six-year-old daughter. Anything to see the Dawgs.

He contacted Butler's alumni office in an attempt to secure tickets, but none was available. He kept searching websites of online brokers, finally settling for seats high in the 600 level. He reunited with friends and former band members, some of whom he had not seen in 20 years.

"To me, I was just a proud alum and big college basketball fan who all his life has wanted to attend a Final Four," he said via e-mail. "The planets all aligned this year, and it worked out for me to attend not only in my 'hometown,' but with my home team. . . . I just had to travel 7,000-plus miles to get there!"

Distance was a Final Four coverage theme, with recurring references to the six miles from Hinkle Fieldhouse to Lucas Oil Stadium. That badly underestimated the expedition.

As with Chapman, the Bulldogs' journey crossed oceans, continents, time zones. Including travel by Hayward and Mack to Colorado and New Zealand, the summer tour of Italy, and games at Anaheim, New York, Birmingham, San Jose, and Salt Lake City, the distance was about 44,000 miles. That equaled more than 7,000 trips from fieldhouse to stadium, or nearly six times around the Earth.

The Road to the Final Four was longer than anyone presupposed.

Butler's players received another ovation when they went to dinner at Palomino on Friday night. When they returned to the hotel, they headed for bed and thanked floor security employees for being with them throughout the hectic weekend.

Stevens and his wife had previously agreed to cochair that night's inaugural Coaches' Huddle event, which benefited the American Cancer Society. They kept the commitment, although Stevens, understandably, left long before the late-night party and dancing. Some of the sport's most prominent coaches attended the event at Union Station, sitting with the 400 who purchased tickets. More than $45,000 was raised.

This was only the second Final Four that Stevens ever attended. His first was in 2001, his first year on Butler's staff, and Duke won the championship. Stevens's view from his seat was terrible. He vowed not to attend another unless the Bulldogs were playing. He had an up-close-and-personal view in 2010.

For the weekend, he came into possession of a talisman—a tie clasp commemorating Butler's 1929 national championship. The granddaughter of Cleon Reynolds, who played for that Butler team, gave the tie clasp to Collier, who in turn delivered it to the Butler coach. Maybe it wouldn't bring the luck that a piece of net did for the Horizon League championship game, but it wouldn't hurt.

On Saturday morning, former Butler players mingled with the current ones before an alumni brunch at the Crowne Plaza, the epicenter of Butler Nation. J. J. DeBrosse, a former Butler director of sports marketing, was corporate and athletics sales manager at the hotel. He placed his own framed collectibles in Stevens's suite, decorated the wall of the bar with Butler items, and had Butler banners decorating the interior. The hotel borrowed basketball jerseys for bar staff, making it look like homecoming weekend.

Brandon Crone traveled from Sweden, where he played professionally, to be there. So many former players made it to Indianapolis, in fact, that Joel Cornette asserted it would be a Final Four record for one school.

"I didn't know one of the greatest moments of my life would have nothing to do with me," said Cornette, the center on the Sweet Sixteen team of 2003.

Brian Ligon, a third-year dental student at Meharry Medical College in Nashville, Tennessee, was as immersed in the experience as if he were playing. He was the center on the Sweet Sixteen team that nearly beat national champion Florida in 2007. Another ex-Butler player, point guard Thomas Jackson, couldn't make it back from his pro team in Germany. Yet his thoughts echoed those of the others:

"This is by far the most memorable moment of my collegiate basketball career at Butler, even though I am not a part of this team."

They felt connected for two reasons: the Bulldogs had been building toward such a climax throughout the 2000s, and a national championship had long been a goal.

"That's what's great about this," said Drew Streicher, a former player in his second year of Indiana University's medical school. "Even back then, the ultimate goal was to go as far as you can go. Why set your goals any lower?"

Cornette had recently lost his job as an assistant coach when Iowa fired former Butler coach Todd Lickliter and his staff. Cornette said he kept a respectful distance from the team but felt close to these Bulldogs. Asked how they compared to his own teams, he replied simply: they had more talent. The realization was humbling.

"They're about as cold-blooded a team as I've seen in playing and coaching," Cornette said.

Many Bulldogs of the 2000s attended the alumni event, whose main speaker was Lickliter. Although Lickliter's three-year Iowa tenure resulted in a 38-58 record and player departures, he was warmly received by the Butler audience. Fong bragged that his first hire as president was Lickliter. After going more than four decades without a Sweet Sixteen appearance, Butler made it twice under the coach. Lickliter joked that he made an important contribution to the program.

"I left," he said, "and turned it over to Brad Stevens."

Signs of Final Four fever permeated the room, including an actual sign. Fong held up a poster from the 1980 Final Four, held in Indianapolis at Market Square Arena, that featured Tony Hinkle's signature. Joe Forgey, an Indianapolis-area dentist and Butler graduate, stood to reveal a new Bulldog tattoo on his arm. He had bet his sons that if the Bulldogs ever reached a Final Four, he would get the tattoo.

The Bulldogs were making their mark in ways they could not have foreseen.

Butler's defense was not easily explained nor easily solved. It was man-to-man that sometimes resembled a zone. Butler freshmen struggled to absorb it. Often, opponents never did.

To play offense against Butler was to be a trout swimming into a fisherman's net. Move about the net, but there was no escaping the net. Nose ahead, but there was no splitting the net.

Want easy baskets? Buy some for Easter. Butler did not sell them. Throughout the NCAA Tournament, opponents were drawn into Butler's vortex, playing as the Bulldogs wanted them to play.

Four tourney opponents all scored less than 60 points, and they shot a collective 42 percent. Beginning in February, 13 of Butler's 14 opponents scored under 60 points, and 20 of 21 averaged less than 1 point per possession—a more accurate measure of defensive efficiency.

The Bulldogs weren't winning low-scoring games because they intentionally slowed the tempo. If the pace lagged, it was because opponents needed so many seconds of the 35-second clock to find a shot they wanted, or would be forced to take.

"We didn't care about tempo," Stevens said. "We weren't trying to pound the ball into the ground. We just wanted to be hard to score on."

Michigan State coach Tom Izzo compared the Bulldogs to two Big Ten teams: Purdue, "because they have toughness," and Wisconsin, "because they don't take chances." Butler was, in a word, solid.

Because Horizon League coaches confronted the Bulldogs so often, they understood them better than major-conference colleagues. Cleveland State coach Gary Waters said Butler approximated what coach Bob Knight once employed at Indiana. That is, Butler defenders stayed in front of the ball.

"So you have to shoot a contested shot every time you shoot it," Waters said. "Every time there's any degree of penetration, there are at least two people ready to help out against you."

Moreover, the Bulldogs were committed to preventing transition. Wright State coach Brad Brownell said Butler made so few turnovers that fast-break opportunities were infrequent anyway. It was always five against five. That required opponents to execute a half-court offense, "and most teams in America aren't great at that," Waters said.

Opponents became caught in the net. They floundered.

Pete Campbell, a pro in Germany who played for Butler's 30-4 team in 2007–08, followed the Bulldogs from afar and suggested that they were searching for identity early in the season. Eureka! They found it in the best half-court defense in the country.

"They took the Butler defensive scheme and basically perfected it," Campbell said.

Stevens agreed that this was the best defensive team he had seen in his 10 years at Butler. His contention was that a team must excel at something, and that something was defense. Earlier in the season, Butler's defense was "close to atrocious," Stevens said.

"Our opportunity to win has to be focused on what we're best at," he said. "We have to soar with something."

Butler players repeatedly stated defense was played collectively, not individually. Unidentified coaches who had scouting reports published before the semifinal game reiterated that theme. One coach theorized that what made Butler so effective was that its two best offensive players, Hayward and Mack, didn't guard the other team's two best scorers.

That was left to Veasley, who could guard all five positions at 6-foot-3, and Nored. Such a divided workload was uncommon.

"As a team, their intelligence level on defense is incredible," the scout wrote. "Their reaction to when one of their teammates makes a mistake is impeccable. They see it happen and everyone reacts immediately, giving just the right amount of help and then sprinting back to their man."

The Bulldogs were effective at preventing second shots. Although Hayward was more renowned for his offensive versatility, his proficiency as a defensive rebounder might have been more important to the team. After opponents missed shots, Hayward invariably snatched the ball away.

"It's remarkable how well he flies in above the rim and cleans up," Stevens said. "Sometimes you base your matchups on the fact that you want him to get balls for you."

If the Spartans had an advantage in Indianapolis, it was their experience in the Final Four and in the venue. They defeated Kansas 67–62 and Louisville 64–52 in the Midwest Regional at Lucas Oil Stadium on their way to the final game in Detroit in 2009. Indeed, Michigan State was 7-0 in NCAA Tournament games played in the city. The April 3 semifinal against Butler came on the 10th anniversary of Michigan State's 89–76 victory over Florida for the 2000 NCAA championship at the RCA Dome.

The Spartans weren't counting on the Bulldogs being distracted at home. Nor were the Spartans discounting them.

"That would be completely dumb," Michigan State's Draymond Green said.

Butler, the only team in the tournament to beat both a No. 1 and a No. 2 seed, started and ended the season ranked 10th in the country. So Izzo said, "I'm not drinking the Kool-Aid" of a Cinderella story. (Strangely, the Kool-Aid expression derived from the infamy of a Butler graduate, Jim Jones. The cult leader induced the 1978 mass suicide of more than 900 people who ingested a poisoned, flavored drink in Guyana.)

Butler advanced despite trailing in all four tournament games, but the Spartans lived even more dangerously. Their collective margin of 13 points in four victories—over New Mexico State 70–67, Maryland 85–83, Northern Iowa 59–52, and Tennessee 70–69—was the smallest in tournament history. Certainly, the Spartans missed the injured Kalin Lucas, but Durrell Summers was playing spectacularly. He was averaging 20 points in the tournament and shooting 53 percent on 3-pointers. After making only 26 from the arc all season, he had 16 in four tournament games.

As with the Bulldogs, the Spartans' mantra was: Next man up.

"That's a testament to what they've built and to Coach Izzo and his staff," Stevens said. "It's a little daunting to have to play them, but as a hoops junkie, it's been fun to kind of study them and learn from them."

Although the Crowne Plaza was merely two blocks from the stadium, it would have been imprudent for Butler players to wade through crowds to reach the entrance. A bus ride of about eight blocks was required to transport them there. Before the game, so many fans waited outside the hotel to cheer the Bulldogs that witnesses said the scene reminded them more of a movie than real life.

Upon arrival at the stadium, Butler players were directed to the green room to accommodate CBS producers putting together an opening for Monday night's championship game. The three other teams did likewise. Players dribbled and passed the ball, and recited lines from a script. Scenes from the two finalists would be inserted into a music video for a new song, "Hello, Good Morning," by recording artist P. Diddy.

Among the fans making the pilgrimage to see the Bulldogs were three members from the family with whom Shawn Vanzant lived during high school. The father, Jeff Litton, and sons Josh and Zach made the 14-hour drive from Tampa, Florida, and were rewarded with seats 10 rows from courtside.

"They don't know how much that means to me," Vanzant said.

The mother, Lisa Litton, and son Chase stayed in Florida. Chase had a summer tournament game, and Lisa, battling breast cancer and lupus, was in no condition for a long car trip. She would watch the first half in a restaurant and listen to the second half on her car radio, yelling and sending Shawn frequent texts.

The student section had open seating, so some Butler students arrived at the stadium as early as 10:00 P.M. Friday to stand in line. They brought food and laptops, waiting for a game 20 hours away. Those students were not allowed in the gate first, having to wait for Butler's dance team. But the dancers admired their classmates' zeal, so they assembled in the second and third rows so the all-night veterans could sit in the front row.

Ryan Waggoner, the student body president the year before, dressed as the biblical David. He borrowed a shepherd's costume from his church's Easter pageant and brought his staff and slingshot, ready to slay the Goliaths from Michigan State.

Butler and West Virginia fans stood in line next to each other. They chanted, "Da'Sean!" and, "Butler!" back and forth, combining the school name with that of Mountaineer star Da'Sean Butler. Indiana's governor, Mitch Daniels, sat in the stadium between a couple of Hoosier hoops legends, Bobby "Slick" Leonard, who played for Indiana's 1953 national champions and coached the Pacers to three ABA titles in the 1970s, and Bobby Plump.

The oversized crowd wasn't going to affect the Bulldogs. The previous day's rehearsal helped in that regard, and Jukes said the players couldn't see 70,000 people all at once anyway.

"The majority of those are over your head, and you're not going to be looking up at the crowd," he said. "If you look straight out at the stands, you see no more people than you see in Hinkle."

An hour before tip-off, Hayward stopped in the middle of the court and gazed at the spectacle surrounding him. The stadium was slowly filling with fans, many dressed in Butler blue. The colors, the banners, the TV cameras, the courtside media.

Hayward stared, looked around, nodded his head. Yep, this was it. This is what the Bulldogs had prepared for since losing to LSU more than 12 months ago. This is why he began hooping when he was four. This is why he gave up tennis. This was the payoff for Auckland and Anaheim, New York and Birmingham, San Jose and Salt Lake City. For all those Horizon League cities in Indiana, Illinois, Michigan, Ohio, and Wisconsin.

On the other hand, it was basketball. As Mack repeatedly said, they had been playing it most of their lives. It was a virtual home game for the Bulldogs, so no need to change any routines now. That included lineup introductions. Blue II was there. So when Howard forgot to pet him after his name was announced, he went back, stooped down, and stroked America's Dog.

At the game's beginning, Michigan State guard Korie Lucious showed off his shooting stroke. On each of the Spartans' first two possessions he sank 3-pointers, sending them ahead 6–0. As usual, Stevens walked up and down the sideline with arms folded.

Hayward responded with two 3s of his own, coming off assists by Nored and then Mack. Mack capped a 7-0 run with a free throw, and Butler went ahead 7–6. Less than four minutes into the game, Howard bumped knees with a Michigan State player and was called for a foul. He went to the bench and was replaced by Jukes.

Fouls became an issue on both sides. Howard wasn't on the bench long, and after he returned, Michigan State forward Raymar Morgan fouled him on the perimeter. It was Morgan's second foul, benching him with 15 minutes left in the half. Bodies tangled while the Spartans had the ball, and Howard picked up a second foul just 14 seconds after reentering the game. So Howard sat again, and in to replace him was Andrew Smith, who had played high school ball 12 miles away little more than 12 months before.

Draymond Green, the Big Ten's sixth man of the year, sparked the Spartans after he checked in. He carried 235 pounds on a 6-foot-6 frame but demonstrated sure hands and nimble feet. His jump shot completed an 8-0 run that pushed Michigan State's lead to 14–7. After Hayward's leaner ended Butler's drought, Green scored on a layup.

"It's the Draymond Green Show at that end of the floor," CBS announcer Jim Nantz said.

Hayward sank his fourth successive shot, a nifty fadeaway, to cut the Spartans' lead to 16–11. He had 10 of the Bulldogs' 11 points. Mack scored the first non-Hayward field goal, a pull-up jumper that trimmed Michigan State's margin to 18–14.

Morgan's return to the court was brief. With 10 minutes left in the half, he was called for a third foul on Veasley's offensive rebound. Coach Tom Izzo angrily stomped his foot at the call, and the Spartans' star forward sat again. Izzo conceded afterward that Morgan allowed the fouls to bother him.

After the Bulldogs inbounded the ball, Mack spotted an opening, attacked the goal from the left, laid in the ball right-handed, and was fouled. He made his free throw, closing the gap to 18–17. A couple of minutes later, Mack caught the ball in transition, pulled up before the arc, and drilled a 3-pointer.

Michigan State 22, Butler 20.

"You can't allow him to run into that jump shot off the dribble. He'll make you pay," CBS analyst Clark Kellogg said. "I call that breaking it and taking it, pardner."

After Hayward's pass intended for Smith sailed out of bounds, Kellogg recapitulated the criticisms of the Butler sophomore.

"One of the things I'd like to see is Gordon Hayward be more assertive," the TV analyst said. "You got the game he has, you have to be thinking about trying to score the ball and putting pressure on your defender at all times."

Five minutes before halftime, Zach Hahn had an open 3-pointer at the end of a fast break. A field goal would have put Butler back in front, but Hahn missed from the arc for the seventh-straight time over three tournament games.

A collision left Hayward with a puffy lip, and he said later that his mouthpiece prevented him from losing teeth. It wasn't only his lip that was swelling. So was his point total. He rattled in a 3-pointer that gave him 13 points and pulled the Bulldogs within 24–23.

Hayward and Mack had 22 of Butler's 23 points.

Durrell Summers's layup, off a deft pass from Lucious, expanded the Spartans' lead to 28–23 as the clock dipped under three minutes. Stevens called a 30-second time-out so the Bulldogs could regroup.

Summers missed a 3-point attempt that was rebounded by Veasley, who was fouled on the play. Veasley sank two free throws. Finally, someone other than Hayward or Mack had scored for Butler.

Michigan State took a 28–25 lead into the final minute of the half, calling a time-out. However, the Spartans couldn't set up a shot because the ball was stolen by Nored. He passed to Vanzant, who sent the ball on to Mack. Beyond the arc, in transition, ball in Mack's hands.

The Bulldogs welcomed that scenario anytime. Aim and swish. Mack's 3-pointer tied the score at 28.

Summers missed a 3-pointer for Michigan State, and Stevens called a time-out with 2.5 seconds on the clock. Students in the Butler section jumped up and down, delighted that their Bulldogs would be no worse than tied after trailing by seven.

Howard came off the bench to inbound the ball, but his pass was deflected as the clock ran out. He played only four minutes, duplicating his four-minute first half against Kansas State.

Halftime: 28–28.

Hayward and Mack had all but three of the Bulldogs' points. Butler led 10–2 in points off turnovers, underscoring Kellogg's assertion that the Spartans, without the injured Lucas, lacked enough ball handlers.

Lucious began the second half with a 3-pointer, just as he began the first half. Then two free throws by Hayward and Veasley's rebound basket returned the lead to Butler, 32–31, for the first time since the score was 7–6. Mack, dehydrated after losing so many fluids two nights before, developed leg cramps and was in and out of the game thereafter.

Howard, attempting to draw Morgan's fourth foul, threw up a wild shot and didn't get the official's call. Stevens spread his arms, questioning why there was no foul. Yet the Bulldogs were seizing control, pulling ahead 38–33 when Howard slipped underneath for his only basket of the game.

"Unless Michigan State commits to running more," Kellogg warned viewers, "this game favors Butler in a possession-by-possession game."

Howard picked up a third foul with more than 15 minutes to play, returning to the bench. Summers freed himself on a back-door cut and dunked, cutting the Bulldogs' lead to 39–37. That prompted an agitated response from Nored, who pleaded with his arms, wondering why no teammate came to help.

After Jukes's rebound basket, Hayward stole the ball and finally induced Morgan's fourth foul. Hayward made the first of two free throws before another Butler steal, by Veasley, resulted in a dunk. The Bulldogs' 44–37 lead was their biggest, and the seven-point deficit was the biggest for Michigan State in the tournament.

Yet it was not easy for the Bulldogs to protect that lead. Not with Mack on the bench as the trainer used a massage gel to treat the leg cramps. Not with Howard unable to contribute much.

Howard collided with Green or teammate Nored midway through the first half, causing the Butler center to blink his eyes and shake his head. Howard soon made two free throws to make the lead 46–41 and went to the bench afterward. Howard, though woozy, returned to action a few minutes later.

The game's rhythm was slow and rigorous, unfavorable to the Spartans. Green picked up his fourth foul, and Hayward made the first of two free throws. Six minutes remained, and Butler led 47–41.

"This has been Butler's way of winning all season," Kellogg said. "Get out to the lead and win it possession by possession."

Butler couldn't score from the field but stayed ahead because Michigan State couldn't, either. Howard twice missed underneath, extending the Bulldogs' streak of consecutive misses to eight. Howard picked up his fourth foul with 3:06 on the clock, and Green made the first of two free throw attempts to hack the margin to 47–44. Green missed the second, adding to the Spartans' frustrations at the foul line.

Kellogg called Hahn an "Allen wrench" because the sharpshooter had one purpose: to make 3s. Instead, Hahn extended the Bulldogs' streak of misses to 10. The Spartans had held Northern Iowa without a field goal for the closing 10 minutes of that victory, and they were smothering Butler, too.

The Bulldogs needed Mack, who instead was stretching on the sideline or clapping encouragement. They needed Howard, whose condition worsened after taking an elbow to the head when he reentered the game. Howard was wobbly when he went to the bench during a time-out with 2:36 on the clock.

"You're done, man," trainer Ryan Galloy told him.

Coming out of the time-out, Nored stole the ball and passed to Hayward, who delivered the ball to Vanzant. Vanzant was fouled and made the first of two free throws, but Green's leaner quickly halved Butler's lead to 48–46.

Butler's successive misses reached 11 on Hayward's 3-point attempt. However, Vanzant rushed under the basket, tore the ball away from teammate Jukes for a one-armed rebound, and passed out to Hayward in the same motion. Vanzant "came out of nowhere," Hayward said later. Hayward took one long step for a layup, scoring Butler's first field goal in nearly 11 minutes and restoring the four-point lead, at 50–46.

Jukes feared Vanzant was going to knock the ball away and out of bounds. Instead, it was the play of the day. Like the moment when Howard plunged out of bounds in the Horizon League championship game, it was a play Stevens could record and use as a portrait in hustle.

"To make a play like that for my teammates, I can't explain how I feel," said Vanzant, who had averaged about one rebound a game in his 99-game college career. If Jukes wanted that rebound, Vanzant teased, "maybe he should get some hops."

Victory was not assured. Far from it. On the Michigan State bench, the injured Kalin Lucas pounded his chest, imploring his teammates to show heart. They did.

Nored fouled with 1:18 on the clock, scowling because he thought he had touched nothing but the ball. Summers sank the first free throw. His second attempt, a miss, was rebounded by teammate Delvon Roe. Hayward's foul sent Green back to the foul line with 56 seconds to play. After the Spartans made only two of eight free throws in the half, Green made both of his. It was a three-point possession, as good as a 3-point basket.

Butler 50, Michigan State 49.

Stevens sent the ailing Mack back into the game, and the Bulldogs let Hayward bring the ball upcourt. Nored drove toward the basket, leaning in for a shot. The ball hit the top of the glass and bounded around the rim, appearing as if it might expand the Bulldogs' lead. The ball bounced out.

Time-out, Michigan State. Twenty-three seconds remained.

The Spartans were not apprehensive. This was business as usual. For Michigan State's fifth-straight tournament game, the margin was one point inside the final 150 seconds.

The Bulldogs and their coach held their composure, too, as they had for more than three months. In the huddle they said to each other, "This is Butler basketball." Bring it on.

"A lot of people want to take the last shot," Nored said later. "We want to guard the last shot."

The Spartans eventually worked the ball around to Green, who dribbled into the foul lane about eight feet from the basket. He was closely guarded by Hayward, who reached and deflected the shot. Hayward conceded he might have brushed Green on the arm. Green said, "Maybe I did get smacked," but chided himself for not going up stronger.

On the Michigan State sideline, Izzo extended his arms, pleading for a foul. The TV replay was inconclusive. Kellogg said there was no foul.

"Oh, that's good basketball there," the CBS announcer said.

After the miss, Green fouled Nored. It was Green's fifth foul, and he was gone. Like the ancient Spartans at Thermopylae, they were running out of warriors. Lucas was out, Lucious tweaked his ankle, Delvon Roe's knee was injured, Chris Allen's arch was sore. Two former walk-ons played important minutes.

With 6.1 seconds on the clock, the Spartans were not out of it yet. Not with Nored at the foul line. In four previous tournament games, he shot 25 percent from there. Anxiety among Butler fans was manifested by five women watching from the basement of an Indianapolis home, holding hands and praying Nored would make his free throws.

There was a hush at Hinkle Fieldhouse, where thousands watched on four large screens.

After handling the ball, Nored puffed his cheeks, took a deep breath, and shot. Good.

Before his second attempt, he licked his lips as sweat poured from his forehead and face. He shot. Good again.

Butler 52, Michigan State 49.

The Spartans rolled in the ball so that no one would touch it and start the clock, and Izzo railed against the officials after calling time-out. Five-tenths of a second came off the clock, and he argued that no time should have been lost. Izzo was so unhinged—frustration accumulated—that Green wrapped his arms around the coach and walked him down the sideline so a technical foul wouldn't be assessed. Officials went to the replay monitor and put two-tenths of a second back on the clock. So it was 5.8.

Butler led 52–49, so only a three-point possession could save Michigan State's season. Stevens knew what to do. So did his former DePauw University coach, Bill Fenlon. The two had discussed such strategy many times:

If ahead by three points, should a team intentionally foul, or risk being tied by a 3-pointer? Fenlon studied a statistician's conclusion that the odds are much greater of winning if the team leading did foul.

"Guys don't know the numbers. They haven't thought about it," Fenlon said. "To me, there's really no decision to make."

This decision was up to Stevens. His sideline composure remedied such moments. If he kept cool, so would the Bulldogs. If he exuded confidence, the Bulldogs would play confidently. Sitting in the stadium, Fenlon was apprehensive, knowing he had talked his protégé into fouling.

"Man, if this screws up," Fenlon thought, "it's going to be all my fault."

The Bulldogs tried to foul. At midcourt, Jukes swiped at Morgan's waist, but nothing was called. The clock ticked. The ball went to Lucious, who was emphatically fouled by Vanzant. Lucious had his back to the basket, giving him no chance to shoot from behind the arc and be awarded three free throws.

With two seconds on the clock, Lucious sank his first free throw. All he could do afterward was intentionally miss, then hope a teammate would tap in the rebound for a tying basket. Lucious's free throw bounded off the back rim, but Hayward leaped high for his ninth rebound. Defensive rebounds were indeed Hayward's specialty.

He stuck his tongue out and raised his right arm, extending his index finger in the sign for No. 1.

Final score: Butler 52, Michigan State 50.

"Butler is going on to the national championship game," Nantz proclaimed. "What a story unfolding in this NCAA Tournament."

No one was more relieved than Fenlon. He texted Stevens:

> You are coachable after all.

Stevens texted back:

> After 33 years, I finally listened.

The Bulldogs scored eight points over the closing 12 minutes; sent a 25 percent free throw shooter to the foul line with the game on the line; and netted four baskets from players other than Hayward and Mack. And Butler won.

The Bulldogs shot 30.6 percent, the worst figure for a national semifinal winner since 1958. They missed all seven of their 3-point attempts in the second half. And Butler won.

The Bulldogs played most of the second half without their Nos. 2 and 3 scorers, Mack and Howard. And Butler won.

Izzo called it smashmouth basketball, a Michigan State trademark. And Butler won.

Twenty-five straight, and counting.

Izzo complained about the officiating, with some justification. Michigan State caught no breaks. However, the foul totals were close: Michigan State 21, Butler 17. Izzo had no complaints about the outcome.

"I felt like if I was not playing, I would be a Butler fan," the Michigan State coach said. "I like the way they play. They're physical. I like their story. I like the whole thing."

Indiana's governor thought it was revealing that Izzo mentioned how rough the Bulldogs played, that the coach was almost whining about it.

"You're used to people saying that Michigan State pushed them all over the floor," Mitch Daniels said. "And for them to say that these Butler kids were too physical for them was terrific."

After 40 minutes of fierce action, Butler was 40 minutes away from a national championship and the smallest school to play for one in 40 years. Not since Jacksonville University took on John Wooden's UCLA dynasty in 1970 had such a small school been such a short distance from such a big victory.

Fittingly, the Bulldogs won because they forced a key stop at the end. Hayward's blocked shot was an encore to his steal against Murray State. He scored 19 points. But as usual, offense did not produce the victory.

"People will look at us, and think about us, and wonder how we did this," Veasley said. "They'll go back and watch all five games and realize that our defense is one of the best defenses in the nation."

Facts supported Veasley. Butler became the first team to reach the championship game by holding five opponents to fewer than 60 points since the shot clock was introduced in 1985–86. The Bulldogs' victory was their first over Michigan State since December 17, 1969, which happened to be coach Tony Hinkle's last season.

There was subdued celebrating in Butler's locker room. All along the Bulldogs were aiming at a two-game weekend. Besides, the availability of Howard and Mack for the championship game was uncertain.

"If they're not ready, then somebody else is going to have to step up and play well in their place," Stevens said.

Reaction to Butler's victory was more demonstrative nationwide, even worldwide.

A contingent of Butler fans watched from the Sadie Thompson Inn in Pago Pago, American Samoa. A gun was fired in the air outside the home of a missionary in Haiti, where two Butler graduates working on earthquake cleanup watched on satellite TV. On the eastern side of the island of Hispaniola, a former Butler football manager watched with teachers from a boarding school in the Dominican Republic.

Barry Collier walked up a Lucas Oil Stadium aisle, high-fiving fans and shaking hands. He stopped to hug Ed Kelly, a California high school coach who had been an assistant on Collier's first Butler staff. Twenty years before, in a cramped office, Collier first shared his vision with Kelly, who remembered goal number one: to compete for a national championship.

A former Butler football player from Inverness, Florida, was inside the stadium as he received 50 congratulatory texts from friends back home within three minutes of the victory. A Butler graduate who taught high school in Henryville, Indiana, was crying and shaking so much while trying to film the scene that she blurred the video. Another Butler graduate, Justin Brown, tears streaming down his face, hugged his six-year-old son, who confidently predicted victory during the long scoring drought. "This was bigger than basketball for me. I cannot imagine something like this ever happening again in my life," said Brown, a former high school player from North Vernon, Indiana.

Euphoria enveloped the campus, much as it did when the Bulldogs beat Kansas State to reach the Final Four. Students again gathered on barricaded Hampton Drive, some sprinting there after watching on large screens inside Hinkle Fieldhouse.

While Dan Wojcik, the Butler tennis letterman who sat in the UTEP section in San Jose, was cheering from the stadium, his daughter was delivering a baby boy in Austin, Texas. After giving birth, Wojcik's daughter commandeered a hospital room and watched on TV with her mother, alarming nurses who didn't know what the clatter was about.

A 44-year-old fan collapsed in his wife's arms, weeping. Fans on spring break watched from Hawaii, where a husband and wife were surrounded in an airport bar after making it known they were Butler alumni. By the end of the game, everyone in the ESPN Club on Disney World's Boardwalk Waterfront was cheering the Bulldogs. Butler students studying in Washington, D.C., for the semester, plus alumni, celebrated in the Penn Quarter sports bar.

Similar scenes played out across the land. The Bulldogs, representing a small university that many Americans had never heard of, had not won the national championship. But the Bulldogs had won their hearts.

CHAPTER 9

THE LONG SHOT

For the NCAA championship game, Duke was cast as a killjoy against Butler. Yet Duke, a private school of high academic standards featuring a collection of scrappers, resembled Butler as much as any other school in the NCAA Tournament. According to the NCAA, the combined enrollment of Butler (4,200) and Duke (6,340) would be the smallest for a national championship game since San Francisco met LaSalle in 1955.

Duke used 52 percent shooting on 3-pointers to defeat West Virginia 78–57 in the second semifinal, on April 3. The Blue Devils' big three—Jon Scheyer (23), Kyle Singler (21), and Nolan Smith (19)—combined for 63 points, or 6 more than West Virginia's team. No team in the nation had a higher-scoring trio than Duke's.

Scheyer sank 5 3-pointers, Smith 4, and Singler 3. Duke tied a record—set by UNLV in 1987 against Indiana—by sinking 13 from the arc in a national semifinal. The Mountaineers tried to stop Duke with man-to-man and zone defenses, and neither worked. Scheyer said the Blue Devils had prepared for anything.

Or almost anything. They hadn't prepared to play the championship game in the opponent's hometown. Scheyer was from suburban Chicago, about a three-hour drive from Indianapolis, and conceded he didn't know much about Butler while growing up.

Coach Mike Krzyzewski was going to fill him in, as well as the rest of the Blue Devils. Considering that the Bulldogs consecutively beat Syracuse, Kansas State, and Michigan State—and were the only team to beat both a No. 1 and a No. 2 seed—they probably had the toughest road to the championship game, Krzyzewski suggested.

"I think they're a very outstanding basketball team who, because Butler hasn't been to the Final Four, create that Cinderella thing," Coach K said. "But they're one of the best teams in the country, or else they wouldn't be playing for the national championship. They've earned it."

Butler coach Brad Stevens scouted the game, and when he finally retired to his hotel room, his wife, Tracy, was waiting. She wanted to see her husband before taking their two young children home. She smiled at him, a figure of encouragement amid the tumult.

"You guys are playing for the national championship," she reminded him.

"Yeah," Stevens replied. "But we're playing Duke."

The next day's dawn brought Easter Sunday, and several Butler players attended worship services. Garrett Butcher accompanied Gordon Hayward to Brownsburg for services at Hayward's home church, Messiah Lutheran.

Harder than getting up early was getting out of the sanctuary. Hayward accepted congratulations, and he autographed church bulletins.

"People were swarming us, which is really weird, especially at church," Hayward said. "You don't ever get that. It was obviously exciting for all of them."

At the St. John African Methodist Episcopal Church, where Ronald Nored's aunt preached, Lenore Williams told the congregation that they were there "to not only celebrate Butler, but also to praise the Lord for what happened to Butler." Around Indianapolis, Easter churchgoers kept the Bulldogs in their minds and in their prayers.

On Sunday evening, some Butler players gathered at the Crowne Plaza for a service conducted by a pastor from Stevens's home church, St. Luke's United Methodist. Coincidentally, the pastor, David Williamson, was a graduate of Duke Divinity School. God wasn't taking sides.

When Butler players returned to the stadium for practice, they listened attentively to the scouting report, as usual. They always politely said other coaching staffs watched film of opponents and readied game plans, too, but privately they felt they were always more prepared than their opponents. Didn't matter if the coach on the other sideline was Jim Boeheim, Tom Izzo, or Mike Krzyzewski. Stevens was self-effacing about opposing such coaching giants.

"I think the best way I can put it is, they write books," Stevens said, "and I get to read 'em."

As far as the Bulldogs were concerned, if they had been paired against John Wooden and UCLA, they would have felt comfortable being directed by Stevens. Earlier in the NCAA Tournament, when Nored's grandmother asked if they would be ready, her grandson unhesitatingly replied, "Of course we are. The coach is a genius."

Indeed, Wooden approved. The 99-year-old coach, who died two months after the championship game, said in a telephone interview from his daughter Nan's house in Reseda, California, that he liked the way the Bulldogs played.

"They don't hurry things," Wooden said. "They're not wild. They're in control. I'd like to see them win very much. Not just because they're Hoosiers, but because they're the underdogs."

Wooden was recruited in the late 1920s by Butler coach Tony Hinkle. Wooden acknowledged that if Hinkle "pushed it a little more," he probably would have gone to Butler rather than Purdue. Wooden also referred to Hinkle as "the great one." He respected the modern-day Bulldogs, too.

"Any coach would be proud of this team," Wooden said.

At the practice, Stevens addressed precise details. Throughout the Horizon League season, a Saturday-afternoon game often followed a Thursday-night game. Stevens could prepare for upcoming opponents quickly and thoroughly. Butler's players studied as they did for a classroom exam.

"They had a good feel for what Duke was going to do offensively," assistant coach Matthew Graves said.

The Bulldogs' defensive principles were such that they never overhauled how they played anyway. They merely adjusted to the opponent. Or, more often, made the opponent adjust to Butler. Could anyone do that to the Blue Devils?

"Brad had them scouted to a T," said Horizon League commissioner Jon LeCrone, who watched the team's closed Monday walk-through.

The biggest question of the championship game was the condition of Shelvin Mack and Matt Howard. Mack took intravenous fluids and shot the ball at practice. He appeared okay. Howard had a headache, and Butler released a statement that he was diagnosed with a mild concussion. Stevens accepted that judgment. If Howard could not play, he could not play.

But he could be playful. Howard and Smith were sitting in the Crowne Plaza atrium when a four-year-old boy, after a Sunday afternoon at Bracket Town, walked into the hotel. The boy recognized Howard and said hi, and Howard told him he heard something in the foliage around the elevators. Must be an alligator, Howard said. So the big center and the little boy spent the next 20 minutes looking for the "alligator."

Police had to wall off a pathway for the players to enter for dinner at Harry and Izzy's restaurant, where the Bulldogs received their customary ovation. Stevens was occupied elsewhere and arrived late, the only passenger on the bus.

There were pressroom rumors about the futures of Stevens and Hayward. After the championship game, Stevens was supposedly going to accept a multimillion-dollar contract to coach at the University of Oregon. Hayward was said to have chosen an agent and decided, for sure, to leave Butler early for the NBA. Neither rumor was true, and no such stories were published.

Journalists and coaches pondered two themes on the eve of the championship game: Where would a Butler victory rank in the history of college basketball, and would Butler really have a chance?

On the latter issue, the consensus was that as compelling as the Bulldogs' magic act had been, it was time to shut it down. Oddsmakers made Duke a 7-point favorite. Izzo said he expected Duke to win by 10 or 15. Georgetown coach John Thompson III, who had faced both teams, told CNN that Duke would win.

There was agreement on the first issue, too. A Butler victory would be epic, probably the greatest in college basketball history. Playing at home. Small school. Storied opponent. David versus Goliath. *Hoosiers*. Underdawgs.

"I think the dynamics of the whole package make this absolutely unique," Gannett News Service columnist Mike Lopresti said. "I can't think of another one that would come close."

Four NCAA championship games of the previous half century produced cultural milestones or momentous upsets:

- 1963: Loyola 60, Cincinnati 58, overtime.
  Loyola, a 100-to-1 shot, overcame a 15-point deficit to prevent the Bearcats from winning a third consecutive title. The small Chicago

school—later belonging to the Horizon League with Butler—was the first champion to start as many as four black players.

- 1966: Texas Western 72, Kentucky 65.

Texas Western, now known as Texas–El Paso, inspired the movie *Glory Road*. Texas Western was the first champion with five black starters, beating a traditional power, coached by Adolph Rupp, featuring an all-white lineup. That was a big story, but long before ESPN and CBS's billions turned college basketball into a mainstream sport.

- 1983: North Carolina State 54, Houston 52.

Houston was 31-2, and the Phi Slama Jama fraternity boasted future NBA stars Hakeem Olajuwon and Clyde Drexler. North Carolina State barely made it into the tournament, then barely made it to the Final Four. The Wolfpack won its tournament opener in double overtime by two points, then won twice more by one point each. North Carolina State won when Lorenzo Charles dunked Dereck Whittenburg's air ball as time expired. That resulted in one of college basketball's most enduring images, that of North Carolina State coach Jim Valvano running around the court looking for someone to hug.

- 1985: Villanova 66, Georgetown 64.

Villanova had lost to Georgetown by only 52–50 and 57–50 in Big East games. But with a 35-2 record, the Hoyas were seemingly headed for a second-straight national championship. Instead, the Wildcats played a virtually perfect game in the last championship without a shot clock, shooting 79 percent (22 of 28).

The press, having established that Villanova–Georgetown was the first game Stevens could remember watching, asked him what he could take from that game. He quipped, "I guess if we shoot 78 [*sic*] percent, we'll have a better chance than if we shoot 15 for 49."

At Sunday's news conference, Stevens and Butler players appeared at ease on the podium, as they did throughout the tournament. Although Butler had risen to prominence in the 2000s, played in Sweet Sixteens, and won the NIT Season Tip-Off, the cascade of media attention was unlike anything the players, or the school, had ever encountered.

They were invigorated by it. Zach Hahn said to play on such a stage against the best teams in the country was something they wanted all their lives. They were ready for it, and they showed it.

Stevens and players were questioned about Howard's concussion, Hayward's future, the Butler Way, underdog status, childhood impressions of Duke, scheduling, scouting, and specifics about matching up against Duke. When a journalist asked them to elaborate on the differences between college football and basketball, they all looked at Nored because he was from football-crazed Alabama. He was such a Crimson Tide football fan that he once cried when they lost an important game. But what was happening in the Final Four could never happen in college football.

"I think this is what makes college basketball great," Nored said. "I honestly believe on any night, five guys can beat five guys. It's about going out and competing, sticking to your system, and doing what you do."

Nored was also the one revealing that his coach was not always as serene as he seemed.

"I've gotten yelled at pretty often," he said. "I got yelled at in practice last week for getting back-cut. Things like when you're supposed to trail a guy, you go up through the middle, things like that, he'll jump on you pretty quickly. Don't let him fool you."

Coincidentally, both teams pointed at losses to Georgetown as turning points in their respective seasons. Butler was 27-1 since losing to the Hoyas 72–65 on December 8, and Duke was 17-1 since an 89–77 loss on January 30.

If the insatiable media believed they could prod Duke into making statements that might inflame the Bulldogs, create sound bites, or spice their written accounts, they were disappointed. These were Duke players and Coach K, after all. The words "stupid" and "Duke" did not belong in the same sentence.

The Blue Devils said all the right things, and actually looked like they meant them. Singler could have been reading from Butler's script, saying that "understanding who you are and playing the right way" were big parts of the tournament.

Krzyzewski was forthcoming and insightful, especially in identifying why Duke was an object of derision. Duke was a private university without an obvious constituency.

"You know, people wouldn't take the shots at us they do if we were a state school because the people of the state wouldn't like it, and there would be a filter there," Krzyzewski said. "And there's no filter for us, a Notre Dame. So if we're gonna be really good, we're gonna get that because there's nobody to hold anybody accountable before you even start talking. It's just true.

"That's just the way it is, and I'm okay with it. I think it helps us keep our edge."

The championship game was not Krzyzewski's introduction to Butler. The Blue Devils beat Butler 80–60 on January 30, 2003, and the coach invited Butler players into a team room afterward for a private meeting at Cameron Indoor Stadium. Among those who attended was Darnell Archey, the Butler coordinator of basketball operations, who led the Bulldogs that night with 14 points.

"I figured Coach K doesn't speak to every team," Archey said. "Butler, he saw something in us that he wanted to congratulate us. He could probably see it climbing. Climbing and climbing, and now, seven years later, we're in the national championship game."

The Bulldogs were dispirited after that defeat but felt better when Krzyzewski told them the game was scheduled because Butler was the kind of team Duke might face in the NCAA Tournament. Both teams reached the Sweet Sixteen in 2003, then were eliminated in regional semifinals.

Twenty-nine hours before the game, the line began to form outside Lucas Oil Stadium. Butler students began camping out on Easter with a store of provisions, and spent the afternoon playing cards, eating, swapping stories, and napping on the concrete. A 12-pack of Dr Pepper made a makeshift pillow.

When the students were ready to turn in for the night, police told them that tents weren't allowed on stadium property. So the tents were converted to tarps stretched between barricades and trash cans. High winds and heavy rain struck at about 2:00 A.M. Police returned, saying the makeshift tarps were prohibited, too.

Finally, students stood under a small awning to stay out of the rain. TV news cameras began filming them at about 6:00 A.M., and they spent the day drying out in the sun, being interviewed by reporters, playing games, and relishing what they considered to be a once-in-a-lifetime opportunity.

Some students left the line to attend class, and saw Hayward coming out of a campus building. Nored went to his eight-o'clock class, posing for pictures with others in his classroom. As many as eight Butler players were in morning classes.

Trainer Ryan Galloy and Howard tried to be inconspicuous as they arrived at Hinkle Fieldhouse that morning so that concussion-test software could be used to evaluate Howard's condition. Students saw him and wondered what was going on. Howard said he felt fine.

At least he wasn't being pestered by reporters, as the trainer was. It was something out of a bad spy novel, sneaking Howard into the training room and trying to respond to media requests without divulging too much.

A few hours before tip-off, Howard would be cleared to play.

At another noon pep rally on Monument Circle, about 2,000 blue-clad fans turned out supporting the Bulldogs. Rob Chapman, the alum who traveled from China, joined musicians in the Butler pep band and played alto saxophone. Butler athletic director Barry Collier and Mayor Greg Ballard reprised their "back bump."

Carson Kressley, a former cast member of the Bravo hit TV series *Queer Eye for the Straight Guy,* surprisingly appeared at the rally. Kressley, who was in town performing male makeovers for *The Oprah Winfrey Show,* was lifted by male cheerleaders and shouted over a megaphone.

The presidents of the two universities, Butler's Bobby Fong and Duke's Richard H. Brodhead, met in Fong's office that afternoon at Brodhead's request. Besides having winning basketball teams on their campuses, both had doctorates in English literature, shared an interest in baseball, and were longtime fans of the New York Yankees.

Local pro teams rallied around the Bulldogs. The giant inflatable Colts football player outside the team's northwest Indy training complex had a GO BUTLER sign attached to him. An aerial photograph of Victory Field, home to the Indianapolis Indians' Triple-A baseball team, showed GO DAWGS spelled out in the upper deck.

Fans from all four teams mingled in downtown restaurants and bars. Some from Duke were relieved to be able to have drinks with Butler counterparts, speak with them, and shake hands. At North Carolina or Maryland, the Duke fans sometimes endured spitting or cursing. This was a relative safe haven, as illustrated by the Butler professor who lodged 17 Duke students because they were his stepson's fraternity brothers.

Because of a mission trip, a member of Butler's pep band missed the Kansas State and Michigan State games, flying back from Salt Lake City so she could join a church group traveling to Nicaragua. But Erin Mueller was back in Indianapolis for the championship game. Rather than play in the band near courtside, she joined her sports junkie father, Dave, in the stands.

"That was special," Dave Mueller said.

When the Butler players emerged from the Crowne Plaza that night for the short trip to the stadium, there were some 1,000 fans awaiting them, about 400 in the lobby and more outdoors. They were 10 deep by the team bus. With all the screaming, cheering, and popping flashbulbs, the scene looked like a 1960s newsreel of the mania provoked by the Beatles.

At the stadium, pride in their school filled Butler alumni who looked around and saw young and old supporting the Bulldogs. In one aisle sat a couple of Butler graduates who had been married more than 50 years. Near them was a 10-year-old boy with his face painted, wearing a Matt Howard jersey.

Among those arriving early was Lou Taylor, a 59-year-old confined to a wheelchair by a severe case of multiple sclerosis, a chronic and unpredictable neurological disease. Taylor once played basketball for coach Tony Hinkle's Bulldogs. Because of his condition, Taylor rarely left his home in Simpsonville, Kentucky, and had not attended a game in years. But a former insurance colleague arranged for tickets and drove him to Indianapolis.

Taylor spoke to a fan in the next seat. They realized they had a mutual acquaintance, Pat Fagan, who was Taylor's college roommate and Lambda Chi fraternity brother. The roommates hadn't seen each other in 35 years.

Fagan was in the stadium, too. The fan called his cell phone, and Fagan came down to the wheelchair section from his upper-level seat. Fagan was allowed to stay there, the two of them watching their Bulldogs. It was as if they had never left the campus.

In Anaheim, California, baseball fans on opening day watched the Angel Stadium scoreboard for updates and were transfixed by TV sets in the concourses. Former Butler pitcher Pat Neshek, in the bullpen for the Minnesota Twins, couldn't figure out what the random "ooohs" and "aaahs" were about until he realized the fans were watching basketball, not baseball.

Lieutenant Colonel Dave Sigmund, a 1988 Butler graduate, submitted a photo of himself with two Iraqi allies who became Butler fans from 8,000 miles away. They were going to watch the game on the Armed Forces Network at 1:00 A.M., local time.

It was as if the whole world were watching.

An anonymous benefactor paid the airfare so that Lisa Litton, the mother of the family that took in Shawn Vanzant, and son Chase could fly in from Tampa, Florida. ABC produced a segment for *World News Tonight with Diane Sawyer*, interviewing the family via cell phone outside the airport terminal. Vanzant himself declined to be interviewed.

"You know what, Pops," he told Jeff Litton, "I'm going to concentrate on basketball."

The Littons had never traveled to Indianapolis to see their adopted son play. Jeff Litton regretted that time on the interview could have been spent with Vanzant. The segment never aired anyway, bumped by coverage of a West Virginia coal mine disaster. The Littons did see Vanzant briefly in the Crowne Plaza, where Lisa gave him a kiss and said she loved him.

"Do what you do," she told the son she called Shawnie.

When the national anthem began, Vanzant looked into the stands and spotted "Moms." She blew him a kiss, and he nodded and touched his heart.

Vanzant would receive an unusual transcript of the play-by-play. Lisa often sent him texts that he never saw until after the games. She sent 75 texts from the championship game, beginning with:

Well today is your time Shawnie! Stay Focused, Work Hard and Play Pink Strong for Moms!!! I Love You and know that you also have a mom angel from heaven who's wings will lift you to a victory. Use your wings and my love and your strength to win tonight Shawnie! We both will be watching and cheering you on. . . . LUV U.

This was the game of a lifetime for Butler players, the game of the century for their university. It was the destination that completed a long journey. But it also was another game, in many ways no different from every other game the Bulldogs had played since going for an unbeaten league record back in February at Valparaiso.

Brad Stevens shortened practices approaching March to forestall fatigue, but he had never seen a team work so vigilantly so deep into a season. It was as if they had an inexhaustible reservoir of resolve. The Bulldogs were like the front-running marathoner who, once past the midpoint of the race, renewed strength and pulled even farther ahead.

"All the games I feel like, we got better," Avery Jukes said. "We definitely got better, and more of a team. We played better together and played smarter—everything that came with experience."

Butler won the opening tip against Duke and worked the ball inside to Matt Howard, who was fouled and made the second of two free throws. After Nolan Smith's jumper put Duke ahead 2–1, Howard caught the ball inside again but missed a layup. A pattern was established.

Duke surged ahead 6–1 after Brian Zoubek tapped in a miss and Smith scored again. Three minutes hadn't elapsed, and Butler had already missed four shots—all good looks, including a left-handed hook by Howard and Shelvin Mack's layup.

Gordon Hayward drove into the lane for a dunk, but he was fouled before the shot. No basket. No Butler baskets at all.

Mack's step-back 3-pointer ended that, trimming Duke's lead to 6–4. Willie Veasley had a chance to tie the score on a rare Butler fast break, but Duke's Jon Scheyer knocked the ball from his hand and out of bounds. Howard spun inside for another left-handed attempt, missing for the third time.

Scheyer's basket in the foul lane pushed Duke's lead to 8–4. The Bulldogs continued to be successful passing the ball inside to Howard, who was fouled by Kyle Singler. Usually, no matter how errant Howard's shooting was, he made his free throws. But he missed twice.

The Bulldogs were no easier to score against than they had been throughout the tournament, so Duke couldn't exploit the shooting drought. Mack pulled up behind the arc in transition, cashing another 3-pointer that pulled Butler within 8–7. Then he stole the ball and drove for what would have been a go-ahead basket, but Scheyer blocked the shot.

Little more than six minutes into the game, Singler scored his first points on two free throws to make it 10–7. With the shot clock running out on Butler's next possession, Veasley missed an off-balance 3-pointer. Hayward streaked toward the rim, rebounded the ball, and laid it in all in the same motion.

Duke 10, Butler 9.

Zach Hahn, who had been in the game barely 90 seconds, finally ended his streak of eight straight 3-point misses. His 3-pointer from the right wing—five feet beyond the arc—produced a 12–11 Butler lead and prompted a clamorous response from the overwhelmingly partisan crowd. Hahn exhorted his teammates and clapped his hands when he retreated to the other end of the floor.

"He can shoot from out there, as you can see," CBS announcer Jim Nantz said.

Singler's first basket, a 3-pointer, propelled Duke back in front, 16–14. Seconds later, Ronald Nored picked up his second foul, causing Butler's defensive ace to exit for the final 11 minutes of the half. Stevens showed mild concern on the sideline, and Nored looked up at the scoreboard before heading to the bench.

Shawn Vanzant snapped away a defensive rebound, keeping the ball as he dribbled all the way to inside the top of the key. He rattled in a long 2-pointer, tying the score at 16. It was a memorable moment for Lisa Litton, whose 850-mile flight that morning allowed her to be in the stadium. Texting gave her an outlet for all that emotion.

Keep leading them and firing them up!!

Singler scored again for the Blue Devils, stroking a jumper that restored their lead, to 18–16.

"Boy, he is so smooth. Silky smooth," CBS analyst Clark Kellogg said. "And ever so patient, Jim. He doesn't really force things. Much like Hayward. You mentioned Hayward has not gotten into the offense yet. . . . He's not going to force it."

The Bulldogs were staying close by banging the boards on offense. Mack rebounded his own miss and scored, tying the score at 18. On the Bulldogs' next possession, on their third attempt, the 6-foot-3 Veasley slipped underneath to tap in the ball and send them ahead 20–18.

"Here comes sneaky, streaky Willie Veasley," Kellogg said. "A terrific offensive rebounder for his size."

Hayward came up empty on Butler's next two trips, first on an open 3-point attempt from the left corner, and then losing control as he failed to reach the rim on a drive. Veasley couldn't expand the lead, either, having his shot blocked by Singler on a play featuring considerable body contact.

A second foul sent Howard to the bench, causing the Bulldogs to play the final eight and a half minutes of the half without their point guard, Nored, or center. Howard's absence also pressed Hayward into duty as a post defender.

The 7-foot-1 Zoubek scored over the shorter and lighter Hayward, tying the score at 20 and beginning an 8–0 spurt by the Blue Devils. Around Veasley's two 3-point misses, Scheyer sank a free throw and a 3-pointer off Smith's assist. Singler's driving bank shot capped the 8–0 run. That extended Duke's lead to 26–20, sending Butler into what Kellogg called "the danger zone."

Stevens reinserted Jukes with five minutes remaining in the half. Neither the coach nor anyone else could foresee how influential that substitution would be. Almost immediately, Jukes rebounded Hayward's missed 3-pointer and drove in for a layup, cutting Duke's lead to 26–22.

Hayward grabbed a defensive rebound, dribbled the length of the floor, spun in the lane, and scored to make it 26–24. Butler fans, so worried seconds before, filled the stadium with noise. The crescendo grew louder when Jukes, after taking a pass from Mack, shot over Zoubek from the left corner behind the arc. Jukes's 3-pointer completed a 7–0 spurt and shot the Bulldogs into a 27–26 lead.

The Blue Devils went back in front 30–27 but remained unable to protect their own glass. After two misses, and two offensive rebounds by Hayward, Jukes didn't jump high enough to dunk the ball. But Jukes collected his own miss, scoring on a layup.

Scheyer missed a 3-pointer that was rebounded by Veasley, who couldn't control the ball and had it stolen by Scheyer. The open teammate was Smith, whose 3-pointer gave Duke a 33–29 lead with 49 seconds left in the half.

As the shot clock was winding down on the Bulldogs, Veasley passed to the ubiquitous Jukes at the top of the key. Jukes swished another 3-pointer, pulling them within 33–32 and finishing the most extraordinary five minutes of his four-year college basketball career.

Jukes scored 10 of Butler's final 12 points, all in the closing 4:42 of the half. The 10 points tied his season high and were his most in 30 games.

"My shots were open. I mean, I honestly didn't do much," he said afterward. "Just knocked down some open shots and took advantage of the drive when they overplayed the jump shot. I guess it just happened to come back to back in a short period."

With three seconds left in the half, Jukes fouled Smith, who missed the front end of a potential one-and-one.

Halftime: Duke 33, Butler 32.

In a half that counted nine lead changes and three ties, the favored Blue Devils led by one point. Butler's 12 offensive rebounds, and 10–3 edge in second-chance points, compensated for 34 percent shooting.

"Can Butler hang with them? They have," Nantz said.

It was a peculiar first 20 minutes. The Bulldogs attempted 38 shots, the most in 75 halves of basketball all season. They played entire games without taking many more than 38 shots. They fired that often against Duke because they kept rebounding their own misses.

In the locker room, Stevens wrote a giant "20" on the whiteboard. Twenty minutes. Twenty minutes were all that remained in this season.

Trailing was commonplace for the Bulldogs. They were behind in the second half of all six tournament games.

To begin the second half, Hayward was fouled and sank two free throws, allowing Butler to reclaim a lead, at 34–33. Singler responded with a 3-pointer, representing the 11th lead change and putting Duke ahead 36–34. Veasley, after a 1-of-7 first half, missed an open 3-point attempt from the left corner.

"The quality of shots for Butler has been pretty good, Jim," Kellogg said to his announcing colleague. "They've just not knocked down enough of them."

Coach Mike Krzyzewski instructed the Blue Devils to drop back closer to the basket so they could stop penetration by Butler and also rebound more effectively.

"It was an absolute game of cat-and-mouse executed by two really good coaches," said LeCrone, the Horizon commissioner.

Howard slipped inside for a left-handed layup—his first field goal—and tied the score at 36. But seconds later he picked up his third foul and was replaced by Jukes.

Duke and Butler kept trading baskets.

Lance Thomas hit an open jump shot for Duke, and Nored weaved through defenders to score on a layup for Butler. Mack's powerful drive through an open lane sent Butler ahead, but Smith tied it at 40 on a high-degree-of-difficulty shot over Hayward.

"Have to play through contact tonight, Jim," Kellogg said. "Those little bumps are not being called."

With the shot clock nearly expired, Duke's Miles Plumlee fired a sweeping hook off of an out-of-bounds play. The ball bounced softly, and Scheyer was in the right place at the right time, leaping to tip in the ball at the left side of the rim.

Duke 42, Butler 40.

Howard didn't stay on the bench long, and he missed an off-balance scoop shot. He was in long enough to pick up a fourth foul, though, on the rebound. He went to the bench with 14 minutes remaining.

"He has only one speed, and it cost him," Kellogg said. "He has to be a little more discreet when he's in the foul trouble that he's in there." Nored dribbled inside but had his layup blocked. Then he circled around to the right corner, took a pass from Veasley, and launched one of his rare 3-point attempts. Swish. It was only Nored's third 3-pointer of the tournament, but like his pivotal shot against Syracuse, this one came at an opportune moment.

Butler 43, Duke 42.

Singler raised his arm to call for the ball, caught a pass from Zoubek, and hit a step-back 3-pointer. That allowed Duke to reclaim the lead 45–43. CBS cameras panned to Singler's parents, of Medford, Oregon, cheering the Blue Devils and their son.

Jukes had a chance to tie the score when Zoubek fouled him on a drive to the hoop. However, Jukes, attempting his first free throws of the tournament, missed twice. The Blue Devils' lead grew to 47–43 when Zoubek caught an inbounds pass from Scheyer under the basket and easily scored.

Hayward made a strong move to the basket, banked in the ball, and was bumped by a late-arriving Scheyer. But instead of a block against Scheyer, there was a charge called on Hayward. That nullified a potential three-point play that could have cut Duke's lead to one. It was the second basket Hayward had taken away, and it was a damaging development for Butler, whose points were coming sparingly.

"Oh, wow. I think that should have been a block," Kellogg said. "He [Scheyer] hop-stepped into the path of Gordon Hayward. He wasn't there."

After a miss by Singler that was rebounded by Jukes, Hayward dribbled to the goal again and this time was fouled by Zoubek. By then, the Bulldogs had made only three of eight free throws, but Hayward's two trimmed the margin to 47–45.

For a third successive Butler possession, Hayward drove to the basket. He was fouled again, made two free throws again, and cut Duke's lead to two again, 49–47. Jukes went to the bench, effectively leaving the Bulldogs with Hayward and four guards on the floor.

"Butler going small now," Kellogg said.

On another inbounds play, Scheyer nodded at Singler, lofted the ball in front of the rim, and Singler scored to restore the lead to four, 51–47. It was the Blue Devils' third second-half basket off an inbounds play. Butler scouted and prepared for such out-of-bounds plays, but the Blue Devils executed them so well that they scored anyway.

"They scored on everything we thought they might score on," assistant coach Matthew Graves said later. "Our guys did what they were supposed to do."

Mack pulled Butler within two, 51–49, with nine and a half minutes left in what was becoming an instant classic. Crowd noise swelled. Student fans on each end remained standing.

"This place is electric," Nantz said. "No one's been able to pull away. Every single possession challenged."

Veasley had a chance to push Butler back in front but missed a fifth 3-point attempt. Hayward ripped the ball away from Zoubek—no foul was assessed despite the contact—but had his subsequent layup deflected.

Scheyer banked in a basket and was fouled by Jukes—his fourth—with 7:58 on the clock. After the under-eight-minutes media time-out, Scheyer sank his free throw to extend the Blue Devils' lead to their largest of the half, 54–49.

Despite his four fouls, Howard reentered the game. He caught a pass inside from Hahn, was fouled, and sank both free throws. Howard immediately went to the bench, replaced by Jukes, in a platooning ploy that Stevens often used to protect Howard. Insert Howard for offense, take him out for defense.

Duke 54, Butler 51.

Scheyer, fouled by Nored, converted both ends of a one-and-one to restore Duke's five-point lead, 56–51. Then Singler blocked a shot by Mack. It was Duke's seventh blocked shot, compared to none by Butler.

Duke couldn't expand the lead, and Butler couldn't reduce it. Nored missed on a driving layup. Only six minutes remained for the Bulldogs to overtake Duke and secure a place in college basketball history.

"You start to see Duke wearing Butler down just a little bit," Kellogg said.

After Stevens called a time-out with 5:42 left, Nantz echoed his broadcast partner: "Butler without a field goal for nearly four minutes. You feel they're at a crisis point."

Butler kept going to Howard, whose right arm was scraped by Scheyer. Howard sank both free throws—the second rolled around the rim before dropping—to cut Duke's lead to 56–53.

Time and again, Kellogg said, the Bulldogs had risen to the occasion on defense.

"Can they do it again?" he asked.

After the Blue Devils regained possession, Nored stole a pass by Singler and passed ahead to Hayward. Hayward had a clear path to the goal, but his left arm was hooked by Lance Thomas, sending Hayward crashing hard into the padded basket support.

Officials checked the replay monitor, determining whether the foul was flagrant. The review showed Thomas had made a permissible play on the ball and that the momentum sent Hayward falling awkwardly. No flagrant call.

Hayward shook his arms, arched his wrist in a shooting motion, and accepted the ball. He sank both free throws—he was 8 of 8 in the second half—and pulled Butler within 56–55. His mother, Jody, stood and shook her fists as the Bulldogs stayed in the fight.

"This is worthy of an NCAA championship," Kellogg said.

Under the five-minute mark, Singler sank a long jumper to expand Duke's lead to 58–55. Hayward then missed an off-balance, high-arching jumper from the left baseline that was rebounded by Scheyer.

Scheyer missed from 16 feet, but Zoubek kept the ball alive by tapping it out. As the shot clock wound down, Veasley fouled Smith from behind.

"Will this be a Duke night," Nantz asked, "or a *Hoosiers* sequel?"

After a media time-out, Smith rattled in his first free throw, then swished the second with 3:16 left.

Duke 60, Butler 55.

Thomas nearly stole the ball from Mack, who ended up on the floor. Neither could control the ball, and the possession arrow pointed toward the Bulldogs, allowing them to keep it.

Mack missed a one-handed floater from the baseline with 2:34 left, extending the Bulldogs' drought to seven minutes without a field goal. The game had evolved into a possession-by-possession, hard-fought half-court conflict. Butler attempted only six shots over those seven minutes.

Duke not only had the ball, but also a chance to lengthen the lead to a nearly insurmountable seven points. From the right of the lane, Singler drove toward the basket, plowing into Howard and sending both to the floor. Instead of a foul on either player, Singler was called for traveling, and Butler regained possession with 2:04 on the clock.

Nored dribbled all around the half-court but had room neither to shoot nor to pass the ball inside. He threw to Hayward, who headed toward the basket. Instead of continuing with the ball himself, Hayward looped a pass to Howard cutting to the goal. Howard's shot bounced off the rim and dropped through. There was 1:44 on the clock. Butler students jumped up and down as hope, and surround sound, returned to the stadium.

Duke 60, Butler 57.

Duke depleted 25 seconds of the shot clock before Smith's left-handed shot fell off the rim. Nored collected the rebound, dribbled ahead, and passed to Mack. Mack dribbled once and, as he did so often, pulled up behind the 3-point line. But this shot didn't fall.

The hustling Howard fought off everyone else to secure the ball, and passed it out to Hayward. Hayward sent it over to Nored, who passed back to Mack. Mack bounced the ball several times, then, from the free throw line, detected Howard breaking for the goal again.

Howard grabbed Mack's pass and laid it in with 55 seconds left. That gave Howard, whose participation had been uncertain because of the concussion, 8 of Butler's last 10 points.

The reverberation was like something heard in an Olympic stadium for a gold-medal moment by a host nation. After the pep band played the "Butler War Song," new fans took cues from the Butler faithful and began mimicking the chant "B-U, B-U." For one night there was a Butler Nation, and its rallying cry of "B-U, B-U" filled the vast spaces.

Time-out, Duke.

Duke 60, Butler 59.

"Have you ever seen a scene like this, Clark?" Nantz asked.

"I have not, but I'm loving it. I'm loving it, pardner," Kellogg replied.

During the time-out, Howard had his left hand and wrist wrapped in black tape because he was bleeding there. When play resumed, Scheyer saw Singler dart to an open spot on the floor. But the uncontested shot by Singler was short, grazing the front rim.

Under the basket, Zoubek tried to wrestle Howard out of the way, and the ball skittered out of bounds. The official pointed that the ball went off Zoubek's foot, and Butler regained possession with 33.7 seconds on the clock.

For the first time in a long time, Butler had the ball with a chance to seize the lead.

Hayward tossed the inbounds pass to Nored, who dribbled right to left past midcourt. Nored sent the ball to Veasley, then received a return pass and dribbled into the lane. Scheyer cut him off. Nored passed the ball to Veasley, who sent it to Mack.

Mack dribbled backward, then drove toward the free throw line and stopped. Veasley was unguarded by Duke in the left corner. That made sense, given Veasley's cold shooting night. Mack sent a pass intended for Veasley, but Zoubek deflected the ball out of bounds with 13.6 seconds on the clock.

Time-out, Butler.

Tension was so high that the 70,930 in the stadium briefly quieted. Twelve thousand were similarly nervous inside Hinkle Fieldhouse, where a packed audience watched on large screens. Blue II was led near the bench, at the request of CBS, in case the Bulldogs could achieve the improbable.

In the far corner of the stadium, section 449, a group of fans chanted, "Run the picket fence, run the picket fence, run the picket fence." They were referencing a scene from *Hoosiers* in which Shooter called a play for what became a winning basket by Hickory. After the chanting stopped, one fan stood and announced: "I'll make it!"

That, too, was a line from the movie, spoken by Jimmy Chitwood in the climactic scene. For fans seated nearby, it was comic relief.

Stevens had been walking up and down the sideline, hands on his hips. He was at his best in such critical moments. Besides designing appropriate strategy, he infused the Bulldogs with the calm confidence necessary to carry it out.

"We're going to win this game," Stevens told them, as he had throughout the NCAA Tournament. Throughout an entire five-month season, really.

"Every time he says that, it fires us up," Veasley said later.

There had not been a crossroads like this in college basketball. Butler was on the brink of a national championship. Yes, Butler.

The small school that was a 200-to-1 shot, that nearly quit major college basketball and traveled in the Blue Goose, that had 15 season ticket holders and no recruiting budget, that went 12 years without winning a game in its conference tournament, that practiced early in the morning so no one missed classes, that endured coaching changes, a committee's snub, and dispiriting defeats.

Certainly there had not been a crossroads like this since the sport exploded in the 1980s, became an ESPN staple, elevated to the mainstream, required domed stadiums, fetched billions in network broadcast rights, attracted 50 million TV viewers, and millions more from 178 countries watching online.

Substitute "national" for "state," and a *Hoosiers* devotee could have heard the words of Shooter echoing from his hospital room: "No school this small has ever been to the state championship."

First, the Bulldogs would have to pass the ball inbounds. Hayward attempted to do so from the left corner. With Zoubek fronting him, no one was free. Hayward formed a "T" with his hands.

Time-out, Butler. It was the Bulldogs' final time-out.

Stevens wanted Hayward to make a play. Shoot, drive, pass. With the ball in his hands, Hayward could make something happen. One thing Stevens wasn't counting on was inducing a foul. A player "would just have to get creamed" to get a call like that in a national championship game, Stevens said.

This time, from out of bounds, Howard was throwing it in. He passed the ball to Hayward, who jumped and caught it, landing about 30 feet from the basket. Guarded by Singler, Hayward went to his left, dribbled behind his back, and changed direction to go right. Singler shadowed Hayward, who dribbled toward the baseline and Zoubek. Hayward picked up the ball, leaned back, and arched it over Zoubek's extended left arm.

"It's in! It's in!" a Butler fan shouted.

From several angles, the shot looked good.

It was not.

The ball hit the back rim and bounced directly to Zoubek. He was fouled by Mack with 3.6 seconds left. Stevens clapped his hands on the sideline, understanding that it was a sound play and wanting his players to keep believing.

"That's good all the way around," Kellogg said. "It was right on line. Right on line. Terrific job by Gordon Hayward to jump-stop and then lean back. That's outstanding defense by Duke."

Duke 60, Butler 59. The score was unchanged.

Hayward said that he had made that shot many times, although it was not a shot he often took in his college career. Howard said he had seen Hayward make it hundreds of times.

"It was right on, but just long," Hayward said. "I let it go and I thought it was in."

The Bulldogs and the Blue Devils walked to the other end, taking places along the foul lane. Krzyzewski gestured to where he wanted Duke players positioned. Jukes was a study in concentration as he kneeled in front of the Butler bench. Butler fans around the globe peered into TV screens, home computers, and laptops, wondering if the Bulldogs could do the extraordinary.

Zoubek dribbled three times, squared his shoulders, and shot the ball. Swish.

Duke 61, Butler 59.

Krzyzewski did not want to risk going into overtime. Five more minutes in this environment, he calculated, would be disadvantageous to Duke. So he instructed Zoubek to miss the second free throw intentionally. With 3.6 seconds left, a miss would lessen the chance of Butler retrieving the ball, advancing it, and attempting a makeable shot.

The only problem with that tactic is that, with a two-point lead, Duke could be beaten by a long 3-pointer or a half-court shot. But what were the odds?

Hayward, with no one between himself and Howard on the foul lane, leaped and grabbed Zoubek's miss off the back rim. Hayward took two short dribbles, then two long ones, advancing the ball. Howard stopped abruptly before the midcourt line, setting a screen. Singler crashed into Howard, falling backward. Who would have the presence of mind to set a screen for a desperate heave? Howard did.

Hayward took another long step and a half, aiming at the rim from half-court. He was about 50 feet away when he sent the ball arching toward the basket. It was not a heave, and Hayward had a running start. The trajectory was such that the ball appeared to have a chance to pass through the rim.

But there was nothing like Plump's Last Shot. No Jimmy Chitwood promising, "I'll make it," and then making it.

Hayward's 3-point attempt hit the glass backboard and rim, bounding away.

"Oh, it almost went in! Almost went in!" Nantz said.

Final: Duke 61, Butler 59.

The miss elicited a collective gasp from those who witnessed something transcendent in American sports, but who also instantly understood what might have been.

Duke players celebrated amid blue and white confetti falling from the ceiling, and Krzyzewski and his assistant coaches jumped in one another's arms. Hayward walked away from the court toward the Butler bench, looking into the distance. Howard stayed on the floor and had to be pulled to his feet. Veasley stared, blankly and numbly. Nick Rodgers, the nonscholarship senior who carried the West Regional trophy, said all feeling left his body.

Hayward's half-court shot was close. Oh, so close.

So close that Singler, down on the court and twisting his body to watch the ball's flight, said it looked good. Howard thought so, too. Nored said he had no doubt, that he was just waiting for it to go in.

A video analysis by John Brenkus for ESPN's *Sport Science* separated the shot into three components: launch angle, release velocity, and aim. The launch angle (54 degrees) was good. Velocity was 28 miles per hour, or 0.5 more than would have given the ball a chance to strike the inside of the front rim and drop through. Aim was three inches too far to the right.

Duke won by two points and about three inches.

It was not Hollywood fiction. It was not a *Hoosiers* reincarnation of the Milan miracle. It was not, as many suggested it could have been, the greatest shot in the history of a sport invented in 1891. It was not the greatest ending in any team sport, any nation, any era.

It was real. For the Underdawgs, it was over. After 25 successive victories over more than three months, they lost. They had forgotten what it felt like.

"We almost had an aura of we thought we were going to win every game," Stevens said.

In many respects, it was amazing that the Bulldogs almost won six NCAA Tournament games. They shot less than 40 percent—38.7 percent—for the tournament.

In the championship, the Bulldogs' two forwards, Hayward (2 of 11) and Veasley (1 of 9), shot a collective 15 percent. Butler went nearly eight minutes of the second half without a field goal after going nearly 11 minutes without a field goal in the second half against Michigan State.

Hayward and Mack scored 12 points each, Howard 11, Jukes 10. Singler, the Final Four's most outstanding player, led Duke with 19. Scheyer scored 15, Smith 13.

Stevens tried to be philosophical and analytical at the same time, stating that in a game of 145 possessions, Butler came up one possession short. If there was doubt whether the Bulldogs were simply happy to be there, the looks on their faces and the sounds of their voices dispelled such a notion. They were "crushed," as Stevens put it. Vanzant said he never hurt so bad after a loss before. Howard said he was in shock. Hayward spoke in a barely audible tone at the postgame news conference.

"Hate losing," Hayward said. "It's one of the worst feelings personally that I have, is losing."

Krzyzewski was both elated and relieved. Later he told John Adams, the NCAA's supervisor of officials, of his displeasure with the blind-side screen set by Howard on Hayward's half-court shot. But Duke won, so it became irrelevant.

"I still can't believe we won," Coach K said. "The game was so good that anybody could have won."

In the 8 national championship games in which he had coached, Krzyzewski said, this was the best. He said it would become historic. And of 40 games over nearly five months, out of 35 victories, Scheyer said this was the toughest. He said he could not imagine what the Butler players were feeling.

It didn't take imagination to know what Veasley was feeling. He sat in the corner of the locker room, his jersey covering his head, sobbing. Awhile later, he said it hit him that it was over. The game. The season. The career.

Like Stevens, Veasley had grown to believe the Bulldogs could not lose. They always found a way.

"I was waiting for that to happen in those final seconds, and it didn't," Veasley said. "The last thing that usually happens just didn't."

In the shelter of their locker room, the seniors took turns speaking to teammates. Rodgers said thanks for letting him in on the ride. Jukes was gratified to be part of something bigger than himself. Veasley choked up again. Rodgers asked if he needed a crying towel, and tossed Veasley a warm-up jacket. The Dawgs laughed together. They were so close that they could razz one another about anything, the way brothers do. Veasley composed himself enough to say that he, too, was thankful.

Gloom didn't pervade everything. Stevens reminded the players that the run was special and that it would echo beyond that night. Nored actually stood inside the door with a smile and without a tear. This was one game, he said, and they had each other for a lifetime.

"Teams are going to see what we did and know that they have a shot,"

Nored said. "They can know that if they play together, and do the right thing, and listen to their coach, they have a great shot at doing something special."

Hayward was repeatedly asked about the last shot. The last two shots, really. He will be asked about them for the rest of his life. He acknowledged that it was hard, that he could have made history, but that he tried not to think about it.

The women in the principals' lives continued to think about it, processing the events of the preceding months. Stevens's wife, Tracy, said she was at peace with the outcome. She wasn't sure her husband ever would be. Hayward's mother, Jody, viewed the outcome through a spiritual lens.

"I don't know that God really cared, but God might not have wanted him to bear that burden," she said. "And God has a plan for everyone's life, and who am I to question God's plan?"

Before leaving the stadium, Lisa Litton had a final text for her Shawnie:

I just want you to know how proud I am of you and everything you're doing with your life and how you have empowered mine! I love you!

In a storage area where the Butler band and cheerleaders warmed up, the student who was the "Hink" mascot took off his bulldog costume and kneeled to the ground, tears running down his face. The cheerleaders and musicians pet the actual bulldog, Blue II, for comfort. Colts quarterback Peyton Manning surprisingly visited them, telling them they should be proud, and complimenting their school spirit.

Butler players boarded the bus for the six-mile drive back to Hinkle Fieldhouse, where there was no wild celebration in the middle of the night. They were alone except for one another and with their thoughts.

As the players departed the bus, Charles Jones, their previously unbeaten driver, thanked the team for a memorable season. And thanked them for treating him like a person, not just the bus driver. The bus driver was part of the team. On a team, everyone mattered. It was the Butler Way.

Butler was the only team in major college basketball to go unbeaten in January, February, and March, going 105 days between defeats. Butler beat seven conference champions: Ohio State and Michigan State (cochamps of Big Ten); Xavier (Atlantic 10); Siena (Metro Atlantic); Texas–El Paso (Conference USA); Murray State (Ohio Valley); and Syracuse (Big East).

If the Bulldogs were not America's Team, they were representative of Americana:

- Gordon Hayward was a homegrown boy who thought he was going to be a tennis player until a teenaged growth spurt. He was named after his father, as were two other starters, Ronald Nored and Willie Veasley.
- Shelvin Mack was a gym rat ignored by the mighty Kentucky Wildcats in his hometown.
- Ronald Nored was a pastor's son born in Indianapolis, raised in Alabama, and redirected to Butler's campus, where he had played as a boy.
- Matt Howard was the eighth of 10 children born to a couple in Connersville, a basketball-mad Indiana town.
- Willie Veasley was the son of an ironworker whose contributions were so hard to measure that he became the Shane Battier of college basketball.
- Shawn Vanzant rose above family hardships and became as devoted to his teammates as if he had spent his entire life with them.
- Avery Jukes transferred from a larger school, modified his skills to complement those of everyone else, and extended the theme of servanthood by starting a foundation for Ugandan schoolchildren.
- Zach Hahn was a quintessential Hoosier, a sharpshooter from the hoops nursery of New Castle, home of the Indiana Basketball Hall of Fame.

The Bulldogs were more old school than hip-hop. They were more Ivy League than one-and-done. They were more Oscar Robertson and John Havlicek than LeBron James and Kobe Bryant.

But the Bulldogs defied any racial or sociological labels that others attempted to apply. If they conjured up images of white teenagers from the *Hoosiers* of 1950s Indiana, well, that was simplistic.

White? Five of the top eight players were black. Butler's basketball culture was such that skin color was not a singular characteristic. They were all blue.

Hoosiers? The five starters came from four states.

Talent? The whole was greater than the sum of the parts. But Hayward was headed to the NBA, and maybe Mack. Butler's key players would have thrived anywhere, even if that wasn't evident in the recruiting process.

Some fans around the country asserted that they had begun to lose interest in the NCAA Tournament but that they were energized by Butler's noble quest. It didn't take a cynic to recognize that Butler was an antidote to the cheating, excesses, and money poisoning college basket-ball.

Among those taking the defeat hardest was Indiana's governor, Mitch Daniels. He said he grieved for days. He loved everything about the Bull-dogs: where they played, how they played, who they were.

"Even though those two shots didn't go in, never again will anybody be able to say, 'Never,' which people were saying up until Butler," Daniels said. "All these Gonzagas, it's all very cute, you know? Every year, some-body gets lucky. . . . They're never going to really contend against the semipro teams, which is the way I think of most of the rest of them. And they'll never be able to say, 'Never,' again.

"Duke was damn lucky. We all know it."

CHAPTER 10

FALL AND RISE

Brad Stevens watched a replay of the championship game soon after he returned home from Lucas Oil Stadium. He finished at about 5:00 A.M., then went to bed.

"I just kind of wanted to be done with it," he said.

A gratifying moment was a phone call from President Barack Obama that afternoon. Customarily, champions receive such calls, never runners-up. Players and coaches crowded into Stevens's Hinkle Fieldhouse office to hear from the president, a fervent basketball fan, over a speakerphone. Obama told the Bulldogs they grabbed the nation's attention.

"I think he speaks for a lot of people who enjoyed this ride with us," Ronald Nored said.

At a pep rally, several thousand fans turned out to thank the Bulldogs. The question on the minds of everyone there was the future of Butler's coach and star. The answers weren't long in coming.

Two days later, Butler awarded Stevens a 12-year contract extension through the 2021–22 season. Although terms were not disclosed, it was speculated that he became the university's first $1 million employee. Butler's Board of Trustees was discussing an amount like that before the Bulldogs reached the Final Four. Whatever the salary was, it was less than half what Stevens could have made at a larger school.

A week after the championship game, Gordon Hayward met his father for lunch on campus to discuss the pros and cons of leaving school early. He announced April 14 he would submit his name for the NBA draft and reiterated his decision at a May 7 news conference. Hayward attended the June 24 ceremony in New York, where the Utah Jazz drafted him with the No. 9 pick. He became Butler's first NBA player since Buckshot O'Brien, who played two years in the league, 1951–52 and 1952–53.

It was another "can-you-believe-it" moment for Hayward, the formerly skinny teenager who considered abandoning basketball for tennis. Now, here he was in the NBA after winning a state championship, a world championship, and nearly an NCAA championship. His story defied credulity. So did Butler's.

Losing Hayward, Willie Veasley, and Avery Jukes was going to diminish the Bulldogs for the 2010–11 season. Yet there was no reason for players, coaches, or fans to lose faith.

So what if they couldn't advance to another Final Four? That was a once-in-a-lifetime achievement for a university like Butler. The Bulldogs could still win the Horizon League. They could still make the NCAA Tournament and win games there. They could remain relevant in college basketball. Their coach was still Brad Stevens.

The Bulldogs retained 10 players who had been in the program for three years or more. They knew the system and the Butler Way. Few teams across the country had a trio of returning starters to match Shelvin Mack, Matt Howard, and Nored.

For the second successive summer, USA Basketball accelerated Mack's development. He was selected to a team of college players scrimmaging against pros preparing for the World Basketball Championship. His new texting buddies included Rajon Rondo, Chauncey Billups, Stephen Curry, Russell Westbrook, and John Wall. In scrimmages and invitation-only skills camps, Mack said he guarded or was guarded by LeBron James, Derrick Rose, Kevin Durant, Deron Williams, Chris Paul, and Eric Gordon. It was intoxicating stuff for someone yearning to join them in the NBA.

"I think every basketball player playing would love to play in the NBA," Mack said. "I'm not worried about it. I'm taking it one day at a time."

Nored had to do that, too, and not because he was playing. He was coaching. He endured another summer of inactivity because of recurring stress fractures in his shins. To satisfy an outlet for his energy, he became head coach of a 16-and-under AAU team, The Truth, based in suburban Indianapolis. The experience also reinforced his ambition to become a college coach.

Nored was in perpetual motion during the Bulldogs' tournament run, chasing opponents' top scoring guards. Astonishingly, he was not inhibited. He said perhaps because he was so focused on each game's task, he didn't notice any pain. His shins were so bad before the Final Four season, trainer Ryan Galloy said, that Nored "dodged a surgery bullet." Soon after the tournament, the soreness returned as Nored jogged around the track inside Hinkle Fieldhouse.

Throughout the tournament, orthopedist David Brokaw conceded, "I'd hold my breath," worried that his patient might break down. Finally, Nored did. He opted for surgery in which two titanium rods were placed in his legs. For the procedure—bilateral tibial surgery—patellar tendons were moved to allow rods to run from knee to ankle. The surgery is common for elite athletes and soldiers. The rods take stress off the bones, allowing them to heal. Nored hadn't felt so pain-free in years.

"I almost feel completely back to normal," he said. "Almost going back to my freshman and sophomore year of high school, when everything feels good."

Nored, who wore jersey No. 5, began to be called Ron5. In recognition of his new bionic feature, a fan website suggested "Ron5" was as much robot as basketball player. A student began dressing as Ron5 Robot, and the new mascot took on a life of its own. The robot started a Twitter account, commenting on the "humans" with whom it interacted.

"I've got to admit, it's pretty clever," Nored said. "So I kind of play along with the whole thing."

The season was one that many fans in Indianapolis and Connersville had long dreaded, and for one reason: It was the last year for Matt Howard to wear No. 54 for the Bulldogs.

Brad Stevens said Howard influenced the program before he played a game for the Bulldogs. It took courage and vision for Howard, as a 17-year-old, to select Butler over programs offering more exposure. Colleges nationwide pursued the 6-foot-8 Howard, who reduced his choices to Purdue and Butler. Before he could decide, Purdue awarded its last available scholarship.

"I think he's made Butler better. Like, how many guys can say that?" Stevens said. "He has made the whole university better."

As a teenager, Howard's summer play earned him a ranking among the nation's top 100 prospects. In a 2005 game against a team featuring future NBA players Greg Oden, Mike Conley, Eric Gordon, and Daequan Cook, Howard's team nearly won. The summer after that, Howard's

Spiece Central Stars lost 71–66 to a team including NBA-bound Kevin Love and Brandon Jennings.

"That wasn't where it started for Matt," said Pat Mullin, coach of Howard's summer team. "That was kind of the exclamation point."

Howard became as influential at his university as he was in his hometown. And it wasn't the basketball exploits that endeared him to Connersville folks, although he became the high school's all-time scoring leader and led the state of Indiana in rebounding. It was his tireless work ethic and down-to-earth demeanor.

Studying so diligently that he made youths think school was cool. Signing so many autographs that he didn't see any of a high school game he attended. Calling on an elderly woman to show her photos from the team's trip to Italy. Visiting an Indianapolis hospital to cheer up the 17-year-old son of Connersville's sheriff.

"He exemplifies the best of all of us. He really does," said Joe Glowacki, a radio/TV teacher at the high school for 43 years.

Howard was the eighth of 10 children and youngest of 5 sons separated by 12 years. His 5 sisters were 20 years apart. Because he was so much younger, he didn't play organized sports with his brothers. He was home-schooled in seventh and eighth grades.

His father, Stan, played college baseball and was in his 33rd year as a mail carrier. His mother, Linda, an Indiana University graduate, became a stay-at-home mom after her first child was born. When Matt was born, there was one bathroom in their rural home. It was often "extreme chaos," he recalled. The family eventually moved into a house with seven bedrooms and two bathrooms.

"We didn't start out thinking we were going to have 10 children," Linda Howard said. "But we're not ones to outguess what God has for us. We just marched through it."

Matt Howard suggested residents couldn't help but know him because they knew his family. But how do you explain this incident?

One of his teachers once called his mother and, in a trembling voice, said she had upset him. That bothered the teacher. Matt was eight years old. He was in third grade.

"He has that kind of effect," Linda Howard said. "Nobody wants him to be mad. Everybody wants to please him. And he wants to please other people."

Her son also wanted to make his own way. He raised enough money, from the ages of 9 to 16, to buy a used Nissan Maxima by delivering newspapers and mowing lawns. There was enough left over to bank a certificate of deposit. He paid for his own car insurance.

Aptitude for numbers steered him to accounting classes taught by Linda Rosenberger. Not only did Howard achieve in class and in internships, she said, but he helped other students.

"Everything he has done has been with the mentality of the team," Rosenberger said.

If there was one thing about going home that Howard did not like, it was celebrity status. At the Woodridge Inn, on Indiana 1 at the north edge of Connersville, the marquee read: "Good Luck Matt Howard and the Butler Bulldogs." He heeded the advice of his mother: So many people are watching you, don't do something stupid.

Howard's uneasiness with stardom was evident in high school when his coach, Rodney Klein, called time-out. Howard had 42 points, 2 off a school record, and the coach asked if wanted to try for it. Howard declined to go back in the game.

He was no A-lister at home. The coach knew that and persuaded an older brother, Tim, to be on the team as a senior when Matt was a sophomore. Tim was a natural for his assignment: torment Matt in practice.

"He had an elbow that was always somewhere around face level," Matt said. "It was amazing. He said it was all unintentional. It made things that went on in the game a lot easier."

He never lacked for family support. Several siblings lived or worked in Indianapolis. Two of them, Lucas, 30, and Amanda, 26, resolved to attend all of their brother's games in his senior year at Butler.

Over time, Butler opponents came to appreciate Howard, even if he was unconventional. He was accused of flopping, or exaggerating contact to draw fouls. With the ball, he often lurched toward the basket, initiating contact and inducing fouls. He dove onto the floor to retrieve loose balls as if he were 5-foot-8 instead of 6-foot-8.

"You take him off that team, it's a whole different team," Cleveland State coach Gary Waters said. "Howard is a unique basketball player, probably one of the most unique players to be in this league in a long time."

If Howard weren't humble already, his teammates would have made him so with ridicule of his quirkiness. Not that they could embarrass him. Not that they could understand him sometimes. Howard's jokes were so esoteric that teammates didn't always get the punch lines until later.

"He's brilliant. He really is," said Eli Boyer, a team manager. "When he opens up and has a conversation with you, he really is insightful."

No one wanted to watch Howard's favorite TV show, CNBC's documentary series *American Greed*. When the Bulldogs gathered together to watch a movie during a road trip, he acknowledged that he hadn't been in a movie theater since high school. He explained that he waited for the TV release.

Then there was his penchant for reversing the first initials in two-word combinations. For instance: Shelvin Mack became Melvin Shack. Zach Hahn was Hach Zahn. He called himself Hatt Moward.

Assistant coach Micah Shrewsberry compared him to the character played by Tom Hanks in the movie *Big*, in which a 13-year-old boy is magically transformed into a 30-year-old.

Howard's mode of transportation around campus was a bicycle, irrespective of weather. During the week of an ice storm, he rode his bike to practice daily. His trusty, but rusty, bike once betrayed him, with handlebars breaking and Howard skidding. He came away with only a scraped knee.

He wore the same socks so long that they lost elasticity and fell around his ankles. Teammates said his "turtleneck socks" were "gross." Neither did Howard ever wear the new shoes he was issued. The ones he had were adequate.

One teammate, Emerson Kampen, called Howard a "minimalist." Howard preferred to be called low-maintenance.

"You can officially write Matt's the weirdest person I've ever met in my life," Mack said.

At many schools, the first day of college basketball practice is a Midnight Madness event that is entertaining for fans and ESPN viewers . . . and accomplishes little. Although the Bulldogs would have drawn an adoring audience, coach Brad Stevens stuck to what they had always done.

"The last thing I want to do is change that, because I don't want to insinuate to our team that we're changing our focus," Stevens said. "That is, we're preparing for March Madness, and we're trying to be a part of that."

The only change the Bulldogs made to begin the 2010–11 season was to go off campus and hold a minicamp at Franklin College, located 28 miles south of Hinkle Fieldhouse. Although players engaged in informal games through the spring, summer, and fall, they had been awaiting this day since the night they lost to Duke. Intensity and concentration were evident from the first hour.

"Last year doesn't matter anymore," senior guard Zach Hahn said.

The Bulldogs were not impressive in beating Florida Southern 90–70 and Hanover 80–41 in exhibition games, but neither was there cause for anxiety. Stevens experimented with different lineups. In previous seasons, a Butler coach identified a starting five early and kept it. In some ways, the unpredictability of the lineup and infusion of three freshmen energized the preseason. The Final Four banner was raised for the November 13 opener against Marian, a small Indianapolis university that lost to the Bulldogs 83–54. The ceremony represented closure—at least for the fans. The players were ready to move on.

"Let's embrace the guys in the locker room right now," Nored said. "Let's embrace this team and embrace this year that we're going to have. It's going to be a great year."

For their first road test, the Bulldogs left their 82-year-old basketball cathedral for the nation's newest and most opulent facility. Louisville's $233 million KFC Yum! Center was more like an NBA arena. High school prospects were dazzled by the 22,000-seat sportsplex. Louisville coach Rick Pitino wanted a marquee opponent for the first regular-season game there, and Butler agreed to be that visitor.

The environment shouldn't have disturbed the 16th-ranked Bulldogs, who, after all, had played in front of 70,000 little more than seven months before. But from the tip-off, they were decidedly un-Butler-like. If not for Shelvin Mack, returning to his native Kentucky, the first half would have been worse. The Cardinals led 41–23 at halftime, and Mack had 17 points. Stevens was assessed a technical foul—his first in 53 games.

The Cardinals' lead grew to 50–26 and Mack was sidelined by leg cramps, as he was in the NCAA semifinal against Michigan State. Mack finished with 25 points, but Louisville had no difficulty securing an 88–73 victory. Butler had not allowed as many as 88 points in a regulation 40 minutes in more than a decade, a span of 361 games.

The Bulldogs were smothered. They were "exposed," Nored said. They "got caught up in the moment," Stevens said. A large media contingent witnessed the game, and Butler was unrecognizable.

"I think, if anything, that was the beginning of the wake-up call," Matt Howard said. "Yet at the same time, you lose quite a bit of the confidence you had and wonder what's going on. You start to question some things."

Such questions vanished, if temporarily, after Butler returned to Hinkle Fieldhouse and crushed Ball State 88–55. It made Louisville seem more like an anomaly than an alarm. The next opponent, Siena, was a rematch of their *BracketBuster* meeting. The Bulldogs had dropped out of the Top 25 but were an attraction in New York's capital city. Siena had won 38 straight at the Times Union Center before a season-opening loss.

"It's a great opportunity to have a team like this come to Albany," new Siena coach Mitch Buonaguro said. "It doesn't happen very often."

Neither team was the same as before, and the Bulldogs were burdened when they lost Nored in the game's second minute. He dove for a ball and knocked heads with a Siena player. Nored bled from his left eye and left the floor to receive medical attention. He returned to the bench, but concussion symptoms kept him out of the game.

The Bulldogs couldn't stop Siena's 6-foot-9 Ryan Rossiter—he had 26 points and 15 rebounds—but were otherwise crisp in a 70–57 victory. Butler outscored Siena 38–5 in points off the bench.

"Those guys go in there and play. They know their roles," Howard said.

Shawn Vanzant replaced Nored and scored 12 points, and Chase Stigall sank three back-breaking 3-pointers. Howard, who had made only five 3s in his career, hit two from the arc. He called it a personal turning point. After spending an entire off-season shooting 3s in solitude, Howard proved to himself he could make them in games.

Two days after Thanksgiving, the Bulldogs were without Nored against Evansville. But they had performed capably without their point guard and had won 17 in a row at home, so the absence was outwardly no issue. The Purple Aces were 19-point underdogs.

Stevens surprisingly started Alex Anglin, a nonscholarship senior who understood Butler's system as well as anyone. His assignment was to guard Colt Ryan, the sharpshooter who vexed Butler the year before. Ryan was limited to two first-half baskets, and the Bulldogs built their lead to 33–21. At halftime it was 36–29.

But with Nored sidelined, the Bulldogs lacked their usual vigor. Those on the bench were oddly dispassionate. Stevens was troubled and sensed the Bulldogs were not treating this as the in-state rivalry it was. Had they not remembered nearly losing at Evansville the year before? Stevens frequently substituted, partly because of foul trouble.

"He was on us the whole game, trying to light a fire under us," senior guard Grant Leiendecker said.

In the second half, the Bulldogs wobbled and ultimately toppled, losing 71–68 in overtime. Mack air-balled a contested 3-pointer as time expired, finishing a 3-of-13 afternoon. Not since 1994 had Evansville won at Hinkle Fieldhouse. The Purple Aces employed a lineup of small players, and Butler defenders could not keep up with them.

"They beat us. They just flat beat us," Stevens said.

The scene was incongruous for Brandon Gaudin, the Butler play-by-play announcer. He was an Evansville native who grew up cheering for the Purple Aces and had been their radio voice in the previous two seasons. He was also a 2006 Butler graduate, and he jumped at the chance to call games for his alma mater.

"I got quite a few calls and text messages after that game. 'How do you feel about that career move?' " Gaudin said.

Certainly, the Bulldogs were adjusting to new roles. They were evolving, but into what? *Sports Illustrated* labeled Butler the most disappointing team in the country. There was reason for Stevens to chide the Bulldogs because this defeat, for many reasons, was inexplicable and inexcusable.

"There was serious disappointment in his voice," student-manager Eli Boyer said.

Howard reproached himself for what he said were careless fouls. He had 19 points and 13 rebounds, but he played only 27 of the 45 minutes.

"I didn't think it was possible for us to lose to them," Howard said. "I had a really hard time with that one after the game. And I normally don't dwell on those types of games.

"It wouldn't be the last time, either, unfortunately."

The schedule was so demanding, and the Evansville loss so perplexing, that the Bulldogs confronted the possibility of a four-game losing streak. The Horizon League opener at Chicago pitted them against Loyola, which was 7-0 for the first time since the Ramblers' NCAA championship season of 1962–63. After that was a neutral-court rematch with top-ranked Duke, followed by a game at Xavier. If the Bulldogs didn't turn things around immediately, Stevens told them, they would be forever unhappy with their season.

Hahn organized a players-only meeting. They spoke about what they could do better individually and collectively. Hahn's message was essentially this: "I know we're a good team. We know we're a good team. We just have to start showing it."

Before tip-off, Loyola graciously acknowledged its Horizon colleague for the run to the Final Four. The Bulldogs were again without Nored, who participated in the pregame shootaround and sat on the bench in uniform. He could at least furnish energy from there. Stevens awarded 6-foot-11 Andrew Smith his first college start, representing Butler's fourth lineup in six games.

Butler shot 61 percent in the first half and led by as many as 11 points. Soon after the lead was trimmed to 2, Hahn sank a 3-pointer. As the Bulldogs were in transition, he set up behind the arc from nearly 30 feet away.

"No way!" a fan muttered as he saw Hahn cock his left arm from that distance.

Hahn was open, so he shot it. Simple. He swished it again, expanding the lead to 57–49. The Rambers climbed within a point before Hahn sank two free throws to finish off a 65–63 victory. The Bulldogs never trailed in the closing 35 minutes, and the outcome helped restore confidence.

"It's funny. When you lose in overtime by two or three, everyone looks at it differently than when you win by two," Stevens said. "We've got to keep looking at it objectively the same way."

The Bulldogs were looking at Duke. Although the game was in East Rutherford, New Jersey, it was a virtual home court for the Blue Devils. They were 18-1 at the Meadowlands, winning their last 11.

Not only did Duke feature returning stars Kyle Singler and Nolan Smith but also Kyrie Irving, a freshman guard. Irving was coming off a 31-point game and went on to be the No. 1 pick of the 2011 NBA draft. He said he was "on a mission" in his native New Jersey. He didn't have to prove himself to Stevens, who watched him at USA Basketball's under-18 camp.

"He was ridiculous at the trials," Stevens said.

The No. 1 Blue Devils, at 7-0, had trailed for a total of only three minutes all season. They were so impressive that there were suggestions they could go undefeated. No team in college basketball had done so since Indiana in 1975–76. Considering how poorly the Bulldogs had played, the game had the makings of a mismatch. They knew it, and the increased intensity in workouts showed it.

The Bulldogs practiced Friday at Hinkle Fieldhouse before boarding a charter flight for the December 4 game. Traffic was so snarled that their bus arrived late to the hotel, and the team ate there rather than keep a restaurant reservation.

Preparation was unusual because Stevens changed strategy for Duke. Rather than instruct Butler defenders to go over ball screens—i.e., fight through offensive players setting a screen for a teammate possessing the ball—the coach told them to "go under." Going under allows a split-second opening for a shot, but the tactic also cuts off a dribbler's path to the rim for a layup.

"It's a dangerous thing to do," Stevens conceded. "For that game, we felt it was the most calculated and best thing to do. It's the only time we did it."

After a morning shootaround, the Bulldogs welcomed good news. Nored's concussion symptoms had vanished, and he was cleared for action. A crowd of 14,215 filed into the Izod Center, including Duke fans who posed for photographs with "Blue II" near courtside. A donor arranged to have the Bulldog mascot flown to New Jersey on a private jet.

Soon after the game began, it became apparent that Butler players were channeling the old version of themselves. They were ready. They were attentive. They were purposeful. They were Bulldogs.

Little more than five minutes into it, Butler led 10–5. Seldom-used Garrett Butcher came off the bench and scored seven points in an 86-second span, sending the Bulldogs ahead 21–17. Irving was enduring a half in which he had as many turnovers (four) as points. Duke managed only 4-of-16 shooting from the 3-point arc.

Onlookers either cheered or watched in stunned silence. Where had this Butler team been? It took a brilliant drive and dunk by Nolan Smith for Duke to tie the score at halftime, 33–33.

"The first half was unbelievable," Nored said. "Everything in our scout, we did it to perfection. Everything was clicking."

The Bulldogs were clicking until shortly before the midpoint of the second half. Nored picked up his fourth foul on a 3-point attempt by Nolan Smith, whose three free throws sent Duke ahead 45–44. Then Mack, who had 11 points and 5 assists to that juncture, went down. Leg cramps.

"My leg was locked," Mack said. "It felt like somebody shot me or something."

That was the beginning of the Bulldogs' end. Duke completed a 12–0 run to build a 10-point lead, and Butler did not recover. Shawn Vanzant scored 10 points in a 2½-minute span in which he personally trimmed the lead to 60–57, but successive 3s by Irvin restored the Blue Devils' command. Without Mack, the Bulldogs weren't going to exact payback. Attrition depleted them. Andrew Smith was forced to the bench when he was struck in the face, and Howard and Hahn fouled out.

Nolan Smith scored 24 points and Irving 21 in Duke's 82–70 victory. Irving went to the bench late with a toe injury that turned out to be so severe that he didn't play again until the NCAA Tournament. Duke coach Mike Krzyzewski warned Butler would be a "tough out" in the tournament, especially because of Stevens.

"He's not good. He's really good," Coach K said.

Despite an inspired performance, the Bulldogs were not feeling good. Stevens used the initials CBI—College Basketball Invitational—as the Bulldogs' destination if they didn't reverse the decline. CBI wouldn't be a consolation prize, but table scraps for the Dawgs. No Butler player was calling the Duke game a moral victory. Hahn told teammates they had to start winning games.

"You kind of felt like this team had a chance to be special because they wanted to win at the highest level," said Matthew Graves, newly promoted to associate head coach. "They weren't going to be satisfied by just keeping it close."

It was difficult to leave New Jersey with another defeat, Nored said. The game plan was sound. The execution was there. If only Mack had stayed in, the outcome might have been different.

"In the first half against Duke, we were that team in the [NCAA] tournament," Nored said. "That was a glimpse of who we ended up being, that first half against Duke."

Shelvin Mack's leg cramps weren't merely a nuisance. They were imperiling Butler's season. Trainer Ryan Galloy said he felt partially responsible for the loss to Duke because he was supposed to keep players healthy and on the court.

"Sometimes it seemed like we needed a full-time athletic trainer just for Shelvin," Galloy said.

If Mack ingested too many liquids, he developed stomachaches. If he didn't, cramps could result. Galloy and team physician Joel Kary consulted with other trainers and doctors, including the researchers for Gatorade, the carbohydrate-electrolyte beverage that was developed during the 1960s to replenish athletes.

Loss of electrolytes from sweating ranges widely among athletes, from half a gram per hour to as much as seven grams. Mack simply became dehydrated more easily than his peers. He was losing at a rate found among football players during two-a-day workouts in the middle of August.

His body was "cheating him a little bit," Galloy said. "It's not like we waved a magic wand. We just had to realize how significant it was."

Mack began drinking G2 Gatorade, which had fewer calories. There were so many bottles of the sports drink in the trainer's office that other players asked who they were for.

"They're all for Shelvin," Galloy replied.

For several weeks, Mack drank two to three bottles of V8 juice on game days, ensuring he had vitamins and minerals that enhance muscle performance. After workouts and between games, he sat in cold whirlpools, took ice baths, and underwent soft tissue massages, whether at Hinkle Fieldhouse or in hotels. Mack retained his optimism, as evidenced by his near-daily post on Twitter: "Think positive."

One retired doctor told Galloy: "Don't worry. He'll cramp again, no matter what you do."

The doc was wrong. Positive thinking, and all that treatment, worked. Mack played through the next four months without missing action because of leg cramps.

The Bulldogs traveled to Cincinnati to meet Xavier amid discussion of postseason ramifications. At 4-3, the Bulldogs were not creating a respectable résumé. Keep this up, and they would have to win the Horizon League's automatic spot to return to March Madness.

Their margin of error was "nearly gone," ESPN bracketologist Joe Lunardi wrote. Caution was suggested by Sporting News writer Mike DeCourcy. He noted "it didn't look so sweet" after early losses to Minnesota, Clemson, and Georgetown the year before. And that season culminated in the Final Four. Stevens said he wasn't thinking ahead to March.

"What happens in your first eight games doesn't make you or break you," the coach said. "But you can learn a lot from it and get better. And if you don't get better, then it doesn't matter. It's a lost cause."

Outside the Cintas Center, Xavier students lined up and taunted the Bulldogs as the team bus approached. Yelling, cussing, signs, and vulgar gestures awaited them inside the sold-out arena, where beer was served. Many of the 10,200 fans wore white T-shirts to fulfill a request for a "white-out," and some students at the Catholic university dressed in pope costumes. Students chanted, "We hate Butler, we hate Butler."

Xavier fans were steaming about the clock controversy from the previous year's 69–68 loss at Butler. Moreover, the Musketeers had won 27 straight at home—since the 74–65 loss to Butler on December 23, 2008—and had the nation's second-longest active winning streak. Xavier was once so dominant that it left Butler's conference, and here were the Bulldogs usurping Xavier's Midwest mid-major supremacy.

"Their fans really hate us. It's more than even Wright State," Howard said. "And I don't know where that started."

Howard was struck by one fan's towel as he ran out of the tunnel. Another fan, seated in the fourth row, heckled him about choosing Butler over Xavier, a school Howard had considered.

"They were nonstop yelling at me," Howard said. "That's the most hostile environment that I've ever been a part of."

The Bulldogs began by making their first five shots, going ahead 12–5. Then they missed 13 in a row and fell behind 32–22. When 7-foot, 270-pound Kenny Frease dunked in front of Butler's bench, Stevens called time-out in an attempt to restrain the Musketeers' momentum.

Butler's lockdown defense resurfaced in the second half. Xavier shot 20 percent. Xavier guard Tu Holloway, the Atlantic 10 Player of the Year, was muddling through a 2-of-11, 10-point night.

Although Xavier rebuilt its lead to 41–31, the Bulldogs tied the score at 49 on Andrew Smith's three-point play with 1:26 on the clock. Nored missed two free throws with 32 seconds left that would have sent Butler ahead for the first time in the half. Then he undercut and fouled Xavier's Mark Lyons with 3.4 seconds left. Lyons made both free throws, and Mack missed a makeable 3-pointer as time expired. Xavier won 51–49.

Nored sat on the bench, head in hands, devastated. Two teammates grabbed him to help him up. Mistakes happen, they told him.

Stevens accentuated the positive, saying the final 10 minutes were something to build on. The Bulldogs made a stand, he said, and didn't crumble.

He said Nored was resilent. Indeed, Nored was actually feeling renewed nearly six months after shin surgery and 16 days after the concussion.

"Xavier was the point in the season where I started to feel normal again," he said. "Because I felt that way, it really hurt that that was the way it ended."

Bottom line: four losses in eight games. The previous season, Butler had four losses through 37 games.

On the I-70 drive west to Indianapolis, the Bulldogs watched satellite TV on the bus. As they pulled into the Hinkle Fieldhouse parking lot, ESPN showed highlights from the game. ESPN anchor Neil Everett concluded the segment by saying: "Butler's stock. Don't buy it."

As if on cue, the bus driver turned off the engine. No one spoke. Everyone was turning off the Dawgs.

One of the odd occurrences of Butler's 2010 run to the Final Four was the West Regional final against Kansas State in which Stevens sent in Andrew Smith. Smith had not played a minute in the three previous NCAA Tournament games.

"When you know you can play with some of the best teams in the nation, that definitely helps your confidence," Smith said. "I had a good summer of open gyms and playing on my own. It's all carried over."

Indeed, if Butler had featured one big bright spot—big as in 6-foot-11—it was Smith. Teammates, notably Shelvin Mack and Ronald Nored, fed the sophomore a steady diet of encouragement. Howard, after three years, expanded his game, became a power forward, and made room for Smith at center.

In the loss to Duke, Smith scored what was then a career-high 10 points. If there was an additional crossroads, it came at the end of the Xavier game when he scored the Bulldogs' last five points. Big man. Big moments.

"He's not taking baby steps," Stevens said. "He's been taking leaps and bounds."

Smith's growth, in inches, was not so sudden. He was 24¼ inches at birth, which is so rare that it did not register on a newborn chart. Except for a 15-month spurt in which he grew three inches to 6-foot-7, his teenage maturation was gradual.

From a basketball standpoint, though, it all happened so fast. One day he was an obscure player on a summer team, the next he was a hot prospect. One day he was playing before tiny turnouts at a small Christian school, and months later he was in the Final Four before 70,000.

"It's really a great story about a kid who came out of nowhere," said John Meinen, who coached Smith's summer team.

Smith was born in Washington, DC, where his father, Curt, was communications director for Senator Dan Coats. The family soon moved back to the parents' native Indiana. Curt Smith, who is 6-foot-5, played basketball at Pike High School in Indianapolis. Smith's mother, Debbie, is 6-foot-1. She is from Marion, which won two Indiana state championships while she was in high school. Smith was distantly related to former Butler forward Pete Campbell. (Campbell's grandfather and Smith's grandfather are brothers.)

"We've always been a basketball family," Curt Smith said.

As a child, Andrew played multiple sports in Zionsville, which was Stevens's hometown, a suburb northwest of Indianapolis. In one year of grade-school football, Smith carried the ball on virtually every play, callusing him for similar violence underneath a hoop.

He enrolled at Covenant Christian High School, which had successive 3-17 seasons in his first two years there. He averaged 14.5 points as a junior and was essentially invisible to recruiters. Life changed in the summer of 2008 when Smith's Indiana Premier team opposed The Family, a Detroit team whose star was 6-foot-9 Derrick Nix, a Michigan Mr. Basketball who went to Michigan State. The Family won 82–80, but Smith had 28 points in battling Nix evenly.

"That was definitely the turning point," Smith said.

Smith's distinguishing characteristic, Meinen said, was that he was playing as hard in the last minute of a day's last game as in the first minute of the first game. The young center had an "inward fire," Meinen said, even if not demonstrative.

Smith's father said Andrew's three siblings complained about how competitive their brother was.

"He wanted to win at cards. He wanted to win at computer games," Curt Smith said. "It's not about the other guy. It's about him doing his very best."

As a Covenant senior, Smith led the state in rebounding, as Howard had done. He led his team to its first sectional title but missed eight games with a broken foot and was omitted from the Indiana All-Star team.

None of that mattered anymore. He developed an old-school hook that he shot with either hand. He didn't dunk often, but he had unusual lateral mobility. Nored compared him to a statue-sized piece of wood yet to be sculpted.

"We're just chiseling it out to be make it as fine as it can be," Nored said.

Two days after losing at Xavier, the Bulldogs soothed their anguish by beating Mississippi Valley State 91–71. The subsequent week was devoted to final exams, and the team didn't reconvene for practice until a few days later. The Bulldogs had often been clunky coming out of exams, and the circumstances of this game—a national TV date against Stanford— were untimely for a reoccurrence.

"It was a nice, natural break for our team," Matthew Graves said. "They seemed re-energized from that tough little stretch."

No Pac-10 opponent had visited Hinkle Fieldhouse in 45 years. CBS was televising a game from there for the first time.

Hinkle was "an iconic venue," according to Michael Aresco, executive president of CBS Sports. "It's got so much of the *Hoosiers* persona about it, especially after what happened last year. Let's face it: Butler burst onto the scene in a remarkable way."

As if prompted by a TV producer, Butler burst onto the CBS screen in a remarkable way. The Bulldogs led by 7 points before eight minutes elapsed, then increased that to 14. It was 41–22 at halftime. The half's final play resembled a soccer highlight: With 4.1 seconds on the clock, Shelvin Mack took an inbounds pass and threw downcourt to Matt How-ard. Rather than shoot, Howard redirected the ball over his shoulder to Andrew Smith, cutting to the rim. Smith laid it in as time expired.

The goalkeeper didn't have a chance.

In less than three minutes to open the second half, Howard scored 10 points: a 3-pointer, a banked-in goal, a three-point play, and a rebound basket. By then, Butler led 51–22 and Howard led Stanford 23–22.

"Howard's win-ning, Howard's win-ning," student fans chanted in the Dawg Pound.

The Bulldogs' margin increased to 39 before the 83–50 demolition concluded. Butler led by absurd margins in all statistical categories. Howard scored 27 points in 29 minutes. Ronald Nored called it their best game, from start to finish, of the entire season. "I think that gave us some momentum going to Hawaii," he said.

The Bulldogs headed to Honolulu for the Diamond Head Classic, one of the in-season tournaments televised by ESPN networks. Butler needed victories rather than exposure, but this was an opportunity to satisfy both.

Upon arrival, one of the team's first outings was to Pearl Harbor, the site of the Japanese attack on December 7, 1941, bringing the United States into World War II. Players were respectful and attentive, even the "goofy freshmen," trainer Ryan Galloy recalled. The players asked questions and reflected on events of 69 years before.

The Bulldogs worked out in the University of Hawaii practice gym, which lacked air-conditioning. Players sweat as profusely as they did in summer pickup games at Hinkle or in the small arena in Italy. Also working out there was Utah, whose players could be heard shouting, "Butler, Butler," the name of a play copied from the Bulldogs.

When the teams met the next night, Howard scored 23 points and Butler built a 15-point lead in winning 74–62. The Bulldogs shot 18 percent from the 3-point line—Mack was 1 of 8—but compensated elsewhere. Nored tied a career high, scoring all of his 16 points in the second half and sinking 9 consecutive free throws.

"He's a tough kid," coach Brad Stevens said. "Ever since the Xavier game, he hasn't missed very often."

The Bulldogs advanced to a semifinal against Florida State, which beat Hawaii 70–62. Florida State was an Atlantic Coast Conference power but lacked depth. Consequently, Butler players didn't have to absorb as many details because there were fewer Seminoles in the scouting report. The Bulldogs felt prepared, or as prepared as they could be with no day between games.

Neither team shot 30 percent in a first half in which Butler's 10-point lead was trimmed to 21–19. The Bulldogs fell behind 25–23 early in the second half, then outscored Florida State 26–9 over seven-plus minutes to seize a 15-point lead. Mack sank three 3s in that spree and Chase Stigall two. Chris Singleton scored 26 of his 28 points in the second half for Florida State, which rallied furiously but ultimately lost 67–64.

"You just kept thinking: 'Is he ever going to miss a shot?' We stayed the course and battled all the way to the end," Matthew Graves said.

Butler sank a season-high 11 3-pointers, making 7 of 12 in the second half. As players were leaving the arena, there was a bizarre scene in the stands, where a fight broke out between Mississippi State teammates Renardo Sidney and Elgin Bailey.

Problems confronting Butler were strictly related to basketball. The championship opponent was Washington State, which raised its record to 10-1 by beating 15th-ranked Baylor 77–71. Washington State wing Klay Thompson became an NBA first-round draft pick, as did Florida State's Singleton. Thompson, Mack, and Gordon Hayward were on the U.S. team that won the under-19 World Basketball Championship.

"In the scout, our players knew exactly what we wanted to accomplish," Graves said. "We didn't have to repeat things very often. They really wanted to win that championship; there was no question about that. The level of focus was raised to postseason level."

Not that the Bulldogs spent Christmas Eve on edge. They had most of the day free, strolling along the sand next to the Sheraton Waikiki or walking to a shopping mall. With school out of session and without travel between games, the players had more leisure hours than on most trips.

At the beach, Nored stepped on a sea urchin, which punctured the skin of his left foot with brittle spines and left a black dye. The wound stung, and the needlelike spines were not easily removed. Nored and Galloy headed to the trainer's hotel room for treatment.

"I kind of ruined his day off at the beach," Nored said.

The trainer speculated that Nored would be able to play the next day, and he asked Graves if he should speak to Stevens about it. The head coach had a lot on his mind already.

Graves's response: "No way."

The Bulldogs assembled for a short walk-through on game day, which was Christmas morning. Rather than travel to another gym, Stevens directed players to an outdoor court by the beach. No one had thought to bring a basketball, so the Bulldogs passed around a melon-shaped fruit they found on the ground. They never left a practice until someone made a half-court shot, and they didn't deviate from custom. Assistant coach Micah Shrewsberry launched the "ball," banking it off the backboard as the fruit split apart.

Now, they were ready.

Butler didn't break away from Washington State until the second half, going on a 15–0 run that stretched the margin to 58–40. The spurt featured three successive 3-pointers, one by Howard and two by Zach Hahn. The Bulldogs had been awaiting a breakout by Hahn, who was in an 0-of-17 slump from the arc. He scored all of his 14 points in the second half for the Bulldogs, who overcame Thompson's 31 points for an 84–68 victory. Stevens attempted to ignite Hahn at the previous day's practice, employing the left-hander against a zone defense.

"It was awful defensively, but that was kind of the point," Stevens said. "And the next night, he blew up."

Nored fouled out but persevered through 25 minutes on his sore foot. Mack scored 20 points and joined Howard, the MVP, on the all-tournament team. Their awards were wooden oars, unusual items to be checked through baggage claim once the team reached the airport for a red-eye flight. Howard carried the trophy aboard the jetliner and placed it in a storage bin.

The flight connected through Houston, site of the 2011 Final Four. That destination was not otherwise assured. These were Underdawgs, after all, not Houdinis.

Yet a team that was 4-4 just 16 days before had reemerged on the national scene after five successive victories, four over major programs. The Bulldogs endured a schedule that was third-toughest in the nation, according to a computer ranking.

"Hopefully, we can continue to ride this wave that we're on right now for the rest of the season," Hahn said.

Stevens was restrained. The championship was wonderful, he said, but he wanted to create new memories. He said it wouldn't mean much if the Bulldogs could not sustain progress. His was a prescient remark.

The Bulldogs had a week off before resuming Horizon League play on New Year's Day. Although they beat Valparaiso 76–59—and extended their league winning streak to a record 22—there were signs of trouble. Butler allowed a 19-point lead to be trimmed to 5 midway through the second half. The Crusaders shot 46 percent on 3-pointers against a Butler team that was ranked 19th nationally in defense from the arc.

The Bulldogs boarded a charter flight for a game two nights later at Wisconsin–Milwaukee, and Brad Stevens noticed sluggishness in a workout. It was a familiar condition. Excluding Butler, the collective record of teams leaving Hawaii since the Diamond Head Classic was 0-7.

"The trip has an effect on you," Stevens said. "I don't think it's a great time to go to Hawaii and play."

And there was never a great time to visit the Panthers, who were 7-3 against Butler in the previous 10 meetings at Milwaukee. Moreover, Milwaukee was particularly difficult for Butler to defend. The Panthers featured a strong center, 6-foot-7, 230-pound Anthony Hill, and a 6-foot-8 forward, Tony Meier, who could shoot from the perimeter. Butler could perhaps overcome latent fatigue with focus and precision . . . they proceeded to demonstrate neither.

The Panthers led by as many as 10 points in a first half in which they shot 67 percent. Considering all that, Butler was fortunate to trail 37–29 at halftime. Then Matt Howard, who had largely stayed out of foul trouble all season, picked up his second, third, and fourth fouls just 36 seconds apart early in the second half. Soon after he went to the bench, Butler's 7-point deficit swelled to 21.

Frustration accumulated. Howard was incensed at a foul he thought was charged against him, even though it was on Ronald Nored. Stevens walked onto the court to protect Howard, and the coach was assessed a rare technical.

"I think that was the closest I've been to getting a technical foul," Howard said. "I think Brad took one for me, because I was about to."

Butler's misery ended in a 76–52 defeat that was its most lopsided in 198 games. Inexplicably, Shelvin Mack scored three points, the fewest of his college career. Hill scored 22 on 9-of-10 shooting, and the Panthers shot 48 percent from the arc. Butler's defense, the foundation of success extending more than a decade, vanished.

"Butler isn't Butler anymore," a Milwaukee fan shouted gleefully.

Stevens scolded the Bulldogs afterward, telling them he had never been part of a team that played so soft. Without coaches present, Howard addressed teammates in the locker room. He wanted to make sure that it bothered them that the coach would question their effort. Stevens was right, and everyone knew it.

"That was the most frustrating game I've been a part of. Ever," Howard said.

Frustrating, and mysterious. Months later, players still had difficulty explaining the meltdown.

The Bulldogs further contributed to the strangeness by crushing

Cleveland State 79–56 at Hinkle Fieldhouse three days later. The Vikings entered the game 15-1 overall and 4-0 in the league. Yet they were over-matched, especially by Andrew Smith, who had career highs in points (22) and rebounds (10). Butler built a 19-point lead in the opening 10 minutes and delivered Stevens's 100th victory in his 120th game. Only five coaches in college basketball history won 100 faster.

Zach Hahn was so ill that he was treated with intravenous fluids, and Shawn Vanzant replaced him in the lineup. In front of 13 NBA scouts, Mack scored 6 points, dropping his average to 8.5 and shooting percent-age to .303 in league games.

Two days later, Mack scored 28. The Bulldogs needed all of that for an 84–79 victory over Youngstown State, a 22-point underdog that lost a 17th successive league road game. In keeping with the oddity of the season, the Bulldogs overcame an eight-point deficit to escape what would have been a cataclysmic upset. Howard scored 26 before foul-ing out.

Youngstown made a school-record 14 3-pointers, including 10 of 14 in the second half. If Stevens was concerned privately, he stayed positive publicly. He contended that the Bulldogs needed such a game, one in which they found a way despite everything going against them.

"Can we get better technically? Yes," he said. "Can you just all of a sud-den create the inner toughness and that resiliency and resolve? No, you can't. This team has it, and we had to show it today."

No college basketball team sails through a season on a glass-smooth lake, but Butler's was becoming a ride through river rapids.

When confronted with an animated crowd at Detroit, the Bulldogs shot 57 percent and mounted a 22-point halftime lead in an 87–64 vic-tory. Howard sank a career-high five 3s, and Smith and freshman Khyle Marshall each dunked twice.

Yet two days later, Butler couldn't close it out at Wright State. The Bull-dogs led by five points with less than five minutes left—the kind of games they always won—but allowed the Raiders to beat them 69–64. Fans stormed the court and carried off guard N'Gai Evans, who scored 20 of his 26 points in the second half. With three seconds left, Mack's poten-tial tying 3-pointer rattled around the rim, nearly dropped through, and instead spewed out. Those were the shots the Bulldogs always made—until this season, anyway.

Butler, at 13-6, retained a high RPI and strength of schedule. However,

even Howard suggested it was "pretty much out of the question" for the
Bulldogs to reach the NCAA Tournament with an at-large berth.

Howard bailed them out in their next outing, collecting 29 points and
a career-high 16 rebounds in an 81–75 home victory over Wisconsin–
Green Bay. However, the Bulldogs were as uneven in the game as they
had been all season: Behind by 9 points, ahead by 21, then ahead by just 3.

Two days later, on January 23, Stan Howard sang the national anthem
on his son's 22nd birthday. He was in tune . . . and the Bulldogs again were
not. Milwaukee shot 54 percent in an 86–80 overtime victory, becoming
the first Horizon team to win at Hinkle Fieldhouse in 23 months. Butler
played the overtime without Howard, who fouled out. There were 15 ties
and 21 lead changes, but it was Milwaukee making the key plays. Tone
Boyle scored 8 of his 15 points in overtime, and Bulldog-killer Anthony
Hill scored 18 despite foul trouble.

"I think it's only as devastating as you make it," Howard said. "If you
let it fester and bother you all week and don't come ready to play Saturday, then it can be really devastating."

As had been the case for years in this league, everybody came ready
to play Butler. A record-tying sellout of 5,432 turned out at Valparaiso
in anticipation of beating the Bulldogs, who hadn't lost to their in-state
rivals since December 4, 1993. It would be a Crusaders crusade. It was
so important that Valpo guard Brandon Wood, who hadn't practiced in
10 days because of a hamstring injury, decided after warm-ups that he
would play.

The Bulldogs stayed composed, establishing an eight-point lead in the
first half that they extended to nine early in the second. Then a seasonlong vulnerability—3-point defense—foiled them. After beginning 1 of
10 from the arc, Valparaiso shot 9 of 12. Butler, trailing by eight with less
than three minutes left, came back to tie the score at 67 and go into overtime. Yet the Bulldogs couldn't overcome defensive lapses, even with 13
3s of their own. Valparaiso survived 85–79, prompting a court-storming
scene resembling the one at Wright State.

"You saw what the court was like after the game, right?" Stevens said.
"That's the way it's going to be. Deal with it. Have fun with it. Shoot, come
in and play in front of a packed house. That's a blast. That's what I come
here for."

The Bulldogs scanned the box score, stunned to see they allowed 59
points in the second half and overtime. Fifty-nine points after halftime?

"That shouldn't happen," Nored said.

Stevens continued managing the erratic season. What's important, he said, was that the Bulldogs stay together in good times and bad. They hadn't often lived through times like these. They were 0-3 in overtime games. They were 14-8. At 6-4 in the league, they were closer to seventh place than to first.

On the other hand, Stevens believed in two maxims: (1) You're never as good as you think you are, nor as bad as you think are, and (2) A good team in your league is going to play better against you than a team that has never seen you before. Tellingly, Butler was more effective against bigger teams in December—Stanford, Utah, Florida State, and Washington State—than against smaller Horizon teams in January. Stevens was seeing progress from the Bulldogs in practice, even though they weren't finishing off victories.

"We learned a lot as a coaching staff through this time," Graves said. "It made us better coaches. We had to continue to focus on better ways to communicate to our players how we wanted to cover certain things defensively."

With four league losses in January, the Bulldogs began February in a precarious place, but they still had a chance to pull themselves into the race during a trip to northeast Ohio. First stop was Youngstown State, which had beaten Butler once in 20 games since joining the league. But after nearly losing to the Penguins 25 days earlier, Butler was on alert—or should have been.

Butler fell behind by nine early in the second half but eventually went ahead 57–47. Fewer than six minutes remained in a game in which offensive and defensive execution had been admirable, especially on the road. Then, inexplicably, everything unraveled. The Bulldogs botched late possessions, and the Penguins followed with scores.

Freshman guard Kendrick Perry sank a 3-pointer with 21 seconds left, capping a 10–0 spurt by Youngstown that became a 62–60 victory. Nored dove for the ball in the closing seconds and cut the palm of his left hand on a media table, adding injury to upset. Butler was 6-5 in a league that . . . well, was better than usual, but hardly a superpower. Butler had lost three in a row, four of five, and led in the second half of all four defeats. Butler was in crisis, more so than at any time in Stevens's four seasons as head coach. Graves said the coaches were at a crossroads where they could lose the team altogether.

"I thought we were out of lives at that point," Stevens acknowledged.

In addressing the players afterward, Stevens accepted responsibility, saying he needed to get better. Zach Hahn didn't think that was the appropriate message. "No, *we* need to get better," Hahn said. The senior guard went around the locker room, identifying each player's strength and what he contributed.

When responding to a reporter, Hahn spoke with equal parts disapproval and defiance. The Bulldogs weren't making the tough plays, he said. That's what the old Butler teams did. So what was next for this Butler team?

"Win 'em all. Next game we play, Cleveland State, try to win that," Hahn said. "Then win the rest of them."

Howard felt lower than he did after Evansville. It was hard to comprehend it all. What was going on? The Bulldogs weren't getting the breaks they once did. Was there more to it? On the bus ride to Cleveland, Howard approached Stevens, who was reassuring. The Bulldogs were getting there, the coach said.

Other players weren't comforted. Mack and Nored looked at each other. This was awful, they agreed. Grant Leiendecker recalled a feeling of near hopelessness. If the Bulldogs hadn't figured it out by then, they probably wouldn't. The bus ride was silent. It felt as if theirs was the only vehicle on the road. Wheels spun along the pavement, and inside the players' heads.

"The silence felt so loud because they had to be racking their brains," radio announcer Brandon Gaudin said. "They knew what was on that bus was a lot of special talent and a lot of special players. How could we be in the middle of the Horizon League? It felt very weird."

Overnight, something happened to the Bulldogs that can't really be explained. It was as if they rediscovered themselves. Before, those were not Butler players wearing Butler uniforms. Now, the authentic ones were displacing the imposters.

"The spirit of the team when we went to bed and when we woke up was completely different," Ronald Nored said.

That morning, Shelvin Mack, who had not played like the NBA prospect he was purported to be, asked to speak to the team. He shouldered much of Butler's failures himself. He was ordinarily such a quiet leader that teammates were surprised. His voice was shaky, but his message was

strong. Mack attempted to lift up the team, and his words had a unify-
ing effect.

Brad Stevens said what Mack did was necessary. The best players
"have to exhibit your values the best," the coach said. Nored said Mack
showed he was "really buying into who we were," and not distracted by
NBA reverie.

"The one thing I'm really happy we didn't do is overreact to
Youngstown," Stevens said. "We never even mentioned the game the next
day."

Later that day, the players went to a movie, *The Mechanic*, which
was about a professional assassin. The killer's gun had an inscription:
"Victory loves preparation." The maxim could have been copied from
the Butler basketball manual. Nored immediately recognized that, and
before noon tip-off the next day, asked the Bulldogs to apply that mentality to Cleveland State.

"It was an intense movie," Matt Howard recalled, "but maybe what we
needed."

If this was an important game for Butler, it was no less so for Cleveland State, whose 10-2 record led the league. The Wolstein Center welcomed an ESPN2 audience and 8,490 fans for "Butler Blackout Day."
Though the Vikings were home, they wore new black uniforms, compelling the Bulldogs to wear white.

Nored didn't practice the day before because of a bandaged hand
requiring five stitches. So Chase Stigall made his first Butler start. Cleveland State went on an 11-0 run to go ahead 16–10, but Butler soon erased
that deficit. The Bulldogs shot 55 percent in the second half and, except
for 63 seconds, never trailed.

Butler players were usually undemonstrative, but after one sequence,
Mack and Nored chest-bumped each other. In the final two minutes, with
the shot clock expiring, Howard sank a high-arching 3-pointer, bringing teammates on the bench to their feet. Of Butler's final 18 points in a
73–61 victory, Howard scored 9 and Mack 6.

"We weren't confused anymore about what we were supposed to do,"
Nored said. "It all came together. After that game, basketball was fun
again."

What had been an uneven season turned into a fifth consecutive regular-
season Horizon championship. Cleveland State represented such a turn-

around that it was the first of seven successive league victories—as Hahn forecast. Stevens continued to start Stigall instead of Nored, who had been the regular point guard for three seasons. Shelvin Mack and Shawn Vanzant shared duties at the point.

In one week, the Bulldogs won home games over Illinois–Chicago, 72–65, Wright State, 71–63, and Detroit, 66–51. The latter featured Mack's career-high 32 points, including 24 in the second half. Butler went on the road to beat Green Bay 64–62 (on Howard's game-winning drive and dunk) and UIC 79–52.

February's two scariest moments involved the health of Howard and Stevens. At the end of the first half of the first UIC game, Howard cut his head in a collision. His face was so bloodied that he looked like a battered boxer. Not only did he not return to that game but he was sidelined for the next because of concussion symptoms. Howard engaged in heated debate, telling trainer Ryan Galloy he should be allowed to play.

"He wouldn't back down," Howard said, referring to Galloy. "At some point I had to give up. I really wanted to play. I guess it wasn't supposed to be."

Butler closed the regular season by beating Loyola 63–56 on Senior Day, when about 1,500 Connersville residents showed up to cheer Howard in his final home game. The Bulldogs tied Milwaukee and Cleveland State with a 13-5 record—the most losses ever for a Horizon champion. Stevens had to leave during the first half because of blurred vision that was diagnosed as corneal edema. He was disappointed to miss the ceremony for the seniors, and surprised by a vow made by Matthew Graves, who took charge of the team.

"We're gunning for Milwaukee," Graves announced to the sellout crowd. "We're coming there to getcha."

Stevens asked what Graves was thinking to make such a pronouncement, and the assistant coach conceded he was caught up in the moment. "But I meant it," Graves said.

Stevens returned to practice the next day, this time wearing glasses. His vision was returning, and he was directing a team that never lost sight of the season's goal—to win the league tournament and return to March Madness. The bumpy road was underscored by the fact that Mack, the Horizon's preseason player of the year, didn't make the all-league first team. However, without Mack's oration in Cleveland and steady play throughout February, the Bulldogs would not have reversed the decline.

Neither would they have done so without a renewed commitment to, and understanding of, their complex defense.

"Everyone knew their roles," Stevens said. "Guys on the scout team played as hard as they could every day."

The team boarded a flight to Milwaukee for the Horizon tournament and a March 5 semifinal against Cleveland State. The Vikings, featuring league player of the year Norris Cole, had reason to believe they could win this third meeting. They beat Butler at Hinkle Fieldhouse to win the league tournament in 2009, and Cole predicted a month earlier that Butler and Cleveland State would meet again in 2011.

Mack was so adrenalized during the first half that after he sank a 3-pointer, he turned to Cleveland State coach Gary Waters and told him he'd better find someone who could guard him. Butler led 41–35 at halftime.

In the first minute of the second half, Stevens didn't approve of the way Vanzant was playing and benched him. It was as if the coach lit a fuse. Vanzant soon returned, and he helped the Bulldogs surge to a 10-point lead. Cleveland State kept applying pressure, closing within 60–58. Soon thereafter, Vanzant sank a long 3-pointer.

"Most college players don't make that shot," Stevens said. "That's a gut-check shot."

Then Vanzant hit another 3-pointer. It was 66–58, and the Vikings were sinking.

"It took all the wind out of our sails. It just took it out," Waters said.

Vanzant scored all of his season-high 18 points in the final 13 minutes—12 points in the last 5 minutes—to highlight Butler's 76–68 victory. The Vikings had a 26-8 record and league co-championship, but they simply could not beat Butler.

The outcome set up a March 8 championship game against Milwaukee, which won its semifinal over Valparaiso 70–63. With two days off between games, Stevens wanted to transport the team south to a Chicago gym to break up the monotony, but a tournament rule disallowed that. So the Bulldogs stayed in Milwaukee, attending a Sunday night NBA game between the Milwaukee Bucks and Boston Celtics.

The Bulldogs' defense was ineffective in both previous meetings against Milwaukee, so they were altering tactics. For one thing, they were changing defensive rotations around the perimeter, where Milwaukee burned Butler. For another, they were changing strategy against

Anthony Hill, who liked to body up against defenders. To counter that, the Bulldogs would station themselves far enough away to prevent Hill from creating contact. Move your feet like a boxer, Stevens told the Bulldogs.

Stevens considered starting 6-foot-7 Garrett Butcher, who was mostly sidelined since mid-January because of a bone bruise. Then Butcher hyperextended his knee. Galloy advised withholding Butcher from practice, believing rest would be better than stress.

On the bus ride to the climactic game, Butler players were absorbed in thought, steely looks all around. Headphones were in their ears, cell phones set aside. The only assurance they had of returning to the NCAA Tournament was victory over a team that had already beaten them twice.

Nored, as usual, was the first to take the floor for warm-ups. He walked out to a crescendo of boos from Milwaukee students who gathered early. "I loved it. I enjoyed it so much," he said. "It was one of the coolest things that ever happened to me."

Milwaukee was the bully of the league, and coach Rob Jeter was on the verge of putting the Panthers back in the NCAA bracket. On his Twitter account, Hill suggested he would mimic putting on a title belt, as Green Bay Packers quarterback Aaron Rodgers did at the Super Bowl. Not that Butler needed any more fuel.

In the opening minute, Milwaukee guard Kaylon Williams came off a screen and looked to pass out to Tony Meier. That play had always been open before. This time, Meier was guarded. Nored said that set the tone for the game.

"You could almost see the faces of the Milwaukee players was like, 'That wasn't supposed to happen,'" Graves said. "We really dictated how this game was going to be played."

Mack was so animated that he took the ball from the top of the arc, drove all the way to the rim, and dunked—which he *never* did. That contributed to a surge that sent Butler ahead 23–6 midway through the first half. Milwaukee trimmed a 17-point deficit to 42–39, but Butler soon restored the margin to 17. The backbreaker was delivered by Chase Stigall, who ran to the left corner, caught Mack's inbounds pass, and shot in the same motion. The result: 3 points and an 11-point lead.

Mack mimed the title belt maneuver himself as the clock wound down on the Bulldogs' 59–44 victory, putting them in the NCAA Tournament a fifth straight year. Butcher came off the bench and was instrumental in holding Hill to two field goals and 10 points—half of what Hill usually scored against Butler.

Stevens turned to Galloy and said: "See why I wanted to start him?"

Galloy replied: "See why I didn't want to practice him?"

They were both right.

In a postgame news conference, Stevens reflected on the eight-game winning streak and the abyss from which the Bulldogs had climbed. Winning a conference tournament is so much harder than anyone realizes, he said. Stevens declared that it was Butler's best game of the season.

"That was laser focus," he said. "That was pretty special."

Andrew Smith performed an awkward-looking cartwheel on the court, a Butler tradition for important victories. But Stevens aborted most postgame revelry. He didn't want players cutting down the nets because he didn't want to show the host Panthers any disrespect . . . and there was no ladder available . . . and maybe there was more to be won.

CHAPTER 11

BACK-TO-BACK

It wouldn't be an NCAA Tournament without a Butler sideshow. No player's rap lyrics were involved this time. It was a canine controversy.

The tourney talk wasn't that Butler received a No. 8 seed and would play No. 9 seed Old Dominion in Washington, DC. It was that Blue II would be barred from the site. At the 2010 Final Four, the NCAA made an exception to a rule banning live mascots, allowing Blue II in Lucas Oil Stadium.

The 2011 decision was something that Blue II handler Michael Kaltenmark expected, and he wasn't particularly perturbed. But there was an outpouring of hostility from fans, who began using the hash tag #FreeButlerBlue2 on Twitter posts. Kaltenmark speculated the reaction might have been a manifestation of perceived snubs in Butler's tournament selection and seeding over the years.

"I have no hard feelings, honestly," Kaltenmark said. "We're big boys. I think it's been interesting to see the fan reaction on Twitter. This thing just blew up."

Butler filmed a music video—featuring Blue II, Ron5 Robot, and costumed mascot Hink preparing for March Madness—that was posted on YouTube. That video attracted 16,000 viewers, but nothing approached Blue II's popularity. Butler professor Deb Lecklider delivered Norman Rockwell–styled portraits of Blue II to the Verizon Center, and a Blue II mask was featured on ESPN's *Pardon the Interruption*.

The bulldog eventually ended up on the front page of a Montreal newspaper, the TMZ celebrity website, and on ESPN's *First Take*. He received his own Blue II mobile van from a local Ford dealership. Kaltenmark said he hoped the mini-dispute would relieve pressure from the basketball Bulldogs and allow them to "fly under the radar."

There should have been a controversy over the Southeast Regional seeding because Old Dominion's résumé was superior to Butler's in every way. The Monarchs were better in win-loss record (27-6 to 23-9), record against the tournament field (7-4 to 1-3), RPI (20th to 34th), and strength of schedule (64th to 75th). By those numbers, Old Dominion should have been a No. 5, 6, or 7, and Butler a No. 9, 10, or 11.

The selection committee wasn't supposed to consider the name of the school or what happened in 2010, but it was hard to imagine that wasn't a factor. The seeding supported a theory that the Bulldogs would have made the expanded 68-team field as an at-large entry even if they had lost in the Horizon League Tournament. Old Dominion had more wins than any opening opponent Butler had ever met.

Before pairings were announced, ESPN analyst Jay Bilas restated the obvious, saying "it's a stretch" to think Butler could return to the Final Four.

"Last year was a little bit of a perfect storm," Bilas said.

As Butler players watched the CBS selection show in the Wildman Room of Hinkle Fieldhouse, many had coaches' children sitting in their laps. If there was one picture expressing the family atmosphere the program nurtured, that was it. The only reaction during the show was audible relief when the 8/9 pairing opposite Ohio State was revealed. The Bulldogs did not want to be in a bracket with the No. 1–ranked Buckeyes, led by former Butler coach Thad Matta, who hired Stevens in 2000. A Brad versus Thad story line would have been irresistible to the media.

Old Dominion was a difficult assignment. The Monarchs' Norfolk, Virginia, campus was about a four-hour drive from Washington, so they would have plenty of local support. They came from the same conference—Colonial Athletic Association—that sent George Mason to the Final Four in 2006. Some were identifying Old Dominion as the George Mason or Butler of this tournament, the mid-major to make a Final Four run. Most important, the Monarchs led the nation in offensive rebounding, grabbing 45 percent of their missed shots.

"It's a staggering number, something I've never seen before," Brad Stevens said.

ESPN analyst Doug Gottlieb, who covered the Bulldogs in Hawaii, compared Butler to Connecticut for becoming hot at tournament time.

UConn won five games in as many days in the Big East Tournament, and, coincidentally, was also assigned to Washington. The Butler and UConn teams were lodged in the same hotel, the Crystal City Marriott.

Old Dominion was a trendy pick to beat Butler, a 2½-point underdog in the betting line. It was similarly fashionable to pick No. 12 seed Old Dominion in 2007, No. 10 South Alabama in 2008, and No. 12 UTEP in 2010—and all lost. Butler was 5-1 in NCAA Tournament openers since 2001.

Seeing sights in the nation's capital can be inspirational—Butler's team bus drove past the White House—but the Bulldogs were introduced to a real-life symbol of freedom. Trainer Ryan Galloy invited a longtime friend, Kevin Carson, to join the team for dinner the night before Butler's game. Carson was undergoing physical therapy at Walter Reed Army Medical Center, recovering from shrapnel wounds sustained in Iraq.

Carson, who received head injuries and lost part of his hand in the attack, had a Purple Heart personally delivered to him in his hospital bed by President Obama. Carson was a football player and pole vaulter at Jacobs High School in Algonquin, Illinois, and later a sheriff's deputy in Steamboat Springs, Colorado. Carson left his job to enlist in the military.

"One of the toughest guys I've ever met," Galloy said.

Carson became a Butler fan through his connection to Galloy, who gave him a poster of the 2010 Final Four team that was autographed by all the players. Carson rode on the bus with the Bulldogs, seated behind Stevens. One by one, players shook the soldier's hand as they stepped off the bus.

"It was good for the guys," Galloy said. "He has embodied all the values that we talk about."

Old Dominion's rebounding was not the lone issue confronting Butler. The Monarchs featured long-armed defenders whose zone resembled a man-to-man, and whose man-to-man resembled a zone. The Bulldogs appeared as if they could shoot over that zone when Mack sank two early 3-pointers, but points came grudgingly.

Old Dominion's Frank Hassell, a 6-foot-9 forward, scored the final two baskets of the first half to send the Monarchs ahead 29–27. They were every bit as rugged as depicted.

"That game was all about toughness," Butler point guard Ronald

Nored said. "It was way harder than I thought it was going to be. Those guys were physical, one of the most physical teams that we had played."

The lead seesawed until a personal 6–0 run by an unlikely source—Garrett Butcher—put Butler ahead 47–42. It was Butcher's first tournament action; he did not play in any of the 2010 games because of aching knees. Moreover, he was in such pain from his bone bruise that he didn't practice the day before Old Dominion, just as he didn't practice the day before Milwaukee. He fought ferociously on the boards, twice scoring on offensive rebounds.

The Bulldogs carried a six-point lead into the final six minutes but couldn't preserve it. Hassell scored twice more inside, and Old Dominion tied the score at 58 on two free throws with 31 seconds left.

On the last possession, Butler placed the ball in the hands of Shawn Vanzant, who was looking inside for Andrew Smith. Vanzant misread the defense, and with seconds ticking away, had to do something. His feet slipped along the right baseline, so to keep the ball alive, he threw it in the air toward the rim. Smith leaped to tap the ball off the glass. Witnessing all this was Matt Howard, alone at the foul line. Howard rushed from there to the left side of the rim, retrieved the ball, and laid it in right-handed as time expired.

Final: Butler 60, Old Dominion 58.

Butler won the first buzzer-beater of the tournament, setting off an uncharacteristic display by Howard. He pumped his arm, joined teammates in leaping up and down, and pointed to Smith before the two bumped chests. Officials reviewed the sequence and ruled Howard's shot came in time.

"Andrew made that play," Howard said. "He had like three guys jumping with him. They just left me all by myself."

Smith's alert play came seven miles from where he was born. His family moved from Washington to Indianapolis when he was a few months old.

Butler grabbed 18 offensive rebounds, five by Butcher, and outrebounded the nation's No. 1 rebounding team, 32–29. Old Dominion coach Blaine Taylor said the Bulldogs "did a good job of chasing down those ricocheted biscuits."

Butler was 7 of 26 on 3-pointers but followed the plotline from the previous year: trail in the second half, limit an opponent to fewer than 60 points, win in the clutch. Stevens said no team was as tournament-tested as Butler. Mack had watched such finishes on TV and enjoyed being part of one. He called the end "an amazing moment."

For any other team, it would have been. For Butler, it was almost commonplace.

By most yardsticks, Khyle Marshall flourished as a freshman. But the 6-foot-6 Butler forward from Davie, Florida, had gone for more than a month without making a significant impact. Over eight games, he totaled 13 points, and in none of the eight did he play more than 14 minutes. His contribution against Old Dominion was seven scoreless minutes. With top-seeded Pittsburgh looming next, the Bulldogs needed more out of him.

Assistant coach Micah Shrewsberry pulled Marshall aside in an attempt to encourage and motivate him. Down the road, Shrewsberry told Marshall, you will need to make big plays.

"Bring energy," was the message.

Serendipity brought Marshall to Butler. A precocious childhood, a summer camp, and a thunderstorm helped direct him to the Indianapolis campus. If not for all that, he might have become a soccer or baseball player in south Florida.

Marshall wasn't targeted when Shrewsberry and Brad Stevens were recruiting at a summer tournament in Orlando. They were leaving an off-site gym for the main arena when a downpour began. Shrewsberry came back inside the gym, and Marshall's team was playing. The coach saw Marshall but didn't know who he was, and began recruiting him.

Marshall was unusual for Butler in that he became a nationally ranked prospect—as high as 118th—out of high school. Old Dominion and Alabama–Birmingham were among his final three choices, and Kansas State and Auburn made scholarship offers.

Butler was appealing for its winning tradition, small campus, and academic orientation. Marshall's parents underscored how important studies were when they kept him off sixth- and seventh-grade teams because they didn't think his grades were high enough.

"Even at the age of two, we knew he was more advanced than other kids his age," said Myrline Marshall, his mother. "His ability to learn things and retain it was unbelievable."

Marshall's mother was born in Haiti and his father, Joseph, was born in Saint Lucia. They met as students at Florida International University, where Joseph played on a soccer team that won the NCAA Division II championship in 1982. Marshall's father advised his son to earn a championship ring to match his own.

"He never takes his ring off," Marshall said.

The son dabbled in his father's sport but was more interested in baseball. He finally picked up basketball at age 12. He was behind peers in basic skills, but he joined friends at a summer basketball camp for eighth-graders. His athleticism was so evident that he soon attracted the attention of college recruiters.

He could have enrolled at Pine Crest School, a Fort Lauderdale power featuring Brandon Knight, the 2010 national high school player of the year who went to Kentucky. Or Marshall could have gone to Flanagan High School, which had little hoops tradition. Flanagan coach Michael Bentivegna said Marshall believed in him and stayed loyal to the school in nearby Pembroke Pines.

"They really had a plan for me that I didn't see myself," Marshall said.

When Marshall was a freshman, Bentivegna recommended to Florida coach Billy Donvovan that he build a recruiting relationship. Marshall was going to be that good, the high school coach said. Bentivegna went to Donovan's office again two years later and told him the same thing. No offer was forthcoming. Butler was the beneficiary.

Marshall grew from 6-foot-2 to 6-foot-6 between his freshman and sophomore years, and his aptitude began catching up to his altitude. Work ethic was ingrained. If everyone else was doing 100 reps, his mother said, he was to do 120. If everyone else left practice after an hour, his father said, he was to stay another hour. Marshall began to understand this new sport better.

In contradicting those claiming Flanagan could never win, Marshall's teams went 17-11 and 19-5 in his final two seasons and won a district championship. He averaged 28 points as a senior, scoring 52 in one game.

He attended the 2010 Final Four in Indianapolis, stimulating his appetite for college basketball. College was a "huge adjustment," and not only for schoolwork, time management, and the complexities of Butler's system. He had never seen snow nor been so cold.

"I probably have four or five coats in my closet now," Marshall said. "Layers, thick clothing."

That kept him warm. There was no keeping him under wraps.

Movie themes continued to follow the Bulldogs. The previous year, it was *Hoosiers*. This trip, it was *Remember the Titans*. Before taking on Pittsburgh, the Bulldogs' shootaround was in Alexandria, Virginia, at T.C. Williams High School, whose integrated football team was the subject of the popular film.

At a pregame news conference, Pittsburgh and Butler tried to cast themselves as the aggrieved party. Such a role wasn't applicable to either side.

Butler was coming off an appearance in the national championship game, of course. Pittsburgh crushed North Carolina–Asheville 71–54 in the opening game. The Panthers were not only 28-5 but had advanced to the Sweet Sixteen five times in nine years. Criticism stemmed from the fact that the road almost always ended there.

Pittsburgh was a No. 4 seed or higher seven times in those nine years, and reached the Elite Eight once. Pittsburgh had not made the Final Four since 1941, when one victory was required. (Coincidentally, the Bulldogs' opening 35–33 victory over Pittsburgh at newly built Butler Fieldhouse launched them toward the 1929 national championship.)

Pittsburgh players were testy when speaking about what they called "America's team," the Bulldogs. "Pitt's program has always been overlooked," guard Brad Wanamaker said. Coach Jamie Dixon downplayed the comments, saying the Panthers used different sources of motivation.

Butler guard Shawn Vanzant reiterated that he thrived as the underdog, and that it was nothing new. "Last year, every single round, we were picked against," Andrew Smith added. "At this point, I don't even listen to it anymore."

The game renewed an Indiana high school rivalry between Pittsburgh center Gary McGhee (Anderson Highland) and Matt Howard (Connersville). Their schools were in the same conference, and Connersville won every meeting.

Hostility did not extend everywhere. Shelvin Mack was a close friend of Pittsburgh guard Ashton Gibbs, a bond that began when they were on the under-19 national team coached by Dixon. The players continued to correspond via cell phone, texts, and Skype.

History and odds—not to mention size and athleticism—favored
Pittsburgh. Butler was a 7½-point underdog. Since NCAA Tournament
expansion in 1985, No. 1 seeds were 91-13 in the round of 32, winning
87.5 percent. As valiant as the 8s and 9s were, their efforts were futile.
Stevens joked that he was a "stats geek" and knew the data.

"We're just trying to be one of those 12 percent," he said.

Privately, the Bulldogs were confident. Indeed, self-belief was sometimes all they had going for them. Practice was purposeful, and players
were edgy. Mack thought he had picked up some tips from watching
the way Pittsburgh defended against All-America guard Kemba Walker
of Connecticut. When Stevens first started reviewing film, he thought
the Bulldogs would have a better chance against Pittsburgh than Old
Dominion. The Panthers "weren't the most talented No. 1 seed," Stevens
said, but had been well coached by Dixon. The matchup that worried
Stevens was not Gibbs, an All–Big East selection, but Gilbert Brown, a
6-foot-6 forward averaging 11 points a game.

Before tip-off, the Panthers fired themselves up by locking arms and
swaying as one of them performed a dance in the middle of their circle.
Consensus opinion was that they had the easiest path to the Final Four of
any No. 1 seed, and they weren't about to waste this opportunity.

From the beginning against Pittsburgh, the Bulldogs were sharp. They
committed a turnover on their first possession but only one in the rest of
the half. When Chase Stigall caught Mack's lob for a layup, he extended
Butler's streak to six consecutively made shots. Every starter had scored,
and the Bulldogs led 14-10. Mack's long 3-pointer extended that to 17-12.

"That shot was unguardable," TBS analyst Mike Gminski said. "Unlim-
ited range for Shelvin Mack."

The Bulldogs were finding the range, all right, starting 8 of 11 from the
field and 4 of 5 from the arc. Soon after Zach Hahn entered, his 3-pointer
from the left corner increased the margin to 23-16. He came into the
game with Ronald Nored, who attached himself to Gibbs.

"Look at the work being done by Gibbs, trying to get away from
Nored," TBS announcer Tim Brando said.

Hahn missed his second 3-point attempt, but Khyle Marshall
rebounded the ball and dunked to build Butler's lead to 25-18. It was
easier for the Bulldogs to keep firing from outside than to pass inside to
Howard or Smith, so they kept doing it. Howard sealed off a defender
to free Mack, who drove near the rim and banked in a basket to provide

Butler's largest lead of the half, 30–18. Howard made his first two shots—both from the 3-point line—but couldn't convert in the foul lane, repeatedly missing left-handed attempts.

The Panthers went on an 11–0 run to pull within one point. Then Mack found himself open beyond the top of the arc and swished his third 3-pointer, shouting exultantly afterward. Gminski said the Pittsburgh defender had done everything correctly.

"That's just a great shooter beating you," Gminski said.

As the half came to an end, Mack again had the ball at the top of Pittsburgh's zone. Two defenders dropped their hands, and Mack fired again. Three points.

The Bulldogs made eight 3s in the first half, four by Mack, who scored 16 points. They led 38–30. They were 20 minutes from the Sweet Sixteen. Stevens told sideline reporter Lewis Johnson that the Bulldogs executed their offense as well as they had in two months.

"The NCAA Tournament is a chance at immortality," Brando said. "And Shelvin Mack so far has had an opportunity to do just that."

Mack sank his fifth 3-pointer, again from well beyond the arc, to send Butler ahead 41–32 early in the half. But as crisp as the Bulldogs were on offense, they were vulnerable on defense. As Stevens feared, Brown was stinging them.

"We couldn't guard them," Stevens said.

The Panthers' 12–0 spurt propelled them ahead for the first time since the opening moments, 43–41, and Brown's 3-pointer increased the margin to 46–43.

Pittsburgh's alternating coverages blunted Butler's offense. Mack's baseline jumper—with a high degree of difficulty—returned the lead to the Bulldogs, 48–46.

The quality and ferocity of play caused Brando to suggest the game "easily could be played next week," in the Southeast Regional finals. "A remarkable game," he said. "Both teams just absolutely scintillating on the offensive end of the floor."

Nasir Robinson scored over Smith—who flopped without inducing a foul call—to create Pittsburgh's largest lead, 53–48. Moments later, Mack had the ball behind the arc and waited to see if the 6-foot-11 McGhee would come out on him. McGhee allowed space, and Mack rattled in a 3-pointer to tie the score at 57.

"Right on cue," Brando said.

When Brown's three free throws—on Mack's foul behind the arc—restored the Pittsburgh lead to 60–57, Mack responded. With the shot clock expiring, he pump-faked, then sank his seventh 3-pointer. Butler 60, Pittsburgh 60.

"Wow. Mack the Knife," Gminski said.

"Wake up the echoes of Bobby Darin," Brando said, referring to the singer's Grammy-award-winning recording from 1959.

As the Bulldogs seized a 64–60 lead, the TBS analyst elaborated on the offensive sets they performed. This was not really a No. 8 seed, Gminski suggested.

"They have a very deep playbook," he said. "They really cut hard, and they execute as well as any team I've seen in the half-court."

With 2:45 left, Mack made the first of two free throws for his 30th point, an NCAA Tournament record by a Butler player. Then he followed with a rare miss off the back rim. Thus the Bulldogs led only 67–65, and were soon tied by McGhee's inside basket.

Wanamaker's one-and-one pushed Pittsburgh in front 69–67. Howard dumped the ball inside to Smith, who was fouled and, like Mack, made the first of two free throws. So the Panthers held a 69–68 lead when Dixon called time-out with 1:13 on the clock.

"Does it get any better? Would you like to be anywhere else?" Brando asked.

Brown finally missed from the field when play resumed, and Butler called time-out with 60 seconds left. After the break, Howard missed from the arc, Smith flubbed a putback, and Pittsburgh came away with the ball and a one-point lead.

The Bulldogs needed a stop. The year before, they almost always got one when they needed one. This year, and this team, was not like that year and that team. Yet this Butler team was not the team it was earlier in the season, either.

The Panthers were so deliberate that they were whistled for a shot-clock violation as Gibbs held the ball. With 7.1 seconds left, Stevens called time-out. Then Pittsburgh called time-out.

"And the chess game continues. Gotta love it," Brando said.

His TBS colleague, Gminski, speculated the ball would go to Mack or Howard. Instead, Vanzant, who had the ball at the end against Old Dominion, was entrusted with it. He dribbled toward the right side and found a wide-open Smith, who laid it in with a few seconds left.

Butler 70, Pittsburgh 69.

What ensued was one of the most bizarre finishes in NCAA Tournament history. Indeed, one of the most bizarre in any contest in any sport.

With Pittsburgh almost out of chances to reverse the outcome, and Brown dribbling the ball near midcourt, Mack ran toward him. And into him. Mack fouled Brown about 45 feet from the basket with 1.4 seconds on the clock. Two free throws by Brown, and it would be Pittsburgh heading to the Sweet Sixteen.

The prevailing emotion on the Butler sideline was disbelief. A game that the Bulldogs had fought so hard to win, and seemingly *had* won, was all but snatched away. Nored and Howard held their heads in their hands. Smith despaired because he thought Brown was being awarded three free throws.

On the bench, Grant Leiendecker prayed: "God, I cannot end my career on such an unbelievably stupid play. Please allow him to miss one."

The game looked over. Leiendecker was nearly in tears. So was Mack. So were Butler fans in the stands and watching on TV around the country. And those 30,000 feet in the air.

Players on Butler's baseball team, heading to Indianapolis after a spring trip, were on AirTran Flight 856 from Orlando and listening to the broadcast on satellite radio. They cheered and moaned at the ebb and flow. This was a low point. As the ballplayers slouched in their seats, one turned and whispered to another, "We just lost."

On the Butler bench, some were trying to stay optimistic.

A senior, Alex Anglin, told Nored: "He'll miss one."

Trainer Ryan Galloy offered similar assurance: "He'll miss one."

Stevens put his hands on his hips and shouted at the officials but, as usual, kept his mind on the situation. He went to the bench to insert little-used freshman Erick Fromm, who was Butler's best at throwing length-of-the-floor heaves. If Brown made both free throws, Stevens wanted to maximize what tiny chance Butler had on an inbounds play.

Vanzant asked Brown to miss one but said the crowd was so loud, he wasn't sure Brown heard him. Mack went to the middle of the lane in an attempt to distract the shooter. Mack asked where Brown was from, told Brown his hometown was Lexington, Kentucky, and that he had a 3.0 grade-point average. It was "a regular conversation," Mack said later.

Gminski chided Mack for "a little gamesmanship." Brown claimed he wasn't paying attention to Mack.

Brown shot the first . . . swish. 70–70.

Brown shot the second . . . and the ball rattled off the rim. Howard grabbed it. The Bulldogs had apparently survived to play into overtime. Except that wasn't all. An official whistled a foul against Robinson, who hooked Howard's arm as both went for the loose ball. The foul was as obvious and as egregious as Mack's. There were eighth-tenths of a second on the clock.

"I've never seen anything like that. I doubt I'll ever see anything like that again," said Nored, speaking for everyone.

Butler's baseball players erupted as if they had won the College World Series on a walk-off home run. Then they reverted to silent expectancy. Sophomore first baseman Jack Dillon leaned into the aisle and yelled, "Lock it up, boys!" With that, the ballplayers locked arms at the elbows and across the aisles, heads down, eyes closed.

In the arena, with under a second left, Howard went to the foul line. He shot the first . . . good. His two sisters in the stands, Amanda and Susie, raised their fists.

Butler 71, Pittsburgh 70.

Howard, per Steven's instruction, intentionally missed the second. It would be impossible for Pittsburgh to grab a rebound and score from that distance. Wanamaker did throw the ball three-fourths of the length of the court, and nearly made it. It would have been too late, though.

Butler again had won in the last second, again thanks to Howard. The melodrama was over. There was jubilation inside the Verizon Center and six miles up in the sky, where the baseball team shared the joy of their basketball brethren with smiles, hugs, and spilled drinks.

Butler was advancing to New Orleans and the Sweet Sixteen. It became the second team in tournament history to play four consecutive games decided by fewer than three points each, dating to 2010. (Dayton was the other team, and its games were spread from 1985 to 2000.) In the Bulldogs' seven tournament wins over two years, they trailed in the second half of all of them.

For the second year in a row, the Underdawgs ousted a No. 1 seed from the Big East. Behind as time was expiring, they had seemingly lost. Then won. Then lost. Then won.

It was madness, even for March.

Sports Illustrated reporter Tim Layden approached Butler president Bobby Fong and asked, "Does the story ever end?"

No one was more relieved than Mack, who had the game of his life and the blunder of his life, all inside a couple of hours. He might not have qualified for immortality, but he was spared infamy. He turned to Galloy, the trainer with whom he spent so many hours, and said, "Man, that was stupid as hell, wasn't it?" Mack put his arm around Darnell Archey, the coordinator of basketball operations, as the two walked off the floor.

The conclusion detracted from what had been an instant classic. Journalists who had covered the tournament for decades counted it as one of the best games they had witnessed, one of the best in tourney history. Butler/Pittsburgh was nominated for an ESPY award, as the Butler/Duke epic was.

Pittsburgh shot 56.5 percent and outrebounded Butler 33–22. Brown scored 24 points. Gibbs was limited to 11, going scoreless over the closing 19 minutes against Butler and the tenacious Nored. The Bulldogs won because they made so many 3-pointers (12) and so few turnovers (six). And because Marshall reclaimed that missing vitality, supplying six points and six rebounds off the bench.

Stevens said he felt bad for Pittsburgh because of the ending, and that Butler was no better than Pittsburgh or Old Dominion.

"We just had the ball last," he said.

Robinson accepted blame for the defeat, although teammates rallied to his defense and called him the Panthers' warrior. Dixon didn't blame the officials, either. He called them a great crew.

In the news conference, Stevens said he asked Mack if he had fouled, and Mack told him he did. Both Mack and Howard reflected on the craziness of late events, and the foolishness.

"I had probably the worst foul in Butler history," Mack said. "But then the dude from Pittsburgh made up for it."

Mack was asked if teammates would roast or forgive him, and he conceded, "I'm a dead man walking." He was. When he finally retreated to the locker room, teammates booed. All's well that ends well, so Mack gladly accepted the teasing. It beat losing. He made a point to thank Howard for erasing the gaffe.

For Butler, it was fitting that Howard made the two winning plays because he was a symbol of the Butler Way, the basketball program, and the university itself.

"I think that that's Matt Howard's imprint on our program," Stevens said. "You're going to give everything you have as long as you're out there every single day."

Inside the locker room, Stevens and Emerson Kampen reprised the celebratory body bump that they performed publicly in Salt Lake City. At the team's noontime arrival at Hinkle Fieldhouse the next day, about 100 fans were there to cheer them, waiting in the wind and cold. As Nored stepped off the bus, he was hugged by his uncle, Leo Williams. One fan, Butler graduate Ken Menser, brought his family of four from suburban Fishers to welcome the Dawgs.

"I lost my father last week," Menser said. "The joy that this team brings to me helped soften that blow."

Butler's regional semifinal opponent was Wisconsin. If anything, Wisconsin was the Butler of the Big Ten. Always good, always underrated. Wisconsin had played in 13 successive NCAA Tournaments, the fourth-longest active streak.

The Badgers were unpretentious and efficient. They played stout defense, took care of the ball, made 3-pointers. Their coach, Bo Ryan, formerly coached in the Horizon League at Milwaukee. Their perimeter potency resembled that of other Horizon opponents.

"But nobody in our league has close to their size," Brad Stevens said.

Butler buzz was, if anything, exceeding that of the year before. When the Bulldogs arrived in Salt Lake City, there was little thought of them advancing to a hometown Final Four. In New Orleans, there was rampant speculation that they could. Until Butler, no team seeded lower than No. 3 had beaten No. 1 seeds in successive years before the Final Four. And Butler was a lowly No. 8 seed.

"It's almost fairy-tale-type stuff," Stevens acknowledged.

Including the Diamond Head Classic and league, Butler was 7-0 in tournaments. Maybe there was something to what those in the national media referred to as "Butler magic." Luke Winn of *Sports Illustrated* all but compared Stevens to fictional protagonist Harry Potter. Butler was back, Winn wrote, "perhaps because it's coached by a young, bespectacled wizard."

Ryan said no one respected the "Butlers of America" more than he did. Indeed, he was 0-5 against Butler while at Milwaukee. ESPN analyst Bob Knight, the former Indiana coach whose Hoosiers were cheered by young Stevens, asserted Butler "was not a very good basketball team" when he saw them early. "I think it's the greatest story in college basketball today, how they've improved over the course of the season to become the team they are today," Knight said.

Wisconsin was awkward to defend, featuring a prolific guard in Jordan Taylor and three tall outside shooters: 6-foot-10 Jon Leuer, 6-foot-8 Keaton Nankivil, and 6-foot-6 Tim Jarmusz. Taylor's assist-to-turnover ratio was 4.38, best by a college point guard since 1997. Leuer went on to be selected in the second round of the NBA draft. Statistically, the Badgers played at the slowest pace of 345 teams in Division I, but they were No. 2 in efficiency.

Yet Wisconsin was like one of those conventional power conference teams the Bulldogs had handled in December, and this was March. This was the Bulldogs' month. Wisconsin's style resembled that of Milwaukee, whose coach, Rob Jeter, was once a Ryan assistant.

Stevens was taken aback by what he called the players' "blah" behavior in the pregame news conference and other media interviews. The Bulldogs didn't have the same step about them, he thought, and looked tired in practice. Too much tension and travel? Too much been there, done that?

Whatever it was, the aura didn't last. Replacing it was the pitiless resolve that the Bulldogs manifested against Milwaukee.

"Guys were ready. Guys were focused," Stevens said.

Andrew Smith was assigned to Leuer, Matt Howard to Nankivil, and Shawn Vanzant to Taylor. Early on, Leuer twice grabbed his own missed shot. He sank a 3-pointer to give the Badgers a 5–1 lead . . . and, astonishingly, never scored again. Even when he was open, he was stalked.

"Wherever Leuer would catch it, everybody was aware," said Butler assistant Terry Johnson, who prepared the scouting report.

The half was so ruinous for the Badgers that they were fortunate to be within 33–24. They led the nation in fewest turnovers per game (7.5), then made eight in the half. Butler outscored them 15–1 in points off turnovers.

When Wisconsin missed its first 10 shots of the second half, Butler surged ahead 42–24 and 47–27. After climbing so many mountains— and trailing in the second half of all nine tournament games over two years—it was a downhill glide for the Bulldogs.

Indeed, one incident that appeared to be calamity was closer to comedy. Early in the second half, Smith went to the floor, writhing in pain.

He had stepped on another player's foot and rolled his ankle. Shelvin Mack went over to his teammate in an attempt to calm him.

"Shut up, Shelvin!" Smith responded.

Mack laughed as he walked away, wearing one of his trademark smiles. Smith had simply never injured his ankle like that. He went into the hallway and hit his hand on the wall, although not hard enough to do damage. After treatment and tape, Smith trotted back into the game . . . and scored on a lob pass.

He spent the next 48 hours undergoing medical attention, but he was not in the distress that the Badgers were enduring. Wisconsin trailed 53–40 with less than four minutes left and twice pulled within four points, forcing Butler into uncharacteristic mistakes. But the Bulldogs won 61–54. Any angst Stevens felt disappeared minutes after the game ended.

"Let's move on. That's the way I feel about it now," he said. "It's all about pace, it's all about focus, and it's all about attention to detail, and we'll have that again. I'm not worried about it."

The Bulldogs kept Taylor in front of them. He scored 22 points, but he had only 6 through 30 minutes. Mack went without a 3-pointer, a statistic that was irrelevant on a night in which Butler limited Wisconsin to 30 percent shooting.

Howard, taking only eight shots from the field, scored 20 points to go with 12 rebounds. Considering the stage and his efficiency, it might have been the finest game of his college career.

Ryan lamented that the Badgers took the kind of shots they wanted and just missed. And missed and missed. Howard said Butler set a defensive tone early that extended until near the end.

Making the night more confounding was that a year after Butler and Duke met in the championship game, now it was Butler in and Duke out. Arizona defeated Duke 93–77 in a West Regional semifinal. In the New Orleans opener, Florida beat Brigham Young 83–74 in overtime, holding player of the year Jimmer Fredette to 3-of-15 shooting from the arc. Fredette scored 32 points, but Florida had four players with 16 or more.

It was Florida versus Butler for a spot in the Final Four.

Two games were as important as any in the evolution of Butler basketball in the 2000s. Both came in the NCAA Tournament. Both were defeats in which Butler lost late leads. Both were wrenching.

Both were to Florida.

So when the Bulldogs met Florida, it wasn't only about one year and one team. It was about every year, and every Bulldog, since 2000.

Ronald Nored received texts from two former players, LaVall Jordan and Mike Marshall, before the game. Nored knew what a victory over Florida would represent. So did Matt Howard.

"We knew how much those losses to Florida meant to them. And what the name 'Florida' meant to Butler fans," Howard said. "No matter what was said, we knew that."

Florida beat Butler 69–68 in the first round in 2000 as time expired in overtime. The Gators beat Butler 65–57 in the Sweet Sixteen in 2007. The 2000 game, especially, was a turning point.

"It really jump-started what we were doing," said Darnell Archey, a freshman on that team. "I think it just gave us a lot of confidence in our system and our coaching staff and belief in what we were doing."

Archey was not at the 2007 game but edited game film to show new Bulldogs how undersized Brian Ligon and Brandon Crone put on a "clinic" in post defense. Nor until Archey watched the replays did he realize how close Butler came to beating the two-time national champions. The sores healed, but the scars remained.

In the rematch, a couple of Florida natives—Shawn Vanzant and Khyle Marshall—were smarting from newer wounds. After Butler ousted Pittsburgh in Washington, an interviewer asked Vanzant if that made Florida's road to the Final Four easier, which made him fume. Marshall, who was not recruited by the Gators, told TNT analyst Reggie Miller he still had a chip on his shoulder about the snub.

The coaches, Brad Stevens and Billy Donovan, had such mutual respect that Stevens called the Florida coach during the midseason downturn. Donovan coached teams coming off national championships, so he could address some of Butler's issues coming off a Final Four run. Also, Stevens was among the college and pro coaches invited to Donovan's annual self-improvement clinic at Florida.

Stevens knew he would be opposing a wily counterpart in the 45-year-old Donovan. Micah Shrewsberry, the assistant assigned to the scout, and Stevens devised a plan to seal the Gators off the glass because they were such effective offensive rebounders. The Bulldogs also planned to hedge—that is, step into the path of a dribbler—against Southeastern Conference player of the year Chandler Parsons and guard Kenny Boynton. They would trap 5-foot-8 point guard Erving Walker so he could not dribble between defenders.

This game's purpose was clear. On the locker room whiteboard, in giant red letters, were the characters "F4." Not that this game would be decided strictly on X's and O's. Strategy can't account for intangibles.

The Littons made the eight-hour trip from Tampa to see their adopted son and brother, Vanzant. Lisa Litton texted to her son that it was his night: "Play hard, think strong."

Vanzant texted back: "Thanks, Moms, I really love you. I really appreciate you and I want you to know that I believe that my mom sent me to you."

Shortly before tip-off, Nored gathered the Bulldogs in the tunnel next to the court and, in his son-of-a-preacher-man delivery, told them:

"The three regional games that we've won against Syracuse, Kansas State, and Wisconsin, we've gone out and just jumped on them. Just jumped on them. That's what it takes to win at this level. They want to be more physical? They're not going to be more physical than us—it ain't happening today. All right, let's get to Houston, baby. Let's go!"

Mack began as if incited, scoring Butler's first eight points. Inspiration is not always as effective as preparation, though, and the Gators were not going to be outmaneuvered. They aligned in a zone defense, flustering the Bulldogs and causing them to lose aggressiveness. They could not pass the ball inside to Howard or Andrew Smith, and they could not score from outside.

Just as vexing was Butler's inability to contain 6-foot-10 Vernon Macklin, who lowered his left shoulder to score against Andrew Smith and Marshall. When Macklin ran his total to 13 points—with a basket over Howard—he had scored nearly as many as Butler in propelling Florida ahead 25–15.

"And Florida playing bully ball," CBS announcer Gus Johnson said.

Stevens sent in Zach Hahn, who had been calculating how he could make an impact. Never mind that Hahn had made exactly two 3-pointers—in 20 attempts—since mid-February. Selective amnesia served him well in Honolulu, as it did in New Orleans. Those misses were forgotten when Hahn drilled a 3-pointer to cut Florida's lead to 25–18. Howard passed out to Hahn for another, and it was 27–25. Hahn shouted and shook his fists as he ran downcourt. Mack went to the sideline briefly to have an ankle retaped, but he soon returned and sank a 3-pointer in transition to trim the margin to 31–30.

"His ankle's okay, huh?" said Reggie Miller, who lived by the 3-pointer during his Indiana Pacers career.

After a half that Florida mostly dominated, the Bulldogs trailed 31–30. They maintained momentum into the second half, going ahead 37–35 when Mack sank a 3-pointer and muscled to the rim for a layup.

Then it all began to crumble. Macklin reasserted himself, and teammate Alex Tyus scored on successive dunks.

"Tyus! Whew! Explosion!" Johnson said. "The bigs from Florida, complete domination."

The Gators dropped back into their zone, and Butler dropped back on the scoreboard. The Bulldogs missed 11 of 12 shots from the arc in one stretch, declining to 6 of 26. No matter how good a coach Stevens was, CBS analyst Len Elmore said, the Gators plainly had too much talent. By the time the margin widened to 51–40, even the irrepressible Howard was doubting the Dawgs.

"I felt like, at that point, 'Man, what is it going to take?' " he recalled.

Stevens urged Howard to be a leader, play confidently. Tell everyone, the coach said. So Howard did: *Coach says we are going to win this game!* Players spoke to each other about having no regrets. Stevens could sense the game, and the Bulldogs' faith, was fading away. It would take a desperate move to change things, and the coach tested the sweep of his magic wand.

Stevens walked down the sideline and approached freshman Chrishawn Hopkins, who had played all of seven minutes in games since mid-January. Oh, Hopkins had been splendid on the scout team, impersonating the likes of Norris Cole and Jordan Taylor. This was *not* a 6:30 A.M. practice at Hinkle Fieldhouse. This was for the *Final Four.* Hopkins's heart quickened.

"He said, 'Hop, go get him,' and I knew my time had come," Hopkins said.

He checked into the game. At the home of Vince Stennett, a mentor and former AAU coach for Hopkins, about 20 people gathered there went bonkers. On the Butler bench, Stevens was analytical, not animated. His instructions to the Bulldogs were simple and direct: score, stop, score. The game will get a lot tighter, he said.

Two minutes after he was in, Hopkins caught Smith's pass off an offensive rebound, drove into the middle of the floor, and spotted Howard unguarded. Hopkins whipped the ball to him for a layup.

Florida 53, Butler 46.

Boynton missed a jump shot on the other end. On Butler's ensuing possession, Mack dribbled purposefully toward the basket and, pausing, passed to Hopkins, who was wide open behind the arc. Without hesitation, the ultra-novice shot the ball, keeping his wrist bent as he followed through. Three points. It was his first 3-pointer in nearly three months.

Florida 53, Butler 49.

Donovan called a 30-second time-out, and Hopkins leaped to bump hips with Marshall. Hopkins's high school coach, Jim Merlie, jumped around his living room back in Indianapolis.

"Where'd this kid come from?" Johnson asked the CBS audience.

Elmore said Stevens went to his sleeve and pulled out an ace.

"Billy Donovan didn't know he had that card," Elmore said.

The game was far from over, but the Gators' comfort was gone. They became visibly tense. Hopkins soon made a turnover and returned to his seat, but he had reversed the momentum.

Mack drove in for a layup, jumping off his right foot—Johnson called it his "Euro step"—and scored from the left side of the rim to pull Butler within 57–55. Stevens told the Bulldogs at halftime that Boynton and Walker would eventually stop passing and start shooting, and the coach again proved prescient. Stevens leaned forward on the sideline, smiling and clapping. Crunch time was Butler time.

Mack's two free throws cut Florida's lead to 60–59 with 1:34 left. Donovan pulled Macklin from the game. The Florida coach didn't want the Bulldogs fouling Macklin, a poor free throw shooter, but he was also removing his most formidable force. Walker missed as the shot clock expired, and Mack rebounded with one minute left.

On the Bulldogs' next possession, Stevens didn't like the way a play developed, and he called time-out with 33.7 seconds left. They couldn't inbound the ball, and he called another time-out.

"This is Matt Howard time," Miller said.

Howard received the ball for one of the left-handed attempts he so often missed, but he was fouled with 30.7 seconds on the clock. He made the first free throw.

Butler 60, Florida 60.

He missed the second, leaving the Bulldogs in the position they desired. Given a choice between making the last shot or the last stop, they would opt for the latter. Walker dribbled the ball at the top of the key as Nored bent forward, clapped his hands, and scrutinized the small guard. Walker dribbled to his right and prepared to shoot. Nored ran at him, screaming, hoping Boynton missed. The ball, launched from nearly 25 feet, careened off the back rim.

Overtime.

Smith fouled out early in overtime—his first disqualification all season—and brought Marshall back into the game. Marshall snared an offensive rebound and passed to Howard for a reverse layup. Then Marshall grabbed another, tapped it off the glass, and retrieved it himself. He scored, was fouled, and fell to the floor, landing on his rump. He was unusually demonstrative as he sat up, screaming as he shook his right fist three times. He sank the free throw to propel Butler ahead 65–62.

"With all due respect to Andrew Smith, I think that Khyle Marshall is the right guy for this type of game at this point in time," Elmore said. "Maybe it was fortuitous that he did foul out, and Brad Stevens had no choice but to put Marshall in."

Even Butler's minuses were becoming pluses.

Nored, a poor free throw shooter who invariably made them in the clutch, sank two—one that hit the back rim and yet dropped through—for a 67–64 lead. After Boynton's first 3-pointer of the game tied the score, Nored sank two more free throws to restore Butler's lead to 69–67.

With 1:40 left, Walker hit his first 3-pointer of the game and returned the lead to Florida, 70–69. Howard didn't wonder what would happen next.

"We all knew. We knew as soon as that ball went in, we knew Shelvin was going to take a shot," Howard said. "That's the way Shelvin played in that game."

Mack dribbled the ball to the top of the circle, and when the defender didn't step out against him, he launched with 1:21 on the clock. Boom. Three more points.

Butler 72, Florida 70.

Butler players on the bench leaped to their feet, slinging towels and whipping them off chairs. At the broadcast table, Miller, too, was jumping up and down.

"This is an old-fashioned shootout for a chance to move on to the Final Four," said Miller, who was legendary in Indiana for his postseason dramatics.

Walker rolled in the second of two free throws to cut the margin to

72–71. Mack pump-faked and missed badly off the backboard, leaving Florida with a half-minute left and the shot clock turned off. Out of a time-out, the Gators settled for a long 3-point attempt by Boynton, who missed. Tyus nearly grabbed the rebound for Florida, but Howard went to the floor to create a held ball. The possession arrow pointed to the Bulldogs. Those 50-50 balls, Donovan said later, were the difference.

"We all knew who would come up with that rebound loose ball," Miller said. "Matt. Howard."

With 10.6 seconds on the clock, Mack was fouled. His first attempt teetered on the rim, then dropped through. His second increased Butler's lead to 74–71.

The Bulldogs likely would have fouled as the clock wound down to prevent a tying 3-pointer, but Walker missed from far out with eight seconds still on the clock. Nored recovered the ball and threw it high in the air past midcourt. It was over.

Final: Butler 74, Florida 71.

"The Bulldogs do it again!" Johnson exclaimed. "Butler, down by as many as 11, coming back! And they're headed to Houston!"

Bitter memories of losses to Florida were erased. The previous ride to the Final Four was storybook, but this was surreal. Butler started its run in early February with a 14-9 record. Butler started the tournament as a 100-to-1 shot to make it to the Final Four. If it had been any team other than Butler, it would have been unimaginable. It was anyway.

"Immediately after we won, I remembered all the games in the season where things weren't right," Nored said. "We were where we thought we would be at the beginning of the year. It took us a longer time."

Stevens acknowledged the long climb from near oblivion was "the most rewarding thing I've ever been a part of in sports." He shook hands with Donovan afterward, telling his colleague he had been outcoached. Donovan had employed shrewd strategies against Butler, which sputtered against changing defenses. Yet the best strategy of all would have been to bury the Bulldogs. Allowing them life was a template for tournament death.

"They've got the 'it' factor," Donovan said.

They had Mack, who was as pivotal a figure as he was against Pittsburgh. Finishing with a bandaged scrape over his left eye, he scored 27 points and was voted the regional's most outstanding player. Marshall underscored why his coach thought the Gators should have recruited him, delivering 10 points and seven offensive rebounds. For Florida, Macklin scored 25 in just 24 minutes.

The scene was so riotous in the immediate aftermath that a bald fan wearing shorts, Mark Miller, ran onto the court amid the players. Miller, a Butler pharmacy graduate, was handcuffed by police and photographed before being released. His ecstasy was shared by those cheering at Indianapolis bars and restaurants, by students on campus, by patrons of Chicago's Brownstone Tavern, by fans at a Fort Lauderdale beach bar—in Florida. Fans in New Orleans chanted, "We want Blue! We want Blue!" The mascot was indeed going to be allowed inside Houston's Reliant Stadium.

Stevens and Emerson Kampen performed their leaping body bump. Howard was double-teamed, hugging Nored while Hahn jumped into his arms. Coach and players cut down the nets. Mack did the Gator chomp from atop the ladder after he had his turn with the scissors.

The moment was overwhelming for Vanzant. He reflected on his life struggles, all the love he had been given, all the love he had shown. Jeff Litton, or "Pops," bear-hugged him. Vanzant was one player who had never given up. All season, he off-handedly remarked about Houston, no matter how preposterous that sounded. As the on-court revelry continued, he left his teammates to sit alone with his thoughts.

"I'm soaking it all in," he said.

In that, he was not alone.

Alex Anglin was entrusted with the Southeast Regional trophy, carrying it aboard Butler's charter flight out of New Orleans. The trophy had its own seat. It was nearly 2 A.M. before the Bulldogs arrived at Hinkle Fieldhouse, where they were cheered by hundreds of fans, including university president Bobby Fong. Unlike the previous year, fans were allowed inside before the team arrived.

Anglin stepped off the bus first and held the trophy aloft, and players slapped hands with fans lining entry to the fieldhouse. Stevens carried son Brady in one arm as he greeted supporters, then delivered a short address inside. Fans snapped photos of the players, and players of the fans. The Sunday morning coincided with Blue II's seventh birthday, so the bulldog was serenaded with "Happy Birthday." The band played the Butler War Song, and fans lingered as late as 3 A.M. Matt Howard, unsurprisingly, was the last to leave.

Later that day, the NCAA Tournament delivered another shocking outcome: Virginia Commonwealth 71, Kansas 61.

So Butler (27-9) was paired against VCU (28-11). VCU's story was, if anything, more absurd than Butler's. Kansas was the last No. 1 seed left in the tournament, and VCU became only the third No. 11 seed to reach a Final Four. The other semifinal matched heavyweights No. 3 Connecticut (30-9) versus No. 4 Kentucky (29-8).

How improbable was this Final Four? Out of 5.9 million entries in an ESPN contest, two correctly picked the four teams.

The selection committee was roundly criticized for including VCU—which would not have made it without expansion from 65 to 68 teams—but the Rams had actually been dominant. Of their five victories, all against opponents from major conferences, the average margin was 12 points. Their coach, Shaka Smart, 33, was a year younger than Stevens. Both were graduates of small Midwest colleges: Stevens from DePauw University, Smart from Kenyon College in Gambier, Ohio. Smart was the third-youngest coach to reach a Final Four, behind Indiana's Bob Knight (age 32 in 1976) and Stevens in 2010.

Butler and VCU both qualified as underdogs. Stevens wasn't going to dispute that, but there was genuine reason to be wary of the Rams.

"If you re-ranked the tournament right now, they'd be a '1' seed, based on how they've played," Stevens said.

Final Four week is never normal for participating teams, but this was going to be more routine for Butler than in 2010. There was simply no escape anywhere for the Bulldogs around Indianapolis. If they weren't fulfilling media commitments, they were beset by fans, family, other students. By contrast, Houston week felt like a regular road trip. More businesslike. Fewer distractions. Players walked outside their hotel, the Sheraton Suites, and to the Galleria mall.

"That would have been impossible in Indianapolis," Ronald Nored said. "It was nice to have that breathing room and that space."

In Indianapolis, Hoosier Hysteria was nearly as passionate as the year before. Even with the women's Final Four in town, the Bulldogs dominated newscasts, headlines, and talk radio. The *Indianapolis Star,* planning a four-page Butler special section, expanded to 24 pages. Fong, Governor Mitch Daniels, and Mayor Greg Ballard all spoke at a campus pep rally held despite rain and cold. Butler's bookstore was overrun with buyers, who sometimes waited hours for depleted shelves to be restocked. The university was reopening Hinkle Fieldhouse for fans to watch on big-screen TVs.

In Houston, TNT analyst Steve Kerr, a former NBA player and executive, jokingly referred to the tournament as the "Butler Invitational." Matt Howard received the Elite 88 Award as the top scholar in the Final Four, and he shook hands with former president George H. W. Bush. Bush and his wife, Barbara, became such fans that they later asked Butler cheerleaders to pose with them for pictures.

Indianapolis Colts owner Jim Irsay offered to transport Howard's entire family to Houston, but that was against NCAA rules, so he sent a check instead. Enough money was raised, most from Connersville donors, to send Howard's parents and eight of his nine siblings to Houston.

The fact that Howard's teammates also took school seriously was underscored by their attentiveness to studies. Khyle Marshall used Skype to watch a lecture on ancient Greece and a Panapto webcast for a math class. His freshman classmate, Erik Fromm, typed a psychology paper on his laptop in the stadium locker room. Zach Hahn was in his semester of student teaching, so he submitted lesson plans and "reflections" for his secondary education major.

Classwork wasn't all the Bulldogs studied. VCU was unlike any opponent they had played in the tournament, pushing tempo and sinking 12 3-pointers in each of its three tournament victories. Butler could not allow that. Nor could it allow point guard Joey Rodriguez to pierce the defense and pass out to those shooters. Butler could get second shots because, statistically, VCU was one of the worst defensive rebounding teams in the country.

As in the year before, the Bulldogs featured inspiration to accompany preparation. They heard from Matt White, the ALS victim and former Butler runner who made the trip from his Florida home to Indianapolis for that Final Four. He couldn't travel to Houston but e-mailed another address to Stevens, who read it to the team. White compared the Bulldogs' climb through the bracket to those attempting to climb Mount Everest:

> Only two of ten climbers who try to summit make it to the top. Why do they make it when so many don't? The answer to that question helps me live my life and will help you win a national championship. Trust. Courage. Never Quit! . . .

Every step, the climber struggles. Every minute is harder than the last. I live and love life. Most never leave bed or home. You never quit on a play, on a game, on this season. Look at where you are now. On the high slopes of the highest mountain in college basketball. It's your time to summit! Go Win!

Nored had his own message, directed toward Shelvin Mack: VCU players were talking trash, saying you weren't nearly as good as some of the other players they faced in the tournament. Except that no VCU player said any such thing.

"I lied," Nored said.

Mack later said that he suspected Nored was lying, but the ploy worked. Mack *was* motivated. He scored the Bulldogs' first five points against VCU. Meanwhile, the Rams missed their first five shots.

Then the rhythm began to resemble that of VCU's previous tourney games. The Rams sank three successive 3-pointers, beginning an 11–0 run that pushed them ahead 11–5. When Bradford Burgess hit his third basket from the arc, VCU led 15–7. Kerr, the TV analyst, cautioned that Butler had been lured into the Rams' pace.

Soon, leaks in Butler's defense were plugged. The Bulldogs attached themselves to VCU's outside shooters and blunted Rodriguez's drives. When the Bulldogs missed shots, they rebounded the ball, scored, or drew fouls. Mack sank two more 3-pointers before halftime, including one that he arched over the shorter Rodriguez.

"Sized him up, and sprayed him," CBS analyst Clark Kellogg said.

Howard scored the last six points of the half, putting Butler ahead 34–28. The last two points came on his first field goal, a basket in which he tipped a rebound left-handed, retrieved the ball, and laid it in.

"Big-time work by Matt Howard," Kellogg said. "That's been the difference. The free throw game and the glass-eating game."

The Rams were 3-9 when trailing at halftime, but they were a different team earlier in the season, as Butler was. To dramatize that, Smart began March by ripping the month of February from a calendar, using a lighter, and setting the page on fire in a trash can. February was done.

The Rams were not. They reclaimed the lead 35–34, then went ahead 38–36 on Jamie Skeen's 3-pointer—their first basket from the arc in 18 minutes.

The Rams changed to a zone defense to protect Skeen, who had three fouls. That did not protect them from Zach Hahn.

Hahn, whose timely 3-pointers rescued Butler against Florida, renewed his Zach Attack. He made two 3s against VCU, then uncharacteristically drove to the basket for a left-handed reverse layup. ("When Zach takes it to the hole like that, you know he's feeling it," Nored said.) Hahn scored eight points in 100 seconds. He scored nine—total—in the previous four tournament games.

"You know, there's certain guys that think they should be playing in these games," Stevens said later. "He's one of those guys."

Butler 44, VCU 43.

Mack scored Butler's next 10 points, all in a span of 2 minutes, 21 seconds. He scored six on two 3s, finished 5 of 6 from the arc, and set a Final Four record for 3-point percentage (.833).

Butler 54, VCU 47.

Although the Rams pulled within four points on four separate occasions, Butler closed out its 14th consecutive victory, 70–62. The outcome was essentially secured when Mack, instead of taking an open shot, passed cross-court to Shawn Vanzant for a 3-pointer that expanded the margin to 61–54.

Howard scored six of the Bulldogs' final nine points (17 total), and Mack finished with 24. Considering the margin was four points with a minute left, the game was closer than the score. By Butler standards, it was a virtual landslide.

"VCU was the hottest team coming in. Butler was the toughest," Kerr said. "The way they win every close game is remarkable."

The Bulldogs exceeded pregame goals. They limited VCU to eight 3s, outrebounded them 48–32, and committed just nine turnovers. Skeen scored 27 points, but he and Burgess were the only Rams with more than two field goals. Butler had five players with three or more baskets, and five with six or more rebounds. For a team whose whole exceeded the sum of the parts, it added up to a 10th victory in two consecutive NCAA Tournaments.

"We knew it was going to be like this," Howard said. "We haven't had a game that wasn't."

Butler had been playing such games for so long, the national semifinal did not seem like a national semifinal. Seemed like the next game, Mack said.

There was one more game. For the second year in row, Butler was playing for a national championship.

"We've just got to be one shot better than last year," Stevens said. "That's the bottom line."

There was one team in the tournament hotter than Butler: Connecticut. The Huskies blocked the Bulldogs' path to a championship.

UConn had a similarly bumpy season, finishing ninth in the Big East with a 9-9 record. But the Huskies won five games in as many days to capture the conference tournament, then five more to reach the national championship game. Led by 18 points from All-America guard Kemba Walker, UConn held off Kentucky 56–55 in the other national semifinal.

National media tried to reduce the climactic game to good versus evil. Given Butler's pristine image and UConn's rule-breaking, that was a simplistic story line. UConn coach Jim Calhoun, 68, was slapped with a suspension for the next season's first three Big East games for failing to monitor and promote an atmosphere of compliance, which stemmed from a 22-month NCAA investigation. Butler's biggest issue was whether Blue II could appear at tournament sites.

Yet Calhoun, if crusty, was respected in the sport. Before he arrived at UConn in 1986, basketball there was as irrelevant as it was at Butler in the 1980s. Calhoun won NCAA championships in 1999 and 2004 and already belonged to the Naismith Basketball Hall of Fame. If teams were a reflection of their coach, his fervor was manifested in the toughness with which the Huskies played. Calhoun lost his father at age 15 and worked as a granite cutter, scrap yard worker, and grave digger to support his family. Moreover, he survived three cancer fights.

Butler associate head coach Matthew Graves said UConn, throughout the tournament, was consistently more physical than any other team. Brad Stevens once heard Calhoun speak at a clinic and appreciated the extent to which the UConn coach stood by his players.

"He has a passion for the game," UConn guard Kemba Walker said. "I couldn't see myself playing for nobody else."

Privately, Butler coaches were optimistic about a possible meeting with Kentucky, believing the matchups were something the Bulldogs could manage. There was concern about Connecticut. Although the Huskies started three freshmen, they featured long-armed defenders everywhere.

Walker was 6-foot-1 and freshman backcourt mate Jeremy Lamb 6-foot-5, but other starters were all 6-foot-8 or taller. Charles Okwandu, a 7-foot Nigerian, came off the bench.

The Bulldogs felt prepared, though. They always did. They knew how they wanted to guard Walker coming off screens and rotate players on defense, and how to attack Connecticut's defense.

"I thought we had a great game plan," Matt Howard said.

This time, in game plans, Butler was meeting its match. Two UConn keys were to force the Bulldogs to start offense farther out and to push them off the 3-point line. The scouting report stressed that the Huskies must "stay in the entire possession" because Butler never quit on a play. Lamb was supposed to challenge every shot by Shelvin Mack, and big teammates would hedge, forcing him to drive the ball into tall defenders. Attack Mack, was the plan.

One source of Butler optimism was available in the library. In *White Fang*, a novel by Jack London, a huskylike wolf-dog was indomitable . . . until defeated by a bulldog. Sure, that was fiction. As was this Bulldog run. Or so it seemed.

The late-night tip-off made for a long Monday, but the Bulldogs had endured the long wait once before. They knew how to relax. Ronald Nored took a long nap. Mack played video games. Stevens and the other coaches made their final reviews.

"Behind the scenes, there was not even a pulse in that motel room," radio announcer Brandon Gaudin said. "Everyone was so calm."

Nored was the usual orator when the Bulldogs huddled in a tunnel to take the tournament stage, but Howard took it upon himself this time. He told them to forget about the prize to be won.

"Don't think about the national championship!" he shouted. "This is our last time playing together!"

Soon after play began, it was difficult for the Bulldogs to preserve their pregame calm. Especially difficult was making a basket.

Mack's first attempt, a 3-pointer, was deflected by Lamb. Lamb said Mack appeared timid on his next two attempts, which were missed layups. Butler scored eight points on its first 10 possessions, and had four shots blocked or altered. In falling behind 13-8, the Bulldogs shot 2 of 15, and both baskets were 3s.

The Bulldogs went through scoring droughts and won tournament games before, so this was not unfamiliar. They dug in on defense, taking a 16–15 lead on Chase Stigall's second 3-pointer, launched from 25 feet. It was hard to get much closer than 25 feet against UConn.

Butler held UConn scoreless for the final six minutes of the first half. Mack sank his first 3-pointer to tie the score at 19 with 4:15 on the clock, then beat the halftime buzzer with a longer 3-pointer. In a half in which the Bulldogs shot 22 percent and made one two-point basket, they led 22–19. Offense would surely improve, and Butler's defense was stifling the Huskies.

"I was more confident at that time than I had been in any game in the whole tournament," Grant Leiendecker recalled. "At halftime, there was no doubt in my mind we would be national champions in 20 minutes."

Such conviction appeared warranted when Stigall began the second half by making his third 3-pointer, giving Butler a 25–19 lead that was the largest by either team so far.

From there, the Dawgs descended into darkness. Scoring, which had been a struggle, deteriorated into deprivation. At one point, Stevens turned to his bench and appeared to say, "Our offense is awful."

He wasn't enthralled by the officiating, either. He repeatedly glared at John Cahill, a Big East referee. Stevens tracked all kinds of data. The fact Butler was 0-4 in NCAA Tournament games officiated by Cahill, dating to 1997, likely caught his attention. Butler wasn't catching many breaks, or breaking onto the scoreboard. But it wasn't Cahill. It was Connecticut.

The Bulldogs missed 13 consecutive shots until Vanzant's 3-pointer trimmed the lead to 33–28. They missed nine more consecutively after that. That was an aggregate 1 for 23. "Unparalleled ineptitude," CBS analyst Clark Kellogg called it.

"As it got down right at the end, you sort of had a feeling: 'What else could we have done?' " said Howard, who made 1 of 13 shots.

In a 12-minute span, Connecticut outscored Butler 22–3 and seized a 41–28 lead. Play continued over the last seven minutes, but this one was over.

Final: Connecticut 53, Butler 41.

It was almost universally panned as the worst championship game ever. Calhoun dissented.

"To me, this was beauty," he said.

Butler was 12 of 64 from the field for 18.8 percent, the worst shooting ever in the championship game. Not since Washington State shot 21.5 percent in 1941 had a finalist been so errant. Butler was 3 of 31 on two-pointers (9.7 percent), the worst in that category in any Division I game all season.

For Butler, worst of all was that UConn shot 34.5 percent. Thirty percent shooting, maybe 25 percent, would have produced a national championship for Butler. The Huskies' 53 points were the fewest by a champion in 62 years, and their 1-of-11 shooting from the arc tied a record for worst in a championship game. Walker was limited to 5-of-19 shooting. Butler's game plan actually worked.

"We just didn't score," Howard said.

So many fans nationwide were emotionally invested in the Under-dawgs that the backlash, from fans and media, was scathing. Butler was abominable, critics asserted. Didn't deserve to be there. What wasn't as evident was how magnificent UConn's defense had been. Mack said the Huskies challenged shots as no other opponent did. Film confirmed that.

A detailed analysis by *Sports Illustrated*'s Luke Winn revealed Connecticut blocked or altered 27 percent of Butler's shots, compared to 4 percent by Pittsburgh and 12 percent by VCU. Of Butler's uncontested shots, 80 percent were long two-pointers or 3s, compared with 52 percent against Pittsburgh and VCU. The cumulative effect of all those clanks caused the easy shots—and there weren't many—to become hard.

UConn blocked 10 shots, tying a championship game record. Alex Oriakhi, a 6-foot-9 sophomore, collected 11 points, 11 rebounds, and 4 blocks. Walker had 16 points and 9 rebounds—he was voted outstanding player of the Final Four—but the difference was the Huskies' outstanding defense.

Defeat and despair were inevitable as the minutes ticked away, in contrast to Butler's tense finish against Duke. That was theater. This was torture.

"The hard thing for me was the seniors leaving," Ronald Nored said. "It just stunk that we had to go out their last game in that way. I thought we were more ready this time than the other one."

Butler players brushed off the confetti that fell from the Reliant Stadium roof. In the locker room, they wept. All of them. Not only the seniors who had played their last game but the freshmen who wanted the seniors to go out as national champions. The ever-upbeat Mack cried, and he never did that.

"That was the first time in my five years that everyone on the team was in tears, which says a lot about our chemistry and how close those guys were," Leiendecker said.

Vanzant sobbed in anguish. All he could say was that he wished he could have done more. Nored walked over to pull him up off his stool, and they embraced. Others shared hugs.

The players reminded each other that they were about more than basketball. They were, foremost, a brotherhood. The seniors took turns speaking, thanking each other, telling the younger ones what they could do to improve. That was one thing about Butler. A season might end, but the Butler Way endured. Stevens was visibly moved by what he witnessed, more so than if he had been caught up in delirium of a championship celebration.

"If we would have won this, the title would have been nice, the net would have been nice, the trophy would have been nice," he said. "But it wouldn't have trumped the relationships."

In a college sports culture that had its scandals and scoundrels, this was one shining moment.

CHAPTER 12

A UNIQUE ACHIEVEMENT

There is nothing in the history of American team sports analogous to Butler's successive runs to college basketball's national championship game. Butler did not win, and so its legacy is prolonged underdog achievement rather than a single dramatic upset.

There was a nobility to the quest that was easily understood. Not so easy was putting Butler's two years of March Madness into perspective. Decades will be required for that. Mathematics supply context.

Ken Pomeroy is the statistician whose detailed breakdowns of college teams were used in game plans assembled by Brad Stevens and many other coaches. Based on their season résumé, Butler was calculated to have a 1.5 percent chance of reaching the NCAA Tournament's title game in 2010 and 0.02 percent in 2011. In oddsmaking terms, that's 500 to 1 in the second year.

Using Pomeroy's figures, Butler had a 0.003 percent chance of reaching back-to-back championship games. In oddsmaking, that's 33,333 to 1. The statistician acknowledged that this is probably overstated "since my calculations assume that I have a perfect measurement of a team's ability."

Even if the odds were miscalculated by a factor of 33, that leaves 1,000 to 1. There is no other comparable occurrence in college basketball or any other sport.

The standard by which all other underdogs are judged came at the 1980 Olympic Winter Games, where the United States beat the Soviet Union 4–3 in hockey's medal round in Lake Placid, New York. The Soviet pros had beaten the team of American collegians 10–3 in a pre-tournament exhibition.

"Do you believe in miracles?" TV announcer Al Michaels famously asked.

Sometimes. But the hockey team was not a 1,000-to-1 underdog. Not on home ice.

Two other landmark upsets both occurred in 1969: the New York Jets beating the Baltimore Colts 16–7 in the Super Bowl, and the New York Mets winning the World Series over the Baltimore Orioles. In college football, upstart achievements were Northwestern reaching the 1996 Rose Bowl and Boise State winning the 2007 Fiesta Bowl over Oklahoma 43–42.

Butler's advance to the 2011 championship game would have been a greater shock, but minds were conditioned because of what happened in 2010. As Stevens observed, Butler was "pretty close" to missing the 2011 tournament altogether.

"We improved more drastically than any team I've ever coached," he said. "Other teams had it. This team had to build it."

The entire season felt "weird," Ronald Nored said. He could not explain why. His teammates could not, either.

"The whole course of the year was different," Nored said.

Yet it ended the same, playing in the championship game. Over two tournaments, Butler was an underdog—by seeding or betting line—in nine of its final 10 games. Of the nine games the Bulldogs were supposed to lose, they won seven. They made an imprint that champions rarely do.

Butler became the fourth team in NCAA history to lose successive championship games. The others were among the most memorable in the sport.

- Ohio State, featuring Hall-of-Famers Jerry Lucas and John Havlicek, in 1961 and 1962 (the Lucas/Havlicek team won the title in 1960)
- Houston, featuring Hall-of-Famers Hakeem Olajuwon and Clyde Drexler, with its Phi Slama Jama teams of 1983 and 1984
- Michigan's Fab Five of 1993 and 1994

At a Hinkle Fieldhouse rally commemorating the 2011 Final Four, departing president Bobby Fong, who had a doctorate in English literature, quoted poet Robert Browning: "Ah, but a man's reach should exceed his grasp, or what's a heaven for?"

Butler reached for more than the imaginable—a national championship by a small college whose program was once so decrepit that it could have become small-time. What Butler could not accomplish should not diminish what it did:

- The first team outside the six major conferences to reach back-to-back Final Fours since UNLV in 1990 and 1991, and the first small school to do so since University of San Francisco won national championships in 1955 and 1956.
- Tied for the lowest seed, No. 8, to reach the championship game. (UCLA did so in 1980 and Villanova in 1985.) Even that was understated because, based on its résumé, Butler should have been a lower seed, a No. 9, 10, or 11.
- The first to reach successive Final Fours without being a No. 1 or 2 seed in either year. (Butler was No. 5 in 2010.) Butler was also the first to knock off both a No. 1 and No. 2 seed before the Final Four in consecutive years.
- The first team from Indiana ever to go to the Final Four back-to-back. And that's in a state with college sports giants Indiana, Purdue, and Notre Dame.
- The second team in two decades to reach the national championship game after beginning the tournament unranked. The other was Indiana in 2002.
- As a No. 8 seed, Butler trod the most difficult path possible in 2011, beating the Nos. 9, 1, 4, and 2 seeds, respectively.

"Looking back on it, who has ever experienced that?" Nored asked. "Who has ever experienced what we have experienced?"

If the NCAA Tournament can be characterized as a code to decipher, Butler has cracked it. The reasons were cultural, analytical, tactical, and psychological.

Their Butler Way ethos of we-over-me has proven to be influential and enduring, a culture passed on as an inheritance from seniors to freshmen. It has resulted in adherence to a code of conduct and team-oriented style of play.

"The only way we address the Butler Way with our team is in this regard: People know they've seen and felt something special. They just can't put their finger on it," Brad Stevens said. "That's the only thing we ever talk about with regard to that phrase with our team."

Butler had been building to what became twin peaks throughout the 2000s. Pete Campbell was on the 2007–08 team that finished 30-4 and lost to Tennessee in overtime in the round of 32. He was playing professionally in Germany when the Bulldogs returned to the Final Four in 2011, and he was asked the question repeatedly overseas: How do they do it?

"In my head, the answers are simple, but it's not very easy explaining the culture and identity that goes into being a Butler Bulldog," Campbell responded. "The coaching, teaching, leadership, and values passed down to you are truly invaluable. They are experiences and opportunities that I have realized aren't shared and taught everywhere else. . . . What sets them apart from almost every other team is how prepared they are. How every single guy knows his job, and how every person on the court and the bench are in tune with the game plan. This is a testament to Brad and his staff, but also to the collective effort that went into developing the Butler Way."

Team chemistry is underrated, Matt Howard said. He and others were often asked how Butler did it. There were teams "as talented and much more talented across the country," he said. Yet they didn't win as Butler did. They didn't have the same team dynamic.

"That's it, right there," Howard said.

Additionally, as Butler evolved, the sport changed. With major powers often losing their best players after one or two years, and mid-majors (usually) keeping them for four, the difference in strata became smaller than ever. For instance, the best teams aren't nearly as strong as those of the UCLA dynasty in the 1960s and 1970s. Or even as strong as North Carolina's 2005 champions, who had four of the top 14 selections in that year's NBA draft. Shelvin Mack played against the major powers and spent his college career in a mid-major league, and he suggested those levels are not that far apart.

Recruiting has been as important at Butler as it is anywhere else, although success cannot necessarily be measured in the number of Top 100 prospects collected. That Butler coaches could identify future stars who fit their system was dramatized by future NBA players Gordon Hayward and Mack, neither of whom was on any national list out of high school.

Mack, who left Butler after his junior season, was selected 34th in the NBA draft by the Washington Wizards. Mack carried Butler throughout the tournament in 2011 more than Hayward did in 2010. Mack sank 23 3-pointers in six games, the fourth-highest total in NCAA Tournament history.

Butler has been, in fact, if not in perception, a rebellious program. Maybe the Bulldogs didn't chafe at convention the way that Hoosier rebels John Dillinger, James Dean, and Kurt Vonnegut did, but they stubbornly challenged the so-called natural order. If the Bulldogs were living out a movie, that movie was *Moneyball*, not *Hoosiers*. *Moneyball* dramatized the book detailing how the small-market Oakland A's used unconventional statistical analysis to assemble baseball teams that could compete against big-market teams such as the New York Yankees. Butler's analysis was not all statistical, but it could find players fitting its system and compete against the UCLAs, Michigan States, and Dukes of college basketball.

"I don't think we're rebellious," Stevens said. "Everything that we do needs to be well thought out."

Butler coaches analyzed recruits not only for skills but mentality and personality. Getting them on the roster was just the beginning.

"I think the development is just as critical," Stevens said, "if not more critical."

Tactically, Stevens has been such a savant that he has told players what would happen in a game . . . and the players have watched action unfold exactly as he described. Of course, that did not always happen, but the pieces on Stevens's chessboard moved accordingly in the Marches of 2010 and 2011.

"He does a really good job of analyzing statistics," Ronald Nored said. "There's no one in the country that pays closer attention to the details than him."

Nored contended that tournament success depends on preparation. Butler's preparation over the years—under four different coaches in the 2000s—was keen not only in the postseason. It resulted in five early-season tournament championships from 2001 through 2010.

"It's hard to prepare for us because we're unique," Nored said.

CBS analyst Clark Kellogg said he was "blown away" by the tenacity of Butler's defense during the 2010 tournament, and Butler finally recaptured that late in 2011. Such relentlessness was nearly impossible for opponents to simulate in practice, especially on a short turnaround.

During the telecast of the 2011 Southeast Regional final, CBS analyst

Len Elmore said it was a game in which Florida simply had too much talent for Butler. Before that, he elaborated on Stevens's tactical acumen. "And let's face it, considering the talent by comparison and the teams that he's beaten in the past, he's always found a way not only to play to his strength but to attack the other guys' weaknesses," Elmore said. "And when you have got that one day in between—like the Sweet Sixteen and regional final—to prepare, you've got to have a good understanding of the other guy."

The Bulldogs had an understanding of, and belief in, what they were doing. That was not unique to Stevens's teams. Predecessors Barry Collier, Thad Matta, and Todd Lickliter also engendered such confidence. Psychologically, because the Bulldogs believed they had an edge, they did.

Howard was a freshman on that 2007–08 team with point guard Mike Green and Campbell. Green could be outspoken in arguing that Butler should never lose a game. Howard continued to be influenced by Green's outlook, and he agreed that psychology affects basketball outcomes.

"It's really interesting because before the [2009–10] season, we never really had a reason to say, 'It's the end of the game. We're not losing,'" Howard said. "You continue to build that thought up. 'We're not going to lose this game. We're going to make something happen.' You begin to believe that."

Stevens said the approach that the Bulldogs adopted during the regular season—never too high in victory nor too low in defeat—helped them navigate the tournament bracket. It is easy for a team to get caught up in what it just did, he said. That is a formula for failure.

When the Bulldogs are clicking, the coaches aren't worried about anything other than the next opponent, and the players about anything other than the next play.

"It's a zone like no other when you're doing that," Stevens said.

Although Brad Stevens inherited a thriving program, his impact at Butler can't be overstated. At 34, he became the youngest coach to reach a second Final Four. His record was 117-25, making him by far the all-time leader for victories in his first four seasons. The record was previously held by North Carolina State's Everett Case, who was 107-22 from 1946–50.

Only two other coaches reached a second Final Four by age 35: Indiana's Bob Knight (1973, 1976) and Bradley's Forddy Anderson (1950, 1954).

College basketball writer Jeff Goodman speculated on the CBS Sports website that not even John Wooden, Knight, or Mike Krzyzewski could have directed Butler to back-to-back championship games. Others called Stevens "an unbelievable coach," "an incredible coach," "an iconic figure," a "coaching genius," and "a legend." Indiana's governor, Mitch Daniels, called the coach and his team "the best advertising Indiana's ever had."

President Obama visited Indianapolis on May 6, 2011, just days after U.S. military forces killed Osama bin Laden in Pakistan. The president, after stepping out of Air Force One, was met at the foot of the airport stairs by Daniels, then Stevens. Daniels apologized for the sequence. Under Indiana protocol, the governor said, the basketball coach should have been first in line.

Butler players have a deserved reputation for intellect—Matt Howard, Ronald Nored, and Zach Hahn were three of the five players on the Horizon League's 2011 all-academic team—and they are at times entranced by their coach. Nored, too, called Stevens a genius. Andrew Smith cited the occasions that Stevens introduced a quote from a book that none of the players has ever heard of. The coach has "one of the best minds I've ever encountered," Smith said. Howard was as effusive.

"He probably wouldn't say this, but I would," Howard said of his coach. "He pushes the right buttons."

A whimsical column by sports editor Steven Peek in the *Butler Collegian,* the campus newspaper, compared the coach to Superman. The student editor noted that Clark Kent took the glasses off to become the comic book character, while Brad Stevens did the opposite.

After the 2010–11 season, Stevens reverted to contact lenses, but the glasses did give him a fitting professorial look. So many accolades were showered on him during and after the two NCAA Tournaments that it would test anyone. His equilibrium was aided by that of his wife, Tracy, and by his quiet Christian faith.

"It's come on so fast, I think we realize it could go as fast as it came," Tracy Stevens said. "You try to put it in perspective. The only thing that's different for us is that Brad is recognized more often. So going places has a new dynamic. Traveling with Brad through the airport is a little bit different than it used to be, for example. Besides that, life is pretty much the same."

Stevens is an admirer of Tony Dungy but uncomfortable with comparisons to the former Indianapolis Colts football coach. Stevens said he is "about one-millionth" of the person Dungy is. Dungy often used his winner's podium as a pulpit.

By contrast, Stevens rarely speaks about his own faith. In that, he is "a classic Indiana United Methodist," according to Judy Cebula, director of the Center for Faith and Vocation at Butler. The Rev. Kent Millard was pastor at St. Luke's United Methodist Church, where the Stevens family worshiped. Millard reiterated that humility was a Methodist trait and that faith was not something to boast about. Stevens would say his values are shared by those of many faiths.

"Don't talk about it. Do it. Be it," he said.

On the basketball floor, the Bulldogs showed faith in Stevens, and he in them. That was true, Howard said, irrespective of what was happening in the game.

"Maybe the other team's making a run, you look over and he's moved on to the next play, and he's focused on that," Howard said. "I don't think I've ever once seen any type of look of panic, we're-in-trouble type of talk from him. I think that's really critical for a group of guys to see."

Although valuing process over outcome has become a cliché, it is a methodology that has worked for Butler and Stevens. The 2010–11 season had more twists and turns than an amusement park ride, but the fact that the Bulldogs fought through adversity and stayed together was gratifying to their coach.

If they had not made the NCAA Tournament, "I'm telling you it would not have mattered," Stevens said. He emulated coach Norman Dale in *Hoosiers,* telling the Hickory Huskers: "I don't care what the scoreboard says, at the end of the game, in my book, we're going to be winners."

After all they had been through, Stevens said, a trip to the National Invitation Tournament in 2011 would have represented a good season.

"I know it sounds corny, I know it's not the way the world is viewed, because we're certainly viewed in wins and losses," Stevens said. "But it is so much about the journey. I think when you focus on that, it's so much more fulfilling."

In the aftermath of the 2010 championship game, Duke coach Mike Krzyzewski accurately foretold that the Bulldogs' run would change Butler University.

"And everything that's good about Butler, which are so many things, will now have a chance to be seen in many areas, not just basketball, that people would not have seen Butler in before," he said. "So what can that do for a school that's really good? I think it's scary good, scary good."

Butler's fans, and the university, benefited in ways both measurable and intangible. After each Final Four, those wearing Butler shirts were approached by total strangers on the sidewalk, in grocery stores, anywhere, to talk about the Bulldogs. After the Duke game, a donor with no connection to Butler sent a $1,000 check to the scholarship fund, saying any university represented by a such a classy coach and students must be wonderful.

Bill Templeton, an associate dean in business, was in Greece when he ended up on a late-night train traveling to Athens. Sharing the compartment was a Greek lawyer who wasn't much interested in hearing about the university until he asked if this was the Butler that played in the national championship game. Finally, the Greek lawyer smiled.

"Yes, I know all about this," the Greek said. "I have read everything. This is the university whose very fine players also go to class and are excellent students."

A study commissioned by Butler's athletic department estimated that the two tournament runs generated $1 billion worth of publicity value in television, print, and online news coverage. Factoring in social media, the audience reach exceeded 69 billion.

Butler retained a local television package with WNDY/Channel 23, a rarity in any market, and picked up a new radio partner in 1070 The Fan, the leading sports station in Indianapolis.

For August 2010, the university accepted a record freshman class of 1,049, about 70 more than the previous high. Butler spent $170,000 on furnishings for dorms, squeezing three students into rooms meant for two. Other students were moved down the street to apartments at a seminary. The 2011 freshman class was the first in school history to include more students outside Indiana (54 percent) than inside. That class of 2015 also had the highest average grades (3.76), ACT score (28), and SAT score (1,751) in Butler history.

Applications in 2011 were up 52 percent over 2009. Bookstore gift sales increased by 188 percent and apparel sales by 226 percent over the same period. No matter what was being measured at Butler, the numbers were astounding.

There were other changes. Micah Shrewsberry left Butler to become an assistant coach at Purdue. He was replaced by Michael Lewis, a former Indiana University player from Jasper, Indiana. The Bulldogs welcomed guard Rotnei Clarke, a transfer from Arkansas who was touted as the best 3-point shooter in college basketball. Clarke, the all-time leading scorer in Oklahoma high schools, had one season of eligibility and would not play for the Bulldogs until 2012–13. Bobby Fong ended a 10-year tenure as Butler's president and was succeeded by James Danko, the former dean of the business school at Villanova.

Howard signed a pro contract with a team in Greece and Shawn Vanzant with one in Finland. Butler's involvement in USA Basketball extended to a third successive summer. Khyle Marshall played for the team that finished fifth in the under-19 World Championship in Riga, Latvia, and Stevens was an assistant coach on the team that was fifth in the World University Games in Shenzhen, China.

CBSSports.com columnist Gregg Doyel asserted that Butler was unique, having made "every possible right choice" since 1989. The Bulldogs declined to successive 16-14 and 13-15 records in the middle of the 2000s, but they recovered.

"Butler isn't a one-in-a-million, but only because there aren't a million mid-major programs," Doyel wrote. "If there were, Butler would be the one—because what Butler has done is borderline impossible."

And Doyel wrote that *before* the second Final Four.

In five seasons ending in 2010–11, Butler had a 146-32 record, a winning percentage of .820. The only school in Division I with a higher winning percentage in that period was Kansas (165-22, .882). After those two came Duke (147-34, .812), BYU (139-36, .794), and North Carolina (150-39, .794). In NCAA tourney victories over that five-year span, the top three were North Carolina (16), Kansas (15), and Butler (13).

Kansas, Butler, Duke, North Carolina. Except for the fact that blue was featured in all four schools' color schemes, it didn't seem possible that Butler was among such bluebloods. But conforming to the orthodox way was not the Butler Way. The Underdawgs were an ongoing miracle.

AUTHOR'S NOTE

I didn't expect to be spending three successive summers writing books about the Butler Bulldogs. But after writing *The Butler Way* in 2009 and the first edition of *Underdawgs* in 2010, the second Final Four prompted this updated version. Indeed, from November 2007 to February 2012, my professional life has been largely consumed by Butler basketball. The Bulldogs, in truth, have changed little. It's their audience that has expanded.

During the first Final Four week, a colleague asked me if I was having an "out-of-body experience," and that accurately described it. The only other occasion I labored so much in a week was during an Olympic Games. I had a better seat for the Final Four—courtside near the center circle, next to former Georgetown coach John Thompson, a color analyst for Westwood One radio—than I did for games at Hinkle Fieldhouse.

Before, during, and after the 2009–10 and 2010–11 seasons, I interviewed about 200 people, including sit-down sessions, news conferences, phone calls, and e-mail correspondence. Butler coaches, players, managers, and staff were refreshingly candid. My heartfelt thanks to all.

Several sections required additional sources. Credit goes to AOL Fan-House and the *Tampa Tribune* for background on Shawn Vanzant; to columnists Bob Kravitz of the *Indianapolis Star*, William C. Rhoden of the *New York Times*, and Bill Benner of the *Indianapolis Business Journal* for details on ALS victim Matt White; to digital projects editor Ted Green of the *Indianapolis Star* for his interview with John Wooden; to Jeff Rabjohns of the *Indianapolis Star* for background on Matt Howard; to Dan Wetzel of Yahoo! Sports for the aftermath of the 2011 championship game; and to Luke Winn of *Sports Illustrated* for behind-the-scenes reporting on Butler's team.

Books used were *The Butler Way: The Best of Butler Basketball* by this author; *Butler University: A Sesquicentennial History* by George "Mac" Waller; *Tony Hinkle: Coach for All Seasons* by Howard Caldwell; *Reweaving the Fabric* by Ronald Nored Sr.; *My Personal Best* by John Wooden and Steve Jamison; and *White Fang* by Jack London.

Film sources include the movie *Hoosiers* and footage from CBS-TV, Fox Sports, the Horizon League Network, and YouTube. The Internet made accessing such archives amazingly easy. Also on the film side, information was gathered from websites for Fox Channel 59 in Indianapolis, Turner Classic Movies, and *Entertainment Daily*.

Other websites referenced included those of asapsports.com, Butler University, DePauw University, the University of Louisville, *Sports Illustrated*, ESPN, CBS Sports, the Indiana High School Athletic Association, indianahsbasketball.homestead.com, CNBC, USA Basketball, Yahoo! Sports, and Wikipedia.

Publications used that were not daily newspapers: *Basketball Times, Butler Collegian, Chronicle of Higher Education, High School Sports: The Magazine, Indianapolis Business Journal*, the *Sporting News, Sports Illustrated, U.S. News & World Report*, and the *Wall Street Journal*.

Daily newspapers have declined in circulation and influence during my lifetime, but their print editions and websites usually exceeded all other media outlets in quantity of quality. Invaluable to research for this book were the *Albany Times Union, Bangor Daily News, Charlotte Observer, Chicago Tribune, Denver Post, Deseret News, Fort Wayne News-Sentinel, Green Bay Press-Gazette, Houston Chronicle, Indianapolis Star, New Orleans Times-Picayune, New York Post, New York Times, Peoria Journal Star, Pittsburgh Post-Gazette, St. Louis Post-Dispatch, Salt Lake Tribune, San Jose Mercury News, Santa Cruz Sentinel, Syracuse Post-Standard, Tampa Tribune, USA Today*, and *Washington Post*.

Butler students, parents, alumni, faculty, employees, and fans contributed background, plus season and tournament memories. Although I was unable to use all of their stories, I am grateful to all of the following:

Thomas Abner, Marc Allan, Frank Angst, Bruce Arick, Dawn Armstrong, Robb Barbauld, Bobby Barbour, Eli Boyer, Erick Brown, Justin Brown, Kate Bunten, Rose Campbell, Ben Carson, Jenni Cashen, Scott Cassin, Rob Chapman, Ryan Clarke, Brian and Paula Clouse, Barry Collier, Megan Daley, J. J. DeBrosse, Yancy Deering, Chris Denari, Leigh Ann Douglas, Kerry and Kristen Dunn, Kim (Kutska) Emigh, Bobby Fong,

Mike Freeman, David Frost, Nick Gardner, Brandon Gaudin, Joe Gentry, John Gentry, Chris Grimes, Victoria Guy, Toby Hahn, Gordon and Jody Hayward, Carl Heck, Mark Helmus, Adam Hoog, Alan Horstman, Stan Howard, Levester Johnson, Michael Kaltenmark, Delores Kennedy-Williams, Dan King, Robert Kurtz, Deb Lecklider, Jolie Lindley, Jeff and Lisa Litton, Lindsay Martin, Ryan McLaughlin, Dick McOmber, Dan McQuiston, Mark Minner, Dave Mueller, Kyle Murphy, Ryan Myers, Bruce Nagy, Gary Nash, Emily Newell, Mary Dunham Nichols, Dan O'Reilly, Max and Karen Oyler, John Parry, Bob Parsons, Bobby Phillips, Chris Polhamus, Kara Post, Deanna Proimos, Fred Ramos, Josh Rattray, Marc and Shannon Rueffer, Matt Rutherford, Tony Schueth, Herb Schwomeyer, Rick Sexson, Nate Shadoin, Brian Shapiro, Patsy Shultz, Curt and Debbie Smith, Nick Sproull, Todd and Esther Stanfield, Tim Stark, Bob Steiner, Brad and Tracy Stevens, Jan Stevens, Mark Stevens, Dave Strietelmeier, Tom Surber, Bill Sylvester, Bill Templeton, Mike Trombley, Courtney Tuell, Cameron Twarek, Ann VanMeter, Willie and Rose Veasley, Scott Martin Vouri, John Wasko, Tom Weede, Matt Werner, Tom West, Meg Whelan, Matt and Shartrina White, Linda Williams-Nored, Dan Wojcik, Matthew Yoder, and Peg Zizzo.

Before I wrote a book, I thought it was a solitary endeavor. It is not. As in basketball, it takes a team to achieve desired results.

There are many people responsible for *Underdawgs*, but especially the following:

- Jani Woods, my wife, for her encouragement throughout this process.
- Craig Wiley, my literary agent, for seeing potential in the Bulldogs' story and his enthusiasm for the project, and his brother, George Wiley.
- Brant Rumble, my Scribner editor, for his insights and guidance.
- Doug Carroll, my journalism colleague and best friend of nearly 40 years. He is the leading expert on Butler basketball in the state of Arizona.
- Jim McGrath, longtime sports information director at Butler University.
- Tom Doherty, publisher of *The Butler Way: The Best of Butler Basketball.*
- *Indianapolis Star* editors, who allowed a four-week leave of absence so I could concentrate on writing this book.

Nearly every word was typed in Room 216 of the Fairbanks Center, home of Butler's Eugene S. Pulliam School of Journalism. This book could not have been completed without such a refuge, which I came to call my Author's Lair. It is not as storied as Hinkle Fieldhouse, but it was a cozy place to relive and chronicle one of America's greatest underdog stories.

APPENDIX

2009–10 Butler Men's Basketball Schedule

Overall: 33-5   Conference: 18-0

Date	Opponent	Result
Nov. 14	Davidson	W, 73–62
Nov. 18	at Northwestern	W, 67–54
Nov. 21	at Evansville	W, 64–60
Nov. 26	vs. Minnesota @ Anaheim, Calif.	L, 73–82
Nov. 27	vs. UCLA @ Anaheim, Calif.	W, 69–67
Nov. 29	vs. Clemson @ Anaheim, Calif.	L, 69–70
Dec. 2	at Ball State	W, 59–38
Dec. 5	Valparaiso	W, 84–67
Dec. 8	vs. Georgetown @ New York, N.Y.	L, 65–72
Dec. 12	Ohio State	W, 74–66
Dec. 19	Xavier	W, 69–68
Dec. 22	at UAB	L, 57–67
Dec. 31	Wisconsin–Green Bay	W, 72–49
Jan. 2	Wisconsin–Milwaukee	W, 80–67
Jan. 8	at Wright State	W, 77–65
Jan. 10	at Detroit	W, 64–62
Jan. 14	Cleveland State	W, 64–55
Jan. 16	Youngstown State	W, 91–61
Jan. 21	at Loyola	W, 48–47
Jan. 23	at Illinois–Chicago	W, 84–55
Jan. 29	at Wisconsin–Green Bay	W, 75–57
Jan. 31	at Wisconsin–Milwaukee	W, 73–66
Feb. 4	Detroit	W, 63–58

Date	Opponent	Result
Feb. 6	Wright State	W, 74–62
Feb. 8	Loyola	W, 62–47
Feb. 11	at Youngstown State	W, 68–57
Feb. 13	at Cleveland State	W, 70–59
Feb. 17	Illinois–Chicago	W, 73–55
Feb. 20	Siena	W, 70–53
Feb. 26	at Valparaiso	W, 74–69

Horizon League Tournament at Hinkle Fieldhouse

Date	Opponent	Result
Mar. 6	Wisconsin–Milwaukee	W, 68–59
Mar. 9	Wright State	W, 70–45

NCAA Tournament

Date	Opponent	Result
Mar. 18	vs. UTEP @ San Jose, Calif.	W, 77–59
Mar. 20	vs. Murray State @ San Jose, Calif.	W, 54–52
Mar. 25	vs. Syracuse @ Salt Lake City, Utah	W, 63–59
Mar. 27	vs. Kansas State @ Salt Lake City, Utah	W, 63–56
Apr. 3	vs. Michigan State @ Indianapolis, Ind.	W, 52–50
Apr. 5	vs. Duke @ Indianapolis, Ind.	L, 59–61

2010–11 Butler Men's Basketball Schedule

Overall: 28-10   Conference: 13-5

Date	Opponent	Result
Nov. 13	Marian University	W, 83–54
Nov. 16	at Louisville	L, 73–88
Nov. 20	Ball State	W, 88–55
Nov. 23	at Siena	W, 70–57
Nov. 27	Evansville	L, 68–71 (OT)
Dec. 1	at Loyola	W, 65–63
Dec. 4	vs. Duke @ East Rutherford, N.J.	L, 70–82
Dec. 9	at Xavier	L, 49–51
Dec. 11	Mississippi Valley State	W, 91–71
Dec. 18	Stanford	W, 83–50
Dec. 22	vs. Utah @ Honolulu	W, 74–62

Date	Opponent	Result
Dec. 23	vs. Florida State @ Honolulu	W, 67–64
Dec. 25	vs. Washington State @ Honolulu	W, 84–68
Jan. 1	Valparaiso	W, 76–59
Jan. 3	at Wisconsin–Milwaukee	L, 52–76
Jan. 7	Cleveland State	W, 79–56
Jan. 9	Youngstown State	W, 84–79
Jan. 14	at Detroit	W, 87–63
Jan. 16	at Wright State	L, 64–69
Jan. 21	Wisconsin–Green Bay	W, 81–75
Jan. 23	Wisconsin–Milwaukee	L, 80–86 (OT)
Jan. 29	at Valparaiso	L, 79–85 (OT)
Feb. 3	at Youngstown State	L, 60–62
Feb. 5	at Cleveland State	W, 73–61
Feb. 7	Illinois–Chicago	W, 72–65
Feb. 10	Wright State	W, 71–63
Feb. 12	Detroit	W, 66–51
Feb. 15	at Wisconsin–Green Bay	W, 64–62
Feb. 19	at Illinois–Chicago	W, 79–52
Feb. 26	Loyola	W, 63–56

Horizon League Tournament at Milwaukee

Mar. 5	Cleveland State	W, 76–68
Mar. 8	Wisconsin–Milwaukee	W, 59–44

NCAA Tournament

Mar. 17	vs. Old Dominion @ Washington, D.C.	W, 60–58
Mar. 19	vs. Pittsburgh @ Washington, D.C.	W, 71–70
Mar. 24	vs. Wisconsin @ New Orleans	W, 61–54
Mar. 26	vs. Florida @ New Orleans	W, 74–71 (OT)
Apr. 2	vs. Virginia Commonwealth @ Houston	W, 70–62
Apr. 4	vs. Connecticut @ Houston	L, 41–53

INSERT PHOTOGRAPH CREDITS

All photos by John Fetcho except the photo of the Vanzant and Litton family on page 2, by Tommy Tonelli, courtesy of Jeff Litton; the top and bottom photos on page 3, courtesy of Kristin Enzor; and the bottom two photos on page 5 and the top photo on page 6, by Rachel Senn, *The Butler Collegian*.

ABOUT THE AUTHOR

David Woods is an Urbana, Illinois, native who has won national and state awards for his sports reporting. Woods has covered five Olympic Games for *The Indianapolis Star,* and he has been that paper's beat writer for Butler basketball since 2001. He maintains the "Bulldogs Insider" blog for IndyStar.com and is also the author of *The Butler Way: The Best of Butler Basketball,* a history of the program, published regionally in 2009. He and his wife, Jan, live in Indianapolis. They have two daughters, Karen and Kathy.